Warlords

STRONG-ARM BROKERS
IN WEAK STATES

KIMBERLY MARTEN

Cornell University Press

ITHACA AND LONDON

Cornell University Press gratefully acknowledges receipt of support from the Harriman Institute of Columbia University, which aided in the publication of this book.

First published 2012 by Cornell University Press

Printed in the United States of America

Library of Congress Cataloging-in-Publication Data

Marten, Kimberly Zisk, 1963–
Warlords : strong-arm brokers in weak states / Kimberly Marten.
     p. cm. — (Cornell studies in security affairs)
  Includes bibliographical references and index.
  ISBN 978-0-8014-5076-1 (cloth : alk. paper)
  1. Warlordism—History—20th century. 2. Warlordism—History—21st century.
3. Warlordism and international relations. I. Title. II. Series: Cornell studies in security affairs.

  JZ1317.2.M37 2012
  321.9—dc23   2011051561

Cornell University Press strives to use environmentally responsible suppliers and materials to the fullest extent possible in the publishing of its books. Such materials include vegetable-based, low-VOC inks and acid-free papers that are recycled, totally chlorine-free, or partly composed of nonwood fibers. For further information, visit our website at www.cornellpress.cornell.edu.

Cloth printing   10 9 8 7 6 5 4 3 2 1

To my three best friends,
Mom, Dad, and Jack

Contents

Acknowledgments

I have received valuable help and feedback from so many friends, colleagues, and even relative strangers (whom I have "met" by e-mail or telephone but not in person) that at times this book has felt like a group project. The arguments, narratives, and analysis are my sole responsibility, though. I quite stubbornly did not take all the advice I was given, and the organizations and individuals acknowledged here may not agree with my choices.

It has been a pleasure to work with Roger Haydon, executive editor at Cornell University Press, and I am grateful for his continuing support and advice. I appreciate the good work done by the whole Cornell team, including copyeditor Chris Dodge, Senior Production Editor Karen M. Laun, and Copy Supervisor Susan Barnett. I'm also grateful for the support of the editors of the Cornell Studies in Security Affairs series: Robert J. Art, Robert Jervis, and Stephen M. Walt. Bob Jervis deserves a special note of thanks for his encouragement throughout this project, as do Bob Art and an anonymous external reviewer, who read the entire draft manuscript and provided valuable suggestions for improvement. In addition I am grateful to the Harriman Institute at Columbia University for publication grants that defrayed the costs of the cover photo and indexing of the book. I thank David Prout for excellent professional indexing.

I am indebted to Hew Strachan and Sibylle Scheipers for inviting me to participate in a stimulating March 2009 conference at St. Antony's College, sponsored by the faculty of history at Oxford University, which resulted in an edited volume. An earlier version of some of my arguments (appearing with different wording and scattered throughout several chapters of this book) first appeared as chapter 16, "Warlords," in *The*

Changing Character of War, ed. Hew Strachan and Sibylle Scheipers (Oxford University Press, 2011), used here by permission of Oxford University Press. I also thank Shuja Nawaz and Arnaud de Borchgrave for inviting me to participate in their 2008 team at the Center for Strategic and International Studies in Washington to study Pakistan's Federally Administered Tribal Areas (FATA). An earlier version of some of my analysis in chapter 3 was included in the January 2009 report that resulted, "FATA—A Most Dangerous Place." An earlier version of some other parts of my historical analysis on the FATA, also in chapter 3, was published as "The Danger of Tribal Militias in Afghanistan: Learning from the British Empire," *Journal of International Affairs* (Columbia University School of International and Public Affairs) 63, no. 1 (Fall/Winter 2009): 157–74, and I am grateful to the editors.

The maps included here of the Democratic Republic of Georgia and the Republic of Iraq are used courtesy of the United Nations Cartographic Section. The map of the Federally Administered Tribal Areas of Pakistan is used courtesy of the US Government Accountability Office. The map of Chechnya was created by the Central Intelligence Agency, and is used courtesy of the University of Texas at Austin Perry-Castañeda Library.

My research and writing were generously supported by a grant from the Smith Richardson Foundation administered through Barnard College, and time to work on the book was provided by a Barnard College sabbatical leave. I'm grateful to Nadia Schadlow and Dale Stewart at Smith Richardson, to former provost Elizabeth Boylan at Barnard, and to Gregory N. Brown, Eileen Di Benedetto, Nell Dillon-Ermers, Curtis Harris, Nancy Hirshan, Gwen Williams, and the late Sharon Cauthen at Barnard for their help and support throughout. My earliest work on the project was also supported by an institutional grant from the Carnegie Corporation of New York to the Arnold A. Saltzman Institute of War and Peace Studies at Columbia University. I thank Stephen J. Del Rosso of Carnegie and Richard K. Betts and Ingrid Gerstmann of Saltzman for their support.

The seeds of this book were planted when I visited Afghanistan in May 2004. I was embedded at Camp Julien in Kabul with the support of the government of Canada and with financial assistance from the Andrew W. Mellon Foundation Grant for Recently Tenured Faculty at Barnard College. I thank Daniel Abele at the Canadian embassy in Washington for his help in making the trip possible, the Batallion-Group 3e Royal 22e Régiment of the Canadian Forces for welcoming me, and Luc Gaudet and Mike Mailloux for arranging interviews for me on the ground.

My very preliminary thoughts on warlordism were presented at the University of Minnesota Political Science Department in November 2004.

Michael N. Barnett and Raymond (Bud) Duvall challenged me to rethink my views on the beneficial nature of states, and their comments had lasting impact on this project. Kathryn Stoner-Weiss kindly invited me to present my early research in January 2005 at a joint seminar at Stanford University, cosponsored by the Center on Democracy, Development, and the Rule of Law and the Center for International Security and Cooperation. Special thanks go to Lynn Eden for her prepared comments on that presentation, and to the audience for their helpful and expert feedback. I am also grateful for opportunities in 2005 to present early thoughts from this project at the Global Conference at the London School of Economics (cosponsored by Columbia's Saltzman Institute), and the Workshop on Sovereignty and the New American "Empire," sponsored by the Carnegie Corporation at the Saltzman Institute, and for comments received from the audiences both places.

A draft version of my chapter on post-Soviet Georgia appeared as Working Paper 12 (November 2009) of Columbia's Saltzman Institute, and I again thank Dick Betts and Ingrid Gerstmann for their support in making that happen. I am grateful to an anonymous faculty reviewer for commenting on an earlier draft of that working paper, and to Jack L. Snyder for his comments as moderator in the resulting seminar cosponsored by the Saltzman and Harriman Institutes at Columbia.

I am grateful to Lise Morjé Howard for inviting me to present my work in progress at the Georgetown University Program in Conflict Resolution in April 2010, and for the helpful comments I received from audience members there, including Charles King. In addition, various pieces of the project were presented at multiple annual meetings of the American Political Science Association and the International Studies Association (ISA), and the feedback I received from those presentations was invaluable. Special thanks go to Dipali Mukhopadhyay as the organizer and William Reno, Keith Stanski, and Susan L. Woodward as participants in a particularly inspiring panel and ensuing lunch discussion at the ISA in New York in 2009.

A "book incubator" workshop arranged by the Program on New Approaches to Research and Security in Eurasia (PONARS-Eurasia) at the Institute for European, Russian and Eurasian Studies at the George Washington University played a crucial role in the final shaping and presentation of the analysis in this book. I am grateful beyond words to Henry E. Hale and Cory Welt for inviting me to participate in that incubator, and to Olga Novikova for her support. I'm also exceedingly grateful to the individuals who read my draft manuscript and presented prepared critiques at the workshop, including Nora Bensahel, Henry Hale, Marc Lynch, Sergey Markedonov, Hendrik Spruyt, and Cory Welt, and to those who gave me informal feedback in the discussion, including

Toby Davis, Charles L. Glaser, Michael Johnson, Alexander Kupatadze, and Gerard Toal. I also presented a draft of my Chechnya chapter to an earlier PONARS-Eurasia conference in Odessa, Ukraine, in June 2010. I thank Volodymyr Dubovyk for hosting that conference, Mark Kramer and Ekaterina Stepanova for their prepared critiques of my paper, and all the PONARS-Eurasia members who provided useful feedback both there and throughout the project.

The following individuals have my special gratitude for time they spent in lengthy conversations about the project, for reading and critiquing draft chapters beyond what has already been noted above, and/or for suggesting source material and helping me arrange contacts with interviewees: Akbar S. Ahmed, Mikhail Alexseev, Séverine Autesserre, Deborah D. Avant, Gordon N. Bardos, Nora Bensahel, Sheri Berman, Stephen D. Biddle, Deborah Boucoyannis, Daniel L. Byman, Jonathan Cohen, Alexander Cooley, Georgi Derluguian, Valery Dzutsev, C. Christine Fair, Tanisha Fazal, Archil M. Gegeshidze, Paul Goble, Glen Howard, Colin Kahl, Kornely Kakachia, Jennifer M. Keister, Terrence Kelly, George Khelashvili, Maria Koinova, Mark Kramer, Robert Legvold, Jack S. Levy, Roy Licklider, Alexander Lomaia, Austin Long, Jason Lyall, Sergey Markedonov, Kenneth Menkhaus, Keith Mines, Lincoln Mitchell, Marina Murvanidze Mitchell, Gregory Mitrovich, Michael Mousseau, Mark Mullen, John A. Nagl, Shuja Nawaz, Lauren Ninoshvili, Ghia Nodia, Olga Oliker, Robert Orttung, Nikolay Petrov, Ekaterina Piskunova, Jenik Radon, Almut Rochowanski, Alexander Rondeli, Nona Shahnazarian, Howard J. Shatz, Mark Simakovsky, Hillel David Soifer, Hendrik Spruyt, Brian Taylor, Gigi Tsereteli, Celeste Wallander, Joshua T. White, Temuri Yakubashvili, Kenneth Yalowitz, Mariam Abou Zahab, and Sufian Zhemukhov. I am also grateful to the policy makers, practitioners, and experts who allowed me to interview them (and who often helped me locate additional contacts). Some of these people are named in the footnotes while others prefer to remain off the record.

Robert H. Davis, Jr. of the Columbia University Libraries graciously helped me find key source materials. Katherine Schulman provided helpful research assistance on the Georgian case. Very special thanks go to Marina Murvanidze Mitchell, who gave me unbelievably selfless tutoring to help improve my rusty Russian language skills, in addition to reading chapters. And my research in Georgia would not have been possible (or half as much fun) without my driver (he prefers "transporter") and interpreter Giorgi Chkheidze. A special note of appreciation goes to all of my colleagues in the Political Science Department at Barnard College, for providing an incredibly collegial and engaging work environment throughout.

Acknowledgments

I give my continuing deep gratitude and love to my parents, Lynette and Gordon Marten, whose generosity, emotional support, and pride have been unflagging. Happy fiftieth anniversary year, Mom and Dad! My gratitude and love also go to Jack S. Levy, who throughout this project has provided useful advice and feedback, a stellar example of what it means to be a scholar, and most important, continuing encouragement and loyal friendship through thick and thin. Some of the best parts of the book were written at Jack's kitchen table in New Brunswick, New Jersey, while I watched the birds in his beautiful garden.

Warlords

[1]

Warlords

AN INTRODUCTION

"Warlordism is the default condition of humanity."
—Historian David G. Herrmann

In May 2004 I was embedded as a journalist with the Canadian Forces who were leading the NATO peace enforcement mission in Afghanistan. Kabul and its suburbs were dry and dusty brown, a small tragedy (in a land of great tragedies) given that the city was once famed for its gardens. The Soviet invasion of 1979 and the decades of civil war that followed had targeted civilian irrigation systems and other infrastructure for bombing. Rebuilding was still in its early stages. Yet when we went out on patrol one day in Paghman District, just to the west of Kabul's city limits, a patch of shimmering green appeared in the distance. One small slice of land in this parched desert had well-tended orchards and gardens, alongside a rather opulent compound of buildings. The interpreter pointed it out and told me, "That's our warlord."

He was referring to Abdul Rasul Sayyaf, a former mujahedin commander who used money he received from the United States during Afghanistan's war against the Soviet Union in the 1980s to buy up Paghman land.[1] Sayyaf was a longtime ally of President Hamid Karzai and an elected member of Afghanistan's national parliament. He helped select and appoint prominent judicial officials in the country, while loudly calling for an amnesty for all war criminals. In 2006 he faced down massive local protests—but received no apparent challenge from Karzai's government—when his militia members were accused of illegally forcing ordinary citizens off land that he wanted for himself.

Seeing Sayyaf's lush compound off in the distance in 2004 helped spark the questions that frame this book. Why do state leaders allow warlords to thrive within their territories? What are the consequences of warlordism? Are warlords simply the leaders of microstates or proto-states? What would it take to get rid of warlords, and what are the consequences of trying to overthrow them? In other words, what is the relationship between warlords, sovereign states, stability, security, and peace?

In Afghanistan the United States and its allies were spending lives, money, and political capital on a mission authorized by the UN Security Council to support the state—the sovereign national government—of Afghanistan. A great deal of media attention had been given to Afghanistan's new democratic constitution and its then-upcoming presidential elections. International donors were sending massive development assistance to support Afghanistan's impoverished population. Given all of that, why had the United States and the United Nations continued their tacit support of people like Sayyaf? The international community had allowed warlords to take part in the national *loya jirga* councils of 2002 and 2003 that chose the interim president and passed a provisional constitution, thereby guaranteeing a permanent place for them in the new political system.[2] How was it possible that a man who sat in the (supposedly) democratically elected national parliament and shaped judicial policy under a (supposedly) democratic constitution could still enforce brutal and arbitrary rules on one small piece of territory, with no apparent effort by the state to stop him?

As my research on the NATO operation continued, I heard a wide variety of views from Western experts about warlords like Sayyaf. A US military officer told me that the only way to get stability was to work with the warlords, to tame them and bring them into the government. He proudly recounted the role he had played as a liaison to a different warlord who had joined Karzai's government. This officer saw his work with the warlord as a contribution to state-building and peace. A senior diplomat from another NATO country disagreed. He told me that the warlords were "paper tigers," and claimed they could have been easily sidelined in 2002 if only a different set of choices had been made by the international community. In his view, external support for warlords caused state weakness and instability, not peace. Prominent analysts in the US media were also split about the wisdom of working with warlords.[3]

This book tackles these questions in a new way by placing them in comparative perspective. It examines a variety of recent cases where state leaders, both domestic and foreign, have created, tolerated, actively supported, undermined, and/or overthrown warlords on a particular piece of territory. It then draws lessons from their experiences to build a series of new hypotheses about the relationship between states, sovereignty, "local power brokers" (as the current Washington euphemism calls them), and stability and security in the modern world order. In academic social science terms, this book uses inductive research for the sake of theory-building. I chose not to focus on Afghanistan in my research, since at the time of writing it was still a case in progress where the results of US policy were far from certain. (I also had no desire to make my "war correspondent" status permanent.) Instead I turn to other recent examples of relationships between warlords and states, in order to analyze what happens when state leaders make various choices about warlords and their private militias.

WARLORDS AND SOVEREIGNTY: DEFINING THE TERMS

To use the term "warlord" is to invite controversy. The term is poorly defined, not only in popular usage but also in the relatively small scholarly literature on the subject. People who talk about warlords often mean very different things, making it difficult to compare arguments between analysts or to generalize across cases. Some analysts see the word itself as dangerous and Orientalist, believing that it is used by Westerners to denigrate and pigeonhole people whose political sensibilities are different from their own.[4]

In two previous publications I have worked out a clear and objective definition of the term "warlord" and defended its use:[5] "Warlords" are *individuals who control small pieces of territory using a combination of force and patronage.* They are "lords" (essentially, feudal landlords) who threaten or use "war" (violence unleashed by their militias) to retain their power. As will be detailed in chapter 2, modern warlords who have risen to power in today's universal state system are defined by a further characteristic that distinguishes them from warlords in previous eras: *Warlords rule in defiance of genuine state sovereignty but through the complicity of state leaders.* Warlords today flout and undermine state capacity and state institutions, and they do so by colluding with cost-conscious, corrupt, or frightened officials and bureaucrats. In other words, warlords are parasitic creatures of the state.

My definition is in line with the classical way that the word "warlord" has been used: by Chinese warlords at the turn of the twentieth century who first invented the term to describe themselves;[6] by American scholar Lucian Pye, who studied those Chinese warlords and demonstrated that warlordism is a distinct political system with a logic of its own;[7] by Pakistani anthropologist and government official Akbar Ahmed, who used the term to describe powerful Pashtun landlords with whom he worked in the country's tribal areas in the 1960s and 1970s;[8] and by sociologist Max Weber, who used the term comparatively to distinguish the type of authority that warlords exercise from the types used by both modern

[3]

states and traditional tribal societies.[9] It also fits the description of sub-Saharan African warlords made famous by the work of William Reno.[10] Antonio Giustozzi notes that scholars have recently used the term to describe the Roman Empire, medieval Europe, and premodern Japan as well.[11] In using the term "lord," I do not mean to imply that all warlords are male. Even Afghanistan has had a female warlord, the widow Bibi Aysha of Baghlan whose nom de guerre was Kaftar ("Pigeon"). Her militia was run by her sons, and she was known for her viciousness.[12]

The term "warlord" describes a distinct political phenomenon that has existed throughout history and continues to function across the globe today, wherever states are weak. Indeed, modern warlords are not limited to non-Western societies. The political economy of warlordism bears some resemblance to the political economy of organized crime in highly developed states. Sicilian Mafia bosses in twentieth-century Italy[13] and Chicago housing project gang leaders in the 1990s[14] acted a bit like warlords, operating on a small territorial scale, within a limited scope of policy issues, in states that were otherwise sovereign. Mafia bosses in Sicily colluded with Italian state bureaucrats and politicians, who allowed them a fair degree of control over the local economy and policing. Chicago housing project gang leaders acted as local security providers in areas where police and firefighters were too intimidated to venture, forming a tacit bargain with the state that was maintained until the projects were shut down and their residents dispersed into other housing.

There are a couple of important caveats to keep in mind when making the comparison across these broader cases of organized criminal activity, however. Warlords are autonomous and powerful *individuals*, not members of organizations who are bound by long-standing cultural protocols (such as the Sicilian Mafia's omertà). Furthermore, the territorial nature of warlords distinguishes them from other violent non-state actors who challenge state sovereignty, most notably terrorists who recruit via the global Internet. Warlords rule in particular geographic spaces.

Some other terms are involved in the definition of modern warlords. "Genuine state sovereignty" refers to *the ability of the state to enforce a consistent set of rules over the entire territory it claims*. It requires that state authorities equate de facto control with de jure control over territory, bringing what Stephen D. Krasner terms "domestic sovereignty" (or the ability to enact and enforce consistent policies across territory) in line with what he calls "international legal sovereignty" (or recognition under international law).[15] My definition does not imply that European-style statehood is necessary for genuine sovereignty to exist. Genuine sovereignty merely requires that theorist Max Weber's minimum criteria for modern statehood be met.[16] Weber, writing in the early twentieth century, proposed two criteria for statehood. First, the state must maintain a monopoly over the legitimate use of force on its territory. In other words, state borders must be reliably patrolled by state authorities, state officials must set and consistently enforce rules governing police and army behavior, and private militias must be either illegal or subject to state oversight and regulation. To maintain that monopoly means that if a private militia starts using violence outside the law, the state slams it down. Second—and a crucial piece of Weber's argument that is sometimes neglected by international relations scholars who focus only on violence— the state must enforce some basic common laws across its entire territory, especially over trade, property rights, taxation, and other aspects of commerce. In other words, Weber's concept of modern statehood depends on rational legalism.

Ancient Greek and Chinese city-states, Renaissance Italian city-states, and even the northern European Hanseatic League and the premedieval Carolingian Empire are all examples of territories where Weber's minimal criteria for statehood were met, even though they are not usually thought of as modern. The European Union (if it survives) may eventually become a Weberian state, given its common currency and border controls and its jointly regulated police and judicial systems. At least for now, though, its armies remain outside common control. In contrast to the territorial breadth of enforced law in Europe, some internationally recognized nation-states in sub-Saharan Africa in the 1980s and 1990s did not qualify as genuinely sovereign states by Weber's definition. They were artificial creations whose central governments lacked authority over the space they were allocated by official UN recognition of their borders.[17] Indeed, leaders in those states often cooperated with warlords who controlled pieces of their supposedly sovereign territory.

There is, in addition, a difficult category of states that straddle the gap between Weber's and Krasner's definitions of sovereignty. These states operate by centralized but still personalized patronage networks, not according to legal rules that are impersonally enforced. Such states maintain Krasner's "domestic" sovereignty since their leaders control policies that are consistently enforced across their territory, yet they are not really Weber's rational-legal states. In an extreme form, if they are ruled by a despotic individual, Weber would call them "sultanistic." Much more common, though, are regimes that seem on the surface to be modern bureaucratic states, but have actually been captured by the personal patronage networks of a ruling coalition. Such state "clientelism" can hamper the consolidation of democratic institutions, and is associated with corruption and distortion of free trade.[18] Yet state clientelism can also be seen as a step toward the eventual evolution of liberal democratic states.[19]

Clientelism in states that maintain domestic sovereignty should nonetheless be kept analytically separate from warlordism. States have complex

[5]

bureaucracies, international recognition, and control over wide swaths of territory. Warlords do not. Chapter 2 argues that for a variety of reasons, warlordism is unlikely to evolve into pact-based, clientelistic, organized statehood. Instead, warlordism often marks devolution of centralized control within a state that is already clientelistic.

The word "force" in my definition denotes the fact that *warlords command loyal militias that are not under state control.* Warlords are people who have chosen to become specialists in violence. This sets them apart from other "local power brokers," such as machine boss mayors or the ordinary leaders of autonomous ethnic republics with whom state leaders may have to bargain.[20] Warlords are willing and able to use brute force—not legal niceties and not merely bribes—to defend their control over the territory they occupy. As Diego Gambetta describes Sicilian Mafia dons, warlords use their willingness and ability to employ violence as a tool, in order to maintain economic and political control over the space they inhabit.[21]

"Patronage" is *the ability to distribute resources to supporters based on informal ties and personal preferences, without being subject to laws or other abstract social rules.*[22] The only constraint limiting those who exercise patronage-based rule is that they need to manage shifting power relationships between and among their individual allies and opponents. Because personal patronage is founded on informal relationships, it is subject to constant renegotiation. Warlords are not traditional leaders bound by tribal norms or community decision-making councils. As the empirical chapters on Pakistan and Iraq make clear, warlords may claim tribal privileges to justify and legitimize their rule. Yet they use artificially inflated economic power, threats, and violence—not true traditional cultural authority—to maintain their positions. Force and patronage reinforce each other. The utility of each depends on the warlord's personal reputation for delivering payoffs to supporters. If the individual warlord falters or falls, or if circumstances turn out badly, then followers will desert one leader in search of another.[23]

The use of violence to retain *personal* control over a region's political economy distinguishes warlords from the leaders of many rebel or religious movements.[24] People who see themselves as servants to a larger political or religious cause are often willing to die for that cause, or at least to make themselves personally expendable in the future world they hope to create. In contrast, while warlords may espouse particular ideologies or coerce their followers into particular religious behavior patterns (and may even use such belief systems to create bonds of loyalty through a charismatic leadership cult), their primary goal is to maintain their own individual control over a region, feeding their personal patronage networks by whatever means are necessary. They can be recognized by a behavior pattern that is focused on amassing individual wealth and power through the threat and use of force. The story of warlordism is therefore one that combines structure and agency: certain individuals at any time in human history may be psychologically disposed to become self-interested specialists in violence; weak states provide those individuals with the opportunity to become warlords.

While a few analysts have included cruelty or malevolence in their definitions of warlords,[25] I do not do so. Further, while Reno believes that warlords serve only private interests and never provide public goods,[26] I disagree. Self-interested warlords can provide public goods that benefit their populations. In early twentieth-century China, for example, some warlords established public health and education programs on their territories; one of them abolished the practice of foot-binding for women.[27] The prominent economist Mancur Olson was inspired by the history of these Chinese warlords to craft his widely cited model of how modern development can ensue out of self-interest.[28] (I disagree that his model is fully applicable to modern times, but I will discuss that in chapter 2.) Olson argued that "roving bandits" would become "stationary bandits," as these Chinese warlords were, once they recognized that it would be more profitable to tax their populations and encourage their economic productivity than to pillage them. Certainly, in modern times, wise warlords throughout the world have provided public goods (such as highways and other infrastructure, mosques and other public buildings, and a sense of everyday security for their populations) in order to create local legitimacy for themselves.[29] These warlords help ensure their own personal futures by winning hearts and minds, and thereby removing the costly threat of constant popular rebellion. Warlords often use other ideational tools as well, ranging from clan ties to personal charisma, to bolster their legitimacy.

Yet warlords ultimately resort to violence to maintain their individual power when challenged. They rule from the barrel of a gun, not the boardroom or the ballot box, and their survival is not based on consensual local taxation. They provide public goods when it suits their interests to do so, but their magnanimity is calculated and limited. Fundamentally Reno is right, even if he overstates the case. It is the warlord's ability to distribute patronage to a carefully selected audience that underpins his or her power. Warlords rule by force, not governance.

WHY DOES WARLORDISM MATTER?

State leaders often choose to cooperate with warlords in order to avoid the chaos that they could otherwise unleash, in hopes of avoiding warfare or anarchy in areas that would otherwise be difficult to govern. The absence of immediate warfare and anarchy, however, does not necessarily create long-term security. Bargains with warlords are associated with glaring economic underdevelopment and corruption, and they make "state failure" an enduring outcome.[30] Yet in many cases no one who holds power has an incentive either to replace the bargains with universally applicable state institutions or to consider the pernicious long-term effects of patronage networks on society.

By agreeing to forego violent action, warlords provide a form of passive protection to local businesses and populations. Their militias may also provide active protection from raids by what Olson called "roving bandits." That protection is costly, however. Scholars of organized crime (which is another form of force-based patronage and protection) have long argued that criminal networks can provide some sense of stability and security to private businesses when state legal systems are weak. Criminal networks (including those controlled by warlords) can obtain and distribute information about potential partners, and can enforce business contracts. This allows commercial activity to occur in an environment that would otherwise be anarchic and devoid of trust.[31] But it leads inexorably to a number of major problems. Those problems are shared by warlord rule.

Warlords (like Mafia dons) have an incentive to favor some business enterprises over others in their provision of "protection." Gambetta explains why this is the case in his study of the Sicilian Mafia. He notes that the population believes that the don's unique skills and competencies (and in our example, the warlord's control of the political economy) are necessary or tolerable only when protection is seen as a scarce and valuable commodity.[32] If the average person believed that the world would function just fine without the protected patronage network—for example, because the police and courts did a good job of preventing and punishing burglaries and arson—then the warlord's days would be numbered. The warlord, like the don, has an incentive to make sure that the world seems like a dangerous place. The warlord has an incentive to weaken or damage unprotected spaces and businesses. For "stationary bandits" to retain control, "roving bandits" have to seem like a threat.

As a result, favored businesses are effectively protected from economic competition too. Their rivals are forced out of business. Warlords tend to limit the range of commercial activities in their areas to benefit the members of their personal networks, while ensuring that those outside the network fail. This has the unintended consequence of limiting the incentive for innovation, since business success and increased market share stem from network protection, not from how well merchants appeal to consumers. There may very well be periods of booming economic growth

[8]

on warlord territories, as the favored businesses shine and expand, but these will not lead to sustained and diversified development. Instead all of the development will be controlled by the warlord's patronage network and militia.

An example of this is found in the area controlled by Matiullah Khan, a reputed warlord who operated in summer 2010 in Oruzgan Province in Afghanistan. His private militia provided protection by contract to US military convoys, keeping the major highway from northern Afghanistan into Kandahar open and safe for one day a week.[33] He also owned a rock-crushing company that sold gravel to the US military. He used these various profitable enterprises to employ fifteen thousand people, build seventy mosques on his territory, and endow university scholarships in Kabul for local students. He was simultaneously suspected, however, of colluding in drug smuggling on that same highway. According to a US congressional investigation, it was entirely possible that the militia that protected US military convoys one day a week made the highway unsafe the other six days.[34] Khan certainly shared his wealth and provided public goods and economic development for his population, but if the accusations are correct, he also ensured that growth and development would remain limited (since trade on the highway was limited) and under his forceful control.

A political system centered on one individual is also inherently unstable unless it arises in a context where both the borders of the system and the rules for succession are reliable and permanent.[35] Warlord networks are usually personal and informal, and that means that security and wealth on their territories are subject to contestation. (The exceptional case, discussed in chapter 3, is that of the constitutionally protected Pashtun tribal warlords of Pakistan, whose succession was legally based on primogeniture and whose rule was territorially bounded by the state.) Patronage, when its networks are firmly established and its rules are longstanding and known by everyone, can become a mechanism for organizing society and getting things done.[36] But this does not hold true for the individualistic political systems of most warlords. The assassination of a warlord or even a decline in the warlord's relative fortunes or power can throw the entire local patronage system into disarray, leaving favored merchants in the lurch and scrambling for support as their protection evaporates.

Such occurrences were common in early twentieth-century China.[37] They were also common more recently in Afghanistan. According to a US Senate report, for example, two feuding warlords in the province of Herat (codenamed "Mr. White" and "Mr. Pink" after characters from the Quentin Tarantino film *Reservoir Dogs*) shared a contract for local security provision at a US airbase.[38] They became embroiled in a deadly rivalry over whose supporters would control the contract. After Mr. Pink assassinated Mr. White, Mr. White's supporters—while still working under contract—sought new protection from the Taliban. They then became involved in a shootout against the US forces they were supposed to be protecting when the Americans attacked the Taliban camp. Shifts in which individual warlord was on top had dramatic consequences for patronage and security in the area.

As this Afghanistan example highlights, rational individuals who are informed about the situation have no incentive to make long-term deals or contracts with most warlords, because the future can change so rapidly.[39] While the product in this example is security provision, the principle applies to other kinds of business investments as well. Fruit-tree growers lack the motive to plant new orchards that will only mature in a decade; retail outlets have no reason to plow their earnings back into fixed property improvements; foreign capital owners will shy away from starting long-term development projects; and students tied to the locality may even forego pursuing years of education in local schools that may never pay off. Instead most people will try to earn short-term profits while they can, before an uncertain future comes to pass. The incidence of capital flight, including the human capital flight of emigration out of the territory, will be high. While highly risk-acceptant individuals may invest under the warlord's protection for the sake of immediate profit, their business holdings may disappear in a flash, and this fact will be built into their business models.

They will not have to contend with what Robert Axelrod famously calls the "shadow of the future."[40] This means that they will have no particular reason to be cooperative toward other people in order to protect their personal reputations; reputations won't matter much in the future. By the time the future rolls around, the players will have changed and the winners will have decamped. As a result of this short-term thinking, individuals have an incentive to be predatory. Warlord territory will likely be a place where the favored few prey on those who lack good network connections, even as the warlord showers some public goods on everyone.

Furthermore, the territory that is effectively controlled by each warlord is likely to remain small. In part this is because warlords have to worry about potential competitors arising on their territory, including ambitious followers who may try to topple them. It is harder to monitor people's behavior, and hence to maintain a reputation for effectiveness, if a patronage network grows too large or complex. Just as is true for Mafia dons, trust is easier to maintain when it is verifiable, and verifiability is easier when the number of transactions is limited.[41] Warlords who overexpand risk being overthrown by out-of-control underlings.[42]

Beyond this immediate concern about competitors, warlords also have an incentive to keep the societies they rule relatively simple to understand and monitor, and thus limited in size and geographic scope. As Samuel P. Huntington argued in his classic work on political order, when the variety and complexity of social groups in a society increases, leaders have a harder time making decisions that satisfy all of those in the society who have resources. If no reliable political institution, such as a strong political party bureaucracy, exists to moderate and redirect the groups' demands, then the likelihood of violence also grows.[43] Warlord rule is based on personal patronage, not on strong political institutions. The more that a warlord's territorial purview expands, the more complex the problem of rule is likely to become. The more likely it then becomes that one or another social group will be discontent and turn to violence (or an outside rival patron) to challenge the warlord's ability to maintain control.

This means that warlords are likely to have the most success in relatively small territories with relatively simple economies. Then they can watch the people with whom they do business and use their own personal skills to manage competing social groups. They are likely to remain what anthropologists call "chiefs," ruling thousands or at most tens of thousands of people, rather than overseeing hundreds of thousands of people or more.[44] Individuals like Joseph Stalin or Saddam Hussein may bear a passing resemblance to warlords, given their personalistic style of leadership and their force-based systems of patronage. But each emerged out of a strong political party and inherited a complex state bureaucracy. The institutionalized basis of their rule explains why they were able to control vast territories, while warlords cannot.

The small size and personalistic control of warlord territory in turn impedes economies of scale. Patchworks of warlord rule discourage long-distance trade by raising transaction costs for merchants. When tolls, taxes, and rules vary across small territories and are subject to the unregulated whims of individual warlords, it becomes difficult to make business plans that accurately estimate future costs.[45] Merchants can work around this, as cattle-traders have done in Somalia,[46] but this makes trade inefficient, and dampens prospects for sustained growth and prosperity.

In sum, the combination of small territories, personalistic rule, and force-based patronage leads to economic inefficiency, insecurity, and in most cases instability, even under relatively civic-minded warlords. As Douglass C. North and Robert Paul Thomas have argued, sustained economic development is possible only in a society where reliable institutions guarantee property rights and overcome the natural distrust and collective action problems that arise among strangers.[47] Warlord territories are prime examples of economies operating without institutions. The presence of private militias and the inherent incentive that potential competitors have to overthrow or forcefully steal the warlord's patronage network may also leave warlord territories doomed to what Paul Collier and his colleagues call "the conflict trap."[48] Underdevelopment becomes chronic and subjects populations to ongoing long-term cycles of civil unrest and violence, even when temporary stability is possible.

WARLORDS AS MIDDLEMEN

There is an additional set of negative consequences of warlordism in today's world, beyond these problems that are inherent in any small, force-based, personal patronage system. Warlords often act as "middlemen," working within patronage systems that span international borders. Since warlords are skilled at colluding with state leaders and weak state bureaucracies to manipulate and evade the rules that those bureaucracies are designed to enforce, warlordism is associated with illegal border activities. Warlords smuggle weapons, narcotics, goods, and people across borders, and are adept at avoiding state customs duties. Warlords are often associated not only with economic inefficiency, stunted growth, and weakened states, but also with a range of transnational social ills such as drug addiction, the gun culture, and human trafficking.

Furthermore, warlords make bargains not only with their domestic, titular state leaders but with foreign states who view them opportunistically. Border states can use warlords to sap the resources or challenge the domestic sovereignty of weak neighbors. Distant states can use warlords to gain a measure of influence inside the territories of weak partners or competitors. By working through warlords, foreign states can expand their influence into new territory without paying the costs of direct territorial control.

These relationships are underexplored by political scientists, even though Huntington noted long ago that any corrupt political order is vulnerable to being influenced from the outside as well as the inside.[49] Those who have studied warlordism and criminalized local militias, including Reno, Giustozzi, Charles King, and Peter Andreas, have certainly explored the ways that warlords use and manipulate external actors to garner profits and maintain themselves in positions of power.[50] Warlords bribe and blackmail foreigners who are investing in the mines or oil wells located on their territory, and develop symbiotic relationships with international aid agencies delivering humanitarian goods. But this literature has not explored the reverse pathway in much depth: the fact that external states use and manipulate warlords to undermine sovereignty or gain influence within the states they are targeting.

This may be because middleman warlords fall into the gap that still divides subfields in the discipline from each other. In the international relations subfield there has been an explosion of interest in the concept of sovereignty. Yet scholars have defined sovereignty and its limits from the perspective of direct foreign coercion and contracting between states and state leaders, without discussing the role of middleman warlords or other intermediaries. Krasner demonstrates that the supposed Westphalian norm of exclusive state control over political decisions made on state territory has always been more myth than practice. But all of the instances he notes where states have been coerced into giving up particular aspects of policy control are under direct diplomatic or military pressure from foreign states.[51] Similarly, David A. Lake convincingly argues that sovereignty is divisible, and can be renegotiated as circumstances change. Yet he argues that this divisibility is based on implicit contracts between dominant and subordinate states in an international hierarchy—in other words, in direct bargains between states and their leaders.[52] Alexander Cooley and Hendrik Spruyt analyze a variety of cases where state leaders have voluntarily bargained away or taken back control of particular policy areas for their own self-interested political purposes. But the bargaining they describe is all state-to-state.[53] All of these scholars portray violations of sovereignty norms as if they occur only on the *international* level of relations between states, or between leaders as institutional representatives of different states: one state invades another, sanctions another, makes contracts with another, or enters compacts with others. In contrast, middleman warlords link foreign states through personalistic relationships rather than state institutions, and can serve to weaken domestic sovereignty on behalf of the interests of a foreign entity.

From the other side, comparative politics specialists such as Joel Migdal and Catherine Boone have explored the political and economic interests that link state leaders and low-level state bureaucrats to local "strongmen" or "bosses" who thwart state autonomy and control from within.[54] This long-standing comparative politics literature is quite compatible with the idea that warlords and weak states coexist. State leaders have a strong incentive to affirm their international legal sovereignty since this comes with privileges—prestige, media attention, and access to loans and other resources—that can be translated into domestic political capital.[55] They also have an incentive to publicly claim domestic sovereignty, since patriotism and respect for state institutions provide popular legitimacy for their regimes and levers to influence people's behavior.[56] Yet these interests in furthering the image of state sovereignty sometimes contradict other, careerist interests of state officials and lower-level bureaucrats, who need the support (or at least the indifference) of powerful local clans and the strongmen who head them in order to stay in power. A state that is fully sovereign on paper may be weak in practice, when state representatives have an incentive to negotiate with warlords. Where local interests are threatened by efforts to extend state control, local strongmen protect those interests through bargains with state representatives, thereby thwarting domestic sovereignty.

Migdal and Boone recognize that relationships between bosses and states have been shaped by international interactions, since they are sometimes the result of postcolonial overhang from empires that used local chiefs or bosses to practice indirect rule. Yet Migdal and Boone portray these postcolonial interactions as occurring on what amounts to the *domestic* level. Strongmen, in this model, maintain their authority by using resources that are now locally based, even if their original power relied on assistance from an external colonizer.[57] In contrast, middleman warlords gain at least part of their strength from resources currently supplied by foreign actors.

The literature on the political economy of empires does describe and analyze bridging relationships between local strongmen and external states. For example, Karen Barkey finds that the Ottoman Empire, as well as the Russian and Chinese empires, grew through patrimonialism and bargaining relationships. She argues that Ottoman leaders used these techniques to incorporate local bandits and their militias.[58] The Ottoman Empire made bargains with segmented elites, separate "brokers" (in network theory terms) whose political networks extended up to the center and down to their individual peripheries.[59] Daniel H. Nexon applies these arguments to the early modern era in Europe, where most empires worked out what amounted to separate contracts with various "violence-wielding patrons" or warlords. They used these segmented relationships to create composite states that were internally differentiated, succeeding through divide-and-rule tactics as long as their citizens remained unconnected to each other.[60] There is also a large literature on how the French, British, and American Empires across the nineteenth and early twentieth centuries used patronage to reward particular local actors, who would then use their militias to maintain imperial interests in the periphery through indirect rule.[61] All of these studies, however, focus on eras when universal sovereignty was not yet the norm, and when cooperating with a local boss did not imply that a foreign state was undercutting another sovereign state. The warlords of this era were more like imperial lackeys than middlemen.

Warlords today often work in political spaces that cross recognized state boundaries.[62] The patronage networks that define them are often transnational and benefit actors in one state at the cost of another state's sovereignty. This situation encourages warlords to play one sovereign state off another, while relying on the continued support of both. Dealing with warlords often means engaging in a form of diplomacy, and flirting with the possibility of state-to-state conflict and war.

These negative aspects and challenges of warlordism do not imply that strong states are necessarily better for populations than warlords are. Strong states can be oppressive and authoritarian, genocidal and slaveholding. Charles Tilly reminded us that state-building in early modern Europe was a violent enterprise, at least in part because ordinary people resisted the forced taxation and conscription it entailed. They wanted to be left alone.[63] James C. Scott similarly argues that many people in Southeast Asia in previous centuries tried to flee statehood, for example by migrating to swampy and mountainous areas beyond the margin of state control.[64] While philosopher Thomas Hobbes hoped that the state would relieve humanity's "continual fear, and danger of violent death,"[65] that doesn't always happen in reality.

Yet without state-like structures that have impersonal governance systems and permanent rules, large populations cannot hope to flourish. Long-term, predictable order is provided by institutions that span large spaces, and a modicum of order is necessary for both immediate human security and long-range planning. Even the transnational Al Qaeda terrorist organization seemed to have the ultimate goal of establishing state-like, territorial caliphates in the Muslim world.[66] Al Qaeda actually had a difficult time operating in the failed state of Somalia, in part because of high transportation and operating costs in an area bereft of reliable security institutions.[67] In other words, Hobbes was partly right: in the modern world, some form of minimal statehood is a necessary but not sufficient condition for any complex human activity.

THE PLAN OF THE BOOK

Chapter 2 makes the key theoretical contribution of this book. It argues that warlordism in the modern world—in other words, in the universal state system—is distinct from warlordism in medieval European feudal society. In today's system of universal sovereignty, where all livable space on the globe is claimed by recognized states, warlords have no incentive to build states or state institutions. Warlords now arise and prosper only when they are at least tacitly protected and supported by states, because they are always surrounded by state security forces that could attack them instead. Individuals who choose to become warlords are adept at manipulating weak state structures to their advantage, often penetrating state bureaucracies, and they face incentives to continue their behavior rather than contribute to genuine state sovereignty. Protection by states frees them from the need for self-sufficiency and complex war-fighting capabilities that the state-builders of early modern Europe faced. As a result, warlordism in today's world leads to ongoing state failure, not state-building.

The narrative chapters that follow chapter 2 present case studies of how warlords and states have interacted in recent history. The relationship between warlords and states is an understudied phenomenon, and there were no hypotheses in the existing literature that I could test in this book. Instead, this is an exercise in inductive and policy-relevant theory-building, starting more or less from scratch. I chose cases in strategic hot spots that are likely to be of continuing interest for ongoing international security concerns, where state dealings with warlords were underexplored and sometimes counterintuitive. I did not want to be caught describing a case that was still in motion with my conclusions in danger of being upended by current events, so each of the cases has some sort of end result to observe. I also chose cases where source material allowed me to perform in-depth process tracing of the unfolding relationships between states and warlords using the two languages I know, English and Russian. In each case my goal was to unearth key variables that could be applied across many cases, and to be honest about the limits of their generalizability.[68]

The cases are drawn from two former empires, the British and the Soviet, which both practiced forms of indirect rule that may have laid the groundwork for warlords to emerge later on. In the two cases drawn from the former British empire, large numbers of small-scale warlords grew out of a history of manipulation of tribes in regions that were difficult to rule. In the two post-Soviet cases, single warlords controlled larger discrete areas with the support of state leaders who were unable to control the territory. In each case, nevertheless, the warlords emerged out of very different backgrounds and through very different pathways. There was no shared societal or political factor across the cases that would have allowed analysts to predict in advance the emergence of warlords in some places but not others. All of the warlords had support from some kind of local social network, but the networks differed. Most included a familial element, but this ranged from large tribes connected through many generations to small clans of immediate relatives. Some networks were based more on neighborhood, school, or workplace ties than on family.

Chapter 3 examines Pakistan's Federally Administered Tribal Areas (FATA) in the twentieth century. The British Empire and the postcolonial Pakistani state distorted and manipulated tribal norms to create a system of enduring warlordism, where the warlords were tribal leaders

[16]

appointed by the capital. This system was enshrined in Pakistan's constitution, in a unique state attempt to achieve stability through a decades-long bargain. The bargain protected the state's de jure sovereignty against Afghanistan and its allies, with the warlords acting as middlemen along the border. But it led to grinding poverty and underdevelopment, a lack of real border controls, resentment from residents of the FATA who were cut out of the warlord bargain, and the absence of good state information about what was happening on the ground. When Pakistani leaders decided to end the bargain and support radical Islamists in the FATA instead, they unintentionally created anarchy. The case reveals that another mechanism might have ended the bargain more peacefully: labor migration out of the FATA in the early 1970s began to create a capitalist alternative to the warlord patronage system there, until it was snuffed out by a global recession.

Chapters 4 and 5 examine cases from the post-Soviet empire. Chapter 4 looks at two middleman warlords in Georgia who were first supported by President Eduard Shevardnadze and then overthrown a few years later by President Mikheil Saakashvili. This is the only case in modern history where two state leaders made such drastically different choices toward the same warlords under the same international conditions, and it therefore serves as a natural experiment for studying the consequences of their choices. As was the case for Pakistan and the FATA, Shevardnadze chose to work with these warlords in fear that an external actor—in this case, Russia or Russia-supported Abkhazia—would otherwise use them to unleash havoc. Both warlords were supported by clans of one sort or another. Saakashvili demonstrated that with good state information about clan patronage bargains, the warlord's supporters could be peeled away to help restore domestic sovereignty. But while in one case he worked well with Russia to remove the warlord in question, in the other case his precipitous actions helped lay the groundwork for his disastrous 2008 war with Russia. Working with middleman warlords requires skillful diplomacy.

Chapter 5 looks at the relationship between Russian leader Vladimir Putin and Ramzan Kadyrov in the Russian province of Chechnya. Unlike the other cases presented in the book, Putin did not come upon a case of warlordism and then decide to support it; instead he consciously chose to make Ramzan a warlord.[69] As in the Georgian cases, Ramzan was supported by a clan structure, but in contrast to Saakashvili's efforts to gather information about those clans, Putin increasingly shed potential sources of information about Chechen politics with time, withdrawing security forces command in the region and giving Ramzan more and more legal freedom to maneuver. He did this even though he was a direct observer and participant in the Georgian cases, and hence knew

[17]

what the consequences of these choices were for Russian sovereignty. The chapter explores the potential motives of Russian leaders for making these surprising choices, and their potential future consequences.

Chapter 6 looks at the US choice to support Sunni militias in Iraq through the Anbar Awakening and Sons of Iraq (SOI) programs starting in late 2006. As in the FATA case, a system of warlordism had been established in Iraq when both the British Empire and the postcolonial state under Saddam Hussein chose to distort and manipulate tribal norms. Saddam went even further, encouraging the creation of small militias within his own security forces to prevent a unified military coup. Saddam's patronage of Sunni warlords was first replaced by the patronage of Al Qaeda in Iraq (AQI) after Saddam's fall, and then by the patronage of the United States and its coalition allies when AQI proved an unacceptable ally for the militias. The SOI and the US military used each other to defeat AQI, but Washington never managed to convince Baghdad's Shia leaders to fully support the program, and there were too many warlords and their interests were too diverse for them to take collective action easily. The result was instability and continuing violence (though on a smaller scale) as US forces withdrew and the warlords searched for yet another replacement patron in the absence of Iraqi state support. The United States had not intended to support a system of warlordism, but that was one of the ultimate consequences of its policies.

For each case the chapter analyzes why and how states made the choices they did toward warlords, and what the results of their choices imply for stability, social and economic well-being, and security. The conclusion to each chapter draws out generalizable lessons for policy makers from each case, while noting the conditions that might limit the scope of their applicability elsewhere.

In the final chapter I bring these individual case lessons together to propose a series of inductive hypotheses about the trajectory and consequences of warlordism. My hope is that these hypotheses will be useful both to scholars conducting research on warlordism, and to policy makers who have to face the conundrums presented by dealing with warlords in the real world.

A Concluding Thought on Afghanistan

State leaders sometimes act as if they had no choice except to support warlords. If the only alternative to warlordism is a well-functioning European-style state, the argument goes, what choice is there? Afghanistan in 2002 was, after all, not modern France, and at least the bargains reached with warlords provided some stability. But this is a false dichotomy.

The alternative to supporting warlords is not to create European-style nation-states with well-functioning democracies. It is instead to support the growth of impersonal state-like structures, however imperfect and minimal they might be.

One can imagine an Afghan space in 2011, ten years after the US-led invasion, ruled not by a pseudo-president and a gaggle of warlords who undermine ongoing efforts at real state-building, but instead by traditional, elected, provincial *jirga* councils that retain a great deal of local autonomy. These jirgas would need to have been established quickly in mid-to-late 2002, when local people were still excited about the possibility of change and self-governance, and they would need to have been adequately supported by UN-authorized international forces. In this alterative scenario, Afghanistan's national institutions might have been limited to common tax codes, banking and foreign investment rules, and border and customs laws. These could have been agreed upon by a national-level jirga drawn from the provincial ones, with a small, well-trained executive organization to write and manage the rules, and with federal security forces to enforce them and defend the state from outside attack. Local policing and judicial matters, tax collection, and health and education issues would have been overseen by the provincial jirgas as state-recognized institutions. There would be corruption and human rights violations, as there are in today's Afghanistan, yet there would also be a sense of order and stability, provided not by warlords (or centrally appointed governors) and their feuding militias, but by predictable and enduring mechanisms of popular governance extending across a large space. Institutions would be accountable to their people, rather than having warlords dependent on outside patrons.

State structures in the real Afghanistan may have become too corrupted and distorted to make a do-over possible. But warlordism was not the inevitable outcome of the conflict. Warlords are not the only solution to the problem of weak central states. They are merely the default option.

[2]

Warlords and Universal Sovereignty

Warlords rule by force and personal patronage, rather than governing through institutions. Yet Douglass North, after explaining why institutions are a prerequisite for economic growth, went on to argue that efficient government institutions emerge naturally over time as trading opportunities increase. Powerful actors, in his view, realize that it is in their interests to create institutions to control the costs of increasingly complex transactions with strangers.[1] Might not warlords, then, evolve into state-builders who value the creation of institutions in order to build and protect their profits?

Warlords share important characteristics with many internationally recognized states today. States can also rely on violence and centralized patron-client relationships, not impersonal legality, to maintain domestic sovereignty. Sociologists and political scientists have used a variety of perspectives, including neo-Marxist world systems theory,[2] rational choice theory,[3] and the bounded rationality of cultural norms and habits,[4] to examine the trajectory of such states. In each of these traditions, "patrimonial" or "natural" or "contract-poor" states that are dominated by force and patronage are seen as precursors to the eventual emergence of European-style liberal democracies and open economies. For example, in the view of North, John Joseph Wallis and Barry R. Weingast, state wielders of force and patronage can make binding pacts between themselves to limit their own predatory behavior, eventually creating space for the emergence of liberal state institutions.[5] Why can't warlords simply expand their territorial control and trading interests, and become state-building kings?

This would also seem consistent with Charles Tilly's widely cited model of European state-building. Tilly posited that the people who emerged as the successful kings of early modern Europe were simply those who ran the biggest and most successful protection rackets.[6] Tilly explicitly noted that his model was grounded in medieval European history, however, and that he had doubts about whether it could be transposed to the modern world.[7] Certainly the political system of warlordism today in many ways resembles the political system of medieval European feudalism,[8] and early modern states eventually grew out of feudal incentive structures. Yet there is a crucial difference between medieval Europe and warlordism today. Because of the universal state system, today's warlords arise and exist *inside states* where they are at least tacitly protected by domestic or foreign state leaders. They are creatures of states and they feed off state resources. In turn this has implications for the incentive structures that today's warlords face, in contrast to their medieval forbears.

TERRITORY AND RIGHTS IN THE MEDIEVAL WORLD

Medieval feudal lords in Europe gained control over territory when kings granted them parcels of land in return for their military service. This was a time when communication and transportation over long distances, especially over land, were difficult. Kings could not control outlying areas very well when unpaved roads washed out during the rainy season, and when swamps and mountains could only be crossed by foot.[9] As sociologist Norbert Elias argued in his classic work on state-formation in continental Europe, this had important implications for the relationships that medieval lords had both to the king and to each other.[10]

The difficulty of transportation meant that the wealth of kings and lords depended on what they could produce on their own lands and barter with their immediate neighbors. The only long-distance trade at that time occurred in luxury goods. Hendrik Spruyt argues that luxury trade was possible because those goods were compact, high-value items, easy and profitable to protect with a small band of heavily armed men. Transporting grain or other bulky and low-value goods was unprofitable because protection was too difficult and expensive.[11] Meanwhile, as the Roman Empire disintegrated and neighboring tribes challenged kings' control over their spaces, each king had to fight more and more battles and give away increasing amounts of land to retainers in return for their service. This meant that the king's power declined relative to the feudal lords, because the king had less land to use for generating wealth. While the king may have retained abstract "rights" to the land given away, Elias wrote, in practice territorial control devolved to a lord "strong enough to defend what he possessed."[12] In other words, medieval lords became warlords.

Individuals at that time derived rights and duties from personal loyalties, not from recognized or enforceable property rights or other laws.[13] Loyalties overlapped each other and political control was therefore contested between and among kings, church officials, princes, knights, and lords. There was no clear hierarchy. The writ of one or another authority extended over people as individuals, not over demarcated land.[14] Kings lacked many aspects of what we take for granted today as elements of state power. They had to fight wars with temporary armies of irregular size and uncertain allegiance, cobbled together from local dukedoms or religious orders.[15] They were represented in the hinterlands by people whose own loyalties were mixed, and had to compete for legal and judicial authority with multiple regional courts that had overlapping jurisdictions.[16]

Elias believed that as a result, the feudal lords were really operating in an anarchical, self-help system that resembled the realist state system of the modern era. There was no overarching legal authority that controlled or monitored the relations of feudal lords with each other or the king. When the security of the entire kingdom was threatened, a sufficiently strong king could temporarily count on the support of feudal lords who needed the king's protection. Yet as kings grew weaker by giving away more land, they threatened each other less, while lords simultaneously gained the productive base they needed to maintain horses and armor for their own defense against raiders. As a result the king's protection was rarely needed. "Central authority . . . weaken[ed] in times of peace." The whole purpose and meaning of royal functions declined, and "the king . . . was not much more than a baron, one territorial lord among others of equal power."[17]

Then, according to Elias, a variety of simultaneous transformations extending over centuries eventually allowed kings to once again seize the upper hand. European populations expanded so that there was no longer any unoccupied territory. This spurred increased productivity on existing land, and encouraged the rise of merchants and the expansion of long-distance trade. Transportation technology improved with the invention of horseshoes and shoulder yokes. As long-distance trade increased, easily carried money became the exchange mechanism, replacing barter in goods. Feudal lords who protected merchants could then charge easily collectible customs taxes as a result. Taxation allowed them to build up armies and engage in battles for more territory. In turn, alliances either with kings or against them became more and more necessary as warfare broke out again.

Elias did not specify why traditional royal houses, as opposed to equally or even more powerful dukedoms, became the dominant players in the anarchy of early modern Europe. He left a rather unconvincing answer that it must have been the "personal qualities" of successful kings and accidental factors of succession.[18] There is a better answer to the puzzle, though: kings reemerged on top because society's recognition of their traditional authority roles—in other words, the idea of kingship—gave them an advantage.

Kings could champion the emerging new norm of sovereign territoriality to justify their power and enhance their authority. It wasn't just force and patronage that mattered. It was also the eventual acceptance by lords and dukes over a period of many centuries that sovereign territorial rights were legitimate in return for sovereign protection. There had to be an alternative idea to replace the old understanding of how fealty relationships worked, and that idea evolved from the rediscovery of Roman law.

Sovereign rights, including the marking of territorial boundaries and the claim that public law was superior to personal fealty, were first asserted in Capetian France in the fourteenth century, according to Spruyt.[19] Robert Jackson argues that similar claims emerged in the Italian city-states during the fourteenth- and fifteenth-century Renaissance.[20] Jackson finds, though, that the sovereignty norm did not become widely accepted until kings throughout Europe used it to challenge the authority of the papacy in the Protestant Reformation of the sixteenth and seventeenth centuries. Saskia Sassen believes that sovereignty became the dominant idea only when kings converged on the idea of the mercantilist commonwealth in the late sixteenth century, with the notion that the wealth of the kingdom depended on the wealth of merchants and manufacturers that it could claim as its own.[21]

In other words, large groups of people were convinced by differing pathways and for different reasons that the institution of sovereignty served their own interests. Claims to sovereignty disrupted personal relationships and loyalties, and required people to accept new definitions of rights and duties. Questions included who had the right to claim sovereignty on any particular piece of land and how the exercise of sovereignty should actually be understood in practice.[22] Every authority relationship was being redefined in what amounted to a vast and ongoing experiment. In the process of experimentation, kings learned that alliances with merchants (or sometimes landlords in parliament) could enhance their legitimacy and support their claims of territorial control.[23] This process was helped by the fact that social groups in Europe, on their own initiative, had long formed themselves into recognized corporate bodies. Kings bargained with groups or estates that already had an established sense of legitimacy—not simply with warlords.[24]

Kings now created and enforced reliable laws that favored trade and investment on their territories. This in turn boosted their ability to collect taxes, since their subjects benefited from the protection of those laws and were willing to pay for it. Reliable taxation allowed kings to establish functioning bureaucracies whose loyalty was maintained by the sovereign norm and its related expectations, not just by patronage and force. Bureaucratic agencies regularized taxation and expenditures, enabling kings to fund, fight, and win increasingly complex and technologically demanding wars.[25] These processes established a cycle of expanding sovereign writ over ever-larger pieces of territory.[26] The result was what has been termed the "fiscal-military European state."[27]

Universal Sovereignty and Warlords

In contrast in today's state-centric, postcolonial world, all territory (except for some uninhabitable areas of Antarctica) has already been claimed by states. It is already subject to the agreed international norm of sovereignty, and despite all the talk of states being in decline, no alternative idea for understanding territorial control has yet emerged into wide practice. The only remaining question is sometimes which sovereign states will have their claims recognized by the United Nations, or who will have responsibility to bring new proto-states into eventual sovereign recognition.[28] There are no longer any physical limits to statehood. In a world where railroads, paved highways, and air travel are common everywhere, even far-flung mountains and swamps can be reached by state bureaucracies. (It is noteworthy that Afghanistan in 2011 remained one of the few states in the world without a nationwide railway system.) James C. Scott argues that technological developments made 1950 the defining year for the end of non-state territory.[29]

In turn, sovereign state leaders have resources at their disposal—including seats at the UN General Assembly, widespread media coverage of their statements and activities, and access to loans and aid from international organizations—that warlords do not. Sovereign states today are furthermore protected by international norms that condemn invasion for the sake of territorial expansion, leaving modern state boundaries fairly static.[30] This means that warlords cannot arise and flourish except through their interactions with one or more sovereign states, and the leaders of those states will always have superior resources that warlords cannot claim for themselves. Warlords today are a product of states, and of bargains they make with state leaders. If state leaders did not tacitly agree to the presence of warlords, then warlords would find themselves in constant warfare against the states surrounding them.

Sometimes today's Afghanistan is compared to medieval Europe.[31] What sets Afghanistan apart from that earlier era is that a functioning (if minimal) state existed throughout more than half of the twentieth century. The Afghan warlords of the 1990s were drawn from the ranks of former state military commanders, state university–educated political party members, and the children of state bureaucrats; they gained territorial control in the civil war that followed state collapse. Their current counterparts work with a state bureaucracy (however weak) that is supported by external state military forces and international financial institutions whose members are states. Similarly one might see Somalia as an anarchic exception to universal sovereignty, a stateless society that resembles medieval Europe. Somalia has had no functioning state bureaucracy for over a generation. Yet even in Somalia warlords first arose out of a disintegrating state military organization and later became ministers of weak state institutions. Their later counterparts endured at least in part because of the support of external states, including Ethiopia and the United States. Meanwhile the interests of the international community have converged on re-creating and supporting at least minimally functioning state structures in both Afghanistan and Somalia.

It is true that bargains reached between warlords and state leaders in one sense hark back to medieval forms of authority. Most are based on personal ties, not abstract hierarchies or legal documents like treaties and constitutions (the relationship between the Pakistani state and tribal warlords discussed in chapter 3 is an exception). These relationships are informal, unregulated, and subject to constant renegotiation as political and resource balances shift among the players. Such arrangements can sometimes look on the surface as if they are examples of Weber's rational-legal modern state arrangements, for example when warlords are appointed as official governors or heads of ministries by state leaders. But that is an illusion. In examples of warlordism ranging from early twentieth-century China through modern Afghanistan, a warlord who serves as an official regional governor will collect state taxes with one hand while skimming off profits with the other, in a complex patronage dance with state authorities that is backed by the warlord's private militia.[32]

Despite the similarity of informal patronage relationships, there is a crucial difference between medieval bargains and those of today, and that difference means that warlords are not likely to become state-builders. Warlords in today's world have arisen and consolidated and maintained their power precisely *because* of their ability to manipulate the dangling bureaucratic structures of weak states (or the interests of external states) while challenging genuine sovereign control. That is where their skill set lies; they use the resources of states to their own advantage. They will bargain, cooperate, and collude with state leaders, while continuing to defect from the state institutions whose weakness feeds them. They succeed because they have convinced state leaders to protect them.

This means that bargaining with warlords will not cause Afghanistan's Hamid Karzai to evolve into King Louis XIV of France.[33] The more likely scenario, when warlords in today's world expand their power, is the capture of the state by someone like Charles Taylor, who (according to William Reno) turned Liberia into a "warlord state" that pillaged and plundered its own resources.[34] Taylor was not a state-builder even when he became a state leader. Similarly, warlords whose militias become state military units will likely follow the path of their Chinese forbears under Chiang Kai-shek, proceeding to use their patronage networks to fragment and corrupt the army rather than building its strength as a state institution.[35]

Individuals choose to become warlords in today's world because they are driven to seek power and wealth through the use of violence, and they succeed when they are skilled at arranging tacit bargains with states that allow them to do this. A rare warlord may have a psychological transformation and break free of the given incentive structure to become a truly loyal bureaucrat or party member; several of these rare warlords could perhaps even form the kind of enduring pact between themselves that North, Wallis, and Weingast predict could lead to an institutionalized new state. Yet to make this transition would require a shift in the warlord's personal frame of reference: from being a specialist in violence who focuses on power relationships and coercion within the framework of state protection, to becoming a specialist in governance.[36] It would also require that the warlord buck the surrounding incentive structure that nourishes warlordism. The warlord would have to give up the relative safety of patronage for the long-shot hope that in his or her lifetime institutions based on the public good would emerge to maximize his or her wealth and reputation.

There are no cases of this happening in modern history, to my knowledge. Vadim Volkov's study of individual specialists in violence in Russia in the 1990s seems to want to argue that it happened there: that when Russian organized crime leaders became mayors and legitimate businessmen, they contributed to state-building. What his study actually shows, however, is that reconsolidation of the state occurred when a longstanding *established bureaucratic institution* of violence—namely the remnants of the old KGB—reemerged as the more effective manager of protection, and gained state control over other violent actors.[37] His study does not explain why this re-institutionalization occurred. The message, however, is that a state institution using state resources overwhelmed

[26]

private specialists in violence through the use of superior force—not that those private specialists in violence built new institutions that limited their own use of patronage and force.

Dipali Mukhopadhyay argues that it might happen in Afghanistan. In 2009 she cited the example of Balkh Province, where strongman Atta Mohammad Noor had been appointed governor by President Karzai. Atta sought advisory assistance from Western organizations to help rationalize and coordinate his provincial ministries, even as his private militia continued to control security on the territory and patronage politics dominated his rule.[38] He at least temporarily enforced internationally mandated rules on eliminating poppy cultivation.[39] The relative security of his province led Western donors and outside investors to flock to his province. Balkh's river port of Hairatan on the Uzbekistan border became the transit point for 80 percent of Afghanistan's fuel imports, including half the fuel used by NATO troops.[40] But credible reports indicate that Atta's willingness to cooperate with Karzai faded later that year as he was passed over for Afghanistan's vice presidency. Security in the province began to deteriorate, and outside investment slowed as a result.[41] By 2011 international observers lamented the return of opium poppies to the province (its illegal marijuana fields had never disappeared). Economic growth in Balkh was concentrated in the capital city of Mazar, where Atta's ethnic Tajik patronage network was protected by the police he appointed, and the Taliban took advantage of rural Pashtun discontent.[42] The ultimate consequences of Atta's rule remained uncertain.

Some might see hope for such a transformation in Somaliland, the one region of Somalia that is often cited as a potential new proto-state and a model for the country as a whole. But Somaliland is not the product of warlordism. Somaliland declared sovereignty for a week in 1960, at the end of British rule, before voluntarily merging with the rest of Somalia. Its population always had a sense of sovereign entitlement. It was protected from the warlord predation that wrecked the rest of Somalia in the 1990s by a combination of strong and enduring traditional clan-based governance and market institutions, and by individual leaders who saw themselves as specialists in governance rather than violence.[43] Gang leaders who hoped to become warlords there were quickly quashed by the local government. Somaliland might become an independent sovereign state one day, but if this occurs it will not be because a warlord from Somaliland became a state-builder. The warlords operate elsewhere.

The only apparent case where individual former warlords were successfully integrated into what would become a strong state institution are the few who were inducted into Mao Zedong's Red Army in the 1930s. Mao forced all of his soldiers, including the former warlords, to undergo harsh and continual Communist reeducation, and this appears to have cemented their obedience to the Red Army as an institution.[44] In other words, warlords were cajoled or forced into a different behavior pattern by an institution that had greater power than they did; they did not transform themselves out of the desire to make more profit on their territories by building institutions.

Institutions may evolve out of a warlord society, but they are unlikely to be founded or led by warlords. Instead they are likely to be founded by those fed up with warlord rule. Analysts who hope that warlords in today's world can become state-builders are probably conflating the evolution of societies and social groups over generations with the immediate evolution of individuals during their lifetimes. They may also be misusing the literature. None of the scholars cited at the start of this chapter who talk about the evolution of states provide empirical examples of individuals, as opposed to corporate entities like towns, actually changing their behavior from warlord to state-builder to participate in this evolution.

The Real Protection Racket

Individual warlords and leaders of weak states instead coexist in an uneasy symbiosis, making warlords state parasites and state-drainers, not state-builders. This symbiotic relationship has an important implication for Tilly's model of state-building, and helps further explain why the early modern European model does not apply to today's warlord-plagued states.

Tilly argued that it was the need to conduct complex, large-scale warfare against powerful competitors that caused modern states to grow in western Europe.[45] As warfare grew more demanding, bureaucracies were necessary to manage war while juggling other activities involved in political control. In turn, bureaucracy and war had to be funded by taxation, and successful taxation required successful businesses to provide it. Kings and the capitalists who required their protection had intertwined interests in state-building, either to wage war or to protect themselves from it.

Modern warlords instead coerce or co-opt state leaders into protecting them. Unlike medieval lords, they do not need to be self-sufficient in their production of economic resources. Unlike early modern kings, they also do not need to acquire or maintain the complex bureaucracies or popular tax bases that would support large-scale warfare. They instead rely on patronage bargains with internationally recognized state leaders, not just local citizens, for their protection and resources. In effect, warlords in today's world are the small-scale equivalent of sub-Saharan

African "quasi-states"[46] or oil-producing "rentier states,"[47] protected by a larger patronage system that guarantees their survival. They do not depend on taxpayer loyalty. When states that protect warlords are in turn protected from invasion by international recognition of their borders, the whole arrangement becomes congealed. It changes only when state leaders (or those leaders' interpretations of their own interests) change.

Tilly believed that state-building was not intentional, but instead an accidental by-product of a greedy desire for survival, wealth, and power.[48] Today's warlords may have similarly greedy desires, but they have no incentive to be state-builders. They gain survival, wealth, and power by their location within existing state structures, as long as those state structures remain weak and easy to manipulate. Building state institutions requires removing warlords and their militias as players.

Outsourcing Sovereignty

Why, given threats to their sovereign control, to economic development, and to state security that come from dealing with middlemen, do so many leaders of weak states and their external backers nevertheless bargain with warlords? To a striking degree this has been a preferred strategy followed by the United States and other liberal democratic states working through the UN system in the past few decades. In Afghanistan and Somalia this cooperation was explicit, just as it was in a previous era when the United States encouraged Chiang Kai-Shek to work with warlords in China. In Iraq, the US bargain with warlords was less talked about publicly but every bit as real. Furthermore Russia did the same thing on its own territory in Chechnya, even after Moscow witnessed and participated in the consequences of neighboring Georgia's similar choices.

The following case studies show that in a world of universal statehood with fairly static borders, cooperating with warlords is a way of outsourcing sovereignty. Indirect rule by warlords can save states—both domestic and foreign—budgetary expenditures, the lives of their troops and bureaucratic representatives, and the expenditure of political will that would be necessary for the direct rule of difficult territory. By bargaining with warlords, states gain a measure of influence and stability on a given piece of territory without paying the costs to occupy and defend it. Domestic states can claim de jure recognition on the territory, and foreign states can exert some influence there, even when de facto control would be prohibitively expensive in blood, treasure, and popular support. Warlords allow a form of indirect rule by states.

[29]

As in any example of outsourcing, however, the choice involves what scholars call a principal-agent problem, where the principal actor (the state) relies on an agent (the warlord) to fulfill assigned tasks. Principals often have a difficult time monitoring agents and enforcing their will, ensuring that the agent performs as promised. A warlord bargain is logically akin to the problem faced by states that employ private security contractors as a cost-saving measure, and risk having their overall strategic plans undermined by undisciplined tactical behavior that they cannot control.[49] It also parallels the dilemma faced by intervening states that rely on local informants to provide intelligence when choosing targets, risking the accidental murder of people based on disinformation.[50]

With warlordism, though, the outsourcing choice is potentially even more dangerous. Successful warlords are more powerful and enduring than either contracting companies or individual informants, since they have independent militias and patronage networks that lack transparency. The principal actors (or states) who choose these bargains often have no effective means to monitor or control what the agents (or warlords) do, except through bargaining or coercion. Ultimately what is being risked is the exercise of sovereign authority. That risk can undermine the very survival of the state by hollowing it out from within, leading to enduring state failure.

At the same time, though, external support of one kind or another, by payment, barter, or tacit approval, by domestic states or foreigners, is what keeps warlords functioning. Without some form of collusion by state actors, warlords in today's world could not continue to operate. This means that a warlord who loses one external patron, whether that patron is a domestic state leader or a foreign actor, has a strong incentive to go off in search of another. State patrons are replaceable, and that means that the choice to outsource sovereignty may not be easily revocable. Influence may glide away to another external actor as warlords seek the best deal.

State leaders who choose to outsource pieces of their sovereignty therefore have to hope that the warlords will continue to need and fear them more than they need and fear the warlords. A bargain with warlords may provide a cheap form of stability. It is unlikely to provide lasting security. Once struck it takes on a life of its own, unless and until state leaders are willing to bear the risks associated with breaking it.

[3]

Ungoverned Warlords

PAKISTAN'S FATA IN THE TWENTIETH CENTURY

The Federally Administered Tribal Areas (FATA) of Pakistan became crucial for US and international security concerns in the aftermath of the terrorist attacks of September 11, 2001. When Al Qaeda operatives and their local allies were pushed over the border by the initial US and coalition offensive in Afghanistan in early 2002, the FATA and its neighboring provinces inside Pakistan, the North-West Frontier Province (NWFP) and Baluchistan,[1] became crucial bases for the insurgent movement. Following years of Pakistani state support for radical armed Islamist groups in the region, including the Taliban, parts of the territory evolved into a safe haven for Al Qaeda. It took a few years for the United States to recognize the importance of the FATA.[2] By 2008, however, an intelligence community report to the Senate Armed Services Committee listed Al Qaeda's central leadership location in the FATA as one of the most significant threats to US security.[3] A few months later US President George W. Bush and Gen. David Petraeus separately stated that the next major terrorist attack against US territory would likely be organized in the FATA.[4] Within a year Islamist insurgency in the FATA threatened to destabilize Pakistan as a whole. Violence spread first to important tourist sites in the NWFP and then to the central province of Punjab, as operatives sought to punish the Pakistani state for its alliance with coalition forces in Afghanistan and to undermine its secular government.

Pakistan's responses veered wildly, between negotiation with particular Islamist militants and massive military intervention that destroyed infrastructure and displaced hundreds of thousands of residents. The dilemma of what the United States should do—given its concerns about the long-term security of Pakistan's nuclear arsenal, the location of the FATA on sovereign Pakistani territory, and the opaque bargains reached

[31]

Sources: GAO; USAID and Map Resources (maps).

Map 1. The Federally Administered Tribal Areas of Pakistan. U.S. Government Accountability Office

between actors in the FATA and Pakistan's own security agencies—became one of the defining foreign policy issues for the new US president, Barack Obama. Many observers believed that Pakistan's fate as a functioning state hung in the balance.

This case is therefore likely to have enduring policy relevance. The primary reason it is included in this book, though, is that it provides a unique opportunity to examine a long-standing and legally institutionalized relationship between states and tribal warlords. In the FATA, the Pakistani state's relationship with the men known as "official maliks" was so strong that it was codified into the constitution.

The history of the FATA makes an important contribution to the definition of warlordism. This is because it allows a clear distinction to be
drawn between what Max Weber called "traditional" tribal authority
(where accepted and indigenous social norms of governance have endured for generations) and the arbitrary empowerment of tribal warlords by state actors who seek stability in hard-to-control territory.[5] The
FATA case illustrates better than any other how tribes and their leaders
can be subverted and manipulated to spawn warlordism. In the late
nineteenth century imperial forces in what was then British India used
patronage to disrupt traditional Pashtun tribal norms and create a hereditary class of armed local power brokers in the FATA. The independent state of Pakistan continued this policy after 1947 and codified it into
Articles 246 and 247 of the Pakistani constitution, hoping to maintain
legal territorial integrity over the region against threats from neighboring Afghanistan (and later, from Afghanistan's Soviet supporters). A primogeniture rule ensured that the eldest son of each official *malik* would
eventually take his place in the patronage system. Since the time of the
British Empire, the authority of "tribal" leaders in the FATA emanated
from these state patronage relationships, not tradition.

As a result of this constitutional codification, the FATA showcases the
long-term implications of a choice that seems attractive in the short term
to state actors seeking stability in hard-to-control territory. While warlordism often creates immediate *instability*, since bargains are reached
between individual actors whose relative standing and strength are subject to sudden shifts, the hereditary and legalized FATA system endured
virtually unchanged across a century. (A different example of this will be
considered in chapter 5 on Chechnya. In that case the state legally empowered a single warlord, rather than a system of warlordism, and did
not codify any rules for succession.)

On the positive side, the FATA case demonstrates that stable, legal bargains with warlords can create geographical buffer zones that help prevent warfare from breaking out between contending states. Pakistan
succeeded in holding its contested border with Afghanistan when
the official maliks acted as middlemen. It bought off warlords who
might otherwise have supported independence for their territory as
"Pashtunistan."

The bargain nonetheless had terrible costs. In return for their loyalty
the state gave the official maliks unfettered access to patronage resources
while turning a blind eye to the drug trade and other smuggling that
some of them practiced. The border was held more in theory than practice. Furthermore, the constitution prevented the Pakistani state from
gaining much access to the FATA. Instead the official maliks became the
mediators for the center's aid, trade, and justice policy, embedded in a

permanent force-based patronage system that had no external account-ability and little oversight by Pakistani authorities. The state's only source of information about what happened in the FATA was a small group of appointed political agents (PAs) who had incentives to become enmeshed in private bargains with the official maliks. The result was that the FATA had an abysmal record of economic and political development, an arbitrary justice system, and a porous border with Afghanistan that made it a crossroads for the global heroin trade.

The finale to this seemingly stable tableau was dramatic: when the system broke, it shattered. The official maliks were actually quite weak, since they relied on state patronage for their authority. For a complex set of reasons discussed below, the Pakistani state, alongside its Saudi and US allies, shifted the favored recipients of its patronage over time. Rather than continuing to privilege the official maliks, Islamabad empowered a competing set of political actors in the region starting in the late 1970s: radical Islamists. Their rise was encouraged to counter Iranian influence and to fight the Soviets in Afghanistan, and their evolution was encouraged by the Pakistani state in an attempt to maintain Islamabad's influence over Kabul. In the end, though, Pakistan could not control what this newly empowered class of Islamist warlords did, and the result for Pakistan's own security was disastrous. By the end of the first decade of the new millennium Pakistani military forces were entrenched in brutal warfare in the FATA, displacing almost a third of the region's residents and destroying a great deal of infrastructure in an area that was already impoverished.

While press reports in the United States sometimes portray the Pakistani Taliban's influence as based completely on threats and violence, the truth is that popular resentment against the corruption of the existing order in the FATA helped bolster support for the militants.[6] As was the case for its counterpart in Afghanistan, the Pakistani Taliban gained local supporters in the FATA because it provided order and at least a rough form of criminal justice when the state could or would not. The state instead fell back on the now completely discredited constitutional bargains it had earlier reached with the official maliks. What had ensured stability across decades eventually created blowback against the Pakistani state, and anarchy.

The trajectory of the FATA is also interesting for an unexpected reason, turned up by chance during research on this case. (This happenstance finding supports the claims of qualitative methods proponents that inductive research on the idiosyncratic aspects of individual cases can make unique contributions to the development of social science theory.)[7] The FATA case demonstrates that ordinary people on warlord territory can sometimes gain a modicum of financial independence for themselves and their families through labor migration. During the oil boom of the 1970s, many FATA residents migrated illegally to the Persian Gulf and brought back substantial hidden remittances, avoiding the controls that the official maliks would otherwise have exerted over their actions. This began to create evolutionary social change in the FATA, as new outside resources competed against the old state patronage networks to influence the political economy of the region.

The process was short-circuited by a global recession (leading to falling oil prices) and the effects of the war in neighboring Afghanistan. Yet it suggests a possible causal pathway for undermining warlords: population mobility in a globalized era. As Allen Hicken points out, when low-ranking individuals gain mobility and higher income it becomes harder for patronage systems to operate. Behavior can't be monitored as easily, and the patron (in this case, the warlord) has to expend relatively more resources to keep people loyal, since mobile and wealthier people have more alternatives.[8] Samuel P. Huntington long argued that economic development creates social complexity, and social complexity is hard to manage without complex political institutions.[9] Labor migration leads to economic development that is not under warlord control, and that in turn undermines the effectiveness of the warlord's patronage networks.

This chapter outlines the characteristics of traditional tribal Pashtun culture, in two variations. It describes how that culture was undermined and manipulated by the imperial British Raj in India, and how and why the Pakistani state continued that manipulation throughout the twentieth century. It examines in particular the relations between the state and Pashtun tribal warlords in the early 1970s, when President Zulfikar Bhutto bought off their support against the territorial encroachment of Afghanistan. It then describes how and why an Islamist Pakistani leader, President Mohammad Zia ul-Haq, chipped away at that bargain by empowering radical mujahedin who eventually spawned the Taliban, and what the consequences of that choice were. Finally it describes how the migration of ordinary people from the FATA to the Persian Gulf during the oil boom years might have created an alternative trajectory for the region. The chapter concludes with a set of lessons that can be drawn from the case, and policy recommendations for dealing with warlords elsewhere.

TRIBES AND WARLORDISM

The FATA case raises a fundamental definitional question: is the FATA really representative of other regions in the world that suffer from warlordism? At first glance it would not appear to be an area where the "warlord" label fits. Its very name, "tribal areas," implies that something more traditional than modern warlordism has been practiced there. Indeed throughout recorded history the FATA was considered a wild and "ungovernable" place because of its fierce Pashtun warrior tribes.[10]

Many prominent analysts argue that Pashtun tribal identity continues to explain a great deal of political and social behavior in the FATA in the early twenty-first century. For example, Taliban activity at least in part reflects traditional rivalry among Pashtun tribes.[11] The border between Pakistan and Afghanistan (imposed by the British Empire as the Durand Line in 1893) artificially splits related tribes and their traditional patterns of trade and seasonal migration. The Taliban was an almost wholly Pashtun organization, even though its impact appeared to be growing in non-Pashtun areas of Pakistan by 2009. Key elements of the Taliban were controlled by members of the Ghilzai tribe and their relatives, as opposed to the better-favored Durrani tribe, which ruled Afghanistan for much of its history and includes President Hamid Karzai among its leaders. Some analysts think as a result that the US inadvertently took sides in a long-standing Pashtun tribal rivalry when it sent ground troops into Afghanistan. The fearsome Haqqani network, a different insurgent group, also relies on cross-border tribal connections to support its attacks in Afghanistan.[12]

Further strengthening the idea that tribes are key political actors in the FATA is the special place that they are granted under Pakistani state law. Until 2009 the political and security affairs of FATA were managed through an extraordinary negotiated constitutional arrangement, reached between tribal elders and the state of Pakistan at the declaration of the state's independence from British colonial rule in 1947. Under this agreement, federal laws did not apply to the FATA and federal courts lacked jurisdiction there. FATA's affairs were instead run by elders (the official maliks) through traditional assemblies (or jirgas), subject to direct intervention and oversight by the president of Pakistan (who used the administration of the NWFP governor for this purpose). Both justice and development assistance in the FATA were administered by the PAs through each tribal clan (or *khel*), in a collective manner to the clan as a whole. In August 2009 the Pakistani government announced that it would change this arrangement and work toward integrating the FATA into the normal procedures and structures that govern other provinces.[13] It remained unclear, however, how much change this entailed in practice, and how quickly change would come.[14]

Tribes and their leaders without question played a crucial role in FATA politics. Yet this did not reflect what Weber would have seen as being "traditional" tribal authority. Instead, traditional norms of tribal culture in the FATA were undermined by the lure of economic opportunity. Outsiders, starting with the British Empire and continuing through the age of Al Qaeda, artificially empowered individual men, setting them above the writ of tribal norms by giving them money and weapons that allowed them to create long-lasting patronage systems based on force. The support of outsiders created warlords in the FATA.

An extensive anthropological literature describes the history and mores of the Pashtun ethnic group in Pakistan. This clarifies how "traditional" tribal governance in the region would have looked, and how the reality diverged from the ideal. The culture expressed itself in two different forms, depending on the economic circumstances of the tribes: the *qalang* and the *nang*.

Qalang Society

One traditional form of Pashtun culture is found in areas where adequate rainwater created agricultural wealth. When Pashtuns first migrated into the region from the west at the turn of the sixteenth century, some tribes and khels were able to position themselves in relatively fertile river valleys. In these places natural irrigation from mountain runoff yielded abundant crops, and powerful individuals and families could seize control over large tracts of land. The landholders improved their property by building irrigation canals, and then hired tenants (who were usually not Pashtun) to do their farming. A hierarchical landholding social system became entrenched in these fertile areas.[15]

This sub-type of Pashtun social organization is known as qalang. (The term refers to the lease payments made by tenants to landlords, and the system was somewhat similar to the hierarchical *sardar* system established by the Baluch tribes in neighboring Baluchistan.)[16] Powerful landowners in qalang society were often granted the honorary title of "khan." The clan would turn to the khans for leadership in resolving internal conflicts and to represent the clan and tribe to outsiders. Khan status was often hereditary within the khel, although someone who acted dishonorably might lose the status and have it transferred to another kinsman instead.

While this precolonial Pashtun social system formed a hierarchy between Pashtuns and non-Pashtuns, and while it recognized particular individuals for their leadership and ability to control land, it was nonetheless built on a fundamental equalizing principle. This was because land ownership within each khel periodically rotated in a system called the *wesh*. A complex method of division was supposed to ensure that each family would maintain the approximate relative share (or *daftar*) of the available resources that it had when the Pashtuns first moved into the region, so that no one khan could become too powerful from developing his own lands.[17] In practice, wealthy and powerful khans might be given outsize daftars in return for providing protection or other benefits to surrounding families, but they too would have to rotate the area where that daftar was located. In other words, the accumulation of wealth gained from crop production could not accelerate over time; no one could become a super-khan.

In addition to the equalizing force of the wesh, tribal political affairs (including the resolution of criminal cases) were subject to democratic discussion inside jirga councils. These councils met at each village, khel, and tribal level, and their members included every honorable Pashtun man (honor, or nang, will be defined below). Wealth brought privilege, but there were significant social and structural limits placed on the dominance exercised by individual khans.

These qalang tribes nevertheless turned out to be relatively straightforward for the British Indian empire to control from a distance, because they had established powerful and socially legitimate leaders on their own. The Raj simply had to buy off the support of a predictable set of khans, who were already vested with the authority to deal with outsiders on behalf of the khel and tribe, in a system that brought mutual benefits to both sets of elites and further strengthened select khans.[18] Over time, khan authority came to be based on this outside support.[19] Several anthropologists have used the term "warlords" to describe these British-supported khans.[20] Their authority was based on force and outside patronage.

Qalang areas became the parts of the tribal region that were "settled" by the British Empire, or surveyed and taxed with officially allocated land ownership rights, starting in the late 1860s. The British made the wesh land rotation system illegal, and built canals through the settled areas and gave tax breaks to those who improved their property in order to further discourage its informal practice.[21] After Pakistan gained its independence from Britain, these settled areas were "enclosed" within the Baluchistan and NWFP provinces, becoming subject to the full writ of the state. Over time they gained political institutions that replicated those found elsewhere in the country. (Some Pashtun regions retained an intermediate arrangement called the Provincially Administered Tribal Areas, or PATA, under NWFP oversight. Most national laws applied but property rights were unique, and tenants were still collectively managed by their landlords.)[22] By the 1980s the hereditary khans and their close allies had used their resources to become part of Pakistan's urban upper class.[23]

Nang Society and Pashtunwali

The mountainous Pashtun areas along the Afghan border stand in stark contrast to the fertile qalang areas. These rocky regions have poor soil and little natural irrigation, since rainwater drains away too quickly. Large landholding here would not be profitable, and it is in fact rare. Pakistani anthropologist Akbar S. Ahmed believes that this natural geologic difference explains why Pashtuns in high altitude areas developed a different social system from those in the valley. The highland tribes were characterized by a much more marked equality of participation in the jirga.[24] In these parts of Pashtun society, dominated by the less fortunate, later-arriving tribes and khels (who were later most associated with the spawning of the Taliban), land ownership did not convey recognized political authority. Instead authority came from the maintenance of honor, or nang, conveyed through the consensus vote of the jirga.

The jirga made temporary distinctions among tribesmen. It was always led by a respected and level-headed elder who was chosen in advance. Each jirga also selected an executive enforcement arm to ensure that its decisions were implemented.[25] But there were no hereditary khans in these nang areas. Instead each honorable man had an equal voice in the proceedings.

Nang is defined by a well-established tribal code, the Pashtunwali. The code was so overwhelming in its social authority that Pashtun ethnicity (and hence the right to participate in the jirga) was not bestowed on everyone who had a Pashtun father. Instead it was granted only to those who practiced the code. Pashtunwali was reinforced through strong and constant social pressure and shaming.[26] For men the pressure came from the jirga and other regular social meetings at the public houses of tribal elders. For women it came from everyday interactions such as those at the water well, and especially during preparations for major social events like weddings. The code is misogynistic, treating women as commodities to be controlled, used, and traded by men.[27] Women in the tribal areas have nonetheless told Western anthropologists, even very recently, that they preferred to submit rather than face the lonely ostracism that would result if they demanded more rights.[28]

The code is complex, but the basic tenets of Pashtunwali measure a man's ability to defend his family line from threats, especially those coming from other families in the khel or tribe, and to attract a reliable band of fighters to support him against outside invaders. In other words, it is fundamentally martial. In these rocky and infertile areas, the most important family resource to guard against competitors was the water well.[29] The code lays out numerous and varying measures of a man's capability. A primary duty is hospitality, the protection and feeding of both clan members and strangers in the *hujra* guesthouse. This demonstrates a man's ability to produce extra resources to protect and feed a band of fighters in time of need. Those who are insufficiently hospitable are shamed as despicable misers.[30] Another important duty is *purda*, the covering and seclusion of women, which demonstrates a man's ability to maintain the purity of his hereditary line into the next generation. Paternal genealogy is a key determinant of who is Pashtun and belongs to which tribe and khel, and therefore who is allowed to participate in jirga politics.[31] A key duty is bravery, especially a willingness to take violent revenge and engage in blood feuds when one's family is harmed. This arose from a social system based on interactions between cousin (agnatic) rivals, who historically held adjoining tracts of land and might try to seize or damage their next-door neighbor's resources. The certain knowledge that a transgression would lead to revenge against the perpetrator's immediate family was a strong deterrent to misbehavior. In order to limit the duration and scope of feuds, the code allows both murder and theft to be bought off by an exchange of money or brides supervised by the jirga, if the victimized family agrees.

Alongside the equality of all honorable men, the Pashtunwali code is based on the notion that each family unit is independent and accountable only to itself. This puts a premium on individual male initiative for the family's economic survival, while not placing many limits on the kinds of activities that are pursued. Given the relative lack of arable land in nang regions, it helps explain why raiding and banditry, smuggling, gunrunning, the narcotics trade, and other activities that outsiders would consider criminal have traditionally flourished in the FATA. At the same time, it helps explain why large numbers of Pashtuns have throughout history shown the ambition and resourcefulness to leave the FATA in pursuit of money. Young men from the tribal areas, dating back to the time before the British Empire, frequently served globally as military recruits and often worked as migrant laborers in urban areas in both Pakistan and abroad.[32] Pashtuns have long dominated the long-distance bus and truck transport trade throughout Pakistan, as well as some commercial merchant sectors outside the FATA.[33]

BRITISH SUBVERSION OF THE TRIBAL CODE

The nang areas, like the qalang areas discussed above, soon had their original culture of equality undermined by outsiders. Those who wished to control the area consistently preferred to deal with powerful individuals who could be bought off, rather than with time-consuming and opaque jirga systems. These outsiders introduced the idea that certain maliks in the nang areas, like the khans in the qalang areas, could receive special privileges in representing the jirga to the outside world.

The notion of paying favored maliks in the FATA for their cooperation did not begin with the British. It appears to have extended back in history to every empire that wanted to control the tribes, including the Indian Mughals, the Afghan Durranis, and the Sikhs.[34] Outsiders would often use respected religious leaders or *pirs* as intermediaries to the maliks, hoping that religious authority could convince the maliks to support particular policies toward the friends and foes of whichever empire was in question.[35] In the early nineteenth century the emir of Afghanistan, himself a wealthy and powerful Pashtun, invented the system of allowing the tribes on each side of the Khyber Pass to split the tolls collected from travelers in return for their allegiance, at a time when British observers still believed these tribes to be "independent" and "wild."[36] The British were forced to continue these payments to the Afridi tribesmen when they arrived on the scene, in order to keep the pass open, "compelled to offer them a fixed subsidy to compensate them for the loss of their tolls."[37]

Yet the British were different from other empires in the region that dealt with the maliks, because the British imperial representatives had an Enlightenment-influenced cultural penchant for making categories and rules.[38] Unlike previous outsiders who simply bought off individual maliks as needed, British colonial authorities turned this into a fixed system of permanent genealogical hierarchies. The maliks' supposed relative power and influence among the tribes was laid out in print, creating a table to regularize British payments to them.[39] The lasting effect of this policy was that malik status became official and hereditary, rather than something based on the equality of all honorable men.[40]

British policy toward the tribal areas went through a number of phases over time, starting when the Raj initially seized the neighboring Punjab region away from Sikh control in 1849.[41] All of the variations, however, were centered on a desire by the British to hold the border of the empire against foreign encroachments. The policies relied on a changing combination of sticks and carrots administered by government authorities to the Pashtun tribes, in an attempt to win tribal support for the empire's ability to hold territory against external rivals. Over time those outside rivals ranged from the emir of Afghanistan and the Russian Empire in the nineteenth century, to Turkey during World War I and Nazi Germany in World War II. For example, after the British and their allies secured victory at the close of World War I in 1918, they paid bonuses to the Afridi tribesmen who had supported the Raj.[42]

In other words, the British created warlords in an effort to ensure border stability and security. They also paid the tribes to raise traditional *khasadar* militias to maintain order in the tribal regions, in the hopes that this would permit British troops to man imperial outposts there and construct roads for quick military passage. The British constructed almost 450 miles of paved roads in the Pashtun border areas by the beginning of the twentieth century. The contracts for road (and later, railroad) construction provided needed jobs for impoverished local tribesmen, while the roads themselves brought new trade into the region.[43] Yet the British never did succeed in gaining real control over the tribal areas. Even when the Raj said it was paying the maliks for good behavior, it would often try to forestall further bad behavior by paying the involved tribes *more* after they had unleashed some form of violence against the British. Some British participants at the time believed that this simply allowed the tribes to buy more weapons for rebellion.[44]

If the maliks were willing to accept British allowances to their tribes for cooperation, then they received additional personal compensation—usually amounting to around 7 percent of total disbursements—on top of what was given to the tribe as a whole.[45] Even when the British officially paid the allowances to the jirga, "a portion of the subsidy was reserved for certain individuals whose interests it was impossible to ignore."[46] According to one British colonial observer at the time, "When these people were made chief *Maliks*, then the palms of others began to itch, and by committing offenses in Government territory they too became *Maliks*." The chosen maliks were put forward for the honor not by the jirga as a whole, according to this report, but by small cliques "in the most slip-shod fashion."[47] British construction of such seemingly humanitarian projects as roads, railroads, and irrigation canals also served to further empower the favored khans and maliks, who could use their relative wealth to buy up land that could support cash crops for export, instead of relying on subsistence agriculture.[48]

The fact that the chosen maliks accepted this arrangement means that it was not simply imposed from the outside.[49] Indeed it demonstrates the limits of the Pashtunwali code of equality in influencing the behavior of elites. Outside funding served to disrupt the Pashtunwali, setting apart particular individuals and the militias they controlled for special treatment. In effect it turned them into warlords.

INSTITUTIONALIZING WARLORDISM

The British system was kept in place and institutionalized in the postcolonial era. The new state of Pakistan pledged in 1947 to continue disbursing allowances and subsidies in return for Pashtun tribal loyalty to the state. This was believed to be necessary because neighboring Afghanistan did not recognize the validity of Pakistan's border, which was defined by the British-era Durand Line that cut through Pashtun territory. Afghan leaders preferred that the "Pashtunistan" area should go to them, which would have significantly curtailed the size of the Pakistani state and squeezed what remained between a more powerful Afghanistan and India.

A grand jirga of two hundred maliks from the FATA was convinced by the new state of Pakistan to approve instead a bargain that was recognized in the new state's constitution.[50] Official malik status, as under the British, continued to be governed by primogeniture, in opposition to the Pashtunwali code's stress on the democratic equality of all honorable men.[51] In return for the state's agreement to maintain tribal autonomy in the FATA and to keep paying special subventions to individual maliks and their heirs, the maliks pledged to come to the defense of the Pakistani state when needed.

Immediately following the declaration of statehood, in 1948, this pledge was called in. The state asked the Pashtun tribes to lead their khasadar militias into the disputed Kashmir region as the process of partition took place, in order to drive India out. The official maliks did so, under the rubric of jihad against Hindu rule over a Muslim-majority area.[52] When the Indian army was called in to fight the Pashtuns, it became clear that the tribal militias alone could not hold the territory, and Pakistan soon sent in regular armed forces to back them up. Nevertheless, the militias made great headway, and throughout the twentieth century the official maliks cited this Kashmir service as a reason why the Pakistani state owed continuing allegiance to them and their families.[53]

Administrative matters in the FATA were run, as noted above, by state-appointed political agents. These members of the civil bureaucracy managed overall development assistance, collected revenue, maintained law and order, and acted as judges overseeing the jirga system in criminal cases.[54] This means that the hereditary maliks did not have absolute control in the FATA. For example, the PAs could name new official maliks on occasion, in return for favors they received.[55] Yet the official maliks served as the local power brokers because the rules forbade state security forces to enter the FATA unless specific tribal offenses harmed the state. This meant that the PAs could safely enter tribal territory only with official malik support. The khasadar forces that enforced order were funded, trained, and overseen by the PAs, but the official maliks were responsible for recruiting them and handing out their wages.[56] The PAs and the official maliks needed each other in order to function.

[43]

This did provide more autonomy to the tribal areas to set their own codes of legality and acceptable norms of social behavior through the jirga, since the FATA was not subject to the federal laws that governed the rest of the country. Yet the decisions and even the makeup of the jirga councils were subject to the approval of the PAs and the official, state-subsidized maliks rather than reflecting grassroots "tribal" autonomy. There was no means of redress against their decisions, because the FATA was not under the jurisdiction of the federal courts.[57] In other words, the system was run by personal patronage and the official maliks' khasa-dars, with plenty of opportunity for corruption. The official maliks and the PAs together controlled everything in FATA society, ranging from economic assistance and trade to policing. This allowed them to control political expression as well.[58] The Pakistani state outsourced the sovereignty of the FATA to hereditary warlords.

Until 2009, when it was announced that the system would be changed, the FATA remained governed by the Frontier Crimes Regulation (FCR) set up by the British in 1872. The FCR assigned collective responsibility to the tribes for the criminal actions of any individual member, reinforcing the traditional tribal code of shame and honor. As noted above, state security forces could not enter the FATA under normal circumstances, and policing was the responsibility of the khasadars; but if raiding or other violent criminal activity that affected settled Pakistan emanated from the FATA, the state could impose collective punishment (ranging from fines to brutal military action) against the entire tribe or khel. As late as 2005 state security forces who were battling insurgents in the FATA sometimes closed local schools and hospitals, fired khel members who were distant relations from government jobs in settled Pakistani territory,[59] held khel members (including young children) in jail, and razed the property of khel members living and working in the settled (and supposedly federally governed) NWFP, to punish transgressors in the FATA.[60] Much of the destruction ensuing from the Pakistani military incursions into the FATA in the first decade of the twenty-first century reflected the use of collective punishment against particular tribes.[61] (The state announced as part of its 2009 reform package that it would end such collective punishment.)

Development assistance too was based on a collective system that rewarded the localities of particular official maliks and penalized others. Officially, aid disbursements were based on a traditional system called *nikat* that reflected the population of each khel.[62] In a largely illiterate society ruled by patronage, however, where safe passage by state representatives was subject to approval by the official maliks, one can question the reliability of the censuses of these khel populations. Aid decisions probably depended on political patronage factors rather than the actual number of people in each official malik's territory.

This arrangement also meant that the FATA was not granted the democratic electoral procedures used elsewhere in the country. While it is easy to criticize the frequent subversion of democracy throughout Pakistan, the FATA stood apart even then. It was not until December 1996 that the national franchise was extended to all adults in the FATA. Over the previous two decades, only 35,000 official maliks had the vote, in an electoral college system.[63] The general population had to negotiate all of its dealings with the state through those same official maliks. They controlled the distribution of state-subsidized food rations and local building contracts, and decided who was eligible for state scholarships and employment and visas for foreign travel.[64] In an interesting twist, many of the official maliks chose to live in the more comfortable and "settled" city of Peshawar in the NWFP, and rarely visited their tribal homes.[65]

Even after the franchise was extended in 1996, so that the FATA now elected representatives to Pakistan's National Assembly, it was not clear what those representatives were supposed to do. The federal laws they voted on did not apply to their own region. As a result, they normally just fell in line behind whatever the dominant party in the country wanted.[66] Until 2009 political parties were not legally allowed to campaign in the FATA, so local elites maintained a great deal of influence over popular opinion in a region that was largely illiterate.

This imperial overhang in how the state and the official maliks treated each other helps explain why local observers in the late twentieth century believed that many of these official maliks were by definition not honorable men, but instead corrupt.[67] The official criminal jirga councils were also believed to be corrupt, influenced by the highest bidder.[68] Some state-supported jirgas even adjudicated disputes from the illegal narcotics trade.[69] Reportedly the favored maliks often did not share their bounty with the younger and less favored members of their own khels, who were not blessed by the accident of primogeniture.[70] Instead, many believed, the official maliks were acting in cahoots with the PAs, in a system some local analysts described as a "mafia that controls trade, jobs, construction and development business, and the funds meant for development."[71] As of October 2009, there were "no audits or even recorded accounts of government stipends to the maliks."[72] The favored maliks often stood in opposition to development schemes that might bring new possibilities for wealth generation into their regions, unless they could control the distribution of these resources themselves. At times they even used force to undercut projects that did not benefit them.[73]

An Example: Aid and "Pashtunistan" in the 1970s

Government outreach to the tribal areas in the early 1970s illustrates the impact of the state-malik relationship in practice. The genesis of this program was the civil war that caused Pakistan to split in 1971. Bengal nationalists in East Pakistan wanted their freedom from Islamabad; they were supported in this effort by Indian military intervention that led to a major war. The Bengal nationalists won, establishing sovereignty over the territory of East Pakistan and declaring it the new state of Bangladesh. Pakistani authorities feared that other nationalist groups might also break away from the state, including the Pashtuns living on the northwestern border with Afghanistan.

At that time the left-leaning National Awami Party (NAP), led by Khan Abdul Wali Khan of the NWFP, was continuing to champion the "Pashtunistan" idea.[74] The Pakistani state saw this as a cover for territorial expansion by Afghanistan. Afghanistan had been the only state to object to Pakistan's admission to the United Nations in 1947, arguing that "Pashtunistan" and the FATA territory belonged to Afghanistan, not Pakistan.[75] In 1969, at the time of the Bangladesh crisis, the Afghan state tourist agency actually published maps showing the entire Pashtun region of Pakistan as part of Afghanistan. It put one of these on display at the Afghan Ariana Airlines office in Pakistan's major commercial city and former capital, Karachi.[76] Afghanistan also established a series of "Pashtunistan *madaris*" (the plural of "madrasa," or religious school) in the FATA, where "schoolboys wore uniforms with a miniature flag of Pashtunistan on their sleeves and said a pledge of allegiance to the flag of Pashtunistan in their schoolyards each morning."[77] In 1972 Afghanistan again raised the Pashtunistan issue in the United Nations.[78] In 1973 Afghanistan's monarchy fell to Pashtun nationalist Mohammed Daoud Khan, the former prime minister and a Soviet ally who had earlier advocated military intervention into Pakistan's Pashtun territories. Pakistani leaders believed that Afghanistan might try to take advantage of the Bangladesh crisis, especially given the NAP's support for the Bengali nationalists, to encourage separatism in the FATA and split the country further.

This meant that the official maliks became middlemen who might allow Afghanistan to gain sway over Pakistani territory. Pakistan countered the "Pashtunistan" drive by buying off the official maliks with development assistance. Some saw this as an effort "to win the hearts and minds of the tribal people"[79] while others saw it as "bribe[s] by political authorities."[80] Over the next five years, almost 250 million rupees were earmarked for new FATA development projects, constituting a thirtyfold increase in aid to the region. Projects included the construction of schools, clinics, and roads, as well as electrification.[81] Prime Minister Zulfikar Ali Bhutto visited the tribal areas regularly—he was the first head of government to visit each of the political agencies in the FATA—and held open meetings where ordinary people were invited to sit in the audience.[82] Yet he implemented this assistance selectively, using it to reward his friends and punish his foes in both the NWFP and Baluchistan,[83] with the particular goal to "outflank his Pashtun rivals in the National Awami Party."[84]

The official maliks who agreed to cooperate with Bhutto got "double benefits": development projects were located in the territories that their khels controlled, and they themselves were made the individual contractors for those projects.[85] This increased their ability to dole out patronage favors. Bhutto was careful not to force state penetration too far. For example, some official maliks benefited from poppy growing and the drug trade, and the Pakistani state continued to ignore their activities.[86]

Reportedly the development assistance effort worked, and elite tribal support for the "Pashtunistan" idea declined.[87] Yet the aid that arrived in the FATA had negligible effect, probably because it was siphoned away by the official maliks. It is impossible to find hard data on what economic change in the FATA in the early 1970s may have actually involved, since there seem to have been no official records kept (official sources detail only the amount of money spent, not its consequences). But a comparison of the 1972 and 1981 Pakistani census reports for the FATA is instructive.[88] In addition to providing a household census, the reports include basic descriptions of such things as the number of schools per agency, the length of paved roads, and literacy rates. To the extent that the data in the two reports is comparable (which is questionable, because of differences in the methods used)[89] it provides little evidence of economic advancement during the 1970s. As the following comparison shows, while school construction proceeded apace, literacy rates remained abysmally low, indicating that the schools were not accomplishing much; and paved road construction appears to have been significant only in selected areas.

As of the most recent censuses in 1998 and 2003, the literacy rate in the FATA had increased to only 17.4 percent (still a fraction of Pakistan's overall rate of 44 percent), while female literacy in the FATA remained at only 3 percent. The FATA also had around 80 percent fewer doctors and a third fewer hospital beds per capita than Pakistan did as a whole.[90]

The figures from the earlier censuses may very well reflect the fact that Bhutto's outreach to the official maliks caused the aid to be misused. In the words of Akbar Ahmed, a government representative in the FATA at that time, "Work on the projects is often shoddy, but profits are large."[91] Into the twenty-first century, schools funded by development projects in

Table 1. Comparison of census data, 1972 and 1981, by FATA district

District[a]	1972 census report	1981 census report
Bajaur Agency	73 schools[b] 2.4% literacy rate 41 miles of paved roads	149 schools 2.4% literacy rate 45 miles[c] of paved roads
Khyber Agency	45 schools 8.6% literacy rate 90 miles of paved roads	168 schools 10.9% literacy rate 80 miles of paved roads
Kurram Agency	77 schools 5.6% literacy rate 50 miles of paved roads	179 schools 6.3% literacy rate 74 miles of paved roads
Mohmand Agency	27 schools 2.4% literacy rate 80 miles of paved roads	146 schools 3.6% literacy rate 66 miles of paved roads
North Waziristan	83 schools 8.3% literacy 91 miles of paved roads	209 schools 7.4% literacy 146 miles of paved roads
South Waziristan	98 schools 10.3% literacy 115 miles of paved roads	224 schools 7% literacy 170 miles of paved roads

[a] Only those districts that retained their definition between the two periods are included here.
[b] In each number listed here, the number of "primary," "middle," and "high" schools are combined.
[c] For the 1981 data, kilometers are converted to miles by the author for ease of comparison.

Sources: *Census Report of Federally Administered Tribal Areas (the FATA), 1972* (Islamabad: Pakistan Ministry of Interior Census Organization, 1979); and *1981 Census Report of Federally Administered Tribal Areas (the FATA)* (Islamabad: Pakistan Population Census Organization Statistics Division, 1984).

the FATA continued to be built on land provided by the official maliks, and those maliks continued to get double benefits. They hired their own family members as construction workers, and often the schools were built without plumbing and electricity generators, and without external walls for security. This was intentional. Parents would be reluctant to send their children to these schools, and teachers would not want to live in the faculty dormitories. The official maliks could then claim that local residents did not want the schools after all, and use the buildings instead as their hujra guesthouses.[92] In schools that did open, the guards and custodians tended to be the official malik's tribesmen, ensuring that only the favored children of his tribe or khel were welcome to attend.[93] Many health facilities constructed with development assistance in the FATA

[48]

have reportedly suffered a similar fate, being used by official maliks as their private property.[94] While road construction funded by development aid proceeded rapidly, those roads tended to connect the official maliks to their businesses, rather than being designed for general economic and social accessibility. Some observers believe that road building has received a disproportionate amount of development funds over time as a result of official malik pressure.[95]

Major public claims concerning official malik corruption in the FATA, as well as complaints against the constitutional arrangements reached with the maliks, surfaced as early as 1950.[96] They have grown with time. In recent years, the desire to turn the FATA into a "normal," integrated, state-penetrated province of Pakistan and the question of how to do so has topped the political agenda in the region, especially following the February 2008 elections that brought a civilian government back to power in Pakistan.[97]

Pakistani state outreach to the official maliks in the 1970s had the immediate desired political effect: support for the "Pashtunistan" idea in the FATA waned. The official malik warlords were successfully bought off once again. Yet this changed nothing about the basic relationship between the state and the people of the FATA.

JIHAD AND THE EMPOWERMENT OF THE MULLAHS

Pakistan's relationship with the official maliks began to change in the late 1970s with the rise of jihadist mullahs. Until very recently Islam did not hold much political sway in the FATA. Some analysts have argued that Islamist militants at the turn of the twenty-first century were playing similar roles to the "mad mullahs" who led jihad against the British Empire in the FATA at the end of the twentieth century.[98] A review of the evidence, however, indicates that this claim is incorrect. In previous eras it was the maliks, not the mullahs, who had the resources to maintain local political control. A series of decisions by the state of Pakistan turned this situation on its head by empowering radical mullahs to become a new set of local warlords.

Religious Figures in Pashtun Society

While Pashtuns were Muslims before their arrival in Pakistan, the importance of Pashtunwali as a social code traditionally trumped the importance of following Koranic laws and practices. Ahmed argues that contradictions between Pashtunwali and the Koran were simply shrugged off.[99] Perhaps as a consequence of this, while the roles played by Islamic religious figures in Pashtun society and politics have been complex and varied, they were usually not very powerful in tribal affairs. Islam traditionally only came to the fore when the Pashtuns needed a unifying principle to overcome their tribal rivalries and meet an external threat.[100]

Historically there were two distinct types of religious figures. The pirs or "saints" were mystical Sufi practitioners, revered because they were believed to have direct connections to Allah. The Sufist tradition within Islam is based on the belief that individuals can commune personally with God, seeking the subjugation of the self and expressing religious ecstasy through creative endeavors including music and dance, poetry, and artistic symbolism. Learning and growth among Sufi practitioners takes place through a combination of individual self-knowledge and eclectic continuing study under a master.[101] Pirs and their students were connected to each other through networks that marked their spiritual authority.[102] The pirs were therefore unusual men in the tribal areas, and were exceptionally well connected to the outside world.

The pirs were usually respected non-Pashtuns who were believed to be able to see things from a broader perspective and in ways not influenced by clan rivalry. The tribes would turn to them for political guidance in times of crisis. Throughout most Pashtun history, it was these extraordinary figures who led the battles against outsiders who tried to control tribal territory. They were able to associate threats to the Pashtun people with threats to Islam, and hence warfare in the tribal areas was a form of jihad. In areas like Swat, later part of the NWFP, pirs had wealthy patrons among the khans, and would be given large tracts of land to pass along to their families.[103]

In contrast to the pirs were the ordinary village mullahs in the FATA, Pashtun men who headed the mosques and offered instruction in the Koran to local boys. They had a far lower social status. Mullahs attended meetings of the jirga, but for the most part did not play much of an independent political role there. Unlike the pirs, they were not entrusted with the job of resolving tribal or clan disputes. They tended to be just as poorly educated and even more impoverished than the rest of the population, surviving on alms.[104] Many were functionally illiterate, beyond an ability to read the Koran and hadith (descriptions of the Prophet Mohammad's behavior) in Arabic through rote memorization.

Pakistani historian Sana Haroon argues that the division between pirs and ordinary mullahs in Pashtun society began to break down in the late nineteenth century, when the Indian Darul Ulum Deoband madrasa (established in 1867) started sending students (many of whom were Pashtun) into the NWFP after graduation.[105] The Deobandis arose out of the Sufi tradition, but distanced themselves from the mystical Sufi orders.

Instead the Deobandi curriculum and belief system were based on deep reading and knowledge of Koranic sharia law. Its graduates were disciplined and educated young men, fluent in both Arabic and Urdu (as a language that could unify ordinary Indian Muslims), and able to carry out philosophical debates on questions of Islamic practice.[106] Unlike the pirs, who stood above society, the Deobandi school was based on a reformist desire to purify Islamic society from within. The goal was to return the society to sharia law, in the belief that this would help restore justice to a people beset by what the Deobandis saw as the corrupting influences of the British imperial legal system.[107] They believed it was their duty to establish their own madaris in far-flung locations, to train ordinary mullahs in the correct sharia path. A Deobandi madrasa was established in Peshawar by the end of the nineteenth century.[108]

By the turn of the twentieth century, men trained in this tradition, whom the British called the "mad mullahs," were leading very successful jihads in the Pashtun tribal areas against imperial rule. Haroon argues that people started calling pirs and other exceptional religious figures "mullahs" with the rise of the Deobandi, and that as a result, by the early twentieth century a mullah was a "participant in the tribal jirga and was often asked to dispense justice on the basis of the established and indisputable principles of sharia."[109] Yet anthropologist Jon Anderson argues that tribal leaders feared that this Islamic authority could be unleashed against them, and would "often endeavor assiduously to keep [the mullahs] out of tribal affairs for just this reason."[110]

Since the new village mullahs still lacked both the landholdings and the more widespread fame of the earlier pirs, they continued to be completely dependent on the patronage of local maliks, including for the physical protection of their mosques against raiders.[111] Most were hired by the maliks on a contractual basis.[112] Hence the mullahs with their sharia law and the maliks with the Pashtunwali code reinforced each other's authority.[113] According to Ahmed, the mullahs would be granted leadership roles, as during the jihads, only "in times of extraordinary crisis or political upheaval."[114]

The Pakistani State and the Mullahs

This relationship changed when the state of Pakistan decided to empower certain mullahs. While sometimes this is portrayed as a result of events in Afghanistan, it actually began years before Pakistan started supporting jihad against the Soviet presence in Afghanistan. Journalist Zahid Hussain argues that the foundation was laid under Zulfikar Ali Bhutto in the early 1970s. In an effort to boost his political strength by appealing to new audiences and undercutting old opponents in the wake of the Bangladesh crisis, Bhutto explicitly linked Islam with Pakistani state nationalism. He used this new formulation to reach out to the Arab states of the Persian Gulf for both diplomatic and economic support. When he became prime minister in 1972, he visited fourteen Arab countries over the space of six months, encouraged the establishment of Arab language teaching centers throughout the country, and preached that all Islamic states had a unity of purpose, ensuring that Pakistan became a leading recipient of Arab foreign assistance as the Persian Gulf oil boom hit.[115] In 1976 he chose General Zia ul-Haq, who was enmeshed in a network of Islamists within the armed forces, as his new army chief of staff.[116]

Yet in Bhutto's era, these early Islamizing efforts were not allowed to destabilize the FATA. Because of his continuing bargain with the official maliks, Bhutto did not tolerate mullahs in the FATA who attempted to disrupt the traditional tribal power structure. Ahmed provides an example of this in his discussion of Mullah Noor Mohammad, a member of the Wazir tribe in South Waziristan.[117]

The South Waziristan agency is populated by the Wazir and Mahsud tribes of Pashtuns. The Mahsuds had long been the dominant group, with their official maliks having the most privileged ties to the state. Noor Mohammad, a young Wazir mullah, tried to change this. The son of the previous mullah, he returned to the area after his madrasa studies and received official permission to build a larger mosque where his father's had stood. He then proceeded to foster a growing marketplace, the Wana market, on nearby land (which was technically owned by the state) and taxed the market's commerce to pay for the improvements. As time went on the mosque became quite elaborate (with a fish-bearing stream running through it, for example), and the young mullah continued to build, establishing an associated madrasa for the sons of the nearby Wazir maliks. The graduates from the madrasa would then be given stalls and storefronts in the market, to cement a patronage relationship between the mullah and the malik families.

The mullah next turned to politics, inviting speakers to the mosque to criticize the government. He cultivated a charismatic image by forbidding the locals to listen to the radio, saying it was un-Islamic, and then using the radio broadcasts he himself received to "predict" national events to the illiterate congregants a few days before word traveled about things happening far away. He proceeded to use his charisma and the tax money he received from the market to whip up popular support, including the use of violence, against the more powerful Mahsud maliks whom he called government toadies. He succeeded in wheedling the area's timber permit away from them through clever bargaining with the state. Eventually he used his amassed resources to spark an armed conflict between the Wazir and Mahsud tribes of the area, declaring a jihad against the Mahsuds and paying each side to provoke violence against the other.

In other words, he acted like a classic warlord. But when things got too out of hand, the PA finally arrested him and his men and razed the market in 1976. Under Bhutto, the state may have started moving in an Islamist direction, but it stepped in to maintain status quo relations with the dominant official maliks in the FATA when renegade mullahs threatened their control.

This began to change a year later, when Zia unseated Bhutto in a military coup and eventually had him hanged. Zia empowered the Islamist political parties and individuals with whom he was connected, and for the first time in Pakistan's history Islamists gained government authority within the administration and entrenched positions inside important state bureaucracies, including the security forces.[118] The ties that Bhutto had earlier established with the Arab states of the Persian Gulf now started extending into Pakistan's domestic political realm, since those states sent diplomatic representatives to try to mediate between the opposing factions in the violent and highly contested Zia transition.[119] Simultaneously Zia began to encourage the political ascent of Islamist mullahs in the FATA.

Continuing fears about the Pashtunistan movement certainly help explain this choice: the mullahs were elevated at least in part as an opposing social force against the official maliks. Afghanistan, long supported by the Soviet Union, had become a communist state by 1978, and Zia feared that Kabul could use nationalist Pashtun propaganda to appeal to the leftist NAP.[120] An additional motive for outside Sunni (including Saudi) support for Zia's endeavors arose with the Shiite fundamentalist revolution in Iran in February 1979. The Ayatollah Khomeini's use of extremist Shia rhetoric to marshal popular support for revolution against an established secular state frightened many Sunni leaders (including Zia) whose countries had significant Shia populations. For this reason, funds for sectarian Sunni madaris began to flow in to Pakistan, especially to the province of Baluchistan along the Iranian border. Sunni-Shia sectarian conflict was inflamed by Zia, who encouraged the mullahs to become politically radicalized in a narrow interpretation of correct doctrine that drew on conservative Deobandi roots and even more conservative Saudi Wahhabism.[121]

On the heels of these events came the Soviet invasion of Afghanistan in December 1979, which was intended to prop up one faction in a Communist Party internecine conflict within the country. The United States interpreted the invasion as a Soviet attempt at territorial expansion, and therefore began to fund its Pakistani ally's support for the mujahedin insurgency against Soviet rule. By the mid-1980s the United States had become a lead contributor to the effort, joining Saudi Arabia in sending a total of $7.2 billion of covert assistance (mostly through the Pakistani state) to the mujahedin, including advanced weaponry that eventually featured the Stinger shoulder-held missile.[122] At Zia's insistence, the Pakistani Inter-Services Intelligence (ISI) directorate, an organization within the armed forces, was made the channel for funneling US and Saudi funds to the mujahedin. Much of that funding went to support Islamist clerics in the Pakistani border area who riled up jihadist fighters. USAID supported their madaris directly—for example, with textbooks whose math lessons encouraged students to count Kalashnikovs or dead Russians.[123]

The best estimate is that the Arab Persian Gulf countries established around a thousand new madaris in the NWFP and three hundred in the FATA, all preaching jihad.[124] Much additional funding for the madaris came from Pakistani emigrants living in the West, especially the United Kingdom.[125] More recently a major source of funding came from the Al Qaeda operatives hiding in the Pakistani border areas, in return for the logistical assistance and hospitality shown to them by locals.[126] In other words, unlike their historical counterparts, these radical new mullahs did not depend at all on malik patronage. Instead their funding was completely external.

In 1980, Zia also began financing the madaris himself through state taxes, subtracting the traditional Islamic *zakat* obligation to tithe to charity from all personal bank accounts in the country during the holy month of Ramadan.[127] All state development assistance in the FATA, including such things as the provision and protection of water, pastures, and forests, was redirected toward the jihadist goal,[128] and the amount of such assistance almost sextupled between 1976–77 and 1978–79 alone.[129] In other words, state patronage also shifted away from the official maliks to the radical new mullahs. These outside sources of funding, coming from the Pakistani state, from foreign state supporters, and from private citizens living abroad, all helped the mullahs attain a level of independence from the maliks that was unprecedented in Pashtun history.

COLLAPSE OF THE MALIK BARGAIN

Over time, the influx of new resources led to what amounted to a social revolution. The mullahs had been relatively minor actors until the state empowered and radicalized some of them; now those radicals gained enormous political authority.[130] Their madrasa students tended to come from the poorest parts of society—indeed the madaris attracted many orphans and children from dysfunctional homes, according to Zahid Hussain—who chose the madrasa life because they received free lodging and meals, in addition to a religious education. In short, they attracted boys whose families were cut out of the lucrative old official malik patronage networks. Madaris were also established in the Afghan refugee camps that had been set up in the FATA during the war, drawing strength from the number of impoverished and disaffected Pashtun youths there who had never experienced traditional tribal life.[131] The Pakistani madaris were linked with similar institutions in the cities of Kandahar and Ghazni in Afghanistan through teacher-student mullah networks, cementing the link between Afghan rebellion and the FATA.[132]

At the newfangled, ultraconservative madaris, boys were often isolated from the rest of society, denied television, radio, and most extracurricular activities.[133] This new and very narrow style of madrasa education gave students almost no employable skills, since only the Arabic Koran and hadith (not basic Urdu literacy or numeracy) were on the curriculum. Around 95 percent of mullahs in North Waziristan were functionally illiterate, for example, according to one Pakistani analyst.[134] Few job opportunities were available to graduates. Many joined the jihad because it was the only employment alternative. Other graduates set up their own new madaris in the poorest areas of the NWFP and Punjab, at least in part because they could get funding to support themselves this way even though they lacked the skills for other employment.[135]

The appeal of jihadist preaching was widened by the vast outflow of Afghan refugees over the border into the FATA and Baluchistan. The cross-border movement of Pashtuns strengthened kin social connections among the tribes.[136] Many of the new mullahs in the Swat region of the NWFP, for example, were Afghan refugees.[137] Estimates of the number of refugees in the peak year of 1984 range from 1.7 to 2.9 million people.[138] Many streamed back and forth across the border with the farming season or the movements of battle, thereby mimicking on a larger scale the traditional patterns of Pashtun life.[139] One small-scale survey at a single border crossing, conducted in 2005, revealed that the average traveler had made twenty personal crossings already. Several hundred thousand technically Afghan nationals remained in Pakistan in the early twenty-first century, although most of them had never actually lived in Afghanistan. The number of refugees actually increased after the worst phase of the war was over and the repatriation process began because of the high birthrate in the camps.[140] The refugees penetrated the Pakistani economy remarkably quickly, probably helping to spread the influence of jihadist thinking beyond their immediate communities. Eighty-seven percent of refugee households had at least one member who was a wage earner, whether merchant, tailor, farmer, trucker, or drug trader. The refugees soon dominated the cross-border trucking business, importing low-cost trucks through German aid programs. One analyst estimates that sixty thousand refugee families supported themselves through trucking.[141] As their income grew, the refugees replaced their tents with permanent mud-brick houses in the camps.[142]

It was this milieu that spawned the Taliban movement—literally "students" of Islam—in the mid-1990s. The Taliban were determined to take what they had learned in the madrasa classroom about the need for the purification of Islam, and apply it both to society at large and to the fighting in Afghanistan. They were much more radical even than the state-supported Islamists whose madaris they had attended. They rose to prominence under the administration of Pakistani Prime Minister Benazir Bhutto (Zulfikar's daughter). She supported them because she hoped their purification drive could clear away the warlords who had emerged in Afghanistan out of the anti-Soviet insurgency, who now impeded cross-border trade with their raiding and tolls.[143]

This influx of outsiders further challenged the power of the official maliks, since the newcomers from Afghanistan did not recognize their authority and were not in their patronage networks. The rise of the jihadist mullahs was sometimes welcomed by ordinary people in the FATA, who saw them as a counterweight to the corrupt official maliks. There is evidence that many young men in Pakistan who joined the jihad were those who felt they had no chance to advance in the existing tribal system, and who were economically and politically marginalized.[144] The mullahs as a class were "mythical heroes" because they had not allowed themselves to be bought off by the British in imperial times.[145]

The process of radicalization continued to evolve over time. The radicals turned their violence inward as Pakistan's military alliance with the United States against radical Islamism became more explicit. By 2009 several hundred official maliks had been assassinated by militants in a well-orchestrated campaign that targeted government supporters. Some of the remaining official maliks chose to share their own state patronage funds with the Islamists, in effect buying their own security.[146] In the words of journalist Zahid Hussain, "The influx of huge sums of money and a growing sense of power transformed the mullah's image from that of a docile and humble man to a mafia thug with a four-wheel-drive Jeep and armed bodyguards."[147] In some areas these so-called "Kalashnikov mullahs" took over villages or even city neighborhoods, terrorizing the population with their own version of sharia law, and using their mosques as prisons.[148]

In the end the Pakistani authorities who had empowered this radical Islamization got more than they bargained for. It became clear that they could not control the fervor, the evolution, or the ambition of the political actors they had originally put in place. One set of warlords was replaced by another. Pakistan had once again failed to truly penetrate the FATA, and this time around the problems of the FATA threatened Pakistan as a whole.

It can never be known what would have happened in the FATA without the rise of Islamist militancy. Perhaps the bargain between the PAs and the official maliks could have continued indefinitely. Yet given the economic and political despair of the region, the permanent disempowerment of those not favored by family connections to the official maliks, and the rise of television, Internet, and cell phone networks that have caused disenfranchised people around the world to recognize their relative deprivation, this is unlikely. It is a fair bet that sooner or later some kind of revolutionary idea would have disrupted the warlord bargain.

MIGRATION TO THE PERSIAN GULF

That revolutionary idea did not have to be radical Islamism, however. For a brief period in the 1970s an alternative idea infected the FATA, one marked not by an explicitly political agenda but instead by a popular slogan: "Dubai Chalo"—let's go to Dubai. Illegal labor migration allowed capitalism to enter the FATA, and it began to challenge the patronage system of the official maliks.

The peak era of oil boom migration to the Gulf states began in 1971, when Pakistan turned to Arab leaders for economic assistance following the disastrous war over Bangladeshi independence. It ended around 1988, as oil prices plummeted in a global recession. That was the last year that Pakistani foreign remittances from oil boom migration are estimated to have exceeded $2 billion.[149] While the cost of legal migration to the Gulf was prohibitive, and therefore pursued only by well-connected, middle-class Pakistanis, it was relatively easy to make the trip illegally. Many men got official hajj pilgrimage visas from the Saudi government to go to Mecca, and then overstayed; while they would eventually be expelled, reports indicate that the Saudi government actively encouraged this pattern, to ensure an adequate service-sector seasonal labor force.[150] Others made the risky choice common among illegal immigrants around the world, paying go-betweens to take them on leaky small boats across the Gulf from Baluchistan. Those who chose to migrate at this time were primarily the rural poor, especially unskilled and semiskilled laborers from low-productivity agricultural areas in the NWFP (and its associated tribal areas) and Punjab province.[151] Wages in the Gulf often exceeded the wages for similar work in Pakistan by a factor of ten.[152]

One Pakistani analyst claims that "most of the youngsters from tribal areas migrated overseas to work in the Arab states," noting that "the people from North and South Waziristan Agency were in the forefront."[153] The specific numbers of FATA migrants cannot be verified, as there are no reliable government statistics about how many people migrated from which areas of Pakistan. Both the Pakistani government and the recipient Gulf countries had incentives to underestimate the real numbers. Although migration benefited the economies in both directions (bringing in much-needed low-wage labor to the Gulf, and serving as a major source of foreign exchange earnings and population pressure relief for Pakistan), much of it was illegal and politically sensitive.[154]

According to recent survey data that resulted from questions asked about that earlier period, around 10 percent of all current NWFP households had received remittance payments then.[155] The percentage was probably higher in the more impoverished (and less surveyable) FATA, since it was the unirrigated areas of Pakistan that sent the most migrants. Anthropologist Charles Kennedy believes migration constituted "a safety valve for social and political unrest" among the Pashtuns.[156] The migrants may have included a significant number of Pashtun refugees from Afghanistan living in the FATA and the NWFP.[157]

Overall remittances cannot be accurately measured, since most were either sent through the informal *hundi* banking system or brought back as large durable goods purchases like refrigerators.[158] One local observer believes that the average FATA migrant sent about $200 per month home to his family, along with luxury goods like fancy cloth, watches, and radios.[159] These remittances may have quadrupled the per capita annual income for their households.[160] One mark of the impact that migration had on Pashtun areas was that the wages for unskilled workers at home rose drastically in response to the resulting new local labor shortage. In Peshawar, the NWFP capital that abuts the FATA, day laborer construction wages between 1969 and 1983 were reported to have risen from three to twenty rupees per day.[161]

The new wealth had a significant effect on the lives of local inhabitants. Remittances were used mostly for consumer goods, housing construction, and land purchases, and enabled those who had traditionally been at the bottom of the social hierarchy to obtain access to electricity, toilets, irrigation, and tractors.[162] About one-third of the returnees used their new wealth to open their own businesses for the first time, and those who returned to agricultural employment bought new farm machinery that allowed them increased independence, sometimes enabling them to buy the farms where they had previously been tenants.[163] This temporarily curtailed a longstanding pattern of rural-to-urban migration, since young men were migrating to the Gulf rather than to Pakistani cities for work, but "returning migrants [displayed] a marked preference for settling in cities." According to official figures, 31 percent of Pakistani migrants had originally come from cities, but 45 percent returned to them, and their families often used remittance payments to establish new residences in the cities while the migrants were still abroad.[164]

These choices followed a traditional pattern among tribal Pashtuns who earned money outside the FATA. For example, at the turn of the twentieth century, those retiring from the British Army tended to purchase land in Peshawar and then move there to start their own businesses. About half of the buildings in Peshawar are believed to be owned by Afridi Pashtuns whose families originated in the Khyber Agency of the FATA.[165]

In the early 1980s remittances provided about 10 percent of Pakistan's GNP.[166] They peaked in 1984–85; after that point oil prices started to fall, and the demand for Pakistani labor in the Persian Gulf progressively dried up[167] (although it may have rebounded more recently as oil prices rose again). Many of the newly opened businesses established by returnees at that time failed.[168] Hence the economic boost provided by out-migration was short-lived, and its positive effects in the Pashtun region in particular were undercut by the countervailing in-migration of Afghan refugees, which swelled throughout the 1980s and 1990s and worsened regional poverty. The impact of the returnees' investments was also probably curtailed by the rise of the militants and their external financing.[169]

Despite its short life, migration from the FATA, with ordinary families able to access new resources that were not controlled by the official maliks, holds important lessons. Some scholars, James C. Scott for one, emphasize that people sometimes avoid the state, running to ungovernable territories to maintain their freedom. Yet in the FATA, when the opportunity arose to move from the undeveloped tribal areas to cities that had electricity and running water and other trappings of relative well-being, ambitious men (and their families) went. They valued economic advancement for their families over the ability to avoid the writ of the state. Many wealthier Pashtuns maintained two residences, one in the tribal homeland and one in the NWFP, where they could take advantage of benefits like schools, hospitals, and business opportunities that only existed in an area with a functioning state.

Migration provided the most opportunity to those who had been at the bottom rungs of rural society, so it served (like radical Islamism) as a means for empowerment that upended the existing social order of the official maliks. While those maliks made sure that their sons got legal migration visas to take advantage of Gulf opportunities, they couldn't control illegal migration. Reportedly most of the returnees hid from their tribal elders exactly how much money they had made abroad,[170] and migration served as a means for the "junior, or depressed lineages" of the tribes to challenge official malik dominance.[171]

CONCLUSIONS

The situation in the FATA remains enormously complex. The area is largely impenetrable to most outsiders, and there are continuing incentives for both the official maliks' khasadars and new Islamist militias to limit access to the region's political economy. Yet the history of the FATA provides clear lessons for policy makers elsewhere.

One important lesson is echoed in the Sons of Iraq program. It is this: when policy makers think about "tribes" today, they should be mindful that both the colonial experience and later decisions by independent states may have subverted traditional tribal authority mechanisms. With outside patronage, tribal leaders can become warlords who act in accordance with their own individual self-interests, not necessarily in the interests of the tribal population as a whole. Rather than taking tribes as fixed social institutions that must be accommodated, policy makers should examine the real political economy that lies underneath. Supporting what appear to be tribal leaders may in effect be supporting warlordism, with all of its consequences, especially in any country with a history of empire or absolutism.

The FATA case shows that the bargains reached with warlords can lead to long-term stability, as their proponents in places like Afghanistan argue, especially if those bargains are institutionalized and codified into law. Many states are likely to value stability as a marker of security. They may prefer to aim for calmness in social relations, avoiding the disruptive or even revolutionary activity that would be necessary to enable a more just, and hence satisfied, society in areas that are hard to govern. As one rather sad illustration of this tendency, in 2009 foreign aid to the FATA, including from the United States, still relied on the PAs and the official maliks for safe access to the area, and for identifying the needs of the population and selecting which programs would be implemented.[172] The patronage bargain reached by the British Empire more than a century before was still determining the actions of states dealing with the FATA, despite overwhelming evidence of corruption and in spite of the negligible results of the similar aid bargain from the 1970s. There was no other choice, because the old system still legally controlled who was welcome in the region.

Stability in the FATA did lead to security in many ways, as long as the state did not try to penetrate warlord territory. The British had little success with their efforts to use patronage in the FATA to gain freedom of movement for colonial forces on tribal land. Yet they did gain malik support for external defense and warfare. Similarly the Pakistani state got its most important border security goals met for several decades, by allowing the official maliks to control the region. The independence of "Pashtunistan" was forestalled, the state of Afghanistan and its Soviet occupier were prevented from gaining a foothold on Pakistani land, and Pakistan maintained its territorial integrity in the northwest after the war over Bangladesh in the east. This may very well have forestalled further large-scale warfare in the 1970s and controlled the spread of war after the Soviet intervention in Afghanistan. That benefit should not be underestimated.

Stability nonetheless meant a border open to smuggling and the heroin trade, and terrible human suffering in the FATA. That suffering— both the lack of employment alternatives for men not connected to patronage networks, and popular resentment over state neglect and the inherent unfairness of the aid and justice system—contributed to the radical Islamist militancy that eventually threatened the existence of the Pakistani state. Pakistani authorities (and their Saudi and Cold War US supporters) are without question largely responsible for directly empowering the radical mullahs and militants. In that sense Pakistani leaders brought the scourge of Islamist extremism on themselves, independently of what happened in the FATA. At the same time, though, the bargain between the political agents and the official maliks, perceived by many FATA residents as corrupt, was a key enabler for the Taliban and its Al Qaeda allies. What this case ultimately shows is that even long-term stability in warlord regions can spawn insecurity that threatens state survival. Stability is not synonymous with security.

Furthermore, stability can become stagnation. Legal reform in the FATA began in 2009, but reform required upending the patronage bargains between the official maliks and state officials. It was therefore likely to be stalled and repeatedly thwarted. Legal and constitutional change might eventually arrive in the FATA—a simple act of parliament could alter many of the constitutional provisions underlying the system—but progress was likely to be slow and cumbersome at least in part because it threatened profitable patronage arrangements.

This leads to what may be an unexpected conclusion: sending international development assistance into a warlord region is not likely to be a promising means for building popular support for the state. In 2007 Washington announced an ambitious, multiyear, $750 million economic development package for the FATA, designed to build local support for the state of Pakistan. It was supposed to bolster Pakistan's own 2006 FATA Sustainable Development Plan, and additional funding was promised by US allies, including the United Kingdom and Japan. After damning Congressional and US Government Accountability Office critiques of the program, it was unclear whether or when these plans would go forward, byt it would not be surprising if similar efforts to build state authority through poverty elimination were tried elsewhere in the future. The analysis presented here suggests that such an effort, no matter how well designed, would have its goals thwarted by patronage networks on the ground. It is a mistake to see aid as a counterinsurgency tool in an area where the state lacks control. Whoever manages to seize control of the aid—in FATA, the status quo maliks who alienate the junior lineages and their own better-educated young people, or the radical mullahs who capitalize on that alienation to win recruits for jihad—the very social and political trajectories that threaten long-term security are likely to be reinforced.

Finally, this case holds an unexpected positive lesson. The example of oil boom migration provides a potential alternative mechanism for social evolution. Some analysts have argued that the Pashtunwali code is so overwhelming in its social power that all policies toward the tribal areas must be crafted in accordance with it.[173] Yet the Pashtunwali scorns the pursuit of business and commerce as something lowly and not Pashtun. The word for "shopkeeper" is an insult in the Pashto language, and even farming is considered a demeaning occupation.[174] Trade was traditionally seen as something that diminished the fighting spirit of Pashtun warriors.[175] Real Pashtun men were supposed to spurn the "settled" areas, instead pursuing agnatic rivalry in their barren mountain homeland, and scraping together only enough income (often pooled by the family as an allowance to the traditional malik) to fulfill the duty of hospitality.[176]

Remittances challenged these traditions just as much as state patronage bargains did. Remittances allowed television and pop music to become more attractive as forms of entertainment than the traditional hujra guesthouse. They even made women more powerful in village life, since women could control the income sent home when their men were still abroad, and this began to undercut the purda system.[177] Behavior in the 1970s and 1980s also followed the timeless pattern noted by anthropologist Ahmed: the tendency of the Pashtuns "to move uni-directionally from *nang* to *qalang* in acts of migration," from "wild" to settled areas.[178]

If the ultimate goals of development assistance are to improve the living conditions of the population, to make people less enamored of extremist politics and to extend the authority of the central state to a greater proportion of the country's inhabitants, this case argues that aid should *not* travel through long established channels of resource provision in "ungoverned" areas. What might work better is to encourage ambitious young people to migrate outside those areas for the sake of their own advancement, by dangling economic opportunities nearby.

Large-scale, low-cost migration cannot be controlled by warlords without a huge expenditure of resources to track people and hunt them down. It can bring money into warlord territories, money that gives ordinary people more choices: more confidence in standing up against the status quo because an independent income stream empowers them, and more opportunity to leave if their efforts fail. While we cannot assume that the lessons of this one short-lived example will hold in other countries and circumstances, the logic should fit any case where the losers in patronage bargains have external migration opportunities for profit.

States, even weak states, often have many more economic resources available to them than warlords do. If states get into a bidding war with warlords for popular support, providing more opportunities for people in areas where they do have effective sovereign laws, then states are likely to win. The next chapter shows how a different kind of outbidding effort, one centered in political populism and enthusiasm for change, enabled the Georgian state under Mikheil Saakashvili to defeat warlords on its territory.

[4]

The Georgian Experiment with Warlords

In the early 1990s the newly independent state of Georgia was torn apart by anarchic militia and gang violence.[1] Its two most prominent leaders, the heads of the National Guard and the Mkhedrioni (or "Knights Horsemen") militias, appointed themselves the guardians of the state. With Russian encouragement they invited Eduard Shevardnadze back from Moscow to lead the state out of chaos. Before his famous stint as the westernizing Soviet foreign minister of Mikhail Gorbachev, Shevardnadze had been the Communist Party leader of Georgia. By this time Abkhazia and South Ossetia had effectively seceded from Georgia after bloody civil wars, but Shevardnadze managed to wrest back central control over most remaining Georgian territory. From this milieu, however, two individuals emerged who would act as warlords until they were removed by newly elected President Mikheil Saakashvili in the mid-2000s: Aslan Abashidze in the province of Ajara, and Emzar Kvitsiani in the district of Upper Kodori.

These two warlords had very different trajectories. Abashidze was a high-ranking Communist Party functionary, appointed as governor of Ajara, who tried (but failed) to get his peculiar fiefdom recognized by Georgian law. He built a private militia to guard the border between Ajara and Georgia, and stole the state's customs revenues on his territory bordering the Black Sea. He worked with corrupt bureaucrats in the State Railway Company and elsewhere to line his own pockets. Kvitsiani, in contrast, was a gang leader connected to the criminal underworld. He saw an opportunity during the 1993 civil war between Georgia and breakaway Abkhazia, and seized it. His militia controlled access to a pass in the Caucasus Mountains at the top of the Kodori River that linked Georgia proper to Abkhazia. He used this sparsely inhabited buffer zone to run a protection racket for Georgian electricity supplies and a smuggling ring for timber.

Despite their different trajectories both were warlords: both used patronage and force to control small slices of territory in defiance of Georgian sovereignty, but with Shevardnadze's tacit cooperation. Moreover both were middlemen, using their connections with foreign actors (Russia in the case of Abashidze, and the Russian-supported breakaway region of Abkhazia in the case of Kvitsiani) to sap the strength of the struggling Georgian state.

These historical cases form a natural experiment. Shevardnadze and Saakashvili made drastically different choices toward the same warlords in the same country, in the same basic post-Soviet era. Shevardnadze chose to accommodate them between 1992 and 2003, and Saakashvili chose to overthrow them and extend the geographical reach of Georgian sovereignty in 2004 and 2006. This is the only modern case where state leaders followed such starkly contrasting policies toward warlords on their territories. The case demonstrates what happens when a state leader breaks previous warlord bargains, and provides a clear before-and-after picture of the consequences of warlordism and its end.

Abashidze and Kvitsiani, despite their very different career backgrounds, both used family and clan connections to support their rule as warlords. Shevardnadze had been afraid to tangle with these clans, but Saakashvili's success demonstrates that clan-based warlordism doesn't have to be permanent. Some theorists portray clans as powerful political actors who use webs of reciprocal obligation and emotional ties to provide what amounts to an alternative governance system inside modern states.[2] This can lead to the assumption that the overthrow of warlords will lead to clan-based or tribal violence against the state. Yet what these cases show is that warlords cannot always rely on continuing clan or traditional family interests to support them. The state can use money, threats, and opportunity to break the hold of clan-based warlords. In both Ajara and Upper Kodori, Saakashvili was able to peel away families who had earlier supported the warlords, through promises of future political and economic cooperation. This allowed him to force Abashidze, Kvitsiani, and their few diehard allies to stand down. The most important tool leading to the state's victory in these cases was fine-grained information about how the warlord networks worked and who the individual supporters of the warlords were.

Saakashvili's successes occurred at a time when he had great populist appeal, after soundly beating Shevardnadze in a national election that generated great excitement. Yet the techniques he used against Abashidze and Kvitsiani relied on secret deals that were not subject to institutional oversight. He replaced their local force-based patronage with a state-based

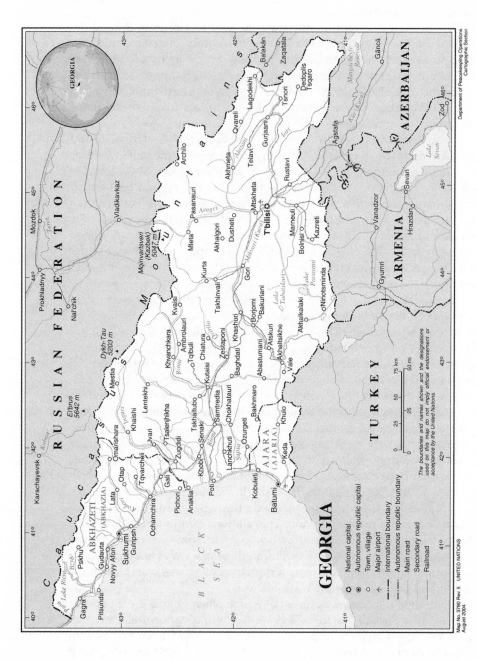

Map 2. Democratic Republic of Georgia. Courtesy of the United Nations Cartographic Section

version of the same thing; loyalty to warlords was replaced with loyalty to the new state and to himself as its leader. These cases suggest that recapturing state control over warlord territory may be easier if state leaders operate in a setting relatively free from public scrutiny and political competition. This is a direct challenge to those who see the end of warlordism as being associated with the advent of democracy building. Saakashvili was widely criticized by human rights advocates for his growing failure over time to support media freedom, free and fair elections, local political decentralization, and judicial reform.[3] But the promises he made to the supporters he peeled from the warlords' coalitions could only be credible in a political system that was not a full-blown liberal democracy. He had to ensure that the judiciary would not prosecute these individuals for their past crimes and corruption as long as they paid an unofficial "tax" to the state, that angry citizens would not vote them out of their new offices as soon as they were appointed, and that their future well-being depended on their continuing support for the penetration of state institutions on their territory.

The Georgian cases also provide a cautionary tale for state leaders who deal with middleman warlords. Leaders who choose to accommodate the warlords on their own territory are also accommodating the foreign actors who are supporting them. Leaders who renege on bargains made with middlemen risk provoking the warlords' foreign patrons. Choices about domestic sovereignty, or the ability of the state to control policy within its territory, are intertwined with choices about what Stephen Krasner calls Westphalian sovereignty, or the exclusion of foreign actors from state territory.[4]

Shevardnadze's choices gave Russian leaders—who in the minds of many people represented the old Soviet empire—a great deal of influence over the security policy of supposedly independent Georgia. Russian economic actors (some of whom had reputed organized crime connections) simultaneously profited from Georgia's weak borders and tax laws. Saakashvili, on the other hand, successfully bargained with Russia to ensure that Abashidze was removed peacefully. Yet his failure to understand the tripwire function that Kvitsiani served in the Upper Kodori buffer zone may have helped precipitate Georgia's disastrous 2008 war with Russia.

This chapter first examines the history of the Abashidze and Kvitsiani cases. For each case it briefly describes the background history of the region and how the warlord emerged. Then it analyzes how first Shevardnadze and then Saakashvili approached each of the warlords, paying special attention to the security and economic consequences of their choices. Each case also discusses the role of Russia. The chapter concludes with an analysis of the lessons to be learned and potential future policy implications from each of the two cases, highlighting the middle-man, clan, and populist authoritarianism factors noted above.

Background

The province of Ajara, lying on the Black Sea in southwestern Georgia, was conquered first by the Ottoman Empire and later by the Russian tsars. It was granted special autonomous status by Bolshevik Russia as part of the Treaty of Kars signed with Turkey in 1921. Some observers have seen Turkey as being protective of Ajara for hundreds of years against Russian expansion. Certainly today Turkish businesses play a significant role in the Ajaran economy. Despite this special Turkish role, however, most of Ajara was not ethnically distinct from the rest of Georgia.

Ajara's special status in the Soviet Union was granted under Turkish pressure because the majority of its population was Muslim, but religion was not recognized as an ethnic category by the atheist Soviet system. The vast majority of Ajarans in fact always considered themselves ethni-cally Georgian. This meant that in contrast to most other autonomous regions in the USSR, Ajara was not recognized by Soviet authorities as having a titular national population. After the 1926 census the category of "Ajaran" disappeared from Soviet documentation. This had an unin-tended consequence. The residents of Ajara, unlike those of other Soviet autonomous regions, did not receive favored promotion to Communist Party and other elite positions during Soviet times, and, unlike those other regions, the territory was left without its own "ethnic machine" to take political control when the Soviet Union collapsed.[5]

It is unclear how deeply Islamic identity really resonated with most of the Ajaran population. Some elite landholders had been converted to Islam under Ottoman rule in the seventeenth century in return for fa-vored treatment, but the majority of the population converted only for the sake of Istanbul's protection during the 1828–29 war between Turkey and Russia. At that point, scholars believe, Turkish started to replace Georgian as the language spoken at home, and some people adopted Turkish names. Turkey continued to be seen as a useful bulwark against Russian predation, and, by the time of World War I, Ajarans were siding with Turkey against the Russian "infidels." Yet unlike the northern Cau-casus regions of Chechnya or Ingushetia, Ajara lacked indigenous Is-lamic brotherhoods to sustain the religion underground during Soviet times, and Islam was maintained only through the link to the Turkish

Islamic hierarchy. This made the province easy to secularize and "Georgia-fy" when it was cut off from Turkey in the Soviet era, especially since native elites spoke Turkish and were therefore disadvantaged in dealing with Soviet Georgian authorities. Leadership positions in the province were taken over by people from elsewhere in the Georgian republic, and intermarriage in urban areas became common. In post-Soviet times a large fraction of the urban population has converted to Georgian Orthodox Christianity,[6] and Islam has been left primarily as the religion of the rural mountain areas.[7] It is common to hear today's Ajaran elites talk about returning to their families' Christian roots, after their ancestors were forcibly converted by Turkish occupiers.[8]

Georgian nationalists had long disdained whatever influence remained of Islam in Ajara,[9] and waged a campaign against it in Georgian newspapers in the 1980s.[10] Georgia's first post-Soviet leader, the former dissident Zviad Gamsakhurdia, was a rabid nationalist who defined Georgian nationhood in Christian Orthodox terms. In 1990–91 he hinted that he might challenge Ajaran autonomy, implicitly linking such a move to Christian supremacy in Georgia.[11] This mobilized Ajaran Muslim religious figures to agitate against his efforts.[12]

Abashidze's rise was supported by these Muslim leaders, and he made his first public political stand by aligning himself with the Muslim movement to retain Ajara's autonomous status. His opponents accused him of trying to lead a fundamentalist Islamist revival in the province,[13] something that played well in the nationalist mood of the time. Abashidze did build some new mosques and continued to work with Ajara's Islamic religious leaders, but there is no evidence of any Islamist resurgence or religious proselytizing under Abashidze's rule. Although he was the descendent of famous Ottoman Muslim nobles, he deliberately left his own faith publicly ambiguous, and even baptized his grandchildren in the Georgian Orthodox Church.[14]

As time went on it became clear that the battle for control over Ajara and its 400,000 residents was not really about ethnicity or religion. Most of the Ajaran population was fairly secular, even those who still considered themselves Muslim. Instead the battle was about which set of Georgian elites, from which locality and which clan, would control the province's border with Turkey, the Black Sea port of Batumi and its oil trade, and the lush citrus orchards, tea plantations, vineyards, and holiday resorts that remained from Soviet times.

Abashidze's Emergence

Abashidze had been a Communist Party functionary in Soviet times. He got his start as a Communist Youth League (Komsomol) activist, and then served as the Ajaran provincial Minister of Communal Services, rising through the ranks to become deputy minister and then minister of communal services for all of Georgia.[15] Georgi Derluguian notes that Abashidze would have dealt with many issues involving legal wrangling and permissions over housing and construction questions, so these positions would have provided profitable opportunities for graft. Eventually Abashidze became the deputy chairman of the Georgian Supreme Soviet in 1991. He was a high-ranking member of the Soviet nomenklatura elite, who would have been vetted by the KGB for loyalty and would have made many strong contacts among the Russian political elites and security service leaders who emerged out of the same milieu.

Abashidze returned to Ajara from Tbilisi when he was appointed acting chairman of the provincial Ajaran Supreme Soviet (a post sometimes termed "governor") by Georgian President Gamsakhurdia in March 1991. His arrival in Ajara followed Gamsakhurdia's late 1990 revocation of the autonomy of a different Georgian province, South Ossetia. Gamsakhurdia's moves against South Ossetian autonomy had sparked an armed confrontation in which five thousand nationalist Georgian militia members carried out brutal attacks against civilians as well as rampant looting in South Ossetia. Gamsakhurdia apparently hoped that Abashidze could prevent similar events from happening in Ajara, by placating the Muslim protestors who objected to the removal of Ajaran autonomy (although there is speculation that Abashidze himself may have organized the Ajaran protests, creating a security problem that he could then solve).

Abashidze's grandfather, the Ajaran political leader Mehmet Abashidze, had helped negotiate the Treaty of Kars that established Ajaran autonomy, and had been close to Gamsakhurdia's father, the novelist Konstantin Gamsakhurdia.[16] Both families had been persecuted and exiled by Stalin. Abashidze's attractiveness to Gamsakhurdia hence lay in the combination of their own intertwined family histories, which presumably made Abashidze trustworthy, and Abashidze's family's prominence in Ajaran politics, which presumably gave him local legitimacy.

But Abashidze's arrival in Ajara was seen locally as the start of a purge.[17] Reportedly the sitting chairman of the Ajaran Supreme Soviet, a member of the Communist Party, was "dragged out of his car and savagely beaten by 'unknown' assailants"; he promptly resigned.[18] Abashidze arrival set off a legal battle between opposition members of the Ajaran Supreme Soviet and Gamsakhurdia, since the Soviet-era autonomous Ajaran constitution stated that only a member of the Ajaran Supreme Soviet, and not an appointee from Tbilisi, could serve as chair.

New elections for the Ajaran Supreme Soviet were scheduled for April but had to be delayed because of continuing protests. Abashidze used these protests to burnish his image as the voice of calm, appearing at a demonstration in Batumi to reassure the protesters that autonomy was secure and that no one would force Ajara's Muslims to convert to Christianity.[19] Days later it became clear that things were far from calm in provincial politics. One of Abashidze's bodyguards shot and killed the acting first deputy chairman of the Ajaran Supreme Soviet, Nodar Imnadze, a member of Gamsakhurdia's Round Table coalition, during a melee that broke out at the parliament building. Imnadze was reportedly drunk and openly carrying a machine pistol at the time (this was an era when armed men roamed freely around Georgia), and there is no question that he started the confrontation. Some believe that Imnadze was angry that Abashidze had been made acting chair, rather than himself.[20] Georgian authorities in 2007 charged and convicted Abashdize in absentia of murder, although Abashidze maintains that the shooting was in self-defense against an assassination attempt. He was wounded in the fight, and claimed that Imnadze used the machine pistol on him first, hitting him once in the neck and twice in the torso.[21] Some believe instead that Imnadze fired only into the ceiling, and that Abashidze's wounds were self-inflicted and for show; in this version, Abashidze used the excuse of the melee to assassinate a potential competitor who may have been spying on him for Gamsakhurdia.

After this inauspicious beginning, parliamentary elections were held in June but the returns were so low that a runoff was necessary. Finally Abashidze was elected to parliament in the next round of elections in July 1991, and his nomination for the chairman's position was immediately put to the newly elected Ajaran parliamentarians. Gamsakhurdia's Round Table supporters had gotten about half the popular vote, which was not enough to assure Abashidze's victory. Those representing the opposition (including the minority Republican Party as well as Communists and others) preferred an alternative representative from the Ajaran capital of Batumi, Rostom Dolidze, for the chairman's post. Reportedly Gamsakhurdia put heavy pressure on the parliamentarians to accept Abashidze's leadership, and forced through a procedural change in the voting to make it public rather than confidential, so that naysayers could be easily identified and punished.[22] At this point Dolidze withdrew his candidacy, and Abashidze was elected chairman.[23] He retained the title of deputy speaker of what became the new Georgian parliament, for several more years, but never again set foot in the capital of Tbilisi, saying that he feared he would be assassinated if he did so.[24]

Abashidze thus came to power in Ajara through means that were technically legal but backed by strong threats of force from Tbilisi. Yet Tbilisi did not control him. He promptly organized his own independent Ajaran militia, saying that this was necessary to protect the province from the Georgian nationalist militias that were raging at the time. At its peak

Abashidze's militia would grow to between five hundred and a thousand men, and he amassed twenty armored vehicles (including four T-72 Russian battle tanks) and a number of helicopters and coastal vessels, including a personal speedboat equipped with a machine-gun that looked like something out of a James Bond movie.[25]

Abashidze was able to create this militia because the Soviet-era laws governing Ajara's status were vague, and had allowed the formation of Ajaran ministries of security and defense.[26] Republican Party deputies in Ajara's Supreme Soviet nonetheless published an open letter in March 1992, when Shevardnadze returned, accusing Abashidze of leaving the police unarmed while illegally distributing weapons to a new private army loyal only to himself. They asked the Georgian state to intervene to restore legality in the province.[27] After he consolidated his power in later years, Abashidze singled out recalcitrant Republican Party members for persecution, destroying the party's offices several times (once with a missile launched from a helicopter), kidnapping and terrorizing several party members, and torching the home of local party leaders Davit and Levan Berdzhenishvili.[28]

It is not clear how real the threat from the Georgian nationalist militias ever was to Ajara, because Abashidze's regime was protected from the beginning by Russian forces located at the Soviet-era military base that remained on the outskirts of Batumi. (This was one of several Soviet military installations remaining on Georgian territory at that time.) Russian press sources and Abashidze himself portrayed the threat as imminent in early 1993, while Shevardnadze dismissed those claims.[29] In any case, there is no doubt that, as Derluguian writes, Abashidze "astutely turn[ed] Ajara] into a Russian military protectorate."[30] Ajara remained free of nationalist violence as the rest of Georgia imploded.

Abashidze had company in this strategy toward Russia, as some members of the opposition like to point out: the new leader of the Georgian state, Eduard Shevardnadze, did something very similar for the country as a whole.[31] In return for Russia's military assistance in ending the civil war in 1993, Shevardnadze agreed to join the Russian-led Commonwealth of Independent States (CIS) and Collective Security Treaty Organization (CSTO). He allowed Russia to maintain four Soviet-era military bases on Georgian territory including the one in Ajara, and consulted Russian leaders when appointing the Georgian ministers of defense, interior, and security (the latter the follow-on to the Soviet KGB).[32] Two Russian military bases remained in the de facto sovereign part of Georgia until 2006, and were removed only after additional negotiations with the Saakashvili regime.

Abashidze maintained a close relationship with the Russian base commanders in Batumi, and spoke out in favor of having the base remain in the province as "one of the guarantees of stability."[33] Amidst 1999 negotiations between Moscow and Tbilisi to finally remove the Russian military bases in Georgia, Batumi base commander Maj. Gen. Vyacheslav Borisov publicly endorsed Abashidze's Union of Democratic Revival (known as the Revival Party) for upcoming national Georgian parliamentary elections for this reason.[34] (Borisov would later go on to command the Russian war against Georgia in August 2008.) Around half of the two thousand Russian Army troops in Batumi were actually Georgian citizens of local Ajaran origin, who saw serving at the Russian base as an alternative to being conscripted into the Georgian Army.[35] A retired Russian officer, Maj. Gen. Yurii Netkachev, who had earlier been the deputy commander of Russian military forces in the South Caucasus at the Batumi base, was the commander of Abashidze's private militia.[36]

Shevardnadze's Approach to Abashidze: Accommodation

During the Shevardnadze era, the relationship between Ajara and Tbilisi was negotiated through backdoor deals and patronage links. Shevardnadze was well known for having a "balancing" or "Byzantine" approach to all political and policy choices, a kind of divide-and-rule technique learned in Soviet times that always kept any one faction from getting too strong. He tried to balance Russian and American influence in Georgia through a complicated dance of alternating partnerships, and to balance the old and the new in Georgian politics by encouraging the rise of a younger, reformist generation in his own party without giving them much policy influence. In Ajara this balancing act meant that he stood back and allowed Abashidze to become a warlord.

Immediately upon his assumption of power in 1992, Abashidze disbanded the Ajaran Supreme Soviet under an emergency decree, making himself the sole authority in the province. He set up checkpoints between Ajara and the rest of Georgia, forcing visitors from elsewhere to show their Georgian passports and get them stamped with a "visa."[37] In addition to gaining fees from these "border" crossings, the checkpoints allowed Abashidze to monitor all traffic in and out of Ajara to enhance his political control. While eventually he allowed the parliament to meet again, he used his paramilitary forces to silence all opposition through intimidation, violence, and imprisonment.[38] His Revival Party was the only party allowed to campaign for elections.[39] The Revival Party gained many seats in Georgia's national parliament over time, apparently through deals worked out with the election authorities who were appointed by Shevardnadze.

In its last major electoral stand, Abashidze's Revival Party negotiated with Shevardnadze to throw the nation's parliamentary elections in

November 2003. These elections were widely seen as crucial antecedents to the next presidential election in 2005, in which Shevardnadze had announced he would not run. Their results would therefore establish the list of credible new presidential candidates.[40] Abashidze was a possible contender for that upcoming presidential election, and his support for Shevardnadze in 2003 had the opposition worried about Georgia's future.[41]

Opposition campaigners and the journalists covering their activities in Ajara were beaten, and their offices and equipment were vandalized.[42] Abashidze accused opposition leader Saakashvili of trying to stage a "coup" in Batumi through his campaigning.[43] On election day, a Georgian election monitor was arrested and roughed up by security forces at an Ajaran polling station, and on the street directly outside Batumi's largest polling station one of Abashidze's former bodyguards, now on the outs with Abashidze, was shot to death in full public view while sitting in his car.[44]

The official national election results released by the Shevardnadze government did not match either the exit polls or the alternative vote-counting results announced by Georgian or international monitoring organizations, which indicated that Saakashvili's party had won.[45] The officially announced returns instead showed Abashidze's Revival Party in the lead for the most parliamentary seats.[46] When pro-democracy demonstrators in Tbilisi began to protest the officially announced results, Shevardnadze flew to Batumi in an apparent bid for support.

Abashidze then sent busloads of his supporters to the Georgian capital to stage a pro-government counterdemonstration on Rustaveli Avenue in front of the parliament building, using the buses as a barrier to keep the Ajarans corralled and set apart from the pro-Saakashvili crowds.[47] The Ajaran group included armed members of Abashidze's militia. In a sign of things to come, however, when Saakashvili and his supporters stormed the building on November 22, 2003, to launch the Rose Revolution, Abashidze's supporters withdrew rather than trying to fight them. Some may have been frightened by the large crowd of Rose Revolution supporters who began to shove their buses out of the way in an attempt to get into the parliament building, and who shouted insults at them.[48] Others may simply have been unmotivated. Many were Ajaran government employees (or their relatives) who had been threatened with job termination if they did not join the pro-Shevardnadze protests in Tbilisi.[49] Some were poorly educated residents of Ajara's rural areas who seemed not to understand what was happening in Tbilisi or why they were there, and at least a few were brought over to the pro-Saakashvili side with simple promises of meals and shelter from the cold.[50] Abashidze thus found himself on the wrong side of the Rose Revolution.

Yet in spite of the long-standing level of political cooperation that Abashidze had with Shevardnadze, he regularly fought with Shevardnadze's government, ignoring state orders and even detaining high-ranking officials who visited Ajara.[51] In many ways Shevardnadze and Abashidze were the best of enemies. Abashidze was able to control all the trade that crossed the province to and from Turkey and other points on the Black Sea, as well as much of the trade from Armenia. (Armenian president Robert Kocharian sent him a Ruger pistol in a gift box, which he kept on display in his Batumi townhouse.)[52] In 1995 Abashidze replaced three hundred Georgian state border and customs officials with local appointees, in defiance of a state directive.[53] According to Georgian authorities, he kept all tax and customs revenues for himself for years, and the lost contributions to Georgia's central budget may have totaled as much as $35 million per year.[54] Abashidze tried repeatedly to legalize this arrangement by having Ajara declared a free trade zone, not subject to taxes, but failed to get Shevardnadze's support for doing so.[55] Reportedly everyone who operated a business in Ajara had to "pay the king" and "grease the paw" of Abashidze, but anyone who wanted to avoid paying Georgian taxes moved their business operations to Batumi and filed their forms locally with Abashidze's tax officials instead.[56]

The trade transiting Ajara included a wide variety of petroleum products that entered Georgia by ship at the Batumi oil terminal, amounting to 60 percent of the country's total.[57] Abashidze privatized the terminal in a move that bypassed Tbilisi in 1999, selling the terminal to the Greenoak Group, a rather shady holding company that had a great deal of business in Ajara.[58] From that point onward Georgian State Railway officials listed more of the oil coming through the terminal as being "in transit" to third countries than was really the case, sending it on "tax free" to various locations that were actually inside Georgia, while Abashidze's customs officials kept the tax revenue paid by the shippers.[59] Beyond the oil terminal scheme, Ajara's profitable enterprises included a hazelnut growing and export business (also owned by Greenoak), in which Abashidze attempted to ensnare two of then-US First Lady Hillary Clinton's brothers in 1999.[60] Abashidze also allowed his family members to bankrupt the Georgian Black Sea merchant fleet through the misappropriation of state funds that were managed via Batumi.[61]

All of the important government positions in the province were controlled not by the Georgian state but by Abashidze's own clan network, based on the Abashidze family and his wife's Gogitidze family.[62] His son Giorgi was mayor of Batumi. Abashidze gained the support of Ajara's former Communist officials by giving them lower-level plum spots in the government.[63] His control was enhanced by the province's ownership of TV-Ajara, which broadcast in five languages and focused on covering him and his activities.[64] Abashidze routinely jammed Georgian national television broadcasts coming into the province, although he was not always successful at shutting them out.[65] He saw Batumi State University in particular as a "corrupt breeding ground of the opposition," and unilaterally replaced its head, a Georgian state official, in 1996.[66] His extended clan retained political command and control of Ajara's security forces through their appointments to the Ajaran Interior Ministry and the Ajaran National Security Council. Georgian authorities allege that he used those forces to run a $100 million per year illegal narcotics trade, and to engage in frequent criminal endeavors, including kidnapping, carjacking, and rape.[67] The former head of the Revival Party in Tbilisi, Tsotne Bakuria, who had a falling out with Abashidze, later even accused him of facilitating the transportation of rogue Russian scientists to Iran to help with that country's nuclear enrichment program,[68] but a knowledgeable American diplomat called that accusation a "joke."[69] Western visitors to Abashidze's palatial home regularly reported being "entertained" with lavish meals essentially at gunpoint or under guard by vicious dogs, and were discouraged from leaving until Abashidze's monologues finally ran their course in the wee hours.[70]

Abashidze's tight grip over Batumi meant that it was in noticeably better shape than the rest of Georgia, according to those who visited it, with cleaner and less dilapidated buildings and better roads.[71] The population was reported to have a higher standard of living than average Georgian citizens.[72] Electricity and heat worked more often than elsewhere in Georgia, at least in part because of a supply deal worked out with Turkey,[73] and official wages were paid on time.[74] Abashidze, in other words, provided public goods to the population.

As the years went by, however, it became clear to the population that Abashidze was not sharing much of the wealth with them. He was notorious for overseeing the construction of beautiful state-of-the-art facilities, such as schools, hospitals, and apartment buildings, that were never used.[75] His son's construction companies got most of the contracts for these.[76] His customs officials raised the "pocket taxes" paid by shuttle traders headed for Turkey, closing the region's profitable post-Soviet smuggling routes to all but big-time players, and causing the locals to mutter about the greediness of his "mafia." The population as a whole became increasingly impoverished as the province's economy declined and unemployment skyrocketed. Abashidze even lacked the grace to open some traditional cultural festivals to the people, instead allowing them to watch only through chain-link fences as visiting dignitaries enjoyed sumptuous banquets and stage shows.[77]

In sum, then, Shevardnadze used Abashidze and his Revival Party to bolster his own political strength, and high-ranking Georgian state officials subverted state control by working out deals with him, in a strongman accommodation model similar to what Catherine Boone describes in some postcolonial African states.[78] Meanwhile Abashidze bled the state dry by stealing customs taxes, and ran what amounted to a miniature criminal police state on supposedly sovereign Georgian territory. Shevardnadze got political stability, including a modus vivendi with Russia, but at great cost for Georgia's economic development and human rights.

Saakashvili's Approach to Abashidze: Overthrow

There was no love lost between Abashidze and Saakashvili. During the November 2003 election dispute, ads on TV-Ajara showed clips of Saakashvili interspersed with snippets of speeches given by Adolf Hitler.[79] When the Rose Revolution occurred in Tbilisi, Abashidze declared a state of emergency and closed Ajara's border to the rest of Georgia, including its rail link.[80] Within a few days, however, the province's dependence on trade with the rest of Georgia became clear, and Ajaran officials announced that truck traffic was being allowed through from Turkey, simply with "increased inspection."[81]

As soon as Saakashvili was elected Georgian president in the snap election of early January 2004, prosecutors in Tbilisi began to investigate the illegal economic activities of Abashidze and his relatives in Ajara. Two of Saakashvili's core campaign promises were to rein in corruption and to reestablish state control over all of Georgian territory. Given Shevardnadze's shady election deal with Abashidze, it is not surprising that resolving the Ajaran situation was one of his top priorities. Abashidze had initially tried to block the January presidential election from being held in Ajara, and his security forces detained (and reportedly threatened the lives of) opposition members.[82] He later relented and Saakashvili won an overwhelming victory in Ajara as elsewhere.[83] During these early weeks of 2004 the United States may have played a key role in convincing Abashidze to temper his actions. US Ambassador Richard Miles had cultivated long-standing relationships with a variety of the major political players inside Georgia, including Abashidze, meeting with him numerous times before the Rose Revolution.[84] Miles had experience with nonviolent protest and conflict resolution techniques dating back to his own participation in the civil rights movement in the American South in the 1960s, and may have been instrumental in convincing both Shevardnadze and Saakashvili to control their supporters in order to avoid violence during the Rose Revolution itself. Now he reached out to Abashidze as well, making frequent trips to Batumi,[85] and urging the Ajaran leader to accommodate the new regime.

In early 2004 Abashidze sent a large tax arrears payment to Tbilisi in an apparent attempt to work out a deal with Saakashvili.[86] Saakashvili's new minister of the interior then carried out a covert operation to arrest the head of the Georgian State Railway, Akaki Chkhaidze, who hid in an Ajaran hospital. Ajaran interior minister Djemal Gogitidze (who had been an outspoken participant in Abashidze's November protests in Tbilisi) complained that he could have done the job of arresting Chkhaidze himself, but Abashidze did not challenge Saakashvili's right to make the arrest,[87] and this was interpreted as a concession by Abashidze and an implicit recognition of Georgia's legal sovereignty over Ajara. Saakashvili next attended a Georgian military parade in Batumi, in another seeming symbol of Abashidze's recognition of Georgian sovereignty, and met with Abashidze privately.[88]

These accommodations did not last, however. As the winter wore on and new parliamentary elections loomed in March, tensions grew between Saakashvili and Abashidze. Abashidze threatened that events in Ajara could "develop like in Abkhazia and South Ossetia," Georgia's breakaway provinces.[89] Meanwhile Saakashvili's new prosecutor general, Irakli Okruashvili, launched an investigation of one of Abashidze's major financial backers, the Omega Group conglomerate, whose cigarette import business was accused of large-scale tax evasion.[90] The Omega Group also owned the pro-Abashidze Iberia television station in Tbilisi, which had been critical of Saakashvili throughout the campaign.[91] Saakashvili supporters in Ajara organized public protests against Abashidze's regime, and there were reports that Abashidze had started issuing weapons to his own supporters in response.[92] Opposition party leaders were abducted and beaten,[93] and opposition party offices in Batumi were ransacked and burned down.[94] The parliament in Tbilisi was disrupted by a brawl between Saakashvili and Abashidze supporters. When opposition protesters and the journalists covering them were repeatedly attacked and severely beaten by Abashidze's security forces in Batumi, Georgian prime minister Zurab Zhvania demanded that Ajaran authorities investigate. Gogitidze, Abashidze's interior minister, instead claimed that the journalists were foreign spies.[95] Georgian finance minister Zurab Nogaideli tried to enter the province on March 13 to campaign, but was briefly detained by Abashidze's forces at the border. The next day Saakashvili tried to enter the province with a group of Georgian officials but was turned away at the border by armored vehicles and hundreds of armed men.[96] Abashidze issued a curfew that essentially shut down the city of Batumi.

Saakashvili responded by ending all attempts at accommodation. He closed Ajaran airspace, put Georgian Army forces on high alert on the other side of the province border, froze the Georgian bank accounts of Abashidze and his supporters (all of which were located in the Batumi-based Maritime Bank), revoked the Georgian legal licenses of all banks that continued to operate in Ajara, arrested some of Abashidze's associates, sent Georgian Coast Guard forces to blockade the port (and oil terminal) at Batumi, and closed the Sarpi customs checkpoint on the Ajaran-Turkish border.[97] This show of the Georgian national government's strength, overwhelming but without resorting to actual violence, seemed to work at first, especially after a number of ships were diverted by Georgian authorities from Batumi to the next port up the Georgian coastline, Poti, to unload their goods.[98] Abashidze agreed to allow parliamentary elections to be held, to demobilize his forces, and to deliver customs duties and taxes, in return for having the blockade lifted. Saakashvili was allowed to enter Ajara on his second attempt, on March 18, and Abashidze reportedly asked in return merely that Saakashvili not have him assassinated.[99]

Yet this seeming resolution was again an illusion. Just a few days later, Abashidze reneged on his commitment to disband his militia, and the Georgian government reported that Ajaran officials were still interfering with border customs collection.[100] Things got worse after the March 28 election, when the Revival Party failed to win enough votes to clear the threshold for representation in Georgia's parliament. In early April the Georgian defense minister relieved the Georgian military commander based in Batumi, General Dumbadze of the 25th Motor-Rifle Brigade, of his command, accusing him of disobeying Tbilisi's orders in March and working on Abashidze's behalf to block the highway connecting Ajara to the rest of Georgia. While a new commander was appointed, Dumbadze mutinied, taking some three hundred Ajaran soldiers and a few pieces of heavy weaponry with him.[101]

Saakashvili ordered an arrest warrant for Dumbadze, while simultaneously urging Abashidze loyalists in the Ajara-based security forces to return to Georgian state command. Most of the officers and soldiers from the 25th Brigade did so, leaving for Tbilisi to rejoin the newly re-formed brigade there.[102] On April 23, the new Georgian parliament in its first order of business declared the actions of Abashidze an encroachment on state sovereignty, and gave Georgian state officials the authority to "neutralize illegal armed groups" in Ajara.[103] A few days later, forty-six members of Abashidze's own special forces deserted to Tbilisi.[104] Abashidze meanwhile reverted to another state of emergency, imposing a curfew that Saakashvili urged the citizenry to ignore.[105]

In late April, Saakashvili staged a major land and naval military exercise in Poti, the Black Sea port city thirty kilometers from the Ajaran border.[106] The Georgian interior minister, Giorgi Baramidze, threatened to carry out a "police operation" in Ajara if it proved necessary.[107] Saakashvili offered a guarantee of safe passage to Abashdize and his "inner circle" if they left peacefully.[108] Hundreds of peaceful protesters continued to stage anti-Abashidze rallies in Ajara, which his remaining security forces continued to break up.

In response on May 2, Abashidze blew up the two highway bridges and tore up the railway line that connected Ajara to the rest of Georgia over the Choloki River, stationing tanks at the crossings.[109] Abashidze said this was to prevent a Georgian military incursion into Ajara, but his opponents claimed that it was done to make it harder for his own increasingly sparse security forces to desert.[110] At that point Saakashvili gave him a ten-day ultimatum to disarm his troops and submit to Georgian authority.[111] Protests against Abashidze in Batumi continued to be broken up by his security forces, including through the use of water cannons against hundreds of students at Batumi State University. Within a few days, though, most of those forces heeded Saakashvili's calls and turned around to join the protests.[112] By May 5, the anti-Abashidze protesters included several members of the Ajaran parliament, a top Ajaran security official, and 175 police officers; and hundreds of troops who had been guarding Abashidze's home all withdrew.[113] Several of Abashidze's militia commanders defected to Tbilisi. In a last-ditch effort, Abashidze's chief commander Netkachev had the Batumi oil terminal mined, but Georgian security forces immediately went in and removed the mines.[114] Eventually Abashidze agreed to go peacefully, and was flown out on a Russian airplane.

Throughout this process Saakashvili used a combination of sticks and carrots to win back Ajara. As soon as Abashidze left on May 6, 2004, Georgian security forces fanned out to patrol the province and offered amnesty to anyone who turned in an illegal weapon.[115] The renegade General Dumbadze was arrested, as were several top Ajaran security officials.[116] Yet Saakashvili managed to wheedle many lower-level officials and even most of the security forces over to his side. Supporters of the Rose Revolution tend to claim that this happened simply because the political mood had shifted so much in the country that there was no real choice; Saakashvili had the massive support of the population, so to fight him would have been illogical. For example, Gigi Tsereteli, who became the deputy chairman of the Georgian parliament, speaks of arriving in Ajara at 4:00 a.m. on the day that Abashidze left and finding a mood of euphoria, with people shouting "Misha, Misha!" (and when they caught sight of him, "Gigi, Gigi!").[117]

Yet there was more to it than that. Saakashvili also promised many wealthy Abashidze supporters that they could continue to live comfortably in the new Ajara, with immunity from prosecution, as long as they paid for their past misdeeds.[118] The proceeds went into a Fund for the Development of Ajara, whose coffers and uses remained opaque.[119] Saakashvili quickly took control over all government appointments in Ajara, effectively removing the province's autonomy through a vote of the province's own parliament.[120] Appointees from Tbilisi now began to fill the spots previously occupied by Abashidze's supporters,[121] but many employees of the previous Ajaran government bureaucracy were kept in their positions.[122] Financial policy and security arrangements for Ajara were brought under the control of the Georgian parliament.

By 2008, most opposition parties were boycotting local elections in Ajara because they believed that Saakashvili's ruling party was winning seats through unfair practices.[123] The primary independent television broadcaster in Ajara, Channel 25, which had also been heavily controlled during Abashidze's time, was targeted for shutdown by the Saakashvili government over a tax dispute. This situation was resolved in October 2009, but only after Philip H. Gordon, assistant US secretary of state for European and Eurasian affairs, highlighted media freedom as a key issue during Secretary of State Hillary Clinton's visit to Georgia in late September.[124]

Saakashvili took control in all of these ways with the help of Levan Varshalomidze, his classmate and friend from university days. Varshalomidze was first appointed the new head of the Georgian State Railway in early 2004 after Chkhaidze was arrested. Then, at the time of Abashidze's removal, he became Saakashvili's personal representative to Ajara. Finally he became the new governor, a position that was now effectively appointed by the president of Georgia, since under a new July 2004 law the refusal to approve the president's appointee leads to the dissolution of parliament and new elections.[125]

Governor Varshalomidze's appointment is significant because he is the son of Guram Varshalomidze, who was Abashidze's prime minister in the early days and later the head of the Georgian State Oil Company with responsibility for the Batumi port. In 2005 Guram Varshalomidze was appointed Georgia's deputy ambassador to Ukraine.[126] The head of the Batumi tax collection department was also named Varshalomidze.[127] One opposition politician claimed in 2005 that eighteen of Varshalomidze's clan members had been appointed to positions of authority in Ajara.[128] Levan Varshalomidze's cousin Kakha Mikeladze became the majority leader in Ajara's parliament.[129] In April 2009 a Georgian human rights organization accused Varshalomidze of using his control over legal and administrative appointments to arbitrarily and illegally reapportion landholdings among his clan members in Ajara, punishing more distant relatives who had supported the opposition.[130] Varshalo-midze's brother and father were accused by the same organization of bullying residents of an apartment building where they owned flats to sell to them in 2006–2007, having one recalcitrant resident arrested and then attempting to involuntarily institutionalize her as insane. (She eventually sold.)[131] It may not be accidental that Varshalomidze donated several dozen newly constructed cottages to residents of the Kodori Gorge in a village named for Ajara, after Saakashvili retook control of that other warlord-controlled area in 2006.[132] In official government documents, the source of funding for those Kodori cottages is listed as "LTD Georgian Railways."[133]

Other prominent Abashidze officials who were "turned" by Saakashvili and went on to positions of responsibility in Ajara include the head and deputy head of the pro-government TV-Ajara, appointed in 2005,[134] and the head of the Ajaran Chamber of Commerce, wealthy businessman Tengiz Bakuridze.[135] Saakashvili also reached a deal with Greenoak, allowing it to enter a joint venture for the Batumi oil terminal with Kaz-MunaiGaz (the Kazakhstan state oil company, which has very good relations with Russia)[136] in 2006. KazMunaiGaz eventually bought out Greenoak's stake. In the meantime Abashidze may have been allowed to maintain his own stake in the privatized terminal after his departure, although the details are unclear.[137]

In other words, Saakashvili did not really bring in a clean sweep. Instead he dusted off the furniture and rearranged it a bit, trashing only the pieces that were no longer suitable. Such a strategy would have been difficult to implement if the Saakashvili regime had practiced liberal democracy. Even though he was elected president in a free and fair democratic landslide, Saakashvili used his high degree of popular support to act in a rather absolutist fashion. He was a populist, not a liberal democrat. If the judiciary had been independent of the president, then it would have been harder to gain a guarantee of amnesty for those who had profited from the corruption of the Abashidze era. If the governor of Ajara were democratically elected, instead of being appointed by Tbilisi, and if elections to the Ajaran parliament were not stage-managed, then there could not have been any guarantee for even the short-term political futures of those individuals whom Saakashvili turned.

This is not to say that political change in Ajara was insignificant; it was marked. There was no longer a "border" with Georgia, and people could come and go freely, something that everyone agrees has changed the psychology of the residents who lived there. The traffic police, reformed from the bottom up throughout Georgia, no longer extorted drivers. Money was poured into the area by the Georgian government, with schools, hospitals, and roads built and reconstructed. A new water and sewer system was being installed throughout the entire downtown area of Batumi in the fall of 2009.

The waterfront was reconstructed to make it attractive to tourists, including plans for an astonishing new aquarium (designed by a Danish architectural firm) that looked like a pile of local beach pebbles.[138] Many international luxury hotel chains invested in new properties in Batumi, and international tourism, primarily from Turkey, countries of the former Soviet Union, and Israel, skyrocketed.[139] In part this was because Batumi was filled with casinos while most gambling was illegal in both Turkey and Israel. There was general agreement that private entrepreneurs could now open new businesses in Ajara without having to pay exorbitant bribes. Opposition politician Davit Berdzhenishvili, who had been victimized by Abashidze and now believed that Saakashvili was impeding liberal democracy in the country, put it this way: No one is crying for Abashidze's time, and it's clear that things are much better, but the situation in Ajara is simply equal to that in the rest of Georgia.[140]

The Role of Russia

In return for supporting Abashidze militarily during his warlord years, Russia received frequent rhetorical support from Abashidze. For example, Abashidze criticized Georgia's cooperation with NATO in the airstrikes against Yugoslavia during the Kosovo crisis of 1999.[141] At one point Shevardnadze appointed Abashidze as his official envoy in negotiations with breakaway Abkhazia, but later fired him for proposals that the Georgian government believed would seal Abkhazia's independence, largely because they were too pro-Russian.[142] In December 2002, Abashidze's Revival Party publicly supported the formation of a new, explicitly pro-Russian party in Georgia, Datvi ("The Bear"), led by Temur Khachishvili, a former paramilitary commander and minister of the interior in Georgia who had been imprisoned for a 1995 assassination attempt against Shevardnadze. Reportedly the two parties' peace plans for Abkhazia were similar.[143]

Abashidze used the opportunity of his brief appointment in the Abkhazia envoy role to cement relations between Ajara and Russia, including in the economic sphere.[144] Over time he made many economic deals with Russian officials. He hosted Krasnoyarsk governor and former military officer Aleksandr Lebed in Batumi, and proposed a number of joint ventures with him, including an airline.[145] He also had a large number of business dealings with Moscow's then-mayor Yuri Luzhkov.[146] Reportedly many of these included Luzhkov's wife, Elena Baturina, a billionaire and at one time Russia's richest woman, who owned the Inteko plastics and construction company.[147] In 1999 Abashidze said that his major business advisor was Grigory Luchansky, the Russian-Israeli dual-citizen billionaire (and reputed organized crime figure) who was reportedly behind the hazelnut deal with Hillary Clinton's brothers.[148] Agreements with Moscow included road and tunnel construction and investment, as well as luxury coastline residences in Batumi.[149]

Throughout the months of crisis in 2003–2004 it had first appeared that Moscow would throw its lot in with Abashidze, who traveled frequently back and forth to Russia and called for Russian "peacekeepers" to be deployed to protect him.[150] Immediately after the November 2003 election, when Shevardnadze was cooperating with him, Abashidze flew to Armenia and met with Russian defense minister Sergei Ivanov there. Ivanov dismissed rumors that Russia would interfere in the election results, but did say that that Russian troops in Georgia—for example at the base near Batumi—would use force "if attacked."[151] Russia gave simplified visa privileges to Ajaran residents after the Rose Revolution, a move the Georgian Foreign Ministry condemned as a violation of Georgian sovereignty.[152] The Russian Foreign Ministry released a statement that called Abashidze's opponents "extremist-minded," saying that Georgia's actions were "extremely dangerous."[153] In March 2004 the Russian Foreign Ministry accused Tbilisi of aggravating the situation and acting to overthrow the "legal leadership" of Ajara,[154] amid unconfirmed rumors in the media that Russian troops had been sent from Armenia to fortify the Batumi base.[155] Moscow warned Georgia not to intervene militarily against Abashidze.[156]

Yet Russian authorities did not react militarily to the crisis, and indeed played a constructive role in the outcome. In February Saakashvili visited Moscow and held a reportedly cordial meeting with President Putin.[157] In March Putin sent a senior officer to the Russian base at Batumi to instruct the commander there not to interfere with what was termed an internal Georgian political matter, and gave assurances to the United States that Russian troops would only use force in self-defense.[158] Russia's ambassador to Georgia officially stated that his country was "neutral" in the crisis.[159] A delegation of Russian representatives, including Luzhkov and Luchansky, convinced Abashidze not to block Saakashvili's second attempt to visit the region.[160] Finally Russian National Security Council chief Igor Ivanov, who had helped resolve the Rose Revolution crisis by easing Shevardnadze out of office, flew to Batumi on Georgia's request.[161] (Ivanov had been the head of Shevardnadze's secretariat when the latter was Soviet foreign minister under Mikhail Gorbachev.)[162] He persuaded Abashidze to leave, and escorted him out of Ajara under the safe passage guarantee of the Georgian government. Abashidze spent his first night in exile at Luzhkov's dacha.[163] As of 2009,

Abashidze still lived comfortably in Moscow and was working on his memoirs. His son, the former mayor of Batumi, reportedly built a business complex in Moscow in cooperation with Luchansky.[164]

Why did Moscow act to dampen tensions, rather than intervening on Abashidze's behalf? Certainly in the spring of 2004 many media and think tank observers, both in Georgia and abroad, were predicting that Russia might take military action. Moscow's passivity was far from a foregone conclusion. In the words of one Georgian analyst, "Russian President Vladimir Putin confounded expectations."[165] Indeed, at least one hardliner politician in Moscow publicly lamented Abashidze's departure, seeing it as the loss of a "counterweight" to Western influence in Georgia.[166]

Part of the explanation may lie in the economic concessions that Georgian leaders made to Russia during 2004. For example, the Georgian parliament lifted an earlier resolution that had vetoed Russia's entry into the World Trade Organization,[167] and Georgia promised favorable conditions for Russian business investment in the country, including in the energy and electricity sectors.[168] That June, Saakashvili named an ethnically Georgian Russian citizen, UralMash heavy industry tycoon Kakha Bendukidze, as his economics minister. While Bendukidze was a free marketer who lauded Western-style privatization, the opposition accused him of selling off Georgian state assets into Russian hands, often in opaque ways.[169] Saakashvili also invited Russian advisory assistance in the rewriting of Georgia's tax code.[170]

Important security concessions were also made. Georgian security forces cracked down for the first time on Chechens who had settled over the border in Georgia's Pankisi Gorge. Russia had long accused this Chechen refugee population of harboring Chechen militants and foreign Islamist militants who used Georgian territory for their operations in the ongoing Chechen war against Russia. Now Georgia welcomed joint patrols with Russian forces on the borders of the region.[171]

Some think that Russia may have expected Saakashvili to be more pliable and cooperative than Shevardnadze became as the years went by. Yet the indications are that if they had expected this of Saakashvili, they began to be disappointed long before the Ajaran crisis was resolved. Reportedly when Saakashvili went to Moscow in February 2004, Putin asked him to keep in place one official from the Shevardnadze regime: the head of the Georgian Ministry of Security, Valery Khaburdzania. This would have been in keeping with the arrangements worked out by Shevardnadze, when Moscow was consulted about the Security Ministry appointments. Five days later Saakashvili reorganized the ministerial structure in Georgia, merged the Security Ministry with the Interior Ministry, and demoted Khaburdzania (who reportedly moved to Moscow).[172]

Saakashvili asserted his control over domestic sovereignty against Russia. Yet several months after this, Russian officials still were willing to mediate in Abashidze's exile.

Georgian officials express perplexity at why Moscow was so cooperative. In the end it may simply come down to what international relations scholars would consider a realist understanding of territory. Russia lacked a land border with Ajara, even if Russian ships could have come to Batumi's assistance over the Black Sea. Some suspect that Turkey may have quietly stood up to Russia on Ajara's behalf. To use military force against the buoyant new Georgian president in 2004 on behalf of an unpopular local dictator may, in the end, have been considered not worth the risk, especially given that the Russian military base in Batumi could easily have been held hostage by Saakashvili if he had chosen to cut off its water and electricity supplies.[173] The Russian base was completely withdrawn in 2006—and indeed that might have been a warning sign that Russia was thinking about a future war with Georgia.

THE CASE OF KVITSIANI IN UPPER KODORI

Background

The steep and rocky Kodori Gorge extends into the mountains just inside the northeastern border of what used to be known as the Autonomous Republic of Abkhazia.[174] Abkhazia was made a constituent part of the Republic of Georgia by a 1931 decree of Soviet leader Joseph Stalin. Upper Kodori, the northeastern leg of the gorge, is a tiny slice of territory about three kilometers wide and fifty kilometers long.[175] The weather there is brutal, with roads open only a few months out of the year; from fall to spring the only transit route is by helicopter on clear days. According to the 2002 census, the population numbered 1,956 individuals, living in around five hundred family units.[176] It has long been dominated by ethnic Georgian Svans.

Ethnicity is a fluid concept in the Caucasus.[177] That having been said, the Abkhazians had seen themselves as ethnically distinct from the Georgians for centuries, with a separate language and clan structure, and these distinctions were encouraged in Soviet times through affirmative action policies that benefited the Abkhazians as national minorities. Yet by 1989, Abkhazians made up only 18 percent of the population in the autonomous republic of Abkhazia, because of state-encouraged inmigration of Orthodox Christians under nineteenth-century tsars and non-Abkhazian Georgians under Soviet rule.[178] Abkhazia was known for its rich orchards and vineyards and beautiful Black Sea tourist resorts in

Soviet times, and in addition to helping explain the reasons behind in-migration, these economic prizes became a major source of Soviet-era criminal activity. Reportedly three hundred of the seven hundred known organized crime networks in the USSR (the so-called thieves-in-law) had roots in Georgia, with many having tentacles into Abkhazia.[179] By the end of the Soviet period, one-third of the thieves-in-law were Georgian, even though Georgians made up only 2 percent of the Soviet population.[180]

The Kodori Gorge feeds into the Georgian province of Samegrelo Zemo-Svaneti, and the Svans, a Georgian ethnic group, were the dominant population in Kodori. The Svans were known throughout history for clan-based resistance to state control, and even in Soviet times it was known that Kodori was a place where criminals could hide and the police would dare not follow.[181] Svans were also exempted from conscription in Soviet times, and tacitly allowed to keep private weapons for defense.[182] Given this potent mix of clan, crime, ethnicity, and resistance, it is not surprising that when Gamsakhurdia stoked Georgian nationalist ethnic violence against the Abkhazians in 1990, a variety of Georgian militias entered Kodori to take part in the fighting. Georgian political scientist Ghia Nodia calls these militias "private armies that served as a cover for smuggling and extortion."[183] The first post-Soviet spasm of violence in Abkhazia ended in 1993, when ethnic Abkhazian militias supported by the Russian military (and ironically also by Chechen and Ingushetian militants who would soon turn to fight Russia) drove Georgian forces out of Abkhazia, along with most of the ethnically Georgian civilian population.[184] A Russian force of military "peacekeepers" supported a new de facto Abkhazian government on the territory.

Only the sparsely populated upper reach of the Kodori Gorge remained under the control of unofficial Georgian militias. The bases of most of these guerrilla groups, including the Forest Brothers and the White Legion, were located in neighboring Samegrelo Zemo-Svaneti province of Georgia proper.[185] As recently as 2002, Russian peacekeepers and Abkhazian forces claimed that the Forest Brothers continued to attack them from Kodori.[186] In February 2004, the new Georgian interior minister, Giorgi Baramidze, successfully led a police raid against the Forest Brothers, charging more than two dozen of them with kidnapping, smuggling, and other crimes, and convinced their leader, David Shengelia, to disarm.[187] But Emzar Kvitsiani's Monadire ("Hunter") militia, centered on his Upper Kodori-based clan, was harder to eliminate, at least in part because Georgian forces with heavy weaponry could not enter the gorge without breaking the 1994 Moscow cease-fire agreement with Abkhazia (discussed below).

Kvitsiani's Emergence

Kvitsiani is an ethnically Svan native of the Kodori Gorge. He is widely suspected of having a criminal history as a young man, and of having spent time in Soviet-era prisons for robbery and hooliganism, where he made connections with the thieves-in-law.[188] He may not have actually been guilty of the crimes for which he was imprisoned; there is a belief that he may have been punished by Soviet authorities in place of one of his relatives, in a sort of blood feud.[189] He is said to have led a youth gang in Upper Kodori whose "uniform" was to go shirtless (a true sign of toughness in the brutal mountain weather). When he got out of prison, he is reported to have run a number of casinos in Abkhazia's tourist areas, further integrating him into the world of the powerful, state-connected criminals who reputedly controlled that industry in Soviet times.[190]

At the end of the first round of warfare in Abkhazia in early 1993, as Georgian nationalist militias were defeated by Russian-supported Abkhazian militias, and Georgian civilians in Abkhazia were targeted for reprisals, one of the routes for displaced Georgians back into Georgia proper was to go up the Kodori River and into the mountainous gorge. Saakashvili's government later accused Kvitsiani's militia of assaulting and robbing refugees along that route.[191] Reportedly some Svan militia members (although it is not clear whether these were members of Kvitsiani's militia, given that this was a time when numerous militias were operating both in Kodori and throughout the country) destroyed pieces of the major road going through the Kodori Gorge, forcing people to leave their cars behind and struggle by foot into the mountains. (The hulks of the deserted cars are said to be still there.) When these displaced people's survival was threatened by starvation and hypothermia, militia members offered them safe passage in return for payment. The militia members also reportedly gave safe passage to retreating Georgian nationalist militias in return for their weapons.[192]

An additional story illustrates how Shevardnadze's officials perceived Kvitsiani's methods. In summer 1993, as part of the cease-fire negotiations, it was arranged that both a Georgian and an Abkhaz official would be allowed to enter Kodori to collect their war dead. Kvitsiani reportedly broke this agreement and took the Abkhaz representative hostage, demanding in return that Tbilisi release all ethnic Svans from prison and give him a shipment of machine guns. The Georgians feared that the Abkhaz would see the kidnapping as a Georgian trick, and that this would collapse the peace negotiations, so they sent two representatives to Kodori as "voluntary hostages" who would stay until the Abkhaz representative was released. Eventually Tbilisi gave Kvitsiani the guns, but did not release the Svan prisoners, and he accepted the compromise.[193]

[88]

Despite (and perhaps because of) his checkered past, Kvitsiani emerged as a guarantor of the buffer zone that was Upper Kodori. A deal was struck with the Abkhaz side that they would not send forces into Georgia through the gorge, and with Shevardnadze that the Georgians would not invade Abkhazia through the gorge. Kvitsiani and his Monadire militia acted as the tripwire, an arrangement that benefited both sides.[194] This deal was ratified in the May 14, 1994, Moscow cease-fire agreement between Georgia and Abkhazia, mediated by Russia, which established Upper Kodori as a demilitarized area. It became a "weapon restriction zone," where "no heavy combat equipment" was allowed, but where "local civil authorities will operate . . . and can have their own weapons."[195] The Monadire, alongside other Svan militias, became the civil authorities. The deal probably benefited the Abkhaz side more than the Georgian: it would have been very difficult to send troops into Georgia through the mountainous Svaneti region, but Upper Kodori sits like the base of an arrow pointing straight down the Kodori River into the Abkhaz capital of Sukhumi.

Shevardnadze's Approach to Kvitsiani: Accommodation

As in the case of Abashidze, Shevardnadze decided for the sake of stability and peace to accommodate Kvitsiani, rather than taking him on. Kvitsiani was a known associate of Abashidze, traveling to Batumi to meet with him several times.[196] After his eventual fall, he was reported to be in contact with Abashidze's militia chief, retired General Netkachev, in Abkhazia.[197] Kvitsiani and Abashidze may have honed their negotiating tactics together.

Kvitsiani is reported to have bolstered and exploited his middleman status with a timber smuggling operation, exporting trees cut down in Kodori to Turkey through Abkhazia tax-free.[198] He is also reported to have been paid by the Shevardnadze government for his cooperation, receiving $50,000 per month in "humanitarian aid" in return for his agreement to protect the major high-voltage elevated power line that entered Georgia from Russia through the Kodori Gorge.[199] This electrical line was shot down by well-aimed bullets several times, plunging Tbilisi into darkness. Kvitsiani claimed that the power-line shootings had been ordered by unknown persons in Tbilisi, and told reporters that he had taken action against them by reporting the incidents to Georgian authorities.[200] The Georgian Interior Ministry argues instead that Kvitsiani held the power line hostage, using the threat of a shutdown to live freely (and operate criminal businesses) in Tbilisi.[201]

Georgian President Shevardnadze made the relationship official by naming Kvitsiani first deputy presidential representative to Upper Kodori in 1998, and in August 2000 by promoting him to be Tbilisi's top official representative there, with duties ranging from socioeconomic oversight to security and self-defense.[202] By 2001, he was the head of the Kodori operations unit of the Georgian Defense Ministry.[203] Shevardnadze moved against some of the Svan militias,[204] but rather than trying to eliminate the Monadire he officially merged it into the Georgian National Guard. In April 2002 Kvitsiani was officially recognized as the Monadire's state-appointed commander.[205] Georgian defense minister Davit Tevzadze announced this move, alongside the deployment of two hundred state border guards to the region, after Russian troops deployed in Abkhazia crossed into Upper Kodori without Georgian approval.[206]

Russia claimed it had made the move because it had reason to be concerned about Kodori, since in late 2001 Chechen rebels crossed into the area and joined Georgian militia forces to fight Abkhazian and Russian troops. Whether or not this movement of Chechen rebels into Abkhazia had been planned by the Shevardnadze government, it was certainly allowed by them; informed observers agree that there is no way that hundreds of rebels could have moved through a large chunk of Georgian territory without the knowledge of Georgian intelligence authorities. The Chechens are believed to have paid off Shevardnadze's minister of interior at the time, Kakha Targamadze.[207] The joint Chechen-Georgian militia grouping reportedly was also responsible for shooting down a UN peacekeeping helicopter flying overhead, killing nine international observers.[208] A few months after these events, the Georgian commander-in-chief for special forces gave Kvitsiani the added responsibility of officially inspecting the Kodori Gorge to ensure that all Abkhazian troops had vacated the Adanga Ridge, a boundary area between the Georgian-controlled area and Abkhazia proper where they had reportedly dug trenches with Russian assistance.[209]

As a result of these state-sponsored security activities, Kvitsiani has been lauded as a Georgian patriot whose Monadire militia of 800–900 members (if the number is correct, it would have employed more than a third of the residents of Upper Kodori) regularly defended the Kodori region from attacks by Abkhazian and Russian forces.[210] On a less laudatory note, his militia also beat up Georgian state authorities when they flew in by helicopter to try to bring him to heel in 1999.[211] He was accused of participating in kidnappings for ransom, including a June 2003 abduction of several UN observers, an event that was reputedly timed to interfere with a proposed repatriation agreement for some Georgian residents of Abkhazia.[212] That was the third abduction of UN observers from the gorge in three years. Georgian and some UN officials believed that the kidnappings were orchestrated by Russia to embarrass the Georgians.[213] Kvitsiani denied that he was involved, claiming that the accusations were part of a long-standing Svan blood feud between his clan and the rival Avaliani family, which dominated the elder council of Kodori and competed for control of the area.[214] Kvitsiani asserted that he had worked through an international crime boss, fellow Svan Tarial Oniani, to negotiate with the kidnappers for the hostages' release, and should thus be given credit for defusing the situation rather than blame for causing it.[215]

In other words, Shevardnadze's regime used Kvitsiani both to contain and to provoke their Russian-supported Abkhazian opponents. In that sense he was a tool of state efforts to maintain what Krasner would call Georgia's international legal sovereignty, protecting and attempting to help re-extend Georgian borders to their previous location.[216] At the same time, though, Shevardnadze allowed Kvitsiani to control the electrical power received by Georgia's capital, something far more crucial for domestic sovereignty and well-being than the smuggling or other criminal businesses Kvitsiani ran. Once again accommodation for the sake of security (if not stability) came at a terrible price.

Saakashvili's Approach to Kvitsiani: Overthrow

According to a knowledgeable US diplomat, the United States had urged Shevardnadze to rein in Kvitsiani, but Shevardnadze believed that Kvitsiani had too much support in Kodori to move against him.[217] Saakashvili disagreed. Monadire members were said to have been inside the parliament building defending Shevardnadze during the Rose Revolution, and this may have intensified Saakashvili's acrimony toward Kvitsiani.[218] One of Saakashvili's first acts as president in early 2004 was to eliminate Kvitsiani's position as head of the Monadire through an official reorganization of the Georgian Defense Ministry. Saakashvili kept him as the official political representative of the president in the region, while taking away his military post and salary.[219]

Yet in September 2004 Saakashvili felt obliged to reestablish the official status of the Monadire battalion (although at four hundred members this time around, apparently at less than half its former strength) following a new round of Russian helicopter overflight and ground incursions into Upper Kodori. Russia claimed that its movements in Kodori were necessary to chase down Chechen rebels who had once again crossed Georgian territory from the Pankisi Gorge, a claim Georgian authorities dismissed. Monadire members, including Kvitsiani, were once again paid from the Georgian state defense budget.[220]

The attempt by Saakashvili to sideline Kvitsiani and his Monadire supporters was drawn out and difficult. In December 2004, a year after the Rose Revolution and following Saakashvili's success in Ajara, the Georgian government officially eliminated Kvitsiani's post as state representative to Upper Kodori. The state National Security Council decided that rather than Kvitsiani, the Council of Ministers of the Autonomous Government of Abkhazia in Exile would supervise Upper Kodori. The chairman of this council at the time was Irakli Alasania, the son of a Georgian KGB general killed in the earlier fighting in Abkhazia. Alasania was himself a Ministry of State Security official for two years under Shevardnadze, and then deputy minister of defense for a few months early in the Saakashvili presidency.

Alasania flew to Kodori by helicopter and met with local residents, including Monadire members, several times when Kvitsiani was away in Tbilisi. He came out of these meetings believing that the Monadire should be preserved, with its members vetted in a system similar to what was used in the US-sponsored Georgia Train and Equip Program for reforming the Georgian Army. Members with criminal records would be fired, under his plan, while the rest would be paid a salary explicitly to defend the power lines. To Alasania's way of thinking, this was reversing the Shevardnadze deal: rather than Georgia being forced to pay for the defense of the power lines, the Monadire would be forced to defend the power lines if its members wanted their pay.[221] Alasania publicly suggested that Kvitsiani would be given a job in Tbilisi with the Autonomous Government in Exile.[222] Kvitsiani, who was living in Tbilisi at the time, claimed to have learned about this decision from journalists.[223]

In January and February 2005, the major power line crossing into Georgia over Kodori was again twice felled by bullets.[224] In April Georgian defense minister Irakli Okruashvili announced that he was washing his hands of Monadire (alongside another Svaneti battalion), and that they would no longer be on his payroll. Monadire refused to lay down its arms and insisted that if it were officially disbanded it would continue to operate as an illegal militia group. Okruashvili called militia members "absurd" and said they were employed only for the purposes of "social relief," adding, "90 percent of this contingent is a gang of layabouts."[225] He suggested that the Interior Ministry could take control of them.[226]

In May 2005 Alasania named a new official envoy to Upper Kodori: Mevlud Jachvliani, a local Kodori resident and a commander of the Georgian border guards, now part of the redesigned Interior Ministry.[227] (Kvitsiani had always allowed ethnic Svan members of the Interior Ministry to live in Kodori, so in that sense there had been some de facto Georgian state monitoring of the area even in the absence of a military presence.)[228] Alasania continued to support Monadire, implying in a July 2005 television interview that the militia would be reformed and retrained and perhaps put under the jurisdiction of the border guards, rather than being disbanded.[229] Okruashvili and Alasania engaged in a public argument over the issue, with Okruashvili claiming that "intrigues" were being planned against him from inside the Defense Ministry with Alasania's help. Okruashvili referred to Monadire as "criminals" and "bandits," and vowed that sooner or later the Georgian state would carry out an operation against them.[230]

Then in March 2006, Alasania was suddenly appointed by Saakashvili to be Georgia's ambassador to the United Nations in New York, in a move that puzzled observers. Alasania was believed to be an effective and perhaps necessary on-the-ground negotiator with Abkhazian authorities, because of his family ties to the region and his demonstrated skills in building trust with them. While Saakashvili argued that Alasania would continue his Abkhazia-focused work in the UN corridors, some expressed doubt that the United Nations had much of a role in resolving the Georgia-Abkhazia dispute.[231] Some observers believe that Saakashvili made the appointment primarily to get Alasania away from Abkhazia, at a time when Abkhazian authorities were eager to reach out to Saakashvili but Saakashvili preferred confrontation.[232]

Although observers in Georgia agree that this new appointment had nothing to do with Upper Kodori per se, it was probably clear to Kvitsiani at that point that he had lost his major advocate in Tbilisi. At the end of March, the Kodori power line was downed by another bullet.[233] That same night a major prison riot happened in downtown Tbilisi, and both the Georgian minister of energy and Saakashvili expressed their belief that the events were connected, and that organized criminals had intended to shut down the power in the capital to allow rioting prisoners to escape.[234]

In July 2006 Kvitsiani contacted journalists in Tbilisi and declared that Defense Minister Okruashvili intended to reassert state control over Upper Kodori by force. Kvitsiani officially announced his "insubordination" to Georgian authorities in a letter to the Autonomous Abkhazian Government in Exile, and returned to Upper Kodori.[235] (This implied that his residence in Tbilisi was part of a deal with the state.) In television interviews on July 23, Kvitsiani said that Okruashvili had asked to talk to him and that when he refused he was told that Georgian forces would attack Upper Kodori on July 27. He said that his Monadire forces would agree to be disarmed only if Georgia first retook control over the rest of Abkhazia, and that if Georgian armed forces came to remove him now, his forces would resist. In one interview he was said to have appeared with a group of armed and masked men.[236] In another he claimed that the United States was pressuring Georgia to remove the Svan population from Upper Kodori.[237]

Nino Burjanadze, speaker of the Georgian parliament and one of the leaders of the Rose Revolution, claimed that Kvitsiani made these statements after being visited by two "Russian" security officials—the defense minister of the de facto Abkhazian government, whom she said was a Russian appointee, and the commander of the Russian peacekeeping forces in Abkhazia. She added that Kvitsiani's actions "serve to benefit only Russia and forces that want to divert Georgia's attention," and posited that either he "rose to the bait" of the Russians or otherwise was "directly carrying out instructions from Russian special services."[238] She urged the population of Upper Kodori not to follow Kvitsiani. In a harsher interview the next day, Saakashvili vowed to "crush anyone who raises his hand against Georgian statehood," and denied that any tension with the Svan population existed.[239] Russia then issued a warning to Georgia not to use force in Kodori, saying that to do so would escalate tensions and violate the 1994 cease-fire agreement that ruled out the deployment of military troops on Abkhazian territory.[240] Masked Monadire gunmen appeared on Russian television.[241]

On July 25, 2006, Georgian forces nonetheless went into Upper Kodori to disarm the militia and arrest Kvitsiani. Tbilisi argued that they constituted a police force without heavy weaponry and were not a military unit that violated the 1994 agreement, but Moscow claimed that Georgia had sent in sixty vehicles led by the defense and interior ministers, with up to five hundred troops.[242] Defense Minister Okruashvili later admitted that Georgian armed forces and special operations forces helped the police action, but said they were immediately withdrawn afterward.[243] The event, in any case, was almost bloodless, and the use of heavy weaponry was not required. Kvitsiani's sister Nora was arrested and charged with participating in an illegal armed grouping and with weapons violations.[244] Kvitsiani and his nephew Bacho Argvliani, Nora's son and reportedly a Monadire commander, escaped with around fourteen militia members.[245] They were believed to have gone into hiding in Abkhazia. The rest of the Monadire melted away, and Georgian authorities say that several dozen assorted criminals hiding in Kodori were caught and prosecuted by the raid.[246] Georgia declared victory the next day, announcing that the Autonomous Abkhazia Government in Exile would relocate to Upper Kodori now that it was back under state control.[247] The Georgian government renamed Upper Kodori, and it now became Upper Abkhazia.

Despite the use of force in this case it is clear that a successful deal was worked out by the Saakashvili administration beforehand to woo Kvitsiani's supporters away from him. The Interior Ministry says that it took Georgian forces thirteen to fourteen hours to make the hundred-kilometer trip up the winding road into Upper Kodori from their base in Zugdidi, which presumably would have given the Monadire plenty of warning about their impending arrival. The Monadire could have laid mines on the mountain road or otherwise harassed the forces, but did not do so.[248]

Both the arriving Georgian troops and the Monadire members are reported initially to have shot into the air, with the Georgian forces returning fire only when they were fired upon by the small group that escaped with Kvitsiani.[249]

There had been a great deal of negotiation between Saakashvili representatives and clan elders in Kodori in particular, giving those who cooperated immunity from prosecution and promising them jobs.[250] Half a dozen experts agreed in interviews that some part of the deal went wrong, however, although none professed to understand exactly what happened.[251] Some say that Kvitsiani had agreed to stay in Tbilisi and broke the deal by returning to Kodori (or that he was tricked into doing so in order to give an excuse for the Georgian action). Others say that the Abkhaz authorities were supposed to arrest Kvitsiani when he escaped the raid, but failed to do so. All claimed not to understand why Kvitsiani's sister Nora was put in jail, given that carrying weapons in Kodori wasn't illegal and that her role in Monadire didn't stand out. Some implied that she might have been jailed as a stand-in for her brother. In any case, Kvitsiani was placed on Interpol's list of wanted criminals.[252]

In October 2006 a joint UN-Russian verification team returned to the area for the first time since the kidnapping in 2003, finding no violations of the 1994 cease-fire agreement.[253] Abkhaz and Russian authorities nonetheless claimed that the Georgian side was trying to trick the United Nations into thinking that the area was not being used for planning aggressive military activities.[254] Later Moscow accused Tbilisi of building illegal military infrastructure and fortifications in the region.[255] When Tbilisi invited UN monitors to establish a permanent post in the area to check those claims, the Abkhaz side refused the proposal.[256]

Kvitsiani did not completely vanish. In September 2006, he sent a video to the Imedi television station in Tbilisi threatening to launch partisan warfare in Kodori. Some small clashes occurred immediately afterward.[257] In November he sent another video, this time to Abkhaz television, accusing Georgian authorities of rigging local elections, and claiming that he was still hiding out in Kodori.[258] Georgian authorities responded that he was not in Upper Abkhazia, but instead "moving along the perimeter controlled by Abkhaz separatists."[259]

In early fall 2006, the Georgian state reestablished administrative control over what was now Upper Abkhazia, setting up a government base in the village named for Ajara in the Chkhalta district, and announcing the permanent deployment of interior minister and state guard service troops there to protect public safety. Within a month, a new electoral district and district council was created for Upper Abkhazia, which had previously not had any official representation in Tbilisi beyond the deals with Kvitsiani.[260]

Already in summer 2005, the year before the overthrow occurred and while Kvitsiani was safely in Tbilisi, the Georgian state had begun a number of new reconstruction projects in Upper Kodori. By the end of summer 2006 a local school was refurbished and two new ones were built, the local hospital was reequipped and three additional doctors were stationed there, food aid including iodized salt and agricultural supplies such as fertilizers were brought in, several major roads were repaired, two hydropower stations were constructed for the electricity needs of the population, and the government reopened the post office, established a bank branch and a cinema, and built two TV towers.[261] The Georgian government decided to make the new Upper Abkhazia a magnet that might attract the rest of the breakaway republic back to the Georgian fold, and set aside $10 million in the annual federal budget for new construction projects. Around 700 of the area's by then 2,500 residents, most of whom had fled the earlier violence in the region, reportedly returned.[262]

While these moves were successful, at least in the short run, this was a very expensive proposition for Saakashvili to undertake. Ten million dollars per year for 700, or even 2,500, people, was an incredible chunk of the budget when the entire amount spent on social benefits for Georgia that year was around $350 million.[263] The program would probably not have gone forward in a country subject to genuine democratic oversight. The government's desire to provide a showcase for Abkhazia would have bumped up against the reality of Georgia's extensive poverty, unemployment, and struggling health and education systems. Some of Saakashvili's opponents also criticized him for taking abrupt forceful action that could be interpreted as violating the 1994 cease-fire agreement. This was especially risky at a time when Abkhaz representatives appeared to be reaching out to Georgia but Russia was being obstreperous—for example, through its March 2006 ban on Georgian wine imports. Had the decision to intervene in this way in Upper Kodori at this time been subject to public debate, there is a good chance the initiative would have failed. Certainly no private deals could have been worked out under a media spotlight.

The Role of Russia

Most Georgian observers agree that Kvitsiani had probably not been cooperating directly with the Russians during his time in Kodori. He had a strong relationship with the Abkhaz leadership, however, and was said to be a relative of the de facto deputy defense minister of Abkhazia, Garri Kupalba. Since the Abkhaz regime has always been funded and defended by Russia, there was certainly an indirect tie.

The Georgian action to remove Kvitsiani and establish a state foothold in Kodori aggravated a deteriorating relationship between Tbilisi and Moscow. In October 2006 Russia tried to introduce a UN Security Council resolution demanding that Georgian troops withdraw from the area, but the United States convinced Moscow to soften its language.[264] By March 2007 Russian planes were once again bombing the upper Kodori Gorge, and Georgian authorities were being blamed by opposition political forces for not providing sufficient air defense to the region.[265] That same month Kvitsiani appeared on Russian state television (in an interview reportedly recorded in Upper Abkhazia), demanding that his sister and other supporters be released by Georgian authorities, and threatening to push Georgia out of Kodori otherwise. Georgian analysts argued that he was being used by Moscow.[266]

Small-scale clashes between Georgian and Abkhazian forces along the Kodori border became a regular occurrence, as the Abkhaz side apparently attempted to interfere with Georgian construction efforts.[267] By mid-2008, Russian paratroopers were reinforcing Abkhaz forces in the area, and each side accused the other of preparing to launch an attack.[268] Russia began extending a railway line to its military base in Ochamchire in Abkhazia, and Georgian analysts argued that this would be used in an attempt to retake nearby Kodori.[269] Kvitsiani was reported to be in Sukhumi, under the protection of Russian special forces.[270] There were rumors that he was to head a propaganda campaign for the Abkhazian side, claiming that Russia would liberate Kodori for the Svans.[271]

At 6:00 a.m. on August 8, 2008, just a few hours after Georgian forces began the fateful shelling of Tskhinvali in South Ossetia, Abkhazian troops headed into Upper Kodori as Russian troops crossed into South Ossetia. The Abkhazian forces were assisted by air support from Russian bombers, and Upper Kodori was shelled for three days.[272] Georgian forces fled. Kupalba told the *New York Times*, "We saw an opportunity and we took it."[273] All of the supplies that the Georgian government had sent to Upper Abkhazia, including state-of-the-art computer and medical equipment, were removed to Abkhazia.[274]

There is no clear picture of exactly what happened in Upper Kodori following the August 2008 war. Most of the Svans who had returned to the area fled again when the fighting broke out, and remained in the western Georgian city of Kutaisi that winter. While Abkhaz officials invited them to return, the United Nations warned them not to, and they could not have navigated the mountain passes in the snow at any rate.[275] Reportedly their homes and farms were looted in their absence, and Georgian officials have claimed that the area remained deserted because there was no way to guarantee the security of returnees. Abkhaz authorities reported that several hundred residents returned before the mountain passes became impassable in the fall of 2008.[276] The Georgian Interior Ministry claims that 135 residents had returned by the fall of 2009.[277] There is no way to verify these numbers.

Some claim that more residents would have returned if they could have gotten Saakashvili's blessing to do so. In this version of events, they considered themselves Georgian patriots and were unwilling to be counted by Saakashvili as traitors, but were willing to take the individual security risk of returning home. It is impossible to verify whether or not their perception of Saakashvili's attitude on this point was correct. But another border area of Abkhazia, Gali district, provides a suggestive tale. Ethnically Georgian Megrelians are the dominant population in Gali, and someone tried to keep them from voting in the March 2007 Abkhaz elections with anonymous phone calls and posters on the street that read, "Abkhaz Megrelians are traitors." Some Gali residents believe that Georgian intelligence services in 2007 targeted those who cooperated with Abkhaz authorities for harassment and arrest when they crossed back into Georgia.[278]

In Upper Kodori the de facto Abkhaz government announced that it had appointed an ethnic Abkhazian, Sergei Dzhonua, rather than an ethnic Georgian Svan as its presidential representative. But Georgian officials announced that the Abkhaz government had appointed a close associate of Kvitsiani's, Zaza Gurchiani, as the governor of the district.[279] Then in February 2009, Georgian state television reported that Gurchiani had been shot dead in the Abkhaz capital of Sukhumi by Kvitsiani's renegade nephew.[280] Georgian government officials interviewed in the fall of 2009 were mostly mum about these events, although there were vague hints that Kvitsiani's nephew might later have taken charge of the district. Sukhumi announced that it intended to support the permanent stationing of a Russian military base in Kodori, and that it would rebuild the area the same way that the Georgian government had earlier tried to do.[281] The Georgian Interior Ministry claimed that a Russian battalion was newly stationed there.[282]

Whatever the details, Saakashvili's seeming success at state reintegration in Upper Kodori was short-lived. While it is impossible to know what Russia would have done if the Monadire had been left to guard the pass by themselves, it is clear that Saakashvili's moves in 2006 provided an excuse for Russia to say that Georgia violated the 1994 cease-fire agreement first. He fanned the flames by declaring Upper Abkhazia a showcase. Democratic oversight of Saakashvili's actions might have restrained what Russia saw as a provocation, and that constraint over his state-based patronage might have better served Georgia's long-term security interests.

Even if Kvitsiani himself was not necessary for the actual defense of Kodori, the Monadire played an important symbolic middleman role along a tense border. If it is correct that Kvitsiani's nephew had retaken political control of Upper Kodori by 2010, this might be a sign that the tripwire was restored under Abkhazia's attempt at negotiated sovereignty.

CONCLUSIONS

Shevardnadze's accommodation with warlords gave him a measure of stability in both Ajara and Upper Kodori, but at the cost of rampant criminality, the bleeding of the state budget, and significant human suffering in Ajara in particular. He also discovered to his chagrin that stability for the middlemen was no guarantee of cooperation from Russia. He did not convince Russia to remove its military bases from Georgia, nor did he achieve a settlement with Russia or even discernible progress on resolving the conflict over the breakaway regions of Abkhazia and South Ossetia. Eventually his alliance with Abashidze helped lead to his own overthrow. Shevardnadze's policies cannot be said to have had productive results.

Saakashvili gained state control in both places, but only through methods that would probably have been impossible in a liberal democratic political system. Life was much better in Ajara than it was under Abashidze, so Ajara can be counted as a measured success for the population, even if it still lacked a truly democratic political system. But Saakashvili lost Upper Kodori when Russia eventually fought back, losing tens of millions of dollars in state investments there as well. Russian actions were not a direct result of Saakashvili's removal of Kvitsiani, and one can imagine a different outcome there that would have restored more state influence, without such a show of state power. Russian aggravation was made more likely by Saakashvili's insistence on showing the Georgian flag so vividly—as well as flaunting the support of the United States—in what had previously been seen as a buffer zone.

These cases lead to several observations that may be useful for policy makers elsewhere. Most importantly, this chapter suggests that warlords may sometimes be more pretense than peril. It is striking how quickly Saakashvili was able to separate both Abashidze and Kvitsiani from their supposedly loyal militias, once each of them demonstrated that he was not leaving power voluntarily. Longstanding fears of civil unrest in both places were laid to rest quite easily. Clans and their traditions gave way in the face of a strong state, especially when backed by promises of money, power, and safety from prosecution. Bargaining, backed by force, worked. This may provide a new strategy for overcoming warlordism in other countries: rather than either defeating a warlord militarily or bringing him or her on the payroll, it may be possible to reach a deal with the warlord's patronage group. This may be an especially promising strategy if individuals connected to the warlord are tired of the costs that the warlord's obstreperousness entails for their own personal and business interests.

To accomplish this it was crucial that Saakashvili's promises were credible. He came to power with overwhelming popular support, and then made clear that he was in charge and not subject to democratic whim or the niceties of a liberal judicial system. He was originally elected in a democratic process lauded for its freeness and fairness, but he then used the populism he had generated to turn in an authoritarian direction. While Saakashvili can be criticized for his violations of human rights, he had a strong state apparatus behind him and it was clear that he was going to be around for a while.

This point may appear anomalous. The literature on bargaining in international relations argues that democratic states make more credible bargains because they give actors more confidence that contracts are likely to endure over the long term.[283] The difference here is that what mattered was speed and momentum, not endurance. Saakashvili made similarly speedy and opaque deals elsewhere in Georgia as well—for example, in his reform efforts in the ministries of security and interior, where some officers accused of corruption were allowed to retain their positions in return for payments to a Law Enforcement and Development Fund.[284]

Saakashvili needed to get rid of the warlords quickly to build momentum for change. The actors he bargained with were likely well schooled in corruption and in some cases criminality. They were survivors and short-term thinkers with high risk-acceptance levels, who had confidence they could find options for themselves if the bargain started to fray at some point. This may have especially been true because Saakashvili demonstrated that it was possible to leave the country and live in peace: Abashidze was prosecuted in absentia, but continued to live a comfortable life in exile.

Yet the very strength of Saakashvili indicates that there is a limit to how broadly generalizable Georgia's experience is for cases of warlordism today. Georgia was a weak state but it had a continuous state bureaucracy, and in 2004 it had a popular state leader. For all of the anarchy it experienced in the early 1990s, and all of the violence it suffered over Abkhazia and South Ossetia, Georgia still had a strong sense of nationhood and patriotism.

It also had a bureaucratic apparatus left over from Soviet times, which spanned the entire country and could be modified into an independent set of functioning agencies. That new bureaucracy, most importantly, inherited the information resources held by the Soviet-era KGB. Old records undoubtedly helped Saakashvili identify the businesses to target in his shakeups, as well as the personnel networks and relationships that surrounded the warlords. This may limit the applicability of Georgian lessons in Somalia, Afghanistan, and other failed states, since it is not clear that such de jure states without any de facto territorial control can produce either the kind of populist leader or the bureaucratic tools (including information) that make the expansion of state authority possible.

Furthermore, it is not clear that the Georgian experience could easily be repeated in areas that are ruled not by a single large warlord, but instead by a fabric of smaller-scale warlordism. In the FATA or Afghanistan, webs of patronage are so complex and small-scale that it would be difficult for any new state authority to make headway. Saakashvili had a huge advantage in Ajara in particular: he was the university classmate and friend of a member of one of the clans that had cooperated with Abashidze. This provided him both with a trusted colleague to use in the overthrow, and with crucial information about potential new allies and their likely resources. In Upper Kodori, Saakashvili's move followed years of negotiation between Georgian authorities and the local population, including Alasania's recent trips to the region in Kvitsiani's absence. Knowledgeable, well-networked, individual people mattered for Saakashvili's success.

Finally, Saakashvili's biggest mistake was to bait the bear. Neither of these warlords mattered all that much to Russia in the abstract. As individuals they were not worth going to war for. In the case of Ajara, Russia was even willing to cooperate in removing Abashidze in return for minor concessions. But by loudly declaring that the Upper Kodori buffer zone was now under Georgian state control and a magnet for the rest of breakaway Abkhazia, Saakashvili brought Georgia ever closer to the August 2008 war. Middlemen are expendable, but the realist interests of external states that they represent are sometimes not.

It is better to work with a powerful external actor to remove a warlord, even if this necessitates small compromises, than to take unilateral action that threatens that external actor's security interests.

[5]

Chechnya

THE SOVEREIGNTY OF RAMZAN KADYROV

After fighting two brutal civil wars to keep and control its own Republic of Chechnya, the Russian state effectively gave the territory away to one man and his militia. By early 2010, Ramzan Kadyrov and his appointees had legal command over the vast preponderance of security forces located in the republic. Moscow, in other words, granted Ramzan a virtual monopoly over the legitimate use of force in Chechnya, ceding the basic building block of sovereignty outlined by Max Weber. Ramzan then received unfettered access to the outside world when Moscow recertified the airport in Grozny, the Chechen capital, for international flights piloted by his own personnel. Russia, in other words, gave Ramzan the opportunity to become a middleman warlord, linked to external actors with little to no state oversight.

Ramzan constantly trumpeted his fealty and indebtedness to Prime Minister Vladimir Putin—for example, by renaming the main street of Grozny in Putin's honor.[1] He volunteered to give up his earlier title of president of Chechnya so as not to be seen as competing against his boss, President Dmitry Medvedev of Russia.[2] Yet his requests to Moscow and his actions in Chechnya proved that his goal was to replace Moscow's control over the security forces, trade, and infrastructure on Chechen territory. Ramzan claimed that he controlled security operations in neighboring Ingushetia as well, and many commentators believed (although Ramzan denied it) that he wanted to expand his power and reunite the two territories into the Chechen-Ingush Autonomous Republic of Soviet times.[3] He followed this path even as he continued to accept hundreds of millions of dollars in reconstruction assistance from the Russian state budget each year. While some Russian authorities expressed irritation at his behavior, and some commentators believed that popular resentment about the funding could become an election issue for Putin in 2012,[4] Moscow's concrete support for him remained strong. Indeed Moscow gave away so much to Ramzan that Russian authorities may never be able to take back control of Chechnya without another bloody war, this time against Ramzan's forces and their patronage networks.

The underlying argument presented here, that Moscow decided to let Ramzan escape Kremlin control, is not new but it is controversial.[5] It has not been developed in detail elsewhere or placed into a generalizable theoretical framework. A major goal of this chapter is simply to demonstrate through careful process tracing that Chechnya is a case that fits this book's warlord model.

Chechnya is a striking example of an otherwise sovereign state methodically choosing to create a warlord on its own territory. Scholars have often thought of "big men" or local bosses as preexisting power brokers with whom new or expanding states had to bargain.[6] But Ramzan was chosen and groomed by Putin for his role, after a long period of Russian and Soviet rule over Chechnya. Russia was not forced to bargain with Ramzan. Instead warlordism was something that state leaders chose to inflict upon themselves.

Russian actions in this regard are puzzling. Why did Moscow do what it did? Elsewhere in Russia during the Putin years, Moscow acted to consolidate federal control over regional ethnic power brokers—for example, by neutering and eventually replacing the obstreperous leader of Bashkortostan, Murtaza Rakhimov.[7] Moscow was furthermore an outside supporter of both Abashidze and (indirectly) Kvitsiani in neighboring Georgia. Putin must have understood from direct observation and participation in those Georgian cases that warlords threaten important components of state sovereignty, including the ability to collect taxes and customs revenues. He further must have known, given Russia's own actions in Georgia, that foreign actors can work with autonomous warlords to gain economic and military influence inside otherwise sovereign states. At the close of those Georgian cases, and at the same time that Ramzan was first gaining strength in Chechnya between 2003 and 2006, Putin saw how relatively easy it was for Georgia's president, Mikheil Saakashvili, to overthrow Abashidze and Kvitsiani by working with their peripheral supporters to undercut and replace them. It is thus surprising that Putin made the choices he did, and that the pathway he established in Chechnya became more and more entrenched over time.

This case challenges the common belief that Putin restrengthened the Russian state. The previous Russian leader, Boris Yeltsin, was forced to bargain away state strength to governors, organized criminals, and oligarchs in the uncertainty of the post-Soviet transition. Putin's reign was

Chechnya

Map 3. Chechnya. Central Intelligence Agency

widely seen as a time of state reconsolidation and recentralization. But Moscow's choices in Chechnya since 2003 instead indicated profound state weakness.

This chapter first describes the rise of Ramzan from out of his father's entourage. It chronicles his growing sovereignty over Chechnya, following his father's assassination, and then discusses several common explanations for Moscow's behavior in this case. For example, some claim that events reflected a personal deal between Putin and Ramzan (later foisted on Medvedev), darkly connected to Putin's own KGB past. Others argue that Moscow's actions stemmed from the profits to be made by exploiting Chechnya's oil resources and refining industry. The Russian state officially argued that Ramzan made Russia more secure by eliminating a safe haven for terrorists on Chechen territory. Other prominent analysts saw Ramzan's rule as being necessary to tamp down clan or other factional violence in Chechnya, arguing that it was better to work with one big warlord than many small ones.

While all of these explanations contribute to an understanding of Moscow's choices, none is completely satisfying. To better explain the trajectory of the case as a whole, I make a new argument: that Russian leaders effectively outsourced Chechnya to a private contractor because they no longer wished to expend the state resources and political capital that would be required for direct control over Chechen territory. In the absence of archival evidence it is impossible to know whether Russian leaders anticipated this effect from the start and consistently pursued policies for this reason, but it is the effective outcome they have achieved, and this argument explains more than the other theories do. Indeed, the new explanation is the simplest, because Moscow's actions fit a global (and historical) pattern: states choose to cooperate with warlords as a low-cost method for achieving immediate, short-term security benefits, without concern for the long-term consequences of their decisions. The chapter concludes with policy lessons that can be drawn from this case to evaluate the wisdom of such choices.

BACKGROUND: THE RISE OF AKHMAD-HADJI

Ramzan first emerged as the commander of his father's personal bodyguard militia, informally known as the *kadyrovtsy*. It is worth making a small diversion to describe the rise of Ramzan's father, Akhmad-Hadji Kadyrov, because his biography helps establish Putin's possible expectations for Ramzan as Akhmad's successor. Akhmad's path to power had its origins in the Chechen independence movement of the early 1990s.

At the beginning of the first war with the Russian state in 1994–96, Chechen rebels were mainly secular and ethnically nationalist in orientation, drawing on a long historical memory of invasion and persecution by Russian forces.[8] Part of what was at stake was control over the republic's oil production, pipelines, and refineries. While the amount of oil in Chechen oilfields was small and in decline, a major pipeline connecting Russia to Kazakhstan and Azerbaijan crossed Chechen territory. Also at stake was something Moscow feared: that Chechnya would set a precedent. If Chechnya were allowed to secede, the entire Russian Federation might go the way of the Soviet Union. An uneasy three-year truce was reached after both sides had exhausted themselves in this grinding and savage counterinsurgency war.

With time the conflict became radicalized. Foreign Wahhabi Islamists infiltrated and helped split the rebel movement.[9] Russian forces resumed operations in Chechnya in 1999, this time following a series of violent attacks elsewhere on Russian territory. Some of these attacks, like an incursion into neighboring Dagestan, were clearly the work of Chechen Islamist extremists, supported by foreign Wahhabists. Others, like a series of apartment bombings in Moscow and elsewhere, were rumored by some to be the work of Russian security services to provide an excuse for the resumption of warfare.[10] While these rumors may simply be conspiracy mongering, they gained credence among some sober analysts after Moscow failed to conduct a detailed public investigation into the events, and then thwarted an independent investigation by a former FSB (Federal Security Service) officer, Mikhail Trepashkin, and imprisoned him on unrelated charges.[11]

In the midst of this resumption of warfare, Akhmad Kadyrov was appointed the head of Chechnya's new temporary administration by Putin in June 2000, shortly after Putin himself was elected the new president of Russia. Akhmad provided many political benefits to Moscow. He practiced a moderate form of Islam and opposed the violent Wahhabism of some Chechen rebels. He had no strong political beliefs of his own, but instead followed a lifelong pattern of serving whomever the dominant authorities were at any particular time. He lacked much of an independent power base, but using his son's militia he was skilled at turning former rebels to the side of the state. Since Ramzan was young and politically inexperienced at the time of his father's assassination, Moscow might reasonably have expected that Russian authorities could shape Ramzan in his father's mold, and hence control him.

Akhmad's appointment occurred amid brutal Russian military campaigns that included mass imprisonments and massacres, torture pits, and other forms of collective punishment against the family members of rebels and villages perceived to be sheltering insurgent sympathizers.

(The Chechen rebels were equally brutal in their tactics.) The city of Grozny was leveled by Russian bombing in 1999–2000, and there were numerous well-documented cases of random kidnapping for ransom and of rampant thievery by Russian troops. Violence against civilians was so widespread and so tolerated by the Russian state that many believe it was systematic and intentional.[12] Some thought that Russia's ultimate goal was to depopulate Chechnya and create "free-fire zones" for mowing down any rebels who remained. Around a third of the population became internally displaced, fleeing to Ingushetia or other nearby Russian regions. Akhmad never complained about Russian tactics, and that undoubtedly helped cement his relationship with Moscow.[13]

Akhmad was not widely trusted in Chechnya itself. He had been able to get a religious education at Soviet state institutions in Bukhara and Tashkent in the early to mid-1980s and rise in the ranks of the official Muslim clergy as religious practice opened up during Mikhail Gorbachev's presidency. This meant by definition that in his early career he had had the support of the Soviet KGB.[14] He had been vetted by the Soviet state, and his Islam then was not of the rebellious, state-challenging variety. In the mid-1990s, though, when he was the deputy imam of Chechnya and separatists took control of its government, he became a rebel militia commander. He was named the mufti of Chechnya by Dzhokar Dudayev's separatist rebels in 1995, during the first war. That year he publicly declared jihad against Russia, urging good Muslims to kill Russian soldiers.[15]

Four years later he backtracked again. He began negotiating with Russia in 1999 as the second war began, renouncing jihad in return for a leadership position under Putin. Akhmad bent with the wind, following the lead of whomever had power at the moment. He agreed to accept the imposition of direct presidential rule from Moscow for a two-year period, after which he was promised more autonomy.[16]

Akhmad was also not trusted in Chechnya because he was suspected of corruption. He got the "Hadji" in his name by organizing the first Chechen pilgrimage to Mecca, probably in 1988 when the first large-scale hajj left from Russia.[17] He did so, however, under lingering accusations that he worked this as a shady business deal. Reportedly he collected money from local citizens to finance the trip, but when Saudi Arabia later covered all the expenses he didn't return the funds to local donors.[18] As in the case of other individuals supported by Putin, this weakness may have made him attractive. Putin operated according to the KGB methods of his own early career. He fostered relationships with people who had compromising material (*kompromat*) collected about them, who could be prosecuted or blackmailed if it ever became necessary to punish their disloyalty.

[107]

This distrust meant that Akhmad occupied a rather lonely and empty centrist position in Chechen politics in 2000. Many pro-Moscow officials in Chechnya signed an open letter of protest against his appointment as head of the temporary administration, expressing bitter disappointment that this jihad-leading rebel had usurped their own role in leading the republic. They tendered their resignations when the appointment went through.[19] The anti-Russian resistance had meanwhile splintered, between those who wanted independence or autonomy for Chechnya as a "normal" state, and those who instead wanted to declare an Islamist caliphate throughout the North Caucasus that would include Dagestan and Ingushetia. Prominent separatist rebels who fled abroad, led by Akhmed Zakayev (a former rebel commander and later the prime minister in exile of the unrecognized Chechen Republic of Ichkeria) disdained Akhmad. They saw him as a corrupt and weak puppet of Moscow, and preferred to negotiate with Moscow directly.[20] The more radical Wahhabi militants resented Akhmad's support of moderate Islam and his condemnation of sharia law. Akhmad called Wahhabism a "terrorist ideology," and both he and his son Ramzan survived numerous assassination attempts by the Wahhabis. Wahhabist rebel leader Shamil Basayev put a price on Akhmad's head of $100,000.[21] Aslan Maskhadov, a separatist Chechen leader whom Akhmad had earlier supported but who later joined the Wahhabis, upped it to over $250,000.[22]

Russian leaders nonetheless rewarded Akhmad because he managed to turn many former rebels to Moscow's side in the second war. In October 1999, alongside the leaders of another rebel militia, the Yamadayev brothers, Akhmad convinced a group of Wahhabi rebels in his home city of Gudermes to surrender in the face of a threatened Russian bombardment.[23] Yet Akhmad could not overcome the deep divisions among various power brokers in Chechnya. His clan ties were limited to the northern and especially eastern parts of Chechnya (including Gudermes), where Moscow had historically found it easier to win control of the population.[24] Indeed Gudermes, not Grozny, was where Akhmad originally based his administration, because it was easier for him to control. He did not consolidate his control in the capital until 2002.[25] Once he did so, he proceeded to appoint his own clansmen to every position that mattered in the republic, "from top government officials to ordinary drivers,"[26] making no effort to include other, competing clans.

Putin meanwhile made sure that Akhmad would win the election for the presidency of Chechnya in 2003. A byzantine series of maneuvers were taken against his potential opponents. Yet there were rumors that all three major security services in Russia—the FSB, the Ministry of the Interior (the MVD, Russia's federal police and paramilitary forces), and the Ministry of Defense (the MoD)—sent a coordinated letter to Putin condemning Akhmad, saying that he was corrupt and that he continued to aid the rebels in Chechnya.[27] For whatever reason, Putin cajoled or forced all of Akhmad's opponents to withdraw from the race so that there were no contenders left by election day. Even a candidate originally supported by Putin's FSB, Malik Saidullayev, a wealthy businessman who had also successfully won over some rebel commanders to Moscow's side, was eventually convinced to withdraw.[28] To emphasize Putin's support, Akhmad was shown on state television traveling with Putin to the United Nations just before the election.[29] The voter turnout in Chechnya was officially reported at over 80 percent, at polling stations that international monitors found empty.[30] Akhmad was not a man likely to challenge the authority of the Russian state or President Putin in Chechnya.

Akhmad continued to woo as many former rebels as he could to join his side, while taking harsh retribution (using his son Ramzan's militia) against those who refused. In 2003 the kadyrovtsy began what would become a long process of gaining official status as the legitimate regional security forces. The head of Ramzan's militia was appointed as commander of the special police (OMON) forces of the regional branch of the MVD, several months after the previous commander was run over by a truck (apparently following threats from the kadyrovtsy).[31]

The "Chechenization" of the conflict had begun. James Hughes suggests that this let Russia continue its harsh policies toward Chechnya while "put[ting] itself at one remove from the most brutal forms of repression," lending itself plausible deniability.[32] At least since the dawn of early modern Europe, plausible deniability has always been a motive for empires to use the kind of indirect rule that Chechenization involved.[33] After the 2003 election, locals began to report that the terrifying "sweep" campaigns and resulting disappearances and kidnappings in the region were being taken over by Chechen-speaking, not native-Russian-speaking, forces.[34]

Akhmad himself did not have long to make his mark on Chechnya. He was killed by a bomb planted under his seat on the reviewing stand of the main Grozny sports stadium in May 2004, less than a year after his election as president. Wahhabi militants led by Basayev claimed responsibility, but some analysts think that the assassination demonstrated Akhmad's failure to draw a wider range of prominent Chechens into his government.[35] His movement from place to place was always conducted under tight security, and his schedule was not publicized in advance. The bomb was embedded in the reviewing stand during construction work ten days before the explosion took place.[36] Yet someone in his inner circle must have tipped off the assassins to Akhmad's presence, because he was supposed to be in Moscow that day, and his trip to the stadium was arranged by surprise.[37]

At this point Ramzan, Akhmad's younger son, engaged in a byzantine power struggle of his own to ensure his own succession. No one had expected him to take over the political leadership of the country, as he was young and had no real political experience. The man previously seen as Akhmad's most likely successor, the chairman of the State Council, Hussein Isayev, was also killed in the stadium blast and there were no obvious alternatives left.[38] Ramzan was appointed vice premier of Chechnya immediately after his father's death, but he was underage according to the Chechen constitution, and could not assume the presidency until he turned thirty in October 2006.

In the meantime Alu Alkhanov, the regional MVD chief, was elected president in another vote rigged by Moscow.[39] Alkhanov was a career police officer who had fought in both Chechen wars on the side of Russia. He reportedly had no significant local connections, and his political supporters were instead Chechen businessmen living elsewhere in Russia.[40] His elevation to the presidency was nevertheless significant for Ramzan's eventual success, because Alu Alkhanov's deputy, Ruslan Alkhanov (apparently no relation), was named the head of the regional MVD in Chechnya when Alu Alkhanov became president. Ruslan Alkhanov had earlier been the head of Akhmad's personal security detail, and was one of the rebels turned by the kadyrovtsy.[41] In other words, one of Ramzan's men now controlled the legal local paramilitary police force in Chechnya, even before Ramzan was officially in charge of the republic.

Moscow then appointed Sergei Abramov as the prime minister of Chechnya. Abramov was not ethnically Chechen, and some believed that Moscow had sent Abramov to keep tabs on the republic as minister of finance during Akhmad's reign.[42] Yet Ramzan, not Abramov, was soon appointed the chairman of the local branch of United Russia, the political party associated with Putin. That post gave Ramzan the ability to control parliamentary elections in the republic, and cemented his status as the key Putin ally in Chechnya.[43]

Just before the next round of parliamentary elections in November 2005, Abramov was in a serious car crash in Moscow. He was hospitalized with major internal injuries after a large truck collided with his armored car. Ramzan, the deputy prime minister, automatically became the acting prime minister. Abramov then announced that he would not return to Chechnya from Germany, where he was undergoing medical treatment. He said that he was resigning not for health reasons, but instead to allow Ramzan to take over as prime minister, calling this "most appropriate."[44]

On April 25, 2006, there was a gunfight between the kadyrovtsy and President Alkhanov's private bodyguard militia.[45] On April 29 Ramzan announced that the kadyrovtsy had ceased to exist as an informal militia, and that 1,200 of his men would be transformed into the North (*Sever*) and South (*Yug*) battalions of the regional MVD.[46] His first cousin Alibek Delimkhanov commanded what became the North battalion. While commentators at the time wondered if Russia was punishing Ramzan by taking over the kadyrovtsy, this in fact gave his most trusted forces legitimate status under Russian law. President Alkhanov's guards lacked this status, even though Alkhanov was a career MVD officer. Now the regional MVD was both commanded and increasingly staffed by Ramzan's people.

In November 2006 a Chechen FSB officer, Col. Movladi Baisarov, who had headed the renowned Gorets ("Highlanders") special battalion and at one time commanded Akhmad's personal guards, was killed on the street in Moscow by a group of these new MVD forces from Chechnya. Baisarov had refused to disband his battalion when ordered to do so by Ramzan, and as a result had been stripped of his FSB appointment and charged with kidnapping and murder. He had gone to Moscow in hopes of regaining FSB protection, and with an offer to give evidence to the Military Prosecutor's Office about the situation in Chechnya. He had been refused on both counts.[47] Baisarov was rumored to be a political supporter of Alu Alkhanov.

Finally in February 2007, with no explanation, Alkhanov resigned the Chechen presidency ahead of schedule. Putin appointed Ramzan the acting president, and he was confirmed by a popular election in March. (Ramzan had turned thirty and achieved legal age for the presidency the previous October.) Ramzan nominated a cousin, Odes Baisultanov, who had previously been responsible for overseeing reconstruction in Chechnya, as his new prime minister, and was sworn in as president on April 5.[48] That June the Chechen constitution was changed to lift the term limits on the number of times he could be reelected.

The Kadyrovtsy

Ramzan coerced many of the rebels who came over to Moscow's side, both during Akhmad's reign and later, to join his own militia. His forces had a reputation for being very selective in their targeting: they knew who the rebels were, and their violence was directed at those individuals and their families.[49] They used severe beatings and torture against those who resisted, and sometimes kidnapped family members to convince individual rebels to surrender.[50] When one of the leading Wahhabi rebels, Akhmad Umarov, surrendered in 2006 under a general amnesty, he "told reporters that he wanted to search for his father, who was kidnapped by unidentified abductors a year ago."[51] By 2008 an arson campaign was torching the family homes of rebels who refused to flip, and parents were forced to appear on local television to beg their sons to give in.[52] In April 2010, the mayor of Grozny and another city official threatened in a television interview to punish the parents of rebels.[53]

Not all of those who changed sides did so under negative pressure. The father of the Chechen rebel who had led the infamous Moscow theater siege of 2002 claimed (in a press interview arranged by Ramzan's office) that he simply wanted to come back to his homeland in Chechnya before he died. Ramzan supported his decision by giving him a banquet, a car, and financial support.[54] Roland Dannreuther and Luke March argue that Ramzan was astute at "striking the necessary balance between inducements . . . and threats" in order to convince the rebels to switch sides.[55]

Yet it is not clear how common this softer form of persuasion was, and Dannreuther and March do not provide evidence for their assessment. One rebel who was persuaded by the Kadyrovs' harsher methods after being arrested in 2003, Umar S. Israilov, secretly wrote a memoir of his own detention and torture in gruesome detail. His father, who was also detained and tortured, also wrote a memoir. The two fled abroad, and then filed complaints against the Kadyrovs to the European Court of Human Rights, sending copies of the documents to the *New York Times* (which held the documents but did not publish them). In 2009 Israilov was hunted down by Chechen-speaking assassins and shot to death in exile in Vienna. Afterward the *Times* devoted a lengthy, front-page article to the claims that the Israilovs made about the horrifying methods of the kadyrovtsy, including savage beatings, the use of blowtorches to burn detainees, and electrical shocks.[56] Austrian authorities accused senior officials in Ramzan's administration of ordering the attack on Israilov, which they called a kidnapping attempt gone bad.[57]

In early 2004 the Kadyrovs had an especially notable success using their fear-based methods. They convinced the field commander and defense minister of the rebel Chechen Republic of Ichkeria in Exile, Magomed Khambiyev, to surrender by kidnapping and holding hostage forty members of the man's extended family.[58] After his surrender Khambiyev worked for the government in Grozny to help convince other Chechens living abroad to return home. In July 2009 he was sent into the mountains as Ramzan's personal aide to assist with the counterinsurgency.[59]

Official Russian statistics indicate that seven thousand rebels have "laid down their arms voluntarily" since 1999,[60] making up about half of the fifteen thousand Chechen forces that officially constitute the regional branch of the MVD. The Kadyrovs reportedly used their persuasion process to gain valuable intelligence about the political and security situation in Chechnya as a whole, including among distant and competing clans. This allowed them to expand their influence in the region and their autonomy from Moscow, overcoming Akhmad's original weakness.[61] Ramzan now had information that Moscow could not access without him.

Meanwhile Ramzan instituted a personality cult in Chechnya that rivaled that of former Soviet leader Joseph Stalin, according to some observers. Schoolchildren wore patriotic pins (*znachki*) on their shirts as in Soviet times, but now featuring Ramzan's photo. Schools gave military training to young people and encouraged them to join the kadyrovtsy. Older teenagers joined the "Ramzan Patriotic Club," wearing T-shirts and carrying flags with his portrait while singing songs that praised him and his father.[62]

RAMZAN'S RIVALRIES

To consolidate his control over local security forces Ramzan had to neutralize his rivals. A variety of informal militias had operated in Chechnya during the war years, including Alu Alkhanov's personal guard and the FSB Gorets battalion of Baisarov. The fighters who were not already under Ramzan's control now resisted his leadership. One of Ramzan's deadliest rivalries was with the Yamadayev brothers. Like him they had commanded a militia that fought on the side of the rebels and then flipped, and it was similarly infamous for its violence and use of torture. (It is rumored that both Alu Alkhanov and Baisarov were in fact Yamadayev supporters.) The Yamadayevs were distant relatives of the Kadyrovs from Gudermes, and had originally been close allies of Akhmad.[63]

The elder Yamadayev brothers, Dzhabrail and Sulim, had helped Akhmad broker his famous deal with Russian forces in Gudermes in 1999.[64] At that point, a year before Akhmad came to power in Chechnya, the Yamadayev militia officially went over to the Russian side and was renamed the Vostok (East) battalion under the command of the Military Intelligence branch (the GRU) of the General Staff of the Ministry of Defense. In other words, the Yamadayev militia was given official legitimacy and support by the MoD in Moscow, at a time when Ramzan's forces were still an informal organization.

Brother Ruslan Yamadayev had been the regional head of Putin's United Russia Party before Kadyrov[65] and served as Chechnya's deputy to the Russian State Duma starting in December 2003.[66] Like Ramzan, the Yamadayevs clearly had a Putin connection. They made the mistake, however, of supporting Saidullayev's leadership bid against Akhmad.[67] From that point on their family members seemed to become targets.[68] It must be noted, though, that blood feuds remain a major component of mainstream Chechen society and culture. When a militia commander known for his brutality is killed, it is never quite clear who may have been taking revenge against him or one of his close family members. Ramzan has used this argument to cast doubt on his responsibility for various murders.

Dzhabrail, the eldest Yamadayev, was killed along with his bodyguards in March 2003 when a bomb placed under his bed destroyed his house. Sulim then took command of the Vostok battalion. The conflict between his forces and the kadyrovtsy came to a head five years later, in April 2008, when a convoy of Vostok forces encountered Ramzan's kadyrovtsy convoy on the highway and each blocked the passage of the other.[69] A few vehicles collided and shots were fired on both sides, killing a member of each force. Ramzan negotiated an apparent end to the standoff and the Yamadayev forces backed up and drove away. Later that day, however, their base in Gudermes was surrounded by Ramzan's forces, and two of their men were detained and killed, apparently after refusing to produce identification papers at a checkpoint. The confrontation lasted several days, and in the end showed that Ramzan's forces were in control.

Within a month Moscow fired Sulim Yamadayev as commander of the Vostok battalion.[70] That June the battalion was cut by 30 percent following an inspection by federal forces.[71] By August Chechnya's MVD head, Ruslan Alkhanov, announced a manhunt for Sulim, who had since moved to Moscow and was now wanted in Chechnya on charges of kidnapping and murder.[72] His name was taken off the wanted list in return for his leading the Vostok battalion against Georgian troops in that month's Russian war in South Ossetia.[73]

In September Sulim's brother Ruslan, the former Duma deputy and someone widely seen as the likeliest future rival to Ramzan's presidency, was shot to death while his car was stopped at a red light near the Moscow White House.[74] He had been on his way to meet with President Medvedev.[75] Sulim and his wife and children then fled the country, but he was himself assassinated in Dubai in March 2009. Another brother, Isa Yamadayev, told the Western media that Sulim had been warned several times after Ruslan's death that a hit squad was being sent for him.[76] Authorities in Dubai accused one of Ramzan's first cousins, Adam S. Delimkhanov, of planning and ordering the murder, and gave his name to Interpol for arrest.[77] Reportedly the murder was carried out with a gold-plated pistol,

Delimkhanov's trademark weapon, which he is accused of giving to the assassin. Because Delimkhanov was a Russian Duma deputy, however, he had constitutional immunity from prosecution and international extradition.[78] That September Ramzan dubbed Delimkhanov his "successor," should anything untoward happen to him.[79]

Meanwhile an assassination attempt against the remaining Yamadayev brother, Isa, was reportedly thwarted in Moscow in the summer of 2009. Isa claimed to have received warning of the attack from "an informant," and "Russian police secretly replaced the bullets in [the assassin's] gun with blanks." The assassin was "quickly overpowered and handcuffed" when he fired the gun and taken into police custody. This incident seems to demonstrate the political limits of the kadyrovtsy, since the Russian police were so easily able to thwart an attack in Moscow in order to keep one of the Yamadayevs alive. It also shows what kind of "balance" Ramzan may use in persuading his followers to act. The assassin, one of Yamadayev's bodyguards, claimed in his video-recorded confession to police in Moscow that Ramzan offered him a million dollars for the hit, but threatened to kill his wife and children in front of him if he didn't agree to it.[80] (A similar type of "balancing" is practiced by drug gang kingpins who act as warlords in western Mexico, according to a recent investigative report.)[81]

Ultimately Ramzan seems to have won this competition. In August 2010 Isa Yamadayev returned to Chechnya to hold a wake for Sulim, and said that he was ready to reconcile with Ramzan. Reportedly he did this under strong pressure from the authorities in Moscow.[82] Isa was presumably protected from further assassination attempts, but at the cost of his independence since he now lived in Ramzan's territory.

THE FEDERAL FORCES AND THE KADYROVTSY

The relationship between the kadyrovtsy and federal security forces was opaque and difficult to unravel. Despite its complexity, it is worth reviewing the history of how the kadyrovtsy became the dominant legal security forces in Chechnya. Russia chose to follow a path that somewhat resembles the choices made in Pakistan's FATA: the force-based patronage of a warlord was institutionalized in federal law.

Moscow announced an end to "active combat" in Chechnya in 2001, and transferred leadership of Russian forces in the region away from the MoD and the MVD to the FSB as a "counter-terrorist operation." Around eighty thousand MoD and MVD troops remained in Chechnya at that time.[83] The FSB created the awkwardly named Regional Operational Headquarters for the Implementation of the Counterterrorism Operation in the North Caucasus, which was located in Chechnya but reported to FSB head Nikolai Patrushev in Moscow. All federal and local forces in Chechnya were put under the supposed command and control of this headquarters.[84] According to Dmitry Trenin, Aleksei Malashenko, and Anatol Lieven, though, "in practice, each federal ministry retain[ed] its virtually independent fiefdom in Chechnya," and was "usually scornful" of Akhmad.[85] Mark Kramer argues that the operations were uncoordinated as a result.[86]

In 2003 the leadership of the regional headquarters was switched from the FSB to the MVD in Moscow. However, its directors were career FSB officers who were simply given police ranks, so the switch had little practical significance.[87] Ramzan reportedly developed a close relationship with the new commander of this headquarters, Col.-Gen. Arkadii Yedelev, deputy minister of the MVD (and a career FSB official).[88] Yedelev was not ethnically Chechen, though, and his command position was widely seen as one more attempt by Moscow to keep watch over the republic. Local Chechen representatives of the various power ministries were included on the headquarters staff, but Yedelev and other federal appointees reportedly did not trust them or coordinate operations with them.[89]

In February 2006 President Putin issued a decree that changed this command relationship. Now the regional operational headquarters was given responsibility for "direct leadership" (*nepostredstvennoe rukovodstvo*) over all counterterrorist activities in the North Caucasus, as well as for "organizing the planning and use" of all forces on Chechen soil (including federal troops under MVD command, sent in on contract from other regions of Russia).[90] Federal troops were now ordered to fulfill the tasks set by the local operational headquarters, and to provide the necessary forces, materiel, and equipment to ensure that this happened. While the local headquarters was still overseen by Yedelev in Moscow, local forces now had more leeway to design and direct operations as they saw fit. They had day-to-day command responsibility. Recall that Ramzan's man had been made the head of the regional MVD after his father's assassination in 2004, and that in May 2006, just a few months after the Putin decree, Ramzan's militia was legally integrated into the regional MVD following the gunfight with then-president Alu Alkhanov's guards. Already by 2006, then, Ramzan was effectively given control over all security operations on Chechen territory.

While the February 2006 decree went some way toward placating Ramzan, he was unhappy that Chechnya was singled out in comparison to other federal subjects mentioned in the decree by having its regional operational headquarters remain under the control of MVD commander Yedelev. Everywhere else the decree put antiterrorist forces under regional FSB commanders.[91] Andrei Soldatov considers this exception significant because the regional FSB in Chechnya, like its counterparts in other Russian regions, was weak and unsophisticated in comparison to the federal MVD administration in Moscow.[92] The regional FSB could be bent to Ramzan's will.

In August 2006, President Putin moved further along the path to giving the kadyrovtsy full control. He signed a decree stating that most federal MoD and MVD forces would be pulled out of Chechnya by 2008. Only fifteen thousand MoD and seven thousand federal MVD forces would remain, alongside three thousand federal border guards. It was further announced that these federal forces would stay on their bases except when needed for special operations, while twenty thousand Chechen MVD forces, including the new North and South battalions, would provide day-to-day order in the republic.[93] At this point, then, Ramzan's security forces were given not only titular command, but also growing operational dominance in Chechnya.

Finally in 2009 Ramzan consolidated his control, according to Soldatov. On April 16 the counterterrorism operation was officially lifted after a great deal of pressure by Ramzan.[94] The declaration itself had limited impact; it did not mention any further withdrawal of troops, and some therefore saw it as a purely symbolic gesture.[95] But it was later announced that 15 percent of the remaining MoD forces in Chechnya would be withdrawn, and that the East and West battalions of the GRU (including the Yamadayev forces mentioned above) would be disbanded and reconstituted under the regular forces of the MoD's Forty-Second Division of combined-arms brigades in Chechnya.[96] They would no longer form a separate, even if federally commanded, militia.

Ramzan said in July 2009, "So far I see absolutely no results. . . . Not one soldier [has] been withdrawn."[97] In October 2009 one Russian newspaper reported that the number of federal forces in Chechnya had actually increased.[98] Some argued that the real reason for Putin's announcement was to cut the combat pay bonuses that federal forces had received up until that point for service in Chechnya.[99]

Regardless of the number of federal forces remaining in Chechnya at that time, however, on October 1, 2009, command over the operational headquarters in Chechnya was transferred from the federal MVD to the regional FSB, led by an ethnic Chechen. This made Chechnya parallel to all other Russian regions, and answered Ramzan's demands. Federal troops on Chechen soil would remain under ultimate federal control, but would be subordinate to local FSB operational command. Soldatov interprets this to mean that Ramzan was now given free reign, since the regional FSB staff were his appointees and would no longer report to the MVD in Moscow.[100] It was simultaneously announced that all federal forces would be withdrawn at the end of 2011, leaving security in the hands of the regional Chechen MVD forces.[101]

On November 10, 2009, Medvedev issued a new decree that expanded the earlier decrees even further, to give Chechnya an independent ability to negotiate with neighboring regions, including Ingushetia and Dagestan, on the use of counterterrorism forces on their territories.[102] According to Ramzan, the MVD and FSB had especially encouraged him to expand the activities of his security forces to encompass Ingushetia. Months before this new decree was announced, he told the press that his forces were working side by side with federal MVD troops in these operations, and claimed that his forces also hunted bandits in Dagestan and North Ossetia even in the absence of agreements with regional authorities there.[103]

Also in November Ramzan received the rank of major general in the MVD, cementing his legal authority over its regional Chechen branch. As a thirty-three-year-old, he was the youngest man in the history of either the USSR or post-Soviet Russia to receive that rank.[104] In February 2010 the deputy minister of the MVD who had overseen operations in Chechnya for the past several years, Yedelev, was removed from his position. An MVD representative told the press that since the regional FSB had taken over management of security operations there, "the necessity for a deputy minister in charge of this region disappeared."[105] Yedelev's replacement as deputy MVD minister was a staff adviser to Putin who had worked on personnel issues since 2001, with no recent field experience, and he was given no particular responsibilities for the North Caucasus.[106] Shortly thereafter, Ramzan publicly called for all non-Chechen police to be withdrawn from his republic, arguing that locally appointed security forces were adequate for the situation and that additional deployments were an unnecessary drain on the Russian state budget.[107]

There had been rumors that Ramzan would be given an even higher position. Medvedev had announced in his state-of-the-union speech in November 2009 that a new post would be created for oversight of the North Caucasus region, and it appeared that Ramzan was in the running for this appointment.[108] In January 2010, however, this new position—the head of a new federal district and a deputy prime minister of Russia—went to a seasoned politician and businessman with no Caucasus ties, Aleksandr Khloponin, the governor of the Siberian region of Krasnoyarsk. Yedelev was later named the deputy head of the new North Caucasus Federal District, but had no forces to command in this position.[109] Given his past ties to Ramzan, he may have been given the role to act as a personal mediator and calm the waters, since Khloponin and

Kadyrov publicly quarreled in the media.[110] Whatever Khloponin's significance ultimately turned out to be, he was unlikely to interfere with Ramzan's control over the security situation in Chechnya. He simply had no levers to do so.

Ramzan's authority in Russia remained limited to Chechnya, with perhaps some security authority in neighboring North Caucasus republics. Yet in Chechnya he had absolute control. In the words of Aleksandr Ryklin, Putin "did not think it necessary (or possible) to intervene in Ramzan Kadyrov's anticolonial policies, which are aimed at gradually pushing the generals out of Chechnya."[111] By early 2010 Russia had legally ceded the fundamental basis of sovereignty, as defined by sociologist Max Weber—monopoly (or close to it) over the legitimate use of force on a piece of territory—to Ramzan.

THE INTERNATIONAL AIRPORT

As part of the official end to counterterrorist operations in Chechnya, Medvedev allowed Ramzan to reopen the airport in Grozny to international flights, and gave him control over customs duties there. These plans moved slowly for several months, and Ramzan publicly complained that the delay prevented several thousand Chechens from going on the hajj to Saudi Arabia.[112] He nonetheless rushed to complete the building of a luxurious customs post even before official approval was final, to ensure that it would be ready to go immediately.[113] In November 2009 Russia's Interstate Aviation Committee certified the airworthiness of the facilities, and the airport opened. It was managed by the Grozny-Avia company in cooperation with the Akhmad Kadyrov Fund, a private foundation headed by Ramzan for the purpose of social and economic development. Its own charter planes would be the major users of the airport.[114] That month the first Boeing 757 left the airport, with two hundred pilgrims bound for Mecca.[115] There were fourteen hajj flights overall that winter, with plans to make it an annual event.[116]

Soldatov called the opening of the airport a "smokescreen," belittling its significance in comparison to Ramzan's control over the security situation in Chechnya.[117] The airport director himself complained in the spring of 2010 that the only regularly scheduled flights each week went to Moscow, and that while charter flights went out sometimes he did not know when the next international flight would be.[118] But the airport did have great significance. It now allowed Ramzan, if he so chose, to become a middleman warlord. As this book goes to press it is too early to know whether Ramzan will take advantage of this opportunity, but he certainly will have had the incentive to do so.

Some argued that Ramzan's real goal in opening the airport was to make it easier to deposit his money in foreign bank accounts.[119] It would also make it easier for him to get new funds (and goods) from elsewhere. Ramzan could clearly profit from his control over the customs point. He could use the airport to run drugs or weapons and engage in duty-free import and export, much the same way as the airport had been used in the early 1990s when Soviet control first evaporated.[120] As Trenin, Malashenko and Lieven have pointed out, after Chechnya declared its independence in 1991 Moscow had allowed the Grozny airport to become "an unrecognized internal offshore zone," generating "huge profits to Chechen leaders and their business partners in Moscow."[121] History might now repeat itself.

Perhaps even more important, Ramzan was given the ability to connect easily with foreign investors and foreign states independently of Moscow. Until the airport opened, all international traffic had to go through other Russian cities and was hence under constant federal oversight. (The one exception would have been illegal transit across Chechnya's international border with Georgia in the treacherous, and federally patrolled, Caucasus Mountains.) Now Ramzan could welcome visitors from anywhere in the world and send his representatives abroad without Moscow's direct knowledge.

Mark Kramer reports that in December 2009 he saw guards stationed at the Grozny airport who appeared to be Russian security personnel from outside Chechnya.[122] An officially produced English-language video clip from April 2010 included a shot of the airport's passport control desk, manned by several Russian-uniformed employees (who appeared to be ethnically Russian), not the fatigue- or leather-jacket-wearing kadyrovtsy.[123] At least at that point, then, the airport was not completely under Ramzan's official legal control, and the authorities wanted foreigners to know it. Yet the small number of federal forces stationed at the airport, deep inside Chechen territory, would have to be able to withstand both the temptations of corruption and the threats of the kadyrovtsy in order for Moscow to have constant access to accurate flight manifests. Without those manifests, Moscow would have no way of knowing which individuals were exiting and entering the republic or what the planes were carrying.

It was not immediately clear how profitable the airport's opening would be for Ramzan, in terms of new foreign trade and investment. He earlier claimed to have reached independent oral agreements with foreign investors from Jordan, Turkey, the UAE, and "Palestine" (whether he meant the Palestinian territories or Israel was left unclear), saying that the only thing limiting the implementation of these deals was the absence of an international airport.[124] Indeed in the fall of 2009, the Russian Ministry of Foreign Affairs officially permitted Ramzan to open separate representative offices for Chechnya in six European countries for trade and investment purposes.[125] Ramzan also trumpeted his new ability, because of the airport, to reach out to the Chechen diaspora still living in Kazakhstan from the time of its deportation under Stalin.[126] This had special resonance for him because his own family had been deported to Kazakhstan at that time, but there are also large Chechen diasporas living in Turkey and a variety of Central Asian, European, and Middle Eastern countries that Ramzan could now reach.

There was one immediate example of success in gaining new investment from abroad: Azeri-born businessman Telman Ismailov and his son Sarkhan were welcomed into Chechnya, after Putin shut down Ismailov's Cherkizovsky Market in Moscow and seized $2 billion worth of contraband goods there.[127] Sarkhan became the vice president of Grozny's Terek football club (which is famed for its apparently fixed matches), while Telman was urged to consider investment projects ranging from a hotel complex in Grozny to a canning factory in either Argun or Ramzan's home city of Gudermes.[128]

Yet in early 2010 Ramzan's supporters in the Chechen parliament complained to Khloponin that Russia was not giving state guarantees for deals that Ramzan had reached with foreign investors. Khloponin replied,

> When Kadyrov goes abroad, whose interests does he represent? Does he think that Saudi Arabia will give him money? And what about America, whose influence there is so strong, does he think that's profitable? For such negotiations we have the Ministry of Foreign Affairs and other organizations. He can go on vacation, he's a private person. But in representing his republic, he can never forget that he is a representative of the Russian Federation.[129]

Russia, in other words, did not completely cede sovereignty to Ramzan. It is telling that the disagreement between Israilov and Putin was publicly resolved before Ismailov arrived in Grozny. Yet while Moscow might prevent Ramzan from signing *legally negotiated* deals with foreign representatives that were not in Russian national interests, there was little means left for the state to control any under-the-table deals with foreigners. Such unofficial and illegal trade and investment deals were precisely what hurt the Georgian state so badly when it tolerated its middleman warlords in Ajara and Upper Kodori.

[121]

WHERE DID RAMZAN GET HIS MONEY?

Moscow might actually have hoped that Ramzan would use the airport to make money for himself, since that would free the Russian state budget from paying for his profligacy. Chechnya's reconstruction had long been heavily subsidized by the Russian state, in what analyst Liz Fuller called a "steady intravenous drip of money from Moscow."[130] There is no means to assess how much state money actually flowed to Grozny, and obviously no one who knew the answer had any incentive to talk about it. From the time of the first Chechen war it was clear that most of the federal budget money allocated for Chechnya never reached its intended recipients.[131] The Russian Federal Audit Chamber found in 2005 that only about a third of the money the state sent to Chechnya was listed as having been used, and half of that was being used "inefficiently."[132] Rather than going into the construction of apartments, municipal services infrastructure, and a cement plant, as had been intended, a large loan from the republican budget was instead illegally given to the infamous Terek football club. The prime minister at the time, Abramov, insisted that the fault lay with federal authorities. A similarly critical report was issued concerning Chechnya's spending in the first half of 2007,[133] despite the 2005 creation of an oversight commission for budgetary spending in the entire North Caucasus region.[134]

It was at about that time in 2007, though, that Ramzan began a building and reconstruction spree in Chechnya that impressed many outside observers. Earlier "inefficiencies" in budget expenditures were fixed after a central directorate was created inside Chechnya for managing federal contracts. This presumably gave Ramzan control over the expenditures. By the end of 2008 Chechen reconstruction was being held up as a model for similar efforts in South Ossetia.[135]

Yet in early 2009 the prosecutor for the Republic of Chechnya, who had been appointed to his position by the Russian Federal Prosecutor's Office, announced that he had found ten thousand violations of the budget law in the previous year, with fifteen hundred violations of anticorruption legislation.[136] If nothing else, the fact that this was publicized indicates the Russian state's displeasure with Ramzan's style of doing business.

Ramzan has done a remarkable job of restoring Grozny's city center, providing jobs for thousands of residents, and allowing a measure of normal life to resume after war. Some criticized him in 2008 for overseeing "shoddy construction," building apartments with beautiful facades that lacked running water or electricity.[137] Yet foreigners who regularly visited Grozny said that reconstruction expanded and became more elaborate with time. Ordinary people were increasingly seen on the streets, sitting at cafés, and shopping at attractive and well-stocked retail stores.[138] (Photos posted by the BBC in October 2010 nonetheless showed that the outskirts of Grozny were still in bad repair.)[139]

Much of the reconstruction funding, as in the case of the airport noted above, came not from the official state budget but from Ramzan's personal foundation, the Akhmad Kadyrov Fund. In late 2009, for example, this foundation provided $3.4 million for the reconstruction of a museum honoring the writer Leo Tolstoy in the Chechen village of Starogladovskaya where Tolstoy lived in the 1850s.[140] The Kadyrov foundation lacked transparency and was privately managed, so it was not clear where its money originated.[141] It is rumored that it was financed from an unofficial "tax" that public employees in Chechnya had to pay Ramzan out of their earnings.[142] With time, virtually everyone who worked in Chechnya, from taxi drivers to market stall merchants, had been forced to become a public employee, and therefore to pay this tax.[143] It is also rumored that an additional unofficial "tax" was extracted not only from businesses located on Chechen territory, but also from those owned by ethnic Chechens elsewhere in Russia.[144] Ramzan himself seemed to support this rumor, at least indirectly. When asked by a journalist for a newspaper with close ties to the Russian state whether he collected "tribute" from businessmen, Ramzan replied, "No, there is none of that. Collecting tribute would be humiliating for a Chechen. A Chechen is supposed to help his people and his republic voluntarily."[145] This leads one to suppose that such help was given "voluntarily" in the same way that rebels laid down their arms voluntarily: to the kadyrovtsy in return for protection.

Journalist Jonathan Littell described his perception of how this combination of taxes and transfers from Moscow worked to fund the reconstruction. Anyone whose ministry or other facility was slated for reconstruction had to first pay Ramzan for the work out of private holdings. Then Ramzan submitted the charge to the federal authorities in Moscow, inflating the cost by a factor of four. Moscow kept 20 percent "as a rollback," and the rest was returned by the federal budget to Chechnya, where a portion was redistributed to those who had prepaid. In Littell's words, "they get back their investment."[146] If he is correct, then Ramzan was stealing money from Moscow by inflating the price of reconstruction.

Meanwhile Ramzan regularly showed off his mansion and personal zoo, his constantly renewed fleet of imported luxury cars, and his stable of thoroughbred racing horses to visitors. He reportedly wore a "$1 million watch," and one of his horses, Mourilyan, came in third in Australia's 2009 Melbourne Cup, earning him $420,000.[147] Some of his possessions were gifts from enthusiastic supporters, such as a $450,000

Ferrari that he was presented on his thirtieth birthday and a combine harvester he received from an agricultural manufacturing plant on the occasion of his inauguration.[148] Ramzan did not try to hide his personal wealth.

In 2009 Ramzan said that budget subsidies from Moscow were being reduced by 30 percent, a fact he attributed to Russia's economic crisis following the global recession. He added that Putin had lent the Chechen budget fifteen billion rubles (around $500 million at that time) to cover the shortfall.[149] If Ramzan was telling the truth, this would imply that the state had been sending Grozny almost $1.7 billion annually. A loan, of course, must be repaid; it is not a subsidy. When all of this is added together, it makes sense that Moscow may have tired of the inflated subsidies game, and expected Ramzan to find other resources to pay for his expenses.

THE CONTEXT AND CONSEQUENCES OF MOSCOW'S CHOICES

It is impossible, without open archives, to know exactly why Moscow made the decisions it did. There was probably no long-standing master plan to grant Ramzan sovereignty from the start. Policy toward Chechnya appeared to be the result of ongoing bargains between central and local authorities.

Some have argued that giving Kadyrov effective sovereignty was the "least bad" choice that Moscow had. They have called Chechnya ungovernable, and argued that without Ramzan in place chaos would result. Yet history indicates that other choices would have been possible. In Soviet times, the state maintained sovereignty over Chechnya using bureaucrats and its own security forces, not by bargaining with a warlord. Chechnya had an uncomfortable and sometimes horrifying relationship with the Soviet state. In the 1940s the USSR faced a brief period of open rebellion in Chechnya. In response, at the close of World War II, Joseph Stalin deported the Chechen population wholesale to Kazakhstan and Siberia, with much suffering and loss of life. Soviet leader Nikita Khrushchev later allowed most Chechens to return, but ethnic Russians and Slavs were still given preference in hiring and advancement in the region, and ethnic tension was rife. A criminalized political economy challenged the Soviet state, drawing on support from state bureaucrats, even more than elsewhere in the Caucasus.

Despite all of these very real challenges to the legitimacy and scope of state authority in Soviet times, though, Chechnya was state-governed during the decades that preceded the perestroika era. Separatism may have simmered under the surface, but the Soviet state (like the Russian Empire before it) was able to construct and maintain sophisticated educational, industrial, transportation, and communication infrastructure in Chechnya, particularly in the capital of Grozny. Despite the hardships they endured, ethnic Chechens derived real benefit from the presence of these state institutions, gaining literacy, employment, modern conveniences, and access to Soviet consumer markets (including illegal ones). As Elise Giuliano notes, even those Chechens whose family members had suffered terribly under Stalin later rose within the local Communist Party. While ethnic Slavs had most of the plum jobs in the republic, Chechens were well represented in government service ranks as well as in the arts, science, and education.[150] Chechnya is not inherently or culturally "ungovernable."

A good argument can be made that in fact no one knows what would have happened to Chechnya without a warlord, because in post-Soviet times Moscow never seriously tried anything else. Russian President Yeltsin made little genuine effort to reach a sustainable negotiated autonomy agreement with Chechen separatist leaders in the early to mid-1990s.[151] Instead both he and Putin led brutal, scorched earth wars against Chechnya that targeted civilians and effectively foreclosed the possibility of compromise. Two leaders of the republic who had some real local legitimacy and might have been able to reach compromises with the state, Dudayev and Maskhadov, were first undermined and then killed by Moscow. Furthermore, Ramzan managed to turn his opponents to his side using force. The fact that they were willing to turn at all, rather than fighting to the death, indicates that softer methods of persuasion (like a more gentle form of state-based patronage) might also have been worth trying.

Aleksei Malashenko, a respected Russian analyst of Chechnya, believes that separatist sentiment had actually died out in Chechnya before Ramzan came to power.[152] This implies that some alternative to warlord rule might have been possible at that point. Yet rather than looking for alternatives, Moscow increasingly provided Ramzan with institutional levers that enhanced his relative weight in the relationship and made any change of heart on Moscow's part increasingly dangerous.

In the absence of reliable information about why Moscow has made the choices it has, analysts have had a tendency to work back from the consequences of Moscow's decisions to infer causality. Correlation is not causality, however, so each of these "explanations" should be taken with a grain of salt. They nonetheless highlight important aspects of Moscow's decision making for the interests of both individual actors and the state.

Personal Connections

Malashenko notes the strong personal connection between Putin and Ramzan as individuals.[153] Some have taken this fact and constructed rumors about what supported the connection. For example, one hears that if Akhmad had been vetted by the KGB, then maybe he worked for the KGB and the follow-on FSB, and that his son did too. Maybe Putin, as a former KGB and FSB officer, owed some kind of debt of loyalty to Ramzan. Or maybe Putin was so desperate for a show of success in Chechnya to bolster his own political future that he took a blood oath, in good Chechen tradition, with Ramzan: that if Ramzan killed or turned most of the terrorists, he would get independence. One rather extreme suggestion is that Putin intended to use Ramzan's militia as a personal enforcer for his own national-level disputes.[154]

Rather than simply dismissing these conspiracy theories out of hand, it is worth exploring how one case of rivalry with the Kadyrovs did seem to reflect national-level rivalries in Russia between the FSB and the other security ministries. This is the case of Beslan Gantemirov. Gantemirov was a police officer from the MVD who became a rebel militia leader and organized crime boss during the original Chechen independence movement of 1990.[155] The rebels had appointed Gantemirov the mayor of Grozny in 1991, where he expropriated money from ethnic Russians that his forces drove out of the city, and took a personal stake in the illegally privatized Chechen oil industry.[156] When the first Chechen government disintegrated in 1992–93, Gantemirov switched to Moscow's side, and was appointed mayor of Grozny once more in 1995 when Russian troops seized the city in the first Chechen war. He was arrested in 1996 for embezzling millions of dollars of reconstruction money for Chechnya, and imprisoned after a long trial in 1998. Yet Russian president Boris Yeltsin freed him in 1999 so that he could lead the pro-Moscow Chechen government in exile as the second war began.[157] Gantemirov commanded a group of several hundred pro-Moscow Chechens in the battle of Grozny later that year.[158] When the Russian side once again took the city he was reappointed mayor a third time, despite being a "notorious bandit" who was thought to be simply after oil and other opportunities for illegal wealth.[159] In other words, like Akhmad he was a man whose loyalties bent with the wind; and even more than was true for Akhmad, the Russian state had information about him that could be used to punish him if those loyalties shifted again in the future. He was clearly a Kadyrov rival.

In 2000 Moscow appointed Gantemirov the deputy head of Akhmad's administration, as well as making him the head of Chechnya's regional unit of the MVD police force. Both the general staff of the federal MoD and the federal MVD—the same organizations that were later seen to be supporting the Yamadayevs—were perceived to prefer his police militia, the *gantemirovtsy*, to Ramzan's alternative informal militia, the kadyrovtsy.[160] The kadyrovtsy, in turn, were perceived as the favorites of the FSB.[161] Hence the rivalry between the two men and their forces may have been proxies for an institutional rivalry between *siloviki* (power or force-based) institutions in Moscow. They may also have been a means to keep the Chechen leadership divided and off-balance.

Gantemirov had established a long-standing base in Grozny, while Akhmad's base was in Gudermes. In July 2000, after first taking office, Akhmad fired some of Gantemirov's supporters from their positions in the administration that was theoretically under his control in Grozny. At that point the gantemirovtsy conducted a raid of the Kadyrov compound in Gudermes, with two hundred men sent in "to make sure there were no rebels hiding there." It took an intervention by Putin's representative for the Southern Russia Federal District to calm the crisis. This gentleman then appeared on national television flanked by Akhmad and Gantemirov, who vowed to work together to solve Chechnya's problems.[162] Gantemirov was relocated by Moscow to Rostov-on-Don, outside of Chechnya, to become the chief inspector for the Southern Russia Federal District.

Akhmad then brought him back to Chechnya as his minister of press and information in early 2002.[163] It was only at that point, in 2002, that Akhmad was able to consolidate his political control in Grozny.[164] Gantemirov later refused to support Akhmad in the 2003 election. Akhmad again removed him from his administration, and Gantemirov left Chechnya to pursue his business interests elsewhere in Russia. When it appeared in 2005 that Gantemirov might once again become involved in Chechen politics as Ramzan's thirtieth birthday approached, he was successfully dissuaded from doing so after his family compound in Chechnya was subjected to a raid by the kadyrovtsy.[165]

This story, in addition to illustrating the complexities of force-based patronage relationships in Chechnya, also indicates that Akhmad may have had some kind of FSB connection to Putin. He may have been the FSB's preferred candidate to manage Chechnya. The personal connection could have been so strong that it would explain why Putin stuck with Akhmad even after the FSB leadership turned away from him in 2003. It could also help explain the personal rapport between Putin and Akhmad's son Ramzan.

It does not do a very good job, however, of explaining why Moscow would increasingly give Ramzan sovereignty over more and more institutions in Chechnya, or why President Dmitry Medvedev would later approve the continuation of those policies. Russian actions, including the ceding of security command and the opening of the international airport, increasingly *weakened* the personal connection between Putin and Ramzan, rather than reinforcing it. They made it harder for the FSB or Putin himself to observe and influence Ramzan's choices. The ultimate consequence of Moscow's choices regarding Ramzan was to weaken the state's means for gathering intelligence in and about Chechnya. Unlike the examples discussed in chapter 4 in Georgia, Putin probably lost the ability that Saakashvili maintained over time, to understand well what was happening on the ground in warlord territory. It would be surprising if Putin, the ex-KGB man, trusted Ramzan's good intentions when no one else did.

Chechnya's Oil

Sometimes one hears the claim that oil explains Russia's tenacity in holding on to Chechnya in the early 1990s when the independence movement began. Certainly at that time, major oil and gas pipelines did transit Chechnya on a route linking Russia and the newly developed fields in post-Soviet Central Asia. Yet those pipelines were diverted as a result of the first Chechen war,[166] so they cannot explain Russia's later actions. Furthermore, Chechnya's own oil assets were small in comparison to the rest of the Russian oil industry.

Oil was once prevalent in Chechnya, but its wells had been relatively inconsequential producers for decades and were fast declining, with expectations by 2009 that they would run dry within fifteen years. Ramzan himself noted that production had declined by 20 percent in recent years, from 2 to 1.6 million metric tonnes per year.[167] In comparison, Russia as a whole produced 9.8 million barrels, or approximately 1.55 million metric tonnes *per day* of petroleum liquids in 2008.[168]

Oil did loom large as a *local* asset in Chechnya. Georgi M. Derluguian writes that the illegal seizure and control of Chechnya's state-owned oil assets by a variety of small players was a major contributor to the anarchy that plagued Chechnya in the early 1990s.[169] In the early years of the twenty-first century, after peace had supposedly come to Chechnya, a great deal of violent criminal activity continued within the oil industry, including kidnappings and torching of oil wells and storage tanks.[170] Many privateers drilled into the major pipeline, stealing oil for their own use and refining it with equipment stolen during the war from state refining facilities. In 2005, the federal Interior Ministry reported that a third of the oil produced and refined in Chechnya was still being stolen and smuggled out by criminal gangs.[171] According to investigative journalist Anna Politkovskaya (later slain), federal forces not only routinely looked the other way as this illegal oil trade took place, they rented out their expertise in explosives to support particular gangs.[172] She accused Akhmad of participating in the illegal oil business, and there is speculation that this was a major source for Ramzan's wealth, too.[173]

Ramzan frequently complained that he lacked control over the region's oil deposits. While his government had a 49 percent stake in Grozneftegaz, the enterprise that was founded in 2001 as the sole legal producer of Chechen oil, the controlling stake in that firm was owned by its parent company, Rosneft. Rosneft, a national oil firm, was 75 percent state-owned, and its board of directors had been headed since 2004 by former deputy chief of the Putin administration (and later Russian deputy prime minister) Igor Sechin. Rosneft, in other words, was a conglomerate linked to Putin. A different enterprise, Chechenneftekhimprom, also founded in 2001, was given theoretical ownership of Chechnya's refining and petrochemical industry and infrastructure. However, Rosneft controlled all licensing and management questions for Grozneftegaz, which was in turn the sole source of oil for Chechenneftekhimprom. This made any other ownership effectively moot.[174] In Ramzan's words, "Rosneft ignores us,"[175] and that may have been a coded complaint to Putin personally.

Rosneft also controlled the transport of legal Chechen oil. A different state-owned company, Transneft, owned all the pipelines elsewhere in Russia (except for the Caspian Pipeline Consortium line originating in Kazakhstan, which was jointly owned by Russian state-owned and private companies and foreign companies and states). But Transneft was removed from ownership of the pipeline on Chechen territory during the second Chechen war. The new owner became Chechenneftekhimprom—which, as noted above, was essentially a subsidiary of Rosneft. (Since that time at least two additional, rather shadowy, companies were apparently also involved in local transport.)[176] In 2004, after Rosneft took over the Chechen oil wells, it stopped sending the oil from the Chechen pipeline that it now controlled (via Chechenneftekhimprom) forward into the Transneft-owned pipeline that had previously been used. Instead Rosneft rerouted the Chechen pipeline to a railway line leading to the Russian port city of Novorossiisk, for export through the Black Sea. The president of the state-owned Russian railway system, Vladimir Yakunin, was a close Putin ally. Abramov, the former prime minister of Chechnya who ceded control to Ramzan after his car accident, was by late 2010 the director of Russia's state railway terminals. Deals in oil and politics were clearly intertwined.

In theory, Chechnya was supposed to get the value of the oil produced from its wells back, through the annual budget subsidies it received from Moscow. But the values of the two figures were far apart, and the calculations made by the Russian Ministry of Energy about how to divide the profits between Rosneft and the Chechen government remain secret.[177]

In other words, Rosneft—a state corporation run by a close Putin ally, which supported a state transportation corporation run by another close Putin ally—maintained tight control over the sale of Chechen oil, in a way that was detrimental to other state agencies like Transneft and reflected secret bargains with the Russian Energy Ministry. Once again, local rivalries reflect potential national rivalries. But, given the relatively small amount of oil Chechnya produces, it would seem unlikely to matter all that much in Moscow. It therefore seems insufficient to explain why Ramzan would be preferred to one of his potential rivals, especially since no one has claimed that any of those rivals were either connected to Transneft or unwilling to bargain over oil policy.

Ramzan eventually succeeded in convincing Rosneft to reconstruct and develop an oil refinery inside Chechnya, after Rosneft had tried for years to get the new plant located in neighboring Ingushetia or Kabardino-Balkaria instead.[178] It was announced that this refinery would be state-of-the-art and would begin operations in 2011, a somewhat surprising development given that Chechen oil was running out. The announcement said that the refinery would produce liquefied natural gas (LNG) as well, from gas now sent into Chechnya by pipeline from elsewhere in Russia, and that it would be accompanied by new pipeline development. This may indicate that rather than focusing on oil products produced in Chechnya, the long-term goal was to reestablish Grozny as a refining node on petroleum pipelines entering Russia from Central Asia, especially Azerbaijan. If such pipelines could be secured, against both pilfering and terrorist attacks, then Chechnya could potentially gain both tariffs from transit and income from the refinery, further easing its claims on the Russian state budget.

Ramzan predicted that the refinery would create one thousand jobs in Chechnya.[179] Certainly Russia (and Putin's allies) would benefit from this deal as long as Chechnya remained stable. But it is hard to see it as a tradeoff for the freedoms that Ramzan was given. The refinery deal gave him more of what he wanted, rather than requiring more of him, and the longstanding pipeline diversion proved that Chechnya was not crucial for Russia's energy security.

Russia's Peace and Security

Russian leaders appeared to find Ramzan useful for other forms of state security. In the words of Mark Galeotti, "They need him. . . . Considering the rise of chaos in the rest of the North Caucasus, the irony is that

Chechnya is a haven of peace."[180] There is no question that the level of violence in Chechnya dropped drastically from 2000 to 2010, to a level no longer constituting civil war. Jason Lyall finds that Chechenization made a difference in the outcome of the second war: when "sweep" operations in particular localities were conducted by Chechen forces, rather than Russian forces, the number of insurgent counterattacks from those districts dropped precipitously.[181]

The real irony, however, is that as Ramzan's independence from Moscow became further consolidated as the decade went on, the number of bloody terrorist attacks, including suicide bombings, increased both across the North Caucasus and in Chechnya itself.[182] By 2010 the deputy prosecutor general of the North Caucasus Federal District publicly announced that the annual number of extremist crimes in the district had increased by more than a factor of four, and that 70 percent had happened on Chechen territory.[183] State-supported Russian press sites suggested that Ramzan's forces actually impeded Russian counterinsurgency operations.[184]

From 2008 to 2009, the number of violent attacks carried out by jihadists in the North Caucasus increased by 34 percent, and the number of casualties among their non-jihadist victims (both state security forces and civilians) increased by 28 percent.[185] During the year following the announced end of the counterterrorist operation in Chechnya, the number of deaths and injuries in Chechnya caused by rebel activities increased in comparison to the prior year.[186] Chechen rebels plausibly claimed responsibility for the shocking November 2009 bombing of the major passenger train line between Russia's two largest cities, St. Petersburg and Moscow, which killed twenty-six people and injured hundreds (this would be equivalent to the bombing of the Amtrak Acela line between New York and Washington, in US terms).[187]

Many of the highest-profile terrorist attacks that plagued Russia, including the March 2010 bombing of the Moscow Metro and the January 2011 bombing of Moscow's Domodedovo Airport, appear to have originated elsewhere in the Caucasus and not in Chechnya itself. There is nonetheless an argument to be made that Ramzan's continued use of beatings, torture, kidnapping, arson, and death squads against his own population drove more young people "to the forest," as the North Caucasus rebel movement is known, including for the sake of revenge.[188] There was no evidence that North Caucasus rebels divided themselves by ethnicity or home region, with Chechens having different sensibilities or motives, for example, from Dagestanis. Instead the Wahhabi ideology that motivated much of the terrorism was pan-regional. Some analysts think that Ramzan simply "squeezed" the rebel bases off Chechen territory and into neighboring Ingushetia and Dagestan.[189]

Respected Caucasus analyst Sergei Markedonov argues that the end of federal counterterrorist operations in Chechnya marked the end of a *separatist* threat in Chechnya, rather than any hope that the threat of terrorist violence had been contained.[190] Ramzan's individual targeting of separatist leaders may have successfully prevented the formation of any organized opposition to Russian territorial claims on Chechen territory, without stopping the horrific violence that stemmed from anger or a desire for vengeance.

Meanwhile any Russian citizen who threatened Ramzan's hold on power, including Chechen opposition figures, muckraking journalists, and human rights advocates who uncovered new information about Ramzan's finances or operations had a distressing tendency to be shot to death by assassins. By 2009 this had become an international embarrassment for Russia, and President Dmitry Medvedev publicly called for the Chechen leadership to do more to solve the murders.[191] Russia also found itself paying restitution to more and more victims of violence in Chechnya who brought their claims to the European Court of Human Rights in Strasbourg. In 2009 Russia was the plaintiff in 28 percent of all cases brought before the court, and the majority of the 13,600 claims filed against Russia that year dealt with Chechnya.[192] While many claims were historical, dating from the era when Russian federal forces had primary responsibility for the atrocities, not all of them were. A special subunit for investigating complaints about unjustified detentions and disappearances was set up inside Chechnya in the Investigations Directorate of the federal prosecutor's office, but it remained unclear what effect such an office could have.[193]

Some Western analysts, most prominently Liz Fuller, repeatedly predicted that there would be an attempt to replace the Chechen leadership as a result of these security problems and embarrassments.[194] Clearly this proved incorrect, at least in the short term. Rather than replacing Ramzan, Moscow gave him more and more levers to use to strengthen his own hand in their relationship. It would seem that Ramzan was not actually aiding Russian security against either terrorist threats or reputational decline, but that his power and independence were being solidified anyway. Moscow's de jure sovereignty was preserved as separatism ended, even as its security remained shaky.

Internal Chechen Stability

Many well-connected Russian commentators argue that there was no alternative to Ramzan. This argument has two variants. One variant notes that Ramzan was a leading member of Chechnya's most powerful clan or *teip*, the Benoi, and that his intelligence gathering had made him a master of clan politics. Removing him from power would have left Chechen society fractured into a multiplicity of armed formations.[195] Ruslan Khasbulatov, an ethnic Chechen who served as the head of the Russian parliament in the early Yeltsin years, said: "Get rid of Kadyrov, send in some guy from Moscow, and a new war will start."[196] These fears were magnified by the continuing cultural power of the blood feud in some parts of Chechen society, where cycles of revenge seeking might make war unending.[197]

It is not clear that such a forecast was accurate. For one thing, Ramzan had been criticized for following his father's path, and appointing too many of his own clan members to top positions in the republic.[198] For another, most Chechens seemed exhausted by two decades of war and "counterterrorist operations," and some analysts thought in contrast that people would be relieved to give their acquiescence to any stable and politically savvy leader who allowed them to live normal lives without daily fear.[199] Indeed, fears about endemic clan instability—as opposed to simple personal rivalry between militia leaders—may have stemmed in part from a stereotyped view of Chechnya as a place where everyone is armed to the teeth, engaged in criminal activity of one sort or another, and willing at any moment to take up ancient blood feuds. Chechens whose business or political interests benefited from Ramzan's rule of course had an incentive to promulgate this stereotype. (Ramzan himself appears to have staged a "blood feud reconciliation," led by an imam who just happened to be his uncle, which Al Jazeera television reporters came across "by accident" on the highway.)[200] Hughes believes that an idealized, Orientalist notion of wild Chechen clan warriors is entrenched both in Russian society and in the minds of many Western journalists who write about Chechnya, with references back to racist nineteenth-century colonial anthropology.[201]

Hughes notes that this idealization probably does not fit the reality of Chechen society in Ramzan's time. Traditional clan identities were broken down and altered by a century of migration and urbanization, and especially by Stalin's deportation policies. Family ties continued to matter a great deal in Chechnya, as they do in many traditional societies, but Hughes argues that they were not the only source of personal or political loyalty, and that their political reach did not extend much beyond ordinary nepotism among immediate relatives. This is largely confirmed by Littell, who notes that Ramzan appointed several high-ranking officials who were not from his own Benoi teip, and that corruption "gets narrowed down to a village, or to close and distant relatives," even though Ramzan was known to reserve his deepest trust for Benoi members.[202]

While the Kadyrovs certainly faced rivals from other clan-based militias, those militias were successfully tamed by people they hated. This indicates that self-interest, not affection or emotion, is the dominating motive for their behavior; they are not prepared to commit suicide for the sake of honor. It would be very difficult for a new appointee to decode the various patron-client networks that define the Chechen political economy. A change in regime would certainly look like a bloody mafia war among the involved parties and their militias. But it is not obvious that any political rivals would have an interest in re-fomenting the level of societal warfare that provoked Russian military intervention. It would be immensely costly and challenging for the state to preserve stability in a post-Ramzan Chechnya, but that is a very different problem from the notion that Chechens are by nature wild, alien, and untamable.

The second variant argues that Ramzan was uniquely placed to manage the moderate re-Islamization of Chechen society, given that he was his father's son. Ramzan adopted a number of somewhat Islamist laws, including the requirement that all girls and women wear head scarves in schools and on government property, and that hard liquor sales be limited to the hours of 8:00–10:00 a.m.[203] During Ramadan in 2010 he ordered all restaurants in Chechnya to close for the month-long fast, which provoked local merchants (and some Western analysts) to complain that he was violating Russian law.[204] He opened a Russian Islamic University in Grozny, spent a great deal of money in reconstructing mosques (including the central Grozny mosque which is now dedicated to Akhmad-Hadji), and insisted that television stations cover Islamic stories.[205] In a rather bizarre twist, he established an Islamic hospital where the chief doctor exorcised "jinns" from women who wanted a divorce or who refused to have sex with their husbands.[206] In July 2010, he finally went on a "small hajj" (or Umrah—i.e., not during Ramadan) to Mecca himself.[207]

There is little evidence, however, that Wahhabism per se was very popular in Chechnya or that it would dominate the scene if Ramzan left. Its strict rules and its focus on centralized religious leadership are alien to the more informal, clan-based, mystical Sufism that was traditional in Chechnya. Many Chechens found Ramzan's new version of Islamism intolerable. This included the women who were hit with paintballs by Ramzan's forces during summer 2010 when they chose not to wear head scarves on the street.[208] At least one woman lost an eye; what hit her was a rubber bullet, not a paintball.[209]

Moreover in either case, whether for reasons of clan conflict or Islamism, if Moscow truly believed that the negative consequences of replacing Ramzan outweighed the benefits, this would explain only why Russian leaders chose to keep Ramzan in power. It would support Malashenko's argument that Moscow and Ramzan needed each other.[210] It would not explain Moscow's continued ceding of more and more sovereignty to Ramzan, or the withdrawal of federal forces. Presumably

Ramzan's own ability to reap economic benefit from his relationship with Moscow would have been jeopardized if he unleashed a high level of instability in the republic. The existence of the mutually beneficial relationship did not in and of itself give him leverage.

Indirect Rule Is Cost-Effective

None of these commonly heard explanations for Moscow's behavior explains the pattern of ceding sovereignty to Ramzan. That leaves the major argument of this book as the remaining alternative. Moscow made the same choice that state leaders elsewhere have often made toward warlords, supporting them for the sake of economic expediency and stability while ignoring the long-term consequences for state security.

Every step that Moscow took toward Ramzan detracted from Russian leverage in Chechnya while conserving Russian resources and political capital. Russia progressively withdrew its forces from Chechnya while giving Ramzan the ability to seek funds elsewhere. Having a strongman in place made it easier to practice information control in the media, keeping negative stories about Chechnya out of the news in Russia and dampening any societal pressure there might otherwise be for Moscow to take more action. Moscow effectively outsourced Chechnya's sovereignty, much as imperial powers (including Europe and the Ottoman Empire) have often done in their colonies. As long as de jure sovereignty was preserved, de facto control over the territory was ceded.

The ability to seek funds independently was something Ramzan long sought. He wanted to establish the kind of tax-free economic zone for outside investment that his former Georgian counterparts also wanted.[211] With time there were increasingly good economic reasons for Moscow to agree to this, and this may help explain the sudden acceleration of Moscow's policies toward Ramzan in 2009. Russia was badly hit by the global economic crisis of 2008–2009. In 2009 the Russian GDP fell 7.9 percent, making its performance the worst among the G-20 leading economic powers. This provoked deep soul-searching among government officials and think tank experts about the country's future economic direction.[212] Demonstrations over wages and prices started to reappear throughout large cities in Russia in 2009, resurrecting a means of political protest that was common in the Yeltsin era but had largely disappeared with Putin's rise to power.[213] Russia's state budget deficit for 2010 was projected to reach 7.2 percent, a figure that would completely exhaust the state's reserve fund built up over the prior oil boom years. As a result the Russian Finance Ministry began to seek bond investment by foreigners for the first time in a decade.[214] Balancing the 2010 state budget in Russia depended on oil prices rebounding to $95 per barrel, a level not reached that year.[215] Even when oil prices rebounded in 2011, it appeared that Russia would turn to the emergency fund to pay the pensions of its progressively aging citizenry.

Economic problems were made worse by the heat wave and fires that plagued Russian cities and farms in late summer 2010, curtailing production. At the same time, Moscow faced the prospect of paying for the 2014 Olympics in Sochi. Around the world, the games usually entail huge expenditures for the host state. Concerns about terrorism emanating from the North Caucasus, right next to Sochi, made these games a potential budgetary nightmare.[216] Moscow was also subsidizing two Georgian border areas that it now recognized as independent states, Abkhazia and South Ossetia.

In other words, freeing itself from the need to subsidize Chechnya might be seen as a welcome windfall. Khloponin declared within days of taking office that one of his major tasks would be to oversee the state budget for the region, assuring that funds were used more effectively and ultimately reducing the size of state subsidies.[217] Some hoped this meant he would rein Ramzan in. Instead, given the increasing independence that Ramzan was granted, it appears that his goal may have been to let Ramzan go.

Economic desperation is clearly not the sole explanation for Moscow's policy toward Chechnya. Increasing support for Ramzan's sovereignty began during Russia's oil boom years, and boom and bust cycles have always pervaded the industry. The financial angle merely provided one more inducement encouraging Moscow to write off Chechnya, declaring victory and then effectively going home (even though Chechnya was technically part of the Russian "home"). As long as Chechnya did not threaten to leave Russia or once again become a terrorist safe haven, it retained no particular value to the Russian state.

CONCLUSIONS

Moscow retained the legal right to fire Ramzan at will, since his appointment as head of Chechnya was made by the president of Russia with Russian parliamentary approval. To oust him, however, would require a significant amount of force to be deployed throughout a province now under Ramzan's command. Moscow could have cut off his budgetary subsidies, but that would be unnecessarily risky, at best aggravating the unemployment and despair that many analysts see as a driving force of the Islamist insurgency. Instead Medvedev reappointed Ramzan to another five-year term in 2011. Russian press reports about this said that governors had "two, at most three terms to show how they can work," implying that a third five-year term was in the offing.[218]

In one sense there is nothing unique about Moscow's choice. The pattern of indirect rule follows the line of many past states and empires. Yet the Russian case is unique because Moscow was not forced into this relationship with Ramzan—not by an imperial desire to take new and uncharted territory, not by external pressure exerted through a middleman warlord, and not because an existing local power broker refused to be tamed by the state. Moscow instead consciously created and abetted Ramzan's control, step by step, as an experiment in resolving ethnic and civil warfare at relatively low cost. The leaders of a fully developed and otherwise functioning modern state chose to outsource a piece of domestic sovereignty, largely for the sake of convenience.

What are the consequences of this choice, and what lessons does this hold for other cases where states may choose to cooperate with warlords?

As Gordon Hahn points out, "Moscow's stake on Ramzan leaves Chechnya's stability inordinately dependent on one rather unreliable man."[219] This has strategic consequences for Russia. For example, Rosneft may build a state-of-the-art refinery in Grozny and turn a profit on it, just as other risk-acceptant oil companies do in unstable parts of the world ranging from Nigeria to Venezuela. It would nonetheless be foolish for Russia to stake its energy future on transit routes through Chechnya, given the absence of stable legal and security institutions there. Things in Chechnya could turn very bad very quickly if Ramzan were to be assassinated, for example. Moscow's actions damaged its ability to collect intelligence about networks and power balances inside Chechnya. Furthermore, with the opening of the Chechen airport, Russia may have exposed itself to one more source for the smuggling in of narcotics and tax-free contraband, weakening state legal and fiscal institutions that had started to be rebuilt during the Putin era. Tolerating warlordism means opening the state to ongoing sources of political and social instability.

Moscow's policy also encouraged Ramzan to seek support elsewhere. He would have benefited from having an external hedge against any future attempt by Moscow to re-exert control over Chechnya's security and legal institutions. He would also have benefited from international deals, including illegal ones, that diversified his income at a time of state budget shortfalls. Moscow risked finding itself—as its Georgian neighbor did before it—facing a middleman warlord who gained benefits from under-the-table external connections not under state control.

Weapons and other forms of covert external military support could also flow in through the airport. Ramzan has long been rumored to seek his own secular reunification of broader swaths of the North Caucasus. It is possible that nearby states in Central Asia or even the Middle East would find it useful for him to employ his methods against Islamist extremists elsewhere in the North Caucasus, whose transnational networks might threaten their security too. Moscow may thus have indirectly provided Ramzan with both the incentive and the leeway to better challenge Russian sovereignty in districts that neighbor Chechnya, expanding his geographic control beyond current boundaries. Tolerating warlordism in one location may mean dealing with the consequences of its geographical spread in the future.

Over the long run the Russian choice could also have very negative implications for the human rights of the Chechen population. At the moment there is no reason to believe that Russian security forces deployed in the region are any more professional or less cruel than their kadyrovtsy counterparts.[220] Yet with time Russia might evolve into a more liberal state that respects human rights, extending that concern to the training and management of its military and police forces. This might occur, for example, if Moscow recognizes that the behavior of its security forces in the North Caucasus is contributing to the insurgency by encouraging revenge seekers to join the jihadists.[221] It might also occur if someone like Yunus-Bek Yevkurov, the leader of Ingushetia who was supported by Khloponin, were ever to succeed in his efforts to isolate extremists through establishing and funding a vibrant civil society.[222] If Ramzan and his designated successors remain effectively independent of Moscow's command and control, then changing norms in the rest of Russia would have little implication for Chechnya. Instead Chechnya would remain a holdout of warlord brutality and violence.

Tolerating warlordism means accepting a future of political backwardness and illiberalism, and all of its potential economic and security consequences. Ultimately Moscow may consider the anointing of Ramzan Kadyrov to be one of its biggest security miscalculations.

[6]

It Takes Three

WASHINGTON, BAGHDAD, AND THE SONS OF IRAQ

In late 2005 and early 2006 the process known as the Sahwa (the Arabic word for "Awakening") began in Al Anbar Province in Iraq. Arab Sunni tribal militias,[1] many led by Baathist supporters of the fallen regime of Saddam Hussein, switched sides. Sunnis who had been cooperating with Al Qaeda in Iraq (AQI) against the new Shia-led government and its US and coalition partners now flipped to fight *against* AQI. Similar switches by other militias cascaded in 2007 and 2008 to a total of eight Iraqi provinces. These groups eventually came to be known as the Sons of Iraq (SOI), and the process was widely lauded as a success story.

Yet by fall 2010 the *New York Times* was reporting that hundreds of SOI members were back in the insurgency, working with AQI and undermining security in Iraq.[2] In some cases support for AQI came not from former SOI leaders, but instead from individuals who resented the new parochial control being exercised by those leaders.[3] The pattern of violence had changed from the war years. AQI no longer controlled any territory in Iraq, and overall casualties from political violence in 2010 were the lowest they had been since the start of the 2003 war, despite bitterly contested elections and difficulties in forming a new national government.[4] Nonetheless, Iraq was still not very stable or peaceful. Four thousand deaths and many more injuries in 2010 were caused by suicide attacks, car bombs, gunfire, and executions. While some of the new attacks did involve large-scale sectarian bombings against Shias and Christians, as during the war years, most were targeted killings that seemed motivated by economic disputes or personal revenge.[5]

The Shia-led government of Iraq (GOI) had earlier claimed that US support for the Sahwa and SOI programs would create sectarian "warlords" whom the government would not be able to control. This chapter

[139]

tests that claim. Iraq is extraordinarily complex, and its future remains murky and unpredictable. The long-term results of the SOI policy will not be known for many years. Since the events recounted here are so recent and so sensitive, there is a limit to the quality of information that is available. Conclusions for now must remain tentative, and the chapter does not even touch on a major continuing security issue in the country, the role of Iraq's Kurds. But the preliminary US military withdrawal, leaving fewer than fifty thousand troops in Iraq by September 2010, with units confined to base unless called out by Iraq's own forces, provides an initial end point to the SOI case and the question of whether it fostered warlordism.

A review of the evidence makes clear that external intervention in Iraq did not *create* Sunni warlordism, despite GOI claims, because Sunni warlordism was already well established in Iraq long before 2003. In part this reflected the same kind of tribal manipulation seen in Pakistan, but Saddam's manipulations extended beyond the tribes. His own security forces also operated fragmented militias that thrived under his patronage, and he cooperated with local organized criminal groups as well. Iraq under Saddam was in many ways like the artificial states in sub-Saharan Africa, held together by patronage bargains. The militias survived in the post-Saddam era because they had easy access to small weaponry and explosives. Many homes in Iraq had always had AK-47s. When the US-led intervention began in 2003 and the regime fell, unguarded arms and ammunition depots were easily accessible, allowing private weapons stocks to soar. Additional weapons were smuggled in from Syria and Jordan and sold in local markets.

Nonetheless, the US military and its allies inadvertently *supported* warlordism. External actors, starting in late 2006, essentially replaced (in a new form and under new rules) the previous role of the Iraqi state under Saddam in managing these relationships and providing warlords with resources. Development and security funds were granted to "local power brokers" for patronage purposes by the US Commander's Emergency Response Program (CERP), and some of these individuals received US political recognition and media attention. This allowed their militias to survive and in some cases strengthen.

The US was the glue that held these post-Saddam militias together. Some reports have portrayed the SOI cascade as either a tribal wave or a national sectarian movement. Neither description fits. The Sahwa began as an Iraqi tribal militia initiative in Al Anbar, but an outside actor—the US military—drove its expansion and fostered the ensuing SOI cascade.[6] Information about the SOI program and the value of collaborating with the US military percolated through tribal and sectarian connections, as well as through the Iraqi mass media.[7] But individual

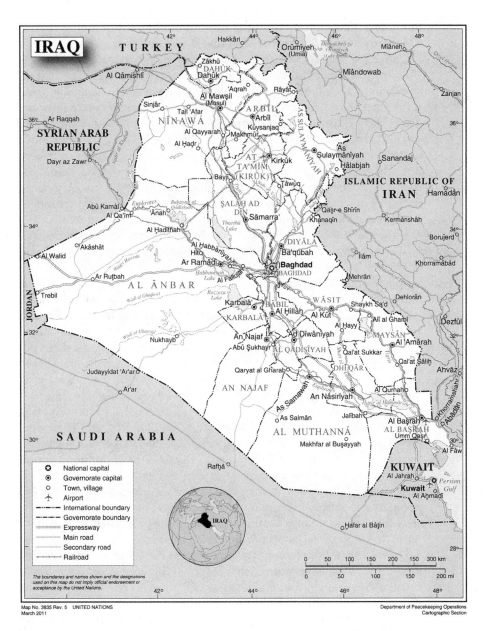

Map 4. Republic of Iraq. Courtesy of the United Nations Cartographic Section

Sunni militias cooperated with the programs for a variety of immediate tactical reasons, not as part of a national tribal or Sunni strategy. Once direct US cooperation with the SOI ended, unity broke down. As an International Crisis Group report quotes one US military officer as saying, "There are a lot of Sunni parties of one."[8]

Unlike the cases of other outside powers explored in this book, though, US commanders did not *consciously* support warlordism. The original US intention had been for the GOI to integrate Sahwa and SOI members into the regular state army and police forces. Official US policy stated that the Iraqi Interior Ministry was responsible for providing additional weapons and ammunition to the SOI units. When the US gave them weapons it was always presented as a temporary stopgap.[9] The Iraqi government publicly went along with the SOI program under US pressure, helping to arrange reconciliation meetings in Jordan and elsewhere and playing up the effort in the media.[10] The Sahwa movement in Al Anbar did more or less become the state-sponsored security provider for that province.

Yet sectarianism acted as a brake on the program's overall success. The GOI never trusted the Sunni-led SOIs in areas with mixed Sunni and Shia populations, including Baghdad and Diyala Provinces. In ways large and small the Shia-dominated GOI instead took vengeance against Sunni SOI members in retaliation for Sunni Baathists and AQI members having made life miserable for the Shia in previous years. The GOI also singled out SOI members for harassment who might have challenged Shia political dominance in the future. Sectarianism and shortsighted political aggression prevented the GOI from doing what a crafty state could have done with the intelligence it had: weeding through the files of Sunni militia leaders to figure out whom to woo to ally with the new state.

GOI representatives told the United States, both publicly and privately, that they were not interested in supporting the SOI program. They were especially not eager to stand up the SOI militias as permanent police forces in mixed areas like Baghdad and Diyala. Desperate for an end to the spiraling violence and eager for a low-cost exit strategy, the United States moved forward with the program anyway, convincing the GOI to put a good public face on things. The Pentagon did not seem to have a clear understanding of what the trajectory of the program might be, or of what would happen once the United States left Iraq.

From an operational combat standpoint the SOI program was a smashing success. Casualties plummeted (for both the US–led coalition forces and the Iraqis, including civilians) as SOI units were formed, and the number of insurgent weapons caches found and neutralized by US and Iraqi forces soared.[11] Province-by-province tracking of the data shows that the timing of each SOI program mattered: as soon as a province had an SOI program, violence fell and normal economic activity increased.[12]

As Sunni extremism became less threatening, the Shia population turned against the extremist (and often corrupt) Shia militias who had defended them from AQI attacks, since they were no longer seen to be necessary.[13] For these reasons the SOI program probably played a crucial role in ending the horrific torture and violence of the 2005–2007 civil war between Sunni and Shia Arabs that had threatened to split the country along sectarian lines.[14] The SOI program succeeded (at least temporarily) in overcoming a disastrous situation, and cooperation with warlords and their informal militias can therefore be seen as contributing to a relative peace.

But an operational military success is not the same thing as a strategic victory. The short-term success of the SOI carried several long-term dangers. One obvious danger, given who the new state leaders were, was that the GOI would ignore Sunni militia demands or terrorize Sunni militia members as soon as the United States turned away. This would tempt the militias to fight back, aggravating ongoing sectarian tensions and deepening Iraq's terrible human rights problems. It would also likely impel the militias to search once again for an external patron to ensure their continued existence and relevance. Warlords have an incentive to search for replacements once their patrons disappear. In this case those replacements could include AQI (or an equivalent extremist movement), or neighboring Arab states who feared Iran's growing influence.

There was also a not-so-obvious danger for the future of US security: that the Pentagon would apply the SOI model heedlessly elsewhere in the world, claiming the program in Iraq as a victory without truly understanding its development or consequences. US forces in Afghanistan in 2009 began creating village-based defense forces that were explicitly modeled on the SOI program. By 2010 the Pentagon planned to spend $35 million from the federal budget on this new Afghan Local Police Initiative, money which otherwise would have gone to support Afghan state security forces at the national level.[15] At least some of these new units were recruited by former mujahedin commanders of the 1990s and other "local power brokers"[16]—in other words, by warlords. All along, many US officials had believed that cooperating with warlords in Afghanistan was a necessity. Now they used the apparent success of the SOI program in Iraq to bolster their original ideas, repeating in Afghanistan the same vague hopes expressed in Iraq about long-term security, while focusing on immediate operational success and an exit date for US troops.

A fuller understanding of the dynamics of the Sahwa and SOI programs, both positive and negative, may lead to better policy choices by the United States as it approaches other conflicts. It might also help convince the government of Iraq to take one final stab at greater inclusion of key Sunni militia leaders into state institutions before it is too late.

This chapter starts by describing the fragmentation of armed Sunni actors in Iraq. These included the security forces of the Saddam era, the Islamist militias who later cooperated with AQI, and the tribes who had been manipulated both by earlier empires and Saddam. It then outlines the development of US policy toward the Sunnis and their strongholds since 2003, highlighting the changes in military and political strategy that enabled the SOI cascade. Next it traces the Sahwa and SOI process in three provinces, Al Anbar, Baghdad, and Diyala, detailing the fragmentation of the Sunni militias and the role of the United States in bringing them together. Finally it describes the ambivalence of the Shia-led government and the important role that sectarianism played in undermining the SOI program, preventing the kind of clever outreach to malleable Sunni actors that might have overcome warlordism. It concludes with some generalizable policy recommendations that emerge from the case.

Fragmentation in Saddam's Security Forces

US military officers and contractors disliked calling the Sahwa and SOI groups "militias," because the GOI used that word as an accusation to question these groups' legitimacy. The SOI were also not equivalent to the large-scale, well-organized, political opposition party militias (such as the Kurdish Peshmerga or the Shia Badr Organization) that predated the US invasion of 2003. Those more formal militias were often led by Iraqis living in exile during Saddam's years in power, and US representatives worked hard to demobilize and integrate them.[17] Nevertheless, the smaller Sunni groups clearly were "militias" by most definitions of the term. They were informal, self-selecting armed bands that were willing to use force to control small slices of territory.

The Sahwa and SOI groups that cooperated with the coalition were not formed spontaneously by random, untrained citizens who simply volunteered to defend their neighborhoods in time of need. They were mostly led by former insurgents and some known criminals. Many were headed by officers from Saddam's former security forces. Stephen Biddle, who worked with coalition forces in Iraq and interviewed a number of Saddam's officers captured in 2003, told the US Senate Foreign Relations Committee in 2008 that many SOI formations "are essentially the same units, under the same leaders, that fought coalition forces."[18] He and others noted that numerous SOI leaders in the Baghdad area had a strikingly military bearing and sense of discipline,[19] indicating they had probably been officers in Saddam's security services. Journalist Jim Michaels cites several examples of former officers participating in the

Sahwa in Al Anbar, including a retired commander in the feared Fedayeen Saddam paramilitary group who brought twenty-five of his men with him.[20]

Some SOI units were not as well disciplined. For example, some were reputed to man checkpoints only when they got word that a US patrol was approaching.[21] Young boys were filmed carrying guns alongside the Sahwa in Al Anbar, indicating that far from all Sahwa and SOI members had served in Saddam's forces.[22] Yet most unit leaders of the Sahwa and SOI were skilled at using weapons and adept at collecting and communicating actionable intelligence about AQI. They were not raw recruits.

The fact that many SOI leaders had come out of the old security forces, however, did not mean that they formed a coherent interest group. The history of factionalism within and across the Iraqi security forces predates Saddam and extends from the time of the British Empire, when the officer corps had been split by personal and tribal network allegiances.[23] Saddam did everything he could to exacerbate this factionalism.

Saddam had been deeply afraid of being overthrown by a coup, with good reason since he himself had come to power through one, and more were attempted during his rule. As a result he intentionally splintered the ruling Baathist Party and his military and intelligence-gathering forces.[24] By sowing distrust and discord he hoped to leave these forces unable to plan and execute a successful overthrow of his regime. He ensured that high-ranking individuals within his regular forces spied on each other, explicitly borrowing methods from Hitler and Stalin, and sometimes forced his closest associates to personally kill those accused of betrayal in order to put blood on their hands.[25] One famous incident illustrates the brutality he used against his own forces. In 1995 he imprisoned a high-ranking Sunni air force officer from Al Anbar who was accused of leading a coup plot against him. When the man's tribesmen pleaded for leniency, Saddam promised that the officer would "be with them" at the upcoming Al Adha feast. On the appointed day, the man's father and brothers were handed his horribly tortured corpse—and separately, his sawed-off head.[26]

Saddam also created many private paramilitary and regional armed units that were funded by the state but not under Defense Ministry command.[27] Their training focused on exactly what the insurgents later used: "small arms, small-unit tactics, sabotage techniques, and military surveillance and reconnaissance tasks" and "commando or terrorist operations." Yet there is no evidence of any nationally coordinated plan for the insurgency.[28] Indeed the fragmentation of Saddam's security forces helps explain why the initial US invasion of Iraqi went so smoothly. Iraqi forces lacked both esprit de corps and coordination. The former security forces that joined the insurgency continued to regard each other warily.

UNDERSTANDING THE INSURGENCY

Sometimes the insurgency in Iraq is portrayed as if it were a unified sectarian action. Sunnis did share a common anger and resentment against the United States and the new GOI, but the insurgency was far from unitary. Instead it involved dozens of ad hoc groups, sharing funding and training but little else.[29] Some coordination in organizing attacks was brought to these groups in 2004 when many Baathist former military officers decided to throw in their lot with Islamist insurgents. Repeated attempts by various insurgent groups to achieve political unity nonetheless failed.[30]

Sunni wrath was fueled by two infamous orders proclaimed by the Coalition Provisional Authority (CPA) immediately upon assuming control of the Iraqi occupation in May 2003. The first fired all government employees, including schoolteachers and civil engineers, who were members of the top four tiers of Saddam Hussein's Baathist Party. The second disbanded the Iraqi Army and Saddam Hussein's various security and intelligence services. A month later the second order was modified to ensure that career military and security personnel would receive small stipends.[31] (The claim sometimes heard that former Iraqi army servicemen joined the insurgency because they were not paid is hence untrue.)[32] As James Dobbins points out, there would have been a great deal of Sunni unhappiness in the new Iraq even without these orders, since minority Sunni interests could never have dominated any representative government.[33] But the orders disenfranchised and humiliated the Sunni elite who had led the country under Saddam Hussein. Humiliation had great import in Iraq's honor-based culture; according to tribal custom, humiliation was supposed to be answered by revenge, and shame may have been a major factor impelling anti-American violence.[34] As Nora Bensahel and her colleagues at the Rand Corporation noted, by disenfranchising Sunni elites who were proud of their service to their country, these orders may also have undermined a nationalist Iraqi identity and contributed to the sectarianism that followed.[35]

Sunni disenfranchisement was unintentionally aggravated by the CPA's efforts to balance competing sectarian and ethnic groups in the interim Governing Council. The new state ministries were divided up by each group's share of the national population. While Sunnis who had opposed Saddam Hussein were able to get at least partial control of the new Defense Ministry, reflecting their overwhelming share of prior military expertise, Shias took the crucial Interior Ministry, responsible for policing, and the Education and Health Ministries that oversaw schools and hospitals. These latter ministries came to be controlled by sectarian Shia militias that provided public services for Shias while at best ignoring Sunni neighborhoods and regions.[36] Some Shia militia leaders actively used the Interior and Health Ministries for ethnic cleansing campaigns, first targeting Sunni enclaves in mixed areas for police raids that were followed by illegal imprisonment and torture, and then murdering the sick and wounded Sunnis who sought hospital treatment.[37] These ethnic cleansing campaigns began in Baghdad in March 2005 as retribution for earlier AQI attacks.[38]

Shia political dominance in post-Saddam Iraq was cemented when many Sunni Arab leaders pressured their populations (including through acts of violence) to boycott Iraq's January 2005 interim assembly and local elections. They quickly realized their error. While new parliamentary elections were held in December 2005 with widespread Sunni participation, the constitution written by the interim assembly had lingering ill effects on Sunni representation. It based seats in parliament on a province-wide party list system, rather than on local district representation. This gave national sectarian parties an advantage in the vote, downplaying the importance of local concerns and preventing the formation of crosscutting policy coalitions based on nonsectarian interests. Iraq's fragmented Sunnis had never needed to establish a broad national party outside of the now banned and discredited Baathists. Sunnis were dominant only in Al Anbar, sharing provincial representation elsewhere with better organized Shias and Kurds, and were therefore left at a national disadvantage. The victorious Shia parties then used their majority status to play up procedural debates that repeatedly delayed new elections for local-level offices. As a result, Shia mayors and governors and city and provincial councils remained in place even in mixed areas that had Sunni majorities, further depriving Sunni populations of adequate government services.[39] New local and provincial elections were not held until January 2009.

Then Prime Minister Nouri al-Maliki's Shia-led national government, which came to office in 2006, created a number of extra-constitutional security agencies that reported directly to the prime minister's office, bypassing Defense Ministry control and regular chains of command.[40] These special security agencies, which in many ways replicated Saddam's earlier model of fragmented security forces, tended to employ former Shia militia members.[41] It was therefore hopeless for Sunnis at that time to work through government channels to get their interests met. The police were either absent or dominated by hostile Shia militia supporters. In 2004–2005 in particular, the United States was supporting the Shia-led government and appeared to show little sympathy for the Sunni plight. Sunni insurgents instead found tactical common cause with AQI. AQI branches rose up in neighborhoods and villages to provide security to Sunnis from Shia attacks. AQI also provided public goods and services in some Sunni areas, including electricity, when the government did not.[42]

FRAGMENTATION AND AQI

AQI's major activities, of course, were offensive, not defensive. Its adherents believed that if insurgents killed enough Americans and other coalition members, they would convince the United States to withdraw from Iraq, leaving the Shia government weak and vulnerable to overthrow.[43] AQI was also a major driver of the developing Shia-Sunni civil war. As early as 2004 AQI and its allies attacked Shia religious sites and population centers for the explicit purpose of provoking a spiral of revenge and retribution, in hopes that the resulting anarchy would discredit and disable the new Shia-led Iraqi government.[44] AQI violence was often shockingly grotesque, involving the same kind of beheading, mutilation, and un-Islamic corpse desecration that had characterized the actions of Saddam Hussein's internal security forces.[45] A favorite tactic was to leave a dead body in the middle of the road, sometimes wired to explosives so that if the family came to claim it they would be killed too. Bodies were often left under armed guard for days at a time so that local residents would smell them rotting.[46]

AQI was never under the complete direction of Osama bin Laden's transnational Al Qaeda organization. Its leaders oversaw several major suicide bombings carried out by non-Iraqis in Iraq in 2003 and early 2004 before becoming attached to Al Qaeda. As a named group it first appeared on the scene in October 2004 under the leadership of Jordanian Abu Musab al-Zarqawi, who had earlier fomented Islamist activity in northern Iraq.[47] Rather than representing an easily classifiable cross-section of the population, AQI was "a hybrid organization of ideologues and criminals, Iraqis and non-Iraqis."[48]

It was overwhelmingly Sunni and originally based in Sunni-dominated Al Anbar Province. But it was far from the only source of Sunni Islamism in Iraq, and far from an agreed representative of those Islamist interests. Some native Iraqi Sunni groups, including the Iraqi Islamic Party (IIP), were Islamists who had long been opponents of Saddam's secular regime.[49] Some independent Sunni clerics in Baghdad urged jihad against the Americans. So did the Association of Muslim Scholars (AMS) in the Al Anbar city of Fallujah, when they perceived that American forces were engaged in indiscriminate violence against Sunnis.[50] The AMS is believed to have served as a sort of ideological coordinator for dozens of disparate nationalist-Islamist groups that led the insurgency.[51] The nephew of the AMS leader became the head of the 1920 Revolution Brigade,[52] one of several nationalist umbrella organizations for the Sunni insurgency.

From the beginning there was friction between the major Iraqi Islamist insurgent groups and AQI. Some Iraqi groups crossed Sunni and Shia lines and objected to AQI's anti-Shia sectarianism,[53] while others objected to AQI's use of suicide attacks.[54] In an apparent attempt to downplay these disagreements, AQI announced in January 2006 that it had created its own Mujahedin Shura Council umbrella organization, based in Ramadi (the capital of Al Anbar), consisting of itself and five Islamist Iraqi insurgent groups. While some analysts saw this as a media stunt,[55] others believed that it marked the start of AQI political overreach and helped drive the spread of the Sahwa movement by alienating other Islamist groups.[56]

In June 2006 al-Zarqawi was killed by US forces. Another foreigner, Egyptian Abu Ayub al-Masri, was named AQI's head. In October AQI (whose leaders had fled Ramadi in the face of the nascent Sahwa movement, discussed below) announced the formation of an "Islamic State of Iraq" in Baqubah, the capital of Diyala Province, complete with a set of shadow ministries.[57] Baqubah and its environs, like Al Anbar, had been a prime recruiting and residential area for Saddam's security forces, and Saddam and his sons regularly took hunting and fishing vacations in the area.[58]

Yet the question of how indigenous the support for AQI actually was is difficult to parse. The original core AQI leaders were clearly foreign Arabs. AQI also brought financial assistance and suicide bombers from abroad to aid the Iraqi insurgency. At one point the money that the suicide bombers carried into the country themselves was the major source of AQI financing.[59] The best public estimates are that by 2008 the total number of foreign insurgents had reached just over three thousand men, or around 10 percent of those who had actively participated in bombings, assassinations, and attacks against coalition forces.[60] (Since many of the foreigners were suicide bombers, they were temporary members of the insurgency.)

It is also not clear from published records what percentage of Iraqi insurgents were members of AQI. In part this is because "membership" in AQI was not a well-defined category. In the words of Omar al-Shahery, the deputy director general of defense intelligence in the Iraqi Ministry of Defense in the early years of the new regime, "AQI don't issue you an ID card."[61] While some news reports mention AQI "cells,"[62] the cells were flexible and temporary. They included unemployed local youths, eager for the cash that would come from planting roadside bombs, who probably did not share AQI's ideology.[63]

Some regional offices of AQI had highly functioning bureaucratic or-ganizations that kept careful financial records and selected bombing tar-gets to achieve maximum impact on local public opinion.[64] The continuation of some well-coordinated large-scale terrorist attacks across Iraq in 2010 indicates that a functioning AQI bureaucracy was probably still in place at that point.[65] Regardless of how many native Iraqis were originally members, it is widely believed that with time the percentage of Iraqis in top leadership positions inside the AQI organization must have grown, since foreigners were singled out for coalition arrest and targeting.

Even if AQI did evolve into a nationally coordinated Iraqi organiza-tion, however, most Sunni insurgents had no interest in the extremist version of Islam practiced by Al Qaeda. Those who led the Sunni insur-gency and formed most of its cadres were instead Iraqi nationalists, more interested in recapturing the dominant political and economic roles they had enjoyed under Saddam Hussein's Baathist regime than in creating a new Islamist caliphate. Many were urbanized and relatively secular: they smoked, listened to Western music, and even drank alcohol. They cooperated with AQI not out of ideological rapport, but because they believed it offered them the best hope of ousting the US military and overthrowing the existing Iraqi government, which they saw as a stooge of Iran.

Cooperation between Iraqi Sunni insurgents and AQI was always un-comfortable and strained. AQI imposed an extreme and unwelcome brand of Islamist discipline on Iraqi communities. It outlawed and se-verely punished what had been considered ordinary behavior (for ex-ample, by cutting off the cigarette-holding fingers of those caught smoking)[66] and enforced onerous dress codes. AQI members took over profitable Sunni businesses and smuggling routes, commandeered pri-vate homes for use as safe houses, and forcibly married (in other words, kidnapped and raped) Iraqi women.[67] AQI kidnapped local Iraqis for both profit and political effect.[68] Its members tortured or murdered any-one who stood in their way, including local authority figures and their families who resisted their influence. From the start, then, the insurgency was ripe for splitting away from AQI.

From Insurgents to Sons of Iraq

While senior US personnel do not like to talk about it, some of the new SOI militia leaders were known by US forces to be former AQI mem-bers.[69] Membership in the AQI organization was fluid. In the words of al-Shahery, AQI membership was "kind of a T-shirt that you can take off if you like, and get back to your more formal bottom shirt again."[70] The United States was fully aware of the risk this fluidity involved. In the words of Col. John W. Charlton, Commander of the First Brigade Combat Team of the Third Infantry Division, who served in Ramadi from 2006–2008, "The guy standing by day on the corner looking like a policeman could be putting out IEDs by night, for all you knew."[71]

As a result, US troops collected biometric information, including fingerprints and retinal scans, from all Sahwa and SOI members, as well as their names and addresses, and recorded the serial numbers of their automatic weapons. This data allowed continued US monitoring of their behavior.[72] If someone turned against the United States and his weapon or fingerprints were found at the scene, he could more easily be hunted down and captured or killed. In Al Anbar and later in Diyala, the tribal sheiks who cooperated with US forces also acted as guarantors. In the words of Colonel Charlton,

> Anytime we went in to recruit, the lists would go to the tribal leadership for vetting. There's no database that you can turn to, to do background checks on these guys. You have to rely on the integrity of the tribal system and the word of the sheik, which carries a lot of weight. It's a personal dishonor to have one of these guys turn out to be an Al Qaeda sympathizer.[73]

These guarantees were considered so strong that by early 2008, the United States was recruiting new SOI members directly out of US detention facilities in Iraq, as long as they had a local sheik to vouch for them.[74]

It remains an open question how many local SOI leaders qualified as preexisting warlords from the start. Some probably were individuals who had long controlled their neighborhood or village territories dating back to the Saddam era, using their militias for personal political and financial gain. It is known that urban gang leaders on the west side of Baghdad were recruited into Saddam's security forces and later became leaders of the local insurgency with the support of wealthy Baathist merchants.[75] Some former regime elements used Saddam's intelligence networks to prey on Iraqi civilians during the years of post-Saddam instability—for example, by targeting kidnap victims using detailed local knowledge of their family's wealth.[76] Certainly the availability of weapons encouraged the rise of criminal activity after Saddam's fall.[77] Presumably some gang leaders later joined the SOI.

It is impossible to demonstrate how common this was because there is no publicly available list of SOI unit leaders. It is certainly not possible to use public sources to trace their backgrounds. At least a few SOI leaders are nonetheless documented to have continued earlier patterns of violence, using their militias to engage in local kidnapping, theft, property seizure, and murder.

One example was Adil al-Mashhadani in the Fadhil neighborhood of Baghdad, a man known for extorting and torturing his own people who was arrested by the Iraqi government with US help after becoming an SOI leader.[78] Publicly the US squadron commander who had liaised with al-Mashhadani as an SOI called him the "don" of a group that "operated like the local mafia."[79] In private some of the Americans who worked with him reportedly called him "our warlord." Another example was a close US ally, Abu Abid, the commander who led the resistance against AQI in the western Baghdad neighborhood of Ameriya. (His role in the Baghdad SOI will be discussed more below.) In front of a journalist from the London-based *Guardian*, he first boasted about assassinating six suspected local AQI commanders in drive-by shootings. Then (with the journalist in tow) he carried out a violent home invasion with his men against a local who reportedly had said, "Al Qaeda is better than you." Later (again with the journalist as witness) he launched a surprise raid against one of his own subunits, looting their weapons and beating up and imprisoning several of his own lieutenants without explaining why.[80]

Beyond these striking examples, there are many documented cases of individual Sahwa and SOI leaders engaging in force-based patronage activities, such as charging local merchants for protection, or charging SOI members a fee to collect their salaries.[81] Many US military officers and other government employees and contractors who worked with the SOI saw patronage schemes as an expected and legitimate component of Iraqi or Arab tribal political culture.[82] If this patronage were in fact based on well-understood and agreed upon social rules (including longstanding tribal norms, for example), then it would qualify as what Max Weber called a "traditional" authority relationship. Given the realities of tribalism in Iraq, however, and the fact that many SOIs were not tribally based, such a characterization is suspect.

TRIBAL AFFILIATION AND FRAGMENTATION IN IRAQ

It is hard to untangle the social and political role of tribal affiliations in Iraqi society. In rural areas tribal leaders and traditions continue to have real cultural impact.[83] Eighty-five percent of Iraqis claim some form of tribal affiliation,[84] and 78 percent of Iraqi prisoners captured and interviewed by US forces said they would turn to a tribal authority for help in resolving a dispute.[85] Yet as British foreign officer Rory Stewart relates from his time serving with coalition forces in Maysan Province in 2003, someone calling himself a "sheik" or tribal leader could have a great deal of social authority, or simply be using his family connections to further his own corrupt agenda. It was hard for outsiders to know which was which.[86]

US forces had similar difficulty when attempting to reach out to tribal leaders during the occupation and its aftermath.[87] US Marines in Al Anbar disagreed about whether or not to work with the relatively minor sheik who ended up leading the Sahwa, as opposed to concentrating on the traditionally revered "paramount sheiks" who had fled abroad.[88] At one point the Americans turned to early twentieth-century imperial British tribal tables in an attempt to help identify who the important sheiks actually were.[89] They did this even though Toby Dodge, a historian of Iraq who served as an occasional advisor to Multi-National Force Iraq (MNF-I) commander Gen. David Petraeus, wrote a scathing critique of the process used by the British to compile these tables.[90] Austin Long, a counterinsurgency expert who served as an advisor to US and coalition forces in Iraq, points out that tribes are not clear hierarchical organizations that can issue commands. The clout or *wasta* of a particular tribal leader is based on personality and current patronage links as much as lineage.[91] It is not clear how much value those old tables had.

But the fact of those British imperial tables does point to the similarity of tribal manipulation in Iraq to that in Pakistan's FATA. Throughout the sweep of modern Iraqi history, from Ottoman times forward, tribal authority was sometimes quashed by those in charge of the country and sometimes inflated as a mechanism for political control. During the Ottoman Empire tribes were encouraged to form confederations led by paramount sheiks, since (as was the case in the FATA) smaller numbers of tribal representatives were easier for the central authorities to handle.[92] In 1858 Ottoman rulers proclaimed an agricultural reform program that made tribal sheiks the private owners of vast tracts of land that had previously been worked collectively by the tribe. The goal was to give the sheiks more of a stake in supporting the empire, but it meant that tribes became "sharecroppers" to their sheiks.[93] The law also gave these new "sheik-landlords" the right to form independent armies on their property, and (again as in the FATA) excluded rural areas from national legal jurisdiction.[94] The British extended this system in their oversight of Iraq in the early twentieth century, including during the League of Nations mandate period.[95] Over the course of imperial history sheiks became what amounted to state-supported warlords.

During Saddam's own years in power, the Baathist Party at first forbade people to use their tribal "last names" publicly.[96] The Baathists, who overthrew the British-installed Iraqi monarchy in 1958, believed that tribes were an archaic relic from imperial times that did not accord with revolutionary progress. They made every attempt to penetrate village life in Iraq and undermine the authority of the tribes, especially the paramount sheiks who posed the greatest risk as an alternative set of leaders.[97] Yet Saddam later turned to the tribes as a means to exercise political and social control. He and his cohort had the knowledge and connections to do this because they came from small rural towns where traditional mores had remained strong, even as Iraqi cities had modernized.[98] Saddam's own Abu Nasir tribe was relatively small so he reached out to more distant relations in other tribes to build his power base, but the division of power among the cooperating tribes was always contested.[99] Tribalism became another source for fragmentation of the Sunnis under Saddam.

Saddam set up a Committee of Tribes in the early 1970s to help with recruitment and vetting of his security forces even as he publicly continued to lambaste tribalism.[100] Then came a series of grueling wars, starting against Iran in 1980, followed by the 1991 Gulf War, and including internal wars fought against Kurds in the north and Shias in the south of Iraq. Saddam used tribal outreach to find more recruits to replace men lost in the fighting and to ensure public order as the regime's popularity declined.[101] The original committee became the cabinet-level High Council of Tribal Chiefs, and tribal law once more functioned apart from the state in outlying areas.[102]

Saddam used an Office of Tribal Affairs to map tribal authority, much as the British had done earlier in both Iraq and the FATA. There had been a traditional hierarchy of tribes in Iraq based on a tribe's relative size and occupation (with Bedouin camel breeders at the top).[103] Saddam's new office disrupted whatever remained of that traditional system. It labeled tribes as A, B, or C, based on their supposed current influence, and Saddam paid their leaders monthly stipends according to their status.[104] He inflated the social position of some tribes over others based on their wealth or loyalty to him, elevating lower-level clans to named tribal status. Locals referred to these as "tribes made in Taiwan." He also named what some have called "fake sheiks," artificially empowering lower-ranking members of tribes to leadership positions if they were useful to him.[105] This made tribal fragmentation worse, since both tribes and individuals within them could now break rank and turn on each other for the sake of political favors.[106]

In return for loyalty to Saddam, "tribal sheiks received payments, access to weaponry, and a blind eye from Baghdad to smuggling and other illegal activities."[107] This gave them the ability to maintain militias and exert local control through patronage. Policing was once again considered a sheik's responsibility in his local area. Tribes were equipped by the state with light arms, rocket-propelled grenade (RPG) launchers, mortars, and howitzers.[108] In 1998, as the sanctions regime and US and British air strikes on Iraq led to growing popular discontent, Saddam called on some of these tribal militias to provide security in and around Baghdad. The favored sheiks used this opportunity to take control over the highways leading out of Baghdad into Al Anbar, engaging in hijacking and smuggling operations.[109]

This does not mean that there was no remaining traditional basis for tribal loyalty. The importance of tribal affiliation in Iraq has always increased at times of uncertainty and government weakness, since it provides an alternative authority structure when the state is absent. Tribes can act as a social safety net, helping members find jobs or to progress in business or government service.[110] Saddam's tribal policies may have been readily accepted by the population because of the hardships they faced, both from Iraq's long and brutal war with Iran from 1980 to 1988 and from the international sanctions that followed the 1991 Gulf War. The safety net aspect also explains the appeal of tribal identification following the fall of Saddam's regime. Especially when Sunni interests had no reliable representation in the new Iraqi government, individuals could turn to tribal authority figures as an alternative means for gaining access to resources.[111] (This was less true in major cities, including Ramadi and especially Baghdad, where tribal connections had atrophied with migration and urbanization.)

Beyond their networking and safety net functions, the most important social mechanism that tribes traditionally served in Iraqi society was to encourage conformity to social norms. Some analysts argue that this was a holdover from the time when Bedouin nomads needed to survive harsh desert conditions by subsuming individual interests to the collective. In such a system, preserving the honor of the tribe was crucial for individual advancement and survival.[112] But while the tribe can compel action when tribal survival or honor is at stake, in a settled environment those threats are rare, and political or military action by the tribes is uncommon. As Michaels says of the paramount Iraqi sheiks, "it had been many generations since they had been called on to fight."[113]

As a result the tribes lacked planning and coordination mechanisms for fighting as well. Concerns about tribal reputation act primarily to restrict or inhibit individual action rather than to compel group action. Austin Long believes that the tribes in Iraq had little organizational capacity. He notes that it was the US Marines (and to a lesser extent the state-trained Iraqi police) who "always provided the organizational backbone for security operations" even in tribal Al Anbar—not the tribes.[114] A similar lack of mobilization capacity prevented the tribal Sahwa movement from becoming a successful national political party beyond its original base in Ramadi, according to Long. It simply could not compete effectively against opposition political parties that had been organized already during the Saddam era.

Members of various US agencies, both civilian and military, had been talking to the paramount sheiks (most of whom were abroad, in Jordan, Syria, Saudi Arabia, Dubai, or Abu Dhabi) since the occupation began in 2003. High-ranking US officers shuttled back and forth to hotel meetings frequently.[115] But the paramount sheiks promised more than they could deliver. They could not compel action back home, especially since the fact that they had not stayed in Iraq meant that they were frightened for their safety and had lost some of their *wasta*.[116] At least some of them also wanted something that the United States could not and would not deliver: an overthrow of the al-Maliki government, whom they regarded as "Iranian stooges."[117]

The lack of unity among the tribes in Iraq was matched by a lack of coordination among the US actors that earlier tried to work with them. According to former CIA director George Tenet, the CIA, the State Department, and the National Security Council were all in favor of giving tribal representatives some seats in the original constituent assembly in Iraq in 2003, but were prevented from doing so by the opposition of Vice President Dick Cheney and Pentagon political appointees. Repeatedly US personnel tried to set up meetings between tribal leaders and senior officials, only to have their attempts rebuffed (and tribal representatives sometimes publicly embarrassed) by CPA Administrator L. Paul Bremer or representatives from the US or British embassies.[118]

Explaining the Cascade

Fragmentation across Sunni society—among Saddam-era security elites, within the Islamists and Baathists who led the post-Saddam insurgency, and between and among tribes—meant that the Sahwa and SOI cascade could not have happened without external support. There simply was no indigenous mechanism to make it happen. Sunni actors, including tribal leaders and insurgent faction members, certainly acted as conduits of information and in some cases provided tactical and technical support across localities. All of the tribal leaders knew each other and communicated regularly, using special address and telephone books that were kept up-to-date by their assistants, even for those living in hotels abroad.[119] There is also evidence that one of the insurgent umbrella groups, the Islamic Army of Iraq, flipped en masse after a public call by its leadership to concentrate on achieving a political presence in the country.[120] But the US presence—and the appearance of US reliability—was the glue and the key motivator for action.

[156]

This argument is not universally accepted. Some have viewed the SOI cascade as tribal. David Kilcullen, who was the special adviser for counterinsurgency to the US secretary of state and became the senior counterinsurgency advisor to Petraeus in MNF-I in 2007, called the Sahwa process he witnessed a "tribal revolt."[121] His terminology was picked up in press reporting about the SOI movement, which was frequently labeled a "Sunni tribal" phenomenon. While previously minor tribal leaders invented and led the original Al Anbar Sahwa process in Ramadi, and while tribal sheiks played important roles in the SOI negotiation process in many locales, the evidence does not support the idea that the cascade of the SOI program reflected coordinated tribal leadership. As will be discussed below, the initial Sahwa process actually made tribal fragmentation worse, especially since many of the paramount sheiks living abroad were largely uninterested in it.[122]

Others have seen the SOI cascade as a national Sunni sectarian movement against the threat of genocide at the hands of Shia militias. Biddle argues that Sunnis as a whole joined the SOI as a defense against Shia ethnic cleansing. The key causal variable in his argument is the Sunni experience of civil warfare in Baghdad during 2005 and 2006. Biddle believes that this war demonstrated that AQI could not provide the Sunni population of Iraq with adequate defense against Shiite militias. He asserts that earlier US outreach efforts toward the Sunnis failed because of a "Sunni leadership that expected to rule Iraq," and that Sunnis only became "interested in American protection" in 2007 after it was clear that they had lost that bid.[123] Nir Rosen, an Arabic-speaking journalist who lived and worked in some of the most violent areas of Iraq, finds that this fits popular perceptions in Sunni areas of Baghdad, noting, "Having lost the civil war, many Sunnis were suddenly desperate to switch sides."[124] But there is no evidence that civil war sectarianism motivated the Al Anbar Sahwa, even if it helped motivate action in mixed areas like Baghdad and Diyala Provinces that suffered from Shia extremist militia violence.

A careful reading of the available evidence shows that the cascade included a wide variety of Sunni actors who for varying reasons calculated that short-term cooperation with coalition forces was more useful than continuing to cooperate with AQI. The key to the cascade was not unified Iraqi action, but instead a newly unified US military strategy, which made the coalition a newly reliable alternative ally and patron. This argument is in line with the understanding held by many US senior officers who served in Iraq and observed the cascade firsthand. Gen. Raymond Odierno called the US presence the factor that allowed the Sahwa in Anbar to "solidify," saying that the United States "carefully shepherded" it into becoming a national program.[125] Colonel Charlton agrees, saying, "The big hurdle was [cleared] when General Petraeus and General Odierno said 'this program has merit, we need to make it work,' and then everything else kind of fell in line."[126] It is supported as well by several prominent analysts who worked with or wrote about US forces and observed the process firsthand, including John A. McCary, Kimberly Kagan, and Jim Michaels.[127] This view is also held by Najim Abed al-Jabouri and Sterling Jensen, writing for the US National Defense University, who stress that the Sahwa in Al Anbar was a "grassroots" movement while the national SOI program was "a U.S.-led and–funded initiative."[128] This explanation does not deny the crucial role that Iraqis played in the movement, but instead emphasizes that it was only possible because an external actor supported and encouraged it.

The US Flip

Before the dramatic change in US strategy there had been plenty of experimental attempts by US representatives in Iraq to cooperate with formerly hostile Sunni forces. Petraeus, back when he commanded the 101st Airborne Division, formed a "civil defense corps" in Mosul (the capital of Ninawa Province) that employed former Baathists in 2003.[129] The security outreach effort of Third Armored Cavalry Regiment commander Col. H. R. McMaster in Tal Afar (also in Ninawa) in 2005 received a great deal of attention.[130] There were numerous attempts to work with tribal and other militias throughout Al Anbar Province starting in 2004, carried out by US Special Forces, CIA and State Department representatives, and civil affairs officers under the leadership of First Marine Division commander Maj. Gen. James N. Mattis.[131] Although some of these efforts had temporarily succeeded, none were sustained, and others simply failed. Some brigade commanders recognized early on the importance of outreach to local actors, but others downplayed and discouraged it.[132]

Keith Mines, the State Department governance coordinator in Al Anbar from August 2003 to February 2004, said that his office received offers from tribal leaders to provide militias for "security contracting," or the defense of power lines, highways, and government buildings, but that the CPA refused to approve the idea.[133] US actors on the ground were constrained in their ability to work with local actors in part because of a higher-level reluctance to engage with people who had been labeled terrorists by Washington.[134]

The outreach process was somewhat eased in November 2005 by the decision to set up what were called provincial reconstruction teams (PRTs) in Iraq. The new US ambassador to the country, Zalmay Khalilzad, brought the PRT idea with him from Afghanistan. US military forces in Iraq at that time were concentrated in forward operating bases (FOBs), large installations located far outside urban areas. The PRTs were designed to bring US and coalition civilian representatives into the FOBs, so that they could coordinate development and security assistance work alongside the military. They were specifically tasked to "work with local leaders."[135]

Yet the overall military strategy through late 2006, mandated by the administration of President George W. Bush, was to stand back and allow the Iraqi state and Iraqi Army and police forces to take the lead. Apart from training Iraqi national forces and fighting alongside them, troops were expected to remain on the FOBs to avoid aggravating anti-American sentiment. This meant that earlier US experiments in working with informal Sunni militias had been piecemeal and uncoordinated. They had not been well resourced in terms of finances, intelligence, or political support from either Washington or the embassy in Baghdad.[136]

Then, in late 2006, following the announcement of the Sahwa in Al Anbar, US forces across Iraq suddenly began to pursue what they called "bottom-up reconciliation," aggressively offering money, training, protection, and humanitarian assistance to tribal leaders and former insurgents who pledged to ally with coalition forces against AQI. The initial flipping of insurgent groups happened in uncoordinated fits and starts whose timing and character varied from place to place. Even the names of the individual groups varied at first: "desert protectors," "emergency response units," "neighborhood watch," "home guard," and "concerned local citizens." The names were negotiated by US forces with the individual local groups with whom they cooperated. As Biddle himself notes, "this model is built not around a national compact, but instead a series of bilateral contractual agreements in which particular groups of local Iraqis agree not to fight the United States or the government of Iraq."[137] While most of the units were Sunni, some were Shia and a few were mixed.[138]

US officers believed that sequencing was crucial for the success of this cooperation. In their view, the United States first had to demonstrate that it had both the military firepower (using air strikes and armored tanks) and the finesse of good technical intelligence (using drones and house-to-house searches) to smash AQI in urban combat when local opposition forces cooperated. That intelligence required initial cooperation from former insurgents. But the standing up of official SOI units waited until after a significant offensive strike had tactically defeated AQI in the locality, to prevent AQI from infiltrating its own men into the new SOI groups.[139]

Next coalition forces deployed in fortified small units throughout these cleared urban areas to provide continuing protection against AQI threats, as well as to dole out humanitarian assistance to cooperative local leaders who could in turn use the aid for patronage. This was only possible after US forces moved off of the FOBs. Rather than avoiding urban areas the United States now concentrated on them. US commanders put up semipermanent outpost structures as a signal of continuing alliance protection to those who cooperated.[140] According to US commanders it was equally important that well-publicized political debates back home at that time made it clear that the United States would not become a permanent occupier.[141] The cascade coincided with strong evidence that the United States was preparing to leave Iraq. The presence inside cities would last awhile, but not forever.

These forceful actions were accompanied by a civil affairs outreach program that rewarded local militia leaders who cooperated. They received development assistance to distribute as they chose to their supporters.[142] Contracts with the US government now allowed local group members to carry AK-47s in order to defend crucial infrastructure, such as highways, schools, and government buildings, from attack. In other words, it was finally legal for US forces to do the security contracting that some tribal leaders had wanted all along. US government attorneys worked with commanders to iron out the legal details of this unprecedented new program.[143]

Sheiks or other local facilitators would be paid approximately $300 per month out of US CERP funds for each member of their units.[144] From the start the United States recognized that the leaders might parcel out the actual salaries in accordance with patronage needs, rather than paying each member equally. Journalist Greg Jaffe describes what this meant in practice: he saw $97,259 in cash sitting "in neat piles on Sheik [Hamid] Heiss's gilded tea table" in Ramadi, inside the marble-floored meeting hall of a private compound built with $127,175 from CERP money.[145] Later in the process, in Baghdad Province, the United States paid some sheiks $1,200 per month to man roadside security checkpoints, and had to be careful to negotiate the resulting competitions between rivals.[146] In other words, the US effort was based on the intelligent use of force and patronage in small slices of territory.

According to Gen. John R. Allen of the US Marines, who served in command roles in Al Anbar from 2006–2008, the United States recognized all along that Sunni cooperation was temporary and tactical, not strategic. He says that the United States simply hoped that the Sunnis would decide to "fight Al Qaeda first and then put us off till later. We would help them to go after Al Qaeda, [and] use that intervening time to create relationships with them, to cause them ultimately to say 'we don't need to fight the Americans, we can use the Americans to solidify our position [and] achieve political advantage.' "[147]

The timing of the US strategic change required both military and political transformation. The military shift happened when US commanders at a variety of levels realized that their previous overall strategy was failing. They communicated with each other (including through the Company Command Net e-mail system) about the experiments that had been tried earlier, and included those lessons learned in a new draft counterinsurgency manual written in late 2005 and 2006.[148] One set of lessons that had particular resonance stemmed from McMaster's work with former insurgents in Tal Afar. When McMaster rotated out as brigade commander in Tal Afar, then-Colonel Sean MacFarland rotated in. He would later use the lessons he learned there to lead the US response to the Sahwa in Ramadi.[149] The Tal Afar experience was also useful outside of Al Anbar, because Tal Afar was a mixed Shia and Sunni city, as were virtually all of the areas where the SOI program spread after the initial Sahwa. McMaster's experiment had emphasized building cooperation between sectarian militias,[150] and US commanders now started employing that tactic in Baghdad and Diyala.

Doctrinal evolution alone cannot explain the timing of the US military shift. Change had to be championed and implemented in the field, and that kind of major change is often impeded by bureaucratic resistance. The speed of the practical shift among US forces was remarkable, and was largely the result of two new senior command appointments.

The one that got the most publicity was the January 2007 appointment of General Petraeus as commander of MNF-I. Petraeus was a crucial advocate and negotiator for the bottom-up reconciliation policy at a strategic and political level.[151] He established a "force strategic engagement cell" (FSEC) of around thirty coalition military personnel (with a State Department liaison) tasked with reaching out to key Iraqi insurgent groups. Because it received high-level support, the FSEC had much better intelligence than earlier ad hoc efforts, allowing it to efficiently target potential partners among the insurgents.[152] It was supported from above by a "reconciliation fusion cell" that integrated efforts with a national-level strategy, and from below by reconciliation sections in each command and reconciliation officers at the brigade level.[153] (The idea for this structure originated with Petraeus's British deputy, Lt. Gen. Graeme Lamb, who had earlier conducted successful outreach programs to insurgents in Northern Ireland.) The FSEC was controversial among some US commanders, who believed they should fight terrorists rather than cooperate with them, and some diplomats from the US embassy who believed that they were better suited than military officers for such delicate political negotiations.[154] Petraeus's role was therefore critical in pushing this idea and sustaining it at the strategic level.

Perhaps even more significant was the prior appointment of Odierno in May 2006 as the operational commander of US forces in Iraq. This made him responsible for ground-level implementation of what became the new strategy, and many officers believe that he played the decisive role in bringing coherence to what had previously been an ad hoc set of initiatives. Odierno "leapt on" the Sahwa idea from Al Anbar and encouraged its spread,[155] championing the movement of US troops off FOBs and into neighborhood outposts even before Petraeus was confirmed in his new command. The dispersion of US forces into urban areas had begun in Ramadi, as another in the line of experiments, in summer 2006. It became an operational directive coordinated by the US high command in November 2006, in the Mansour and Kadhimiyah Districts of western Baghdad, before Petraeus's new appointment. By mid-January 2007, when Petraeus was still being confirmed, preparations for the move off FOBs were in place everywhere in Iraq, and the shift in policy was officially announced by Odierno in February 2007.[156] Later in the year Odierno was also responsible for the authorization to use CERP funds to pay Sahwa commanders in Al Anbar. Before that US officers could "pay" the Sahwa only in rice, cooking oil, and other forms of humanitarian assistance.[157]

The military change in turn depended on political support from top civilian leaders. This is illustrated by a gap in the new counterinsurgency manual, whose penultimate draft was widely circulated in June 2006 (even though it would not be officially released until December 15). While the manual was hailed as the primary marker of a shift in US military thinking, it only mentions reconciliation with insurgents twice in passing.[158] The crucial operational change that underpinned the SOI program does not appear in the manual, which instead advocates separating the insurgents from the population and isolating them, not flipping the insurgents and cooperating with them. According to Lt. Col. (Ret.) John Nagl, the lead writer and one of the editors of the manual, this was because military officers felt unable, on their own initiative, to suggest a shift in strategy that was based on the *political* mechanism of reconciliation with former insurgents. The direction to pursue reconciliation had to come from the US civilian leadership.[159]

The timing of the military shift was enabled by the US congressional elections of November 7, 2006. Iraq had become a hot-button campaign issue that year, placing majority Republicans on the defensive. Defense Secretary Donald Rumsfeld, one of the chief architects of the Iraq War and a strong supporter of the minimal force contact approach of deployment on the FOBs, resigned the day after the Republicans were trounced at the polls. Before his resignation he had offered a classified memo to the president, later published in the *New York Times*, about the need to change direction in Iraq, but none of his preferred changes related either to the move off FOBs or to the effort at reconciling with insurgents.[160] It was not accidental that the US military shift started to be implemented in November 2006. In the words of Nagl, "Petraeus couldn't have done what he did under Secretary Rumsfeld."[161]

Military and political change in the United States explains what enabled the cascade, not its origins in Al Anbar or its acceptance by Sunnis elsewhere. Nothing would have happened without the success of a series of indigenous Iraqi experiments that culminated in the Al Anbar capital of Ramadi. The origins of the Sahwa depended on the local interests of the leaders of minor tribes in the province.

THE AL ANBAR AWAKENING: TRIBES WITHOUT COHESION

Al Anbar Province, the largest in terms of landmass in Iraq, is roughly the shape of a blunted diamond whose eastern tip ends where Baghdad's western suburbs start. The province extends west to Iraq's border with Jordan, its northwest slope borders Syria, and its southwest slope borders Saudi Arabia. The Euphrates River crosses the northeastern part of the province, connecting Syria to the provincial capital of Ramadi and the villages of Baghdad's southwestern flank before heading south. The western part of Al Anbar is a large, empty desert, crossed by a major highway whose forks lead to Jordan and Syria. Both the river valley and the desert highway have long provided profitable smuggling routes for local tribes, whose family networks and traditional trading patterns were artificially disrupted by the imposition of state borders in the early twentieth century.

Al Anbar is said to be 90 percent Sunni (some Shiites were driven out during the recent conflict and live as refugees in the suburbs of Baghdad), and the province was home to many officers in Saddam's military and intelligence forces. During Saddam's regime it was the site of the Habbaniyah military airfield, just to the west of Baghdad, as well as the main Republican Guard compound near Fallujah, on the road between Baghdad and Ramadi. It also housed several huge weapons caches, all of which were looted before coalition forces were able to occupy the area in 2003.[162] The city of Fallujah was long known as a center for Wahhabi mosques and Islamist Sunni political activity even in the Saddam era, and some residents had earlier participated in jihadist activity in Afghanistan and Bosnia.[163] This concentration of means (weapons, training, and smuggling routes) and motives (sectarian, Islamist, or simply based in former security force disaffection) made Al Anbar the cradle of the insurgency. AQI was able to take advantage of this potent mix.

By 2005, though, some of the tribes in the region had begun to turn against AQI. While some analysts argue that this was because of AQI's use of extreme violence against its opponents, John A. McCary points out that residents of Al Anbar had long been used to violence.[164] One example was Saddam Hussein's treatment of the Ramadi air force officer in 1995, noted above. This was just one very visible instance of a pattern of torture and execution that permeated Saddam's regime, sometimes carried out by Al Anbar residents who held ranking positions in that regime. Al Anbar was home to the feared Saddam Fedayeen special forces, at least some of whom later joined the Sahwa. Some tribal leaders who joined the Sahwa had used violence as a criminal tool while engaged in hijacking and highway robbery. Both Long and McCary argue that violence used by AQI actually delayed cooperation with the United States, rather than accelerating it, by punishing those who reached out. For example, Sheik Nasr of the Abu Fahd tribe was beheaded in December 2005 after he met with US ambassador Khalilzad. His kinsmen were intimidated by this and begged AQI to be allowed back into the fold, and it took several more months for the United States to regain ground with them.[165]

AQI drove tribal leaders to switch sides not simply by violence but by making a strategic error: it got greedy. The initial history of the Sahwa in Al Anbar has been detailed in numerous sources.[166] All of them agree that what caused successful cooperation between former insurgents and the coalition was that tribal leaders in different locations at different times came to believe that AQI had begun to harm their political and economic interests. As McCary writes, "upon arrival in the region, al Qaeda immediately began to seek sources of local revenue," and "the easiest sources of revenue were illegal activities, such as smuggling and extortion . . . in which the local tribes had been engaged for decades."[167] AQI set up "snap vehicle control points" on the roads, demanding that Sunnis pay them for safe passage, and murdering anyone whose identity card name appeared Shia.[168] AQI also "destroyed virtually all of the copper-based interchanges" for telephone landlines and then "began to destroy the cell phone towers."[169] This meant that no one could communicate about where those vehicle control points suddenly appeared, or what other threats AQI was using to take over businesses. The sheiks could not exercise their traditional control over the provincial political economy.

At first local tribes had not believed that they had an alternative to cooperating with AQI, because they doubted that the United States was capable of defeating AQI at even a tactical level. This apparently changed with the second battle of Fallujah between AQI and coalition forces in November 2004.[170] The first battle of Fallujah that spring had been a hasty and brutal affair, carried out under heavy pressure from Washington without what commanders on the ground felt was adequate lead time. It strengthened the insurgency because it appeared that the United States didn't care about the huge number of civilian casualties that resulted.[171] The second battle, though it left the physical city and its infrastructure in ruins and did nothing to ease popular resentment, was much more carefully prepared. The United States cooperated closely with Iraqi defense forces in planning the attack; local religious and other leaders were consulted to win their grudging cooperation for anti-AQI coalition action, including with promises of post-battle reconstruction; civilians were evacuated in advance; and AQI was successfully driven out of its home base.[172] The United States did not defeat AQI in that battle—the organization's leaders simply moved elsewhere—but the coalition did demonstrate its ability to successfully clear a locality of insurgents (at least temporarily) when it worked with the locals. In the words of al-Shahery, "Especially after the second Fallujah battle, people there thought that fighting the US was really not [in] their best interests."[173]

The first armed resistance to AQI was led by the relatively small Abu Mahal and Abu Nimr tribes in 2005 in the district surrounding Al Qaim, a key border city for Al Anbar's smuggling trade.[174] AQI had moved into Al Qaim after being driven out of Fallujah. Reportedly the two local tribes "publicly turned on the terrorist group after [AQI] demanded an excessive cut from their smuggling profits" by levying a 50 percent tax on all criminal enterprises.[175] Fasal al-Gaood, sheik of the Abu Nimr and the former governor of Al Anbar, sought US support for what he called his Hamza Brigade of fighters against AQI. He was turned down in April 2005, in accordance with the dominant trend of US military policy toward Sunni militias at that time. The GOI was particularly hostile to the idea of cooperation with the Hamza.[176] When coalition forces led their own operation against AQI in Al Qaim in May, the lack of coordination caused a number of Abu Mahal tribesmen to be killed accidentally by US forces who couldn't tell who was fighting whom. Meanwhile AQI sparked an intertribal war in Al Qaim that summer, leading the Karabil and Salmoni tribes against the Abu Mahal and Abu Nimr. Thousands of Abu Mahal were forced out of the area, and AQI effectively took control of the city.

A paramount Dulaim tribal sheik based in Jordan who was connected to the leader of the Abu Mahal tribe (which is an autonomous branch of the Dulaim) at this point called on an old friend for help: a private American oilman named Ken Wischkaemper. Wischkaemper had worked with him in the past and had been one of the early facilitators of US meetings with the paramount sheiks. Wischkaemper managed to get the Dulaim request for assistance through to US Marines based in Al Anbar (in a process that remains opaque).[177] Additional air strikes were now carried out by US forces in Al Qaim in August, this time in coordination with the Abu Mahal.[178]

Then, as one more experiment in the line of those carried out by mid-level US commanders, Lt. Col. Dale Alford decided to follow up the air strikes by keeping coalition forces deployed in small units in sectors throughout the surrounding countryside. He was able to reach an agreement with the Abu Mahal tribal leader, Sheik Kurdi, that if US forces remained in the area, four hundred tribesmen would cooperate with them as a local police force called the "Desert Protectors."[179] This cooperation allowed coalition forces to drive AQI out of the city of Al Qaim soon afterward because the Abu Mahal gave them crucial targeting intelligence. That cooperation, though, did not mark the start of a unified Sunni or tribal movement in Al Anbar. In fact, according to journalist Bing West, "the Abu Mahal were pissed . . . that they didn't get any credit or funds from Ramadi."[180]

Meanwhile other tribal leaders elsewhere in Al Anbar were also turning against AQI for their own reasons. One of them was Nasser al-Fahdawi, a leader of the Abu Fahd tribe and a ranking Baathist Party member who had been a physics professor during Saddam's rule. He was closely associated with the 1920 Revolution Brigade and was believed to have cooperated with AQI in the past.[181] In December 2005 he formed what he called the Anbar People's Committee. This committee was led by a group of sheiks from different tribes, as well as religious and other local authority figures. Their goal was to allow local Sunnis to vote in the elections that month without fear, and they used their militia forces to protect polling sites across Al Anbar against AQI attacks. Nasser apparently had a tacit agreement with US forces that the Anbar People's Committee would be allowed to do this without interference, even though no official approval had been given by the government of Iraq for such armed action.

The polling site effort was successful. In January 2006 the cooperation deepened and became official when this group of sheiks encouraged their tribesmen to become local police in Ramadi with US and Iraqi Ministry of Interior support. An AQI suicide bomber proceeded to kill fifty of the men who were lined up to enroll as police recruits, and within weeks Nasser and six other sheiks from the committee were also assassinated. AQI attacks were facilitated because the United States and GOI did nothing to protect either the recruits or the sheiks, despite their official cooperation.[182]

Once again, long-standing US connections with tribal leaders were what made security cooperation possible, but again the cooperation did not extend to overall security coordination. Furthermore, like the earlier Al Qaim effort, the committee was not directly connected to what would become the Sahwa. Sheik Sattar, who announced the Sahwa in the fall of 2006, had refused to work with the Anbar People's Committee. Michaels quotes him as saying, "I don't trust those guys. I don't like those guys." Sattar's family had been publicly opposed to AQI from the start, and his father and three of his brothers had been assassinated by AQI. For this reason Sattar did not want to cooperate with former AQI sympathizers. He saw himself as owing a blood debt against AQI.[183]

A vigilante organization called the Thuwar Al Anbar (TAA), made up of friends and relatives of those assassinated by AQI, began to operate at this time.[184] (Publicly available sources do not make clear what role Sattar played in this group.) TAA vigilantism was designed to send the same kind of message that AQI often sent, with bodies being left in the street. The United States did not officially condone these actions, but according to Michaels US forces sometimes looked the other way. Some notable vigilante actions (that may or may not have been coordinated with the TAA) are chronicled by Bing West. They included beatings and a murder against an AQI cell that had taken over a gas station in Habbaniyah; smashing up an Internet café where AQI websites were being maintained; and posting a list of local AQI members in a mosque, and killing all those on the list who did not renounce their AQI ties within the week. In the words of West, "Tribal gangs were changing the atmosphere in a rural community that had resisted control for years."[185]

AQI had meanwhile continued to gain strength in Al Anbar's capital city, Ramadi, calling it the capital of the caliphate they hoped to establish. Local government officials were targeted for assassination, and AQI set up sniper positions downtown that prevented the bureaucracy from functioning. The provincial council met in Baghdad's protected Green Zone instead, while the governor, amidst constant assassination attempts, was shuttled back and forth to his office by a company of US Marines.[186] AQI controlled the local hospital, university, and oil infrastructure.[187]

MacFarland arrived in Ramadi as the US Marines brigade commander in 2006. Using lessons he had learned from McMaster's experience in Tal Afar, he first oversaw a massive coalition assault against AQI. According to Colonel Charlton, "the first thing we did when I got there was kick off a massive campaign to clear Ramadi, to actually go door to door and house to house. . . . We spent about six weeks doing very large-scale attacks using large amounts of Iraqi Army and Iraqi police forces."[188] Coalition forces then set up fortified outposts at locations across the city. Over the summer the brigade began to recruit local police by approaching tribal leaders for help, using some of the same connections that had first been made by Special Forces and US civilians in 2003. According to Colonel Charlton, "There was no other way to do it because if we were to wait and try to generate these through the established police recruiting system, we wouldn't have seen sufficient numbers to hold on to these areas we cleared."[189] In other words, US forces worked with local militias directly, with or without GOI support.

In early September 2006, Sattar (who had helped with this Ramadi recruiting drive) formed a different coalition of tribal leaders whose goal was more ambitious than the Anbar People's Committee had been: now it was to ally with US forces and drive out AQI.[190] Sattar publicized on national television his offer to cooperate with the United States. MacFarland was invited to a meeting of around twenty sheiks who signed the official document declaring the Sahwa. They were all "second- and third-tier sheiks, men who remained behind when the prominent sheiks fled or were killed."[191] They clearly saw outreach to the United States as a means for increasing their own local authority and resources now that the paramount sheiks were out of the picture.[192]

Sattar himself was reported to be functionally illiterate.[193] He was also "an absolutely massive crook" who ran an oil smuggling operation into Syria from an Iraqi refinery, and was believed by US military intelligence officers to be responsible for the murder of an Iraqi border official the previous year. He was a known CIA and US military collaborator from years past, and his rivals accused him of using those connections to win contracts that he used for patronage. The top US intelligence officer in Al Anbar, Colonel Pete Devlin, asked whether Sattar's goal might be to turn the province "into his own personal fiefdom."[194] Sattar fit the description of an ambitious warlord.

The Sahwa organizers pledged to support the Iraqi national government, and to use their security forces within the confines of Iraqi law. Although they had originally called for overthrowing the governor of Al Anbar (who was a member of the IIP) they were convinced by MacFarland to work for electoral change instead. This meant that from the start, the Sahwa was designed as a vehicle to create a political party that could outpoll the IIP, a long-established party that had represented Islamist Sunni opposition to Saddam's regime and was led by former exiles.[195] When most Sunnis had boycotted the January 2005 provincial elections, the IIP had been able to take control over the Al Anbar provincial council and governorship. Only 2 percent of Al Anbar residents voted that January, and the ones who did were diehard IIP supporters.

After some initial push back, MacFarland convinced the US command to ignore Sattar's continued smuggling activity, and to tame his vigilantism by cooperating with the TAA rather than punishing it. As soon as the agreement was reached, coalition forces began to be inundated with actionable intelligence about AQI, and began working with tribal militias in Ramadi to coordinate their actions.

This initial effort won support from the Iraqi Interior Ministry, whose police had no significant presence in Al Anbar (there had been only 140 for the entire capital city of Ramadi before this).[196] The new Ramadi Sahwa members were temporarily called emergency response units (ERUs) until they could get police training. After difficult negotiations between the United States and Iraqi governments, they were accepted as official government employees drawing their pay from Baghdad.[197]

Sattar lacked the political resources that would have enabled the movement to spread on its own to Al Anbar's second major city, Fallujah. Tribal leaders there had long ago fled abroad. Reportedly they were reluctant to cooperate with Sattar now because they did not want to cede any authority to him.[198] Once again, the United States played a critical tribal outreach role, this time as General Allen, now the commander in charge of the province, flew back and forth to Syria and Jordan to meet with the paramount sheiks based abroad. The United States recognized that without enduring local support the tactical success achieved in the second battle of Fallujah would not hold. Eventually Allen convinced one key sheik, Mishan al-Jumaily, to return to Fallujah by promising him both protection and patronage. In return the sheik offered eight hundred men from the Jumaily tribe as a local protection force to cooperate with the coalition.

Rather than marking a successful end to the story, however, this required further negotiation by Allen and his forces, since this sudden surge in tribal authority and action threatened both the Fallujah police chief who had been appointed by the Ministry of Interior (and was from the Zobai tribe), and the Fallujah city council members who were IIP members. Allen had to negotiate who would get control over which sector of the city.[199] One of Allen's overall challenges was to act as a go-between to try to convince tribal and elected political leaders in the province to work with each other—for example, by having tribal leaders put their CERP fund requests into proposals that would be vetted by the Al Anbar Provincial Council.[200]

Sattar, then, was not leading a tribal tide. He was widely disliked, even by those who cooperated with him.[201] Despite his success at forming a coalition of minor sheiks, he had incurred the enmity of many paramount sheiks. The paramount sheiks of the Dulaimi tribes did publicly bless the movement after they were convinced to do by General Allen and the Americans since it was a requirement of GOI support for the Sahwa.[202] Yet they saw Sattar as a publicity-loving upstart, treading on their authority and gaining patronage benefits at their expense.[203] They were especially unhappy that he was trying to get a disproportionate number of seats on the Al Anbar Provincial Council for his supporters.[204]

The situation was aggravated in March 2007 when Sattar received Prime Minister al-Maliki on his first official visit to Al Anbar, in a trip arranged by General Petraeus (who accompanied him from Baghdad).[205] It was made worse when President Bush (who was Sattar's personal hero) visited him in Ramadi and lavished praise on him. These visits were intended by the Americans to showcase Sattar's political legitimacy, but they poured salt in the wounds of the paramount sheiks who had been turned away for years by the CPA and the embassies. Sattar also incurred the wrath of a local rival tribe by threatening one of its sheiks who continued to sell oil to AQI.[206] Sattar had always been an AQI target, but these tribal enmities probably contributed to his demise. A year after Sattar proclaimed the Sahwa he was assassinated by an improvised explosive device (IED) placed on his property, just a week after he shook hands with Bush.[207]

After Sattar's death his brother Ahmad took over the Sahwa movement, but by that time it had fractured.[208] He built one wing into a political party that won a plurality of the vote (25 percent) in the February 2009 Al Anbar provincial elections. The transition to political legitimacy was neither smooth nor complete, however. There had already been a heated conflict, amidst threats of violence, over who had the right to select the provincial police chief—the ruling provincial IIP or the Sahwa movement with its higher degree of current popular support.[209] When initial election results in 2009 showed the IIP in the lead, Sheik Ahmad threatened to go to war with the IIP over what he termed fraud.[210]

Within months of gaining a plurality in the 2009 election, Ahmad was accused by rival tribal leaders of colluding with the new governor to "control how business contracts in Anbar are distributed . . . to freeze them out." This included plans for a lucrative deal for two UAE firms to develop a new gas field in the province, in defiance of the open bidding process conducted by the Iraqi state oil ministry. A rival sheik threatened "a bloody struggle if he takes it all."[211] While it is impossible to say for sure, many observers believe that these business and political conflicts may have played a role in the spate of assassinations and bombings that hit Al Anbar Sahwa members throughout 2010. Despite the success of the Sahwa, peace had not come to Al Anbar.

In sum, the Sahwa was initiated by the entrepreneurial Sheik Sattar abu Risha, but he was not a paramount sheik. Its success was founded on tribal negotiation and cooperation that spread throughout the province, but this cooperation was built on years of low-level US outreach and required senior US officers to spend countless hours "eating sheep with sheiks."[212] It began after US commanders demonstrated US tactical success and staying power, and a willingness to protect local allies from AQI retribution and provide patronage. It was led by upstarts whose success threatened traditional sources of power in Al Anbar, further fragmenting tribal relationships. It did not reflect existing tribal cohesion, and it would not have come together to throw off AQI without US support. Cooperation depended on a US military presence, and seems to have fallen apart after the United States started pulling out of Al Anbar in early 2009.

Baghdad Province

Meanwhile US forces also started cooperating with local militias in the neighborhoods of the capital and the surrounding suburbs of Baghdad Province. Baghdad has a history of local "neighborhood watch" programs dating back over a thousand years. From its founding it was divided into quarters defended by young male residents, paid by government authorities who kept an official list of registered fighters.[213] William S. McCallister, a retired Marine Corps intelligence officer who became a contractor in Iraq specializing in tribal mapping and analysis, argues that there are "striking" similarities with the design of the Sons of Iraq program.[214] It should be kept in mind, as noted above, that Saddam's regime also paid local street thugs in Baghdad to keep watch—and that some of those men may have become SOI leaders.

The city of Baghdad and the surrounding Baghdad Province, with patchworks of Shia, Sunni, and mixed neighborhoods, was the focus of horrible sectarian ethnic cleansing campaigns from 2005 through 2007. At one point the violence was so bad that young men were getting their names and telephone numbers tattooed on their thighs, despite the traditional Islamic prohibition against tattoos, so that their bodies could be identified by their families even if they were beheaded or mutilated.[215] Both AQI and Shia extremists had moved into Baghdad, using it as a staging ground for sectarian expansion from neighborhood to neighborhood as each defended sectarian supporters from the predations of the other.

Odierno had decided that Baghdad Province would be the geographical focus of the US "surge" of twenty thousand additional troops. He believed that reestablishing security in the capital would constitute the "center of gravity" that determined whether the Iraqi population would trust their future to the Iraqi government.[216] In November 2006 US forces began moving off the FOBs and into smaller outposts, co-manned with Iraqi Army troops, in the formerly mixed but now Sunni-dominated Mansour District (including its Ghazaliya neighborhood) and the Shia-dominated Kadhimiyah District.[217] The goal was to disrupt AQI's use of the major highway from Al Anbar to carry explosive materials to the capital and the airport in nearby Abu Ghraib.[218] After hard fighting that cleared insurgent forces from each area, coalition forces built barrier walls that separated Sunni and Shia population centers from each other and set up checkpoints at wall crossings. These were controversial, but they were associated with a dramatic decrease in terrorist attacks.

The growth of "bottom-up reconciliation" in Baghdad was in some ways an expansion of the Al Anbar Sahwa. There was "intertribal and intra-tribal support for this type of activity," and "there was tribal interaction and tribal support for tribes that had a presence in Baghdad but also had a presence in Al Anbar," according to a knowledgeable American who worked in the US Reconciliation and Engagement Program in Baghdad.[219] Yet the tribes did not have much authority in urbanized areas. In the absence of a functioning government, leaders of local mosques in Baghdad ended up as the authority figures behind many militia groupings that were led by former insurgent commanders.[220] And although at least two of the sheiks involved with the Sahwa sent small forces from Al Anbar into western Baghdad Province in fall 2007,[221] the United States actively discouraged this and threatened to punish such actions if they occurred again, by withdrawing its support for the offending sheiks. The US goal was to work with the Shia-dominated (and Sunni-fearing) Ministry of Interior to get each local militia integrated into state security forces; anything that smacked of Sunni expansionism would undermine these efforts.

The first Baghdad Province group to switch sides and make a deal with the United States was on the outskirts of the western suburb of Abu Ghraib, on the Al Anbar border.[222] (It is ironic that the first Baghdad militia to flip was located near the infamous Abu Ghraib prison, notorious both for its use under Saddam's regime and for the torture carried out there by some US troops in the immediate aftermath of the 2003 invasion.) There is no publicly available record of when or how this took place, but the leader of this group, Abu Marouf, had been a 1920 Revolution Brigade insurgent leader who was later targeted for arrest by the Iraqi government, as was his associate Abu Azzam.[223] Right from the start the Abu Ghraib group was harassed by a local Iraqi army unit known as the Muthana Brigade, led by Shia officers.[224] In other words, once the Sahwa moved beyond Sunni-dominated Al Anbar Province, its existence became a sore point for the Iraqi government.

The next area to flip to the American side was Ameriyah. AQI insisted that residents of this Sunni neighborhood provide them with food and housing, and began to kidnap the locals, demanding exorbitant ransoms for their release or otherwise forcing them to become suicide bombers.[225] In May 2007, a sheik who led a local mosque (and who was associated with an Islamist insurgent group) contacted the US commander in the

Mansour District, Lt. Col. Dale Kuehl, and informed him that they would be turning against AQI and wanted the Americans to stay out of the way. Kuehl offered help and was initially rebuffed, but when AQI counterattacked the sheik returned and asked for assistance.[226]

The commander of the insurgents who flipped in Ameriyah was a former Iraqi intelligence officer named Saif Sa'ad Ahmed al-Ubaydi, better known as Abu Abid, whose warlord-like activities were described earlier in this chapter. He too had previously been associated with the 1920 Revolution Brigade, indicating that the initial, yearlong seepage of cooperation with US forces from Ramadi to Abu Ghraib to Ameriyah probably happened because of communication within that umbrella group. He had earlier "catalyzed the uprising" in part of Al Anbar, probably working with his brother who lived in Fallujah, and had been sharing intelligence with the United States since at least 2005.[227] Col. Richard D. Welch, then chief of the Reconciliation and Engagement Program with the US Division Center in Baghdad, said that Abu Abid had a home in Ameriyah and sought permission from the sheik at the mosque to lead the fight against AQI there.[228] After AQI was driven out, Kuehl used CERP funds supplemented by CIA money to hire Abu Abid's militia, known as the Knights of Ameriyah, as a local guard force.[229]

There was no dominant pattern for how and why neighborhood militias in Baghdad decided to turn to support coalition forces. Certainly Biddle is right that one reason for the SOI cascade in Baghdad was Sunni fear of Shia militias, especially the Iranian-trained Jaysh al-Mahdi (JAM). Colonel Welch remembers being in meetings with Sunni leaders in Baghdad, where "they would get a phone call from their families or from other Sahwa members in their areas inside the city and neighborhoods, and you could hear the gunfire. . . . And they would leave the meeting early to go back and join the fight, protecting their neighborhood against Jaysh al-Mahdi."[230] In other cases, the turn happened after AQI-allied militias suffered significant tactical losses against coalition forces. The remnants essentially surrendered and became US allies.[231]

While it may have had a spontaneous beginning in Abu Ghraib and Ameriyah, as the program expanded throughout Baghdad Province it was sometimes deliberately managed by US officers on the ground who chose which neighborhoods to target next. The cascade was not, in that sense, natural or indigenous. For example, in the eastern suburbs of Baghdad in summer 2007, a US squadron "chose the area for expansion based on the presence of an identified leader with whom the ground-owning company commander had a strong relationship and on the need to provide security that neither CF [Coalition Forces] nor ISF [Iraqi state security forces] could provide." These US officers worked with existing nearby SOI groups and the Iraqi Army to wage combat in

AQI-dominated neighborhoods, and then provided development assistance to supportive local sheiks who stood up new SOI groups to hold the areas afterward. This unit's approach became the model used by their entire brigade in "non-permissive areas" in Baghdad—in other words, places where most fighters did not turn away from AQI spontaneously. Continuing coordination between the individual SOI groups in particular districts of Baghdad was arranged through meetings organized by the US forces.[232]

The SOI program in Baghdad eventually included some Shia neighborhoods as well, such as the Rustafa District. Here, in a repeat of the earlier model for outreach in Tal Afar, US forces conducted negotiations first with leaders of the neighboring Sunni district of Al Fahdel (which had turned to the US side) while standing up the Shia Rustafa SOI group, and then encouraged coordinated planning between the two.[233] Eventually, in the eastern suburbs of Baghdad along the approach to Diyala Province, there were some SOI units with joint Sunni and Shia leaders.[234] There are unconfirmed rumors that much of the outreach to Shia neighborhoods was done at the behest of the GOI as part of the agreement, discussed below, to transfer the SOI units to Iraqi government payrolls.

Despite all of its successes, the Baghdad SOI program was fragile right from the start. An illustration of this is provided by Abu Abid, the man who was held up as a hero by US forces for leading the side switching in Ameriyah in 2007 but who also acted like a warlord. He felt he had to leave Iraq in 2008 and take his family into exile in Jordan.[235] All SOI leaders at that time, by agreement between the United States and the GOI, had received a state-supported, two- or three-man bodyguard detail.[236] In April, however, Abu Abid was severely injured in an IED attack when his bodyguards went missing. He believes this was a betrayal by the man who would later take his place as the new leader of the Ameriyah SOI group. When there are no formal rules for warlord secession, the result is instability.

While abroad to get medical treatment and attend a reconciliation conference, Abu Abid learned that he was being investigated by the GOI for several murders. Later one of his brothers was briefly detained by the GOI and then fled to Syria. Some US military officers speculated that Abu Abid was targeted by al-Maliki because he was one of the leaders of the movement to mold the SOI program into a national political party. He himself thought the perpetrators of the betrayal might be leaders of the IIP, the long-standing Sunni Islamist opposition party that was the Sahwa movement's rival in Al Anbar.

In any case, the story of Abu Abid provides evidence of just how little cohesion there was in the SOI movement. It also demonstrates al-Maliki's unwillingness to trust the US vetting of SOI leaders, especially in

Baghdad and other mixed population areas like Diyala. Haidar Abadi, a political ally of al-Maliki, claimed in 2008 that the investigation and arrest of SOI leaders was justified, saying, "The ones in Baghdad and Diyala province just changed their T-shirts. There are large numbers who were really Al Qaeda. We have to really look hard for those elements without blood on their hands."[237] The imagery is striking since it was used by al-Shahery, too. What mattered to the GOI was not that the SOI had taken off their AQI T-shirts to get back to their more formal bottom shirts. What mattered is what they did before they flipped, and what they might do again when the US left.

DIYALA PROVINCE

Diyala starts where the eastern suburbs of Baghdad end. Col. David Sutherland, commander of the Third Brigade Combat Team in Diyala from November 2006 through December 2007, describes Diyala as a microcosm of Iraq.[238] To the northeast it borders autonomous Kurdistan, and it has a significant Kurdish minority population. It extends east from Baghdad to the Iranian border, and served as a transit corridor for weapons from Iran to Kurdistan. Saddam had moved a Sunni tribe into a traditionally Kurdish agricultural area as a protective measure against Iranian influence, but now Kurds were moving back in and challenging Sunni ownership.[239] It also has a significant Shia minority population, but Diyala's majority population is Sunni. It was a major recruiting ground for Saddam's security forces, and US troops reportedly found huge arms caches in the area around Balad Ruz in January 2007.[240] Because of the Sunni boycott of the January 2005 elections, however, its provincial council until 2009 was dominated by Shias. Its official police force remained predominantly Shia into 2010. The province has oil fields as well as date palms and orange and olive trees that were long a source of agricultural wealth. Like Iraq as a whole, Diyala had strong sectarian tensions and natural resources worth fighting over.

By 2007 it was also the deadliest province for US forces.[241] As noted above, AQI established its headquarters in the provincial capital of Baqubah after having been driven out of Al Anbar in 2006. As the year went on, the provincial Shia government stopped functioning and AQI became the de facto government of Diyala.[242] AQI engaged in a campaign of terror to establish its authority. US drones captured images of AQI-affiliated insurgents hauling Shias out of their homes and killing them in the streets.[243] JAM and other Shia militias poured in from Baghdad in response. In fall 2006 in two "wide-cast" sweeps, Shia-led Iraqi security forces arrested around nine hundred military-age Sunni men in

Baqubah, apparently not based on any real intelligence.[244] Fear of Shia death squads caused many Sunni residents to flee.[245]

In the resulting chaos GOI-subsidized fuel and food distribution to residents ended.[246] Some believe that the GOI deliberately stopped providing basic services and subsidies in Sunni areas of Diyala, mimicking techniques used during Saddam's regime to punish a particular region by isolating its economy from the rest of Iraq.[247] Local radio and television stations stopped broadcasting, so residents had little information about what was happening except through rumors spread by personal networks.[248] AQI was left as the default defense and assistance force of the Sunnis who remained. In the words of one former officer from Saddam's army, "Without Al Qaeda, the militias might overrun us."[249]

According to Sutherland, US forces based their approach to local leaders in Diyala on sectarian cooperation, in an effort to overcome this terrible divide. They worked through the joint civil-military PRT on the US side, and through the Shia governor and local director general for tribal affairs on the Iraqi side, to identify the paramount sheiks in the area, both Shia and Sunni.[250] One key interlocutor was a prominent Shia cleric, Sheik Ahmed al-Tamimi, a cousin of the Shia governor, who arranged meetings with Sunni leaders, including several young leaders of the 1920 Revolution Brigade.[251] When al-Tamimi suffered a heart attack, Lt. Col. Morris Goins rushed him to a US military hospital for treatment, cementing a personal bond with the United States.[252] US Army Lt. Col. Keith Gogas also worked to gain the trust of Shias in Diyala by reuniting one sheik with a nephew who had been imprisoned on accusations of working for the JAM militia.[253] By February 2007, Sutherland was regularly meeting jointly with the seventeen paramount sheiks of Diyala, both Sunni and Shia.[254]

In Diyala, as in the neighboring eastern suburbs of Baghdad, the idea for the SOI program was initiated by the US side, not by Iraqi locals.[255] Journalists on the ground in Diyala at the time reported a "sharp change in strategy" by the United States in January 2007—in other words, just as the strategic change had begun in the western suburbs of Baghdad.[256] The change followed the pattern set in Ramadi in 2006: US forces moved off the FOB, fought major urban battles, and then established fortified neighborhood outposts alongside Iraqi Army forces. They used those outposts to find local militia leaders who were willing to cooperate against Al Qaeda, taking the tribal negotiations happening at a higher level in the province as their model.[257] By March 2007, even before the Ameriyah Knights in Baghdad had been stood up, "neighborhood watch" programs were operating in the major Diyala city of Muqdadiyah.[258]

The effort next spread to the town of Buhriz, on the outskirts of the provincial capital. A former intelligence officer in Saddam's Republican Guard and another leader of the 1920 Revolution Brigade insurgents, named Abu Ali, asked for US support as his forces turned against AQI.[259] Sutherland sent a Stryker advanced armored vehicle battalion into the area for a major clearing operation battle in late March and early April.[260] In return Abu Ali's forces pointed out to the Americans a large number of AQI arms caches, buried IEDs, and safe houses. Reportedly Abu Ali was the adopted son of a man named Sheik Khalid, who had cooperated with US forces earlier and convinced Abu Ali to do so now.[261] Once again communication via the 1920 Revolution Brigade network seemed to play a key role.

In late May 2007, what would become the first of the SOI groups in the province (originally called "concerned local citizens" or CLCs in Diyala) was formed in the provincial capital of Baqubah.[262] By that summer, amid some of the fiercest and deadliest fighting of post-occupation Iraq, the US was working with almost seventeen hundred CLCs there. Despite a continuing lack of trust between Sunnis and Shias, each had units co-operating with US forces at checkpoints in the town of Muqdadiyah by early 2008.[263] Indiscriminate JAM violence lessened after al-Maliki scored a political victory against independent Shia militias in March. He unex-pectedly sent the Iraqi Army into the JAM stronghold of Basra in south-eastern Iraq, demonstrating with US and coalition support that he could control Shia militia activity.

The US effort in Diyala did not gain much cooperation from the GOI, however. That summer and fall, US officers publicized the fact that the Ministry of Interior was dragging its feet in hiring the new CLCs as local police officers.[264] Instead of taking any of the 4,600 mostly Sunni names that the United States had on its list, the government hired 548 men who were not on the list and who were mostly Shia.[265] Things got worse as the summer wore on, before upcoming January elections where a Sunni vote could oust Shia leaders in the province. In August, 650 SOI members fled the city after at least five of their top local leaders and hundreds of mem-bers were arrested by the government.[266] Credible allegations were made that Shia-led GOI security forces were torturing and murdering Sunni SOI members.[267] In other words, the US hope of establishing sectarian cooperation in Diyala hit a dead end, not because of the JAM militias but because of the GOI.

Diyala SOIs may have been singled out for such treatment because, in contrast to the Al Anbar case, many were *supported* by the local branch of the IIP. Al-Maliki considered the IIP one of his major political rivals. In Diyala, one local IIP leader donated his party's trucks to help with the US

SOI humanitarian aid distribution effort, and used the opportunity to campaign on behalf of his party.[268]

The SOI program was always presented as being a temporary step, and the ultimate US goal was to integrate these militias into the Iraqi security forces.[269] It was hoped that SOI members would become local police officers so that they could continue to work as units deployed in their own neighborhoods and give residents confidence that they were protected from both sectarian and extremist forces. While some might join the Iraqi Army or another national level force, most were reluctant to join an organization that could assign them to areas far from home where they would face sectarian harassment.[270]

Many SOI members did not have the education or training necessary for police jobs, so the US urged the GOI to show goodwill by offering them civilian government jobs or job training instead. As one US participant who worked on reconciliation issues in 2007 emphasized, however, "this was not a jobs program. It was a security initiative . . . designed to allow recruitment of Sunni military-age males into the legitimate security apparatus."[271] According to the US ambassador to Iraq at the time, Ryan Crocker, "We always felt that they have to link up to the government of Iraq. . . . That has got to happen or nothing good is coming down the line."[272]

In Al Anbar the transition went fairly well after some wrangling between the United States and the GOI. At first the US military could not get Iraqi Interior Ministry cooperation to integrate Sahwa members into the local police because they had not gone through the Iraqi national police training program. Unfortunately the existing police training centers were all in Shia areas. To circumvent this problem, the United States built, paid for, and staffed a new police training center in Habbaniya, at a cost of $10 million; the dean of the Habbaniya academy was a former officer in the Republican Guard, Brig. Gen. Khalid Adulami.[273] There was never complete agreement between the United States and the GOI about the number of police that would be hired from the Al Anbar Sahwa movement.[274] Nonetheless, many Al Anbar Sahwa units were directly transformed into the new provincial security forces, and their salaries were paid by the Ministry of Interior.[275]

As noted above, the Shia-dominated central government had never had much of a presence in Al Anbar, and would have needed to rely on Sunni cooperation for policing in any case. The GOI also seemed to realize that the Sahwa movement had been an effective tool for neutralizing the reach of AQI in Al Anbar.[276] Sahwa leaders threatened to push AQI onto al-Maliki's territory, "close the borders, and let them worry about the terrorists" if the GOI did not cooperate with them.[277] Furthermore, the Sahwa challenged the dominance of the IIP in Al Anbar, and the IIP had been one of al-Maliki's major opponents. In the words of one senior US officer, "Maliki is a politician. . . . The IIP, politically, was like fire and gasoline in regard to the Shia elements that were emerging in power in Baghdad. . . . I think Maliki recognized that he could work with the tribes, and he began to cultivate the sheiks and the Sahwa."[278]

Yet the Shia-dominated GOI never fully trusted the idea that former Sunni insurgents would remain permanently loyal to the new Iraqi state. Iraqi government representatives had publicly complained that the Sahwa program in Al Anbar was elevating Sunni insurgents who had engaged in ethnic cleansing in their province, and expressed fear that the result would be a sectarian bloodbath.[279] At a private level, they reportedly told US officers that they were crazy to pay terrorists not to attack them.[280] In 2009 a close al-Maliki adviser complained that the United States "left us with a security apparatus comprising hundreds of criminals and executioners, because their recruitment policy was anarchic and failed to investigate recruits' prior history."[281]

As the cascade began to show results in marginalizing AQI nonetheless, the GOI did reach agreement with the United States on the transfer and transition plan for the SOI in December 2007. Gradually across 2008, according to this agreement, responsibility for paying the salaries of SOI members would be transferred to the Iraqi Ministry of Interior, even as US forces continued to monitor and work with them on the ground. Eventually legal responsibility for the SOI would also be transferred to the Interior Ministry, as US forces withdrew from urban areas. Then the SOI would be transitioned into government sector jobs. Twenty percent would be offered security sector jobs, while the rest would be offered civilian ministry jobs or retraining (or both).[282] Any who at that point refused the job offers they were given would cease to be the GOI's responsibility. This latter point obviously gave the GOI an incentive to offer Sunni SOI members jobs they wouldn't take, to wash their hands of them.

Beyond its desire to integrate the SOI program into the Iraqi security forces, the United States had another motive for reaching this agreement. It was eager to hand off the expenses of the SOI program to the GOI as the cascade accelerated. By early 2008, eighty thousand SOI members across Iraq were being paid $300 per month each from CERP funds, and Washington was seeking to rein in what amounted to a $288 million per year Pentagon expenditure.[283] At that time global oil prices had skyrocketed to $140 per barrel, so the GOI budget was flush. To prompt the disbanding of SOI groups that were no longer deemed necessary as AQI disappeared, the United States even offered start-up grants of $5,000 to any group of three or more SOI members who wanted to launch a small business.[284]

The minority of SOI members who were Shia, and hence potential supporters of al-Maliki's Shia-based political coalition, were easily placed in army and police structures by the GOI. As of March 2010, however, only 40 percent of the SOIs had been successfully "transitioned" with some kind of government job offer.[285] Many Sunnis who took non–security sector jobs complained about their treatment, saying they were offered jobs they considered humiliating (such as street sweepers or janitors), located far from their homes, and that they faced harsh job-performance judgment and penalties.[286] Those who refused to take such jobs were nonetheless considered successfully "transitioned" because the offer had been made.

Sunni SOIs who were not from Al Anbar or other solidly Sunni areas reportedly had the least luck. For example, in Diyala the hiring process for SOI members to become local police was slated to *begin* only in April 2010, even though it was originally supposed to be completed by the end of 2009.[287] One factor in the slow pace was a policy agreed on between the GOI and United States to keep SOI units functioning to provide election security in spring 2010. But few believe that this is the primary explanation for the police transition delay, since the units could have been transitioned into police who would provide the same protection.

In Baghdad the successful integration level was reported to be almost 75 percent by mid-2010.[288] But since Baghdad also had a very high percentage of the Shia SOIs, and since many Sunni SOI members there were offered unacceptable jobs in Shia-dominant areas, it is not clear how meaningful this number really is. In the absence of good data about exactly what "transitioning" meant, statistics concerning the process are not a reliable indicator of the ultimate success of integration of SOI members into state institutions.

At the beginning the transition process was marred by blatant sectarianism. The GOI agency that oversaw and vetted the SOI units was called the Implementation and Follow-up Committee for National Reconciliation (IFCNR). Al-Maliki chose his friend Bassima al-Jaidri to be the first IFCNR director. She was trained as a rocket scientist and had earlier worked in a clerical job in Saddam Hussein's Defense Ministry, so it is not clear what her qualifications for the job were beyond being al-Maliki's "very close associate."[289] US military officers knew that al-Jaidri was a Shia sectarian because they had intercepted late-night telephone conversations between her and al-Maliki in summer 2006 when she urged al-Maliki to replace selected Sunni military commanders with Shias.[290]

In early 2008 US Army Brig. Gen. David Phillips, who had responsibility for Iraqi police training, called her "one of our significant impediments to reconciliation," who "should be one of the banned leaders in Iraq."[291] Eventually she was replaced under US pressure.

Under her leadership the IFCNR set quotas heavily privileging Shia members of the SOI for the reintegration process. She and her colleagues left large numbers of Sunnis who had been vetted by the US military off police employment lists, instead replacing them with handpicked Shias[292] (as in the Diyala example noted above). Even though Sunnis made up over 90 percent of the SOI membership, they were accepted for state security sector jobs at only a one-to-one ratio with Shias, and many of the jobs they were offered were in Shia-dominant regions where they would be vulnerable to revenge targeting.[293] Many of those who failed the vetting process were apparently rejected simply because of their affiliation with a distrusted tribe, not for any criminal record.[294] Even those who made it through the IFCNR vetting process faced hurdles, since the Ministry of Interior sometimes refused to hire them as police officers anyway.[295] In some districts US soldiers helped SOI applicants "pester" the ministries, filling out round after round of applications until they were eventually accepted.[296]

The Iraqi government was regularly accused of "foot dragging" in integrating the SOI into the regular police and army forces.[297] For example, the IFCNR originally insisted that all SOI members had to be individually vetted by five different Iraqi intelligence agencies.[298] One would have thought that such vetting could have allowed the GOI to find Sunni individuals in the SOI who could be turned to the side of the state and then woo them through offers of state patronage, but there is no evidence that this occurred.

As time went on, commentators disagreed about whether continuing practical problems with the integration program were beyond the control of the Iraqi government, or simply sorry excuses. One issue that slowed down the process was the IFCNR's concern that the SOI rolls had been inflated by local Iraqi commanders seeking additional funds from the Americans; they had to make sure to check each name carefully for possible "dead souls."[299] Then in spring 2009 the GOI announced a temporary hiring freeze on police and army forces, as a result of a budget shortfall.[300] At that time oil prices had suddenly dropped to $40 per barrel because of the global recession, so the funding shortfall was real. The only question was whether the SOI program should have borne the brunt of the budget problem. Another concern was that the GOI didn't have sufficient jobs available to integrate all of the SOIs.[301] Yet that same government had earlier agreed to the arrangement in a document that explicitly stated the number of men for whom it would be responsible. SOI integration was simply not a priority when it came to government expenditures.

Meanwhile Sunnis believed that the al-Maliki government continued to target SOI members for unjust arrest. GOI officials insisted that SOI membership did not give former insurgents immunity for their past criminal actions.[302] It is impossible to determine from publicly available sources what the arrest or warrant rates for SOI members were, but knowledgeable American analysts in fall 2008 called reports about these arrests "disturbing" and rued the "rapidly diminishing leverage" of US forces.[303] US officials insisted in mid-2009 that only fifteen out of eight hundred SOI leaders in the country had been arrested,[304] but many of them fled abroad as they learned that warrants for their arrest had been issued. By the end of that year, the reported number of arrested leaders had gone up to forty.[305] The number of leaders arrested also pales beside the hundreds of SOI *members* known to have been arrested. In 2010, US military representatives were concerned about an uptick in arrest levels of Sunni SOIs occurring immediately before and after the March national elections.[306] This arrest trend continued as the year went on, as wrangling continued over the makeup of the new government.[307] The general sense was that the arrests were conducted for political reasons, including to keep key supporters of the Iraqiya Party (al-Maliki's main opposition) off the street. Unlike Saakashvili's strategy in Georgia, discussed in chapter 4, the GOI seemed unwilling or unable to trade immunity for a switch to state loyalty.

SOI members also feared being targeted for attack by AQI and Shia militias as the GOI averted its eyes.[308] These fears grew as US forces began withdrawing back to the FOBs in 2009, losing their ability to monitor what happened on the ground inside Iraqi cities.[309] By late 2010 it was reported that AQI was back to its old methods, threatening any SOI member it could reach into rejoining the insurgency.[310] In the 2010 words of Colonel Welch:

> Everything from actual influence in the government over the program to our situational awareness of what's going on out there is getting dimmer and dimmer with the drawdown. At the height of the surge, we had troops in every nook and cranny and they were working side by side with the Sahwa. . . . Then after the transfer of our contracts . . . we had to rely on our partnership with the Iraqi Security Forces. . . . We're losing that connection because we have fewer and fewer forces, even in our partnership with the Iraqi forces, to get a clear picture. Plus you now have several thousand being transferred into ministries, and we have no direct connection into the ministries to observe it.[311]

By 2010 some SOI units were believed to be back to supporting insurgents. One sign of this was a series of deadly jewelry store robberies targeting gold merchants in cities throughout Iraq in May and June. Officials believed that the robbers were AQI members struggling for money after successful military raids against the group in the spring. What was most disturbing is that in both Baghdad and Fallujah, these heavily armed and masked robbers arrived in broad daylight, shot into the air to announce their presence to the public, and killed a number of shop owners, but were nonetheless allowed to escape unhindered past guarded road checkpoints.[312] In other words, the local police, presumably including former Sahwa or SOI members, were collaborators.

In theory it was possible that disenfranchised Sunni SOI members could realign into an insurgent movement and reignite a national civil war, especially with foreign support.[313] Certainly Sunnis had an incentive to play up that risk to get the GOI to reach out to them for political support. Yet that risk was small. As Nir Rosen argued in 2005, Sunni insurgents never had the heavy weapons or helicopters of either Saddam's regime or the new Shia-dominant GOI, and Sunni Arabs are a minority in Iraq. Insurgents fought a horrific harassment war with Kalashnikovs and explosives, but never had any real hope of retaking power unless an external state stepped in to help them.[314]

According to one US participant in the SOI integration process, the GOI had been afraid that Baathists would use their connections in Jordan and Syria to "overlay a command and control structure on these 95,000 Sunnis with weapons and create an army capable of taking back the country."[315] Biddle points out, though, that the 2006–2007 Battle of Baghdad in the Sunni-Shia civil war proved that Sunnis simply had no chance of winning.[316] Large numbers of Sunnis were murdered while many more were forced from their Baghdad homes into long-term refugee status, and none of Iraq's neighbors did much of anything to stop the bloodshed. The popular uprisings of the Arab Spring of 2011 further ensured that those neighbors would have to keep their security attention focused inward for the near future. Knowing this, most former insurgents were unlikely to reignite a national civil war.

The possibility was made even more remote by the fact that the Iraqi government ordered a great deal of US weaponry with long-term training and maintenance contracts, ensuring a defense relationship between the GOI and Washington for the foreseeable future.[317] The US State Department also retained contracts for ongoing Iraqi police training and law enforcement. Its largest diplomatic presence in the world was scheduled to remain in Iraq.[318] The GOI and its security apparatus would be watched, and the United States retained tools for sanctioning Baghdad if it failed to control Shia militias.

Yet there was another, much more likely negative consequence of the SOI program that received less attention: the possibility that Sunni SOI groups would remain fractured and fragmented, but locally intact, armed, and frustrated by a lack of cooperation from the state. If this were to occur, the result would be a weak state plagued by warlordism in Sunni communities, with continuing battles for and against the support of Al Qaeda or other external patrons. In the words of Chas Freeman, former US ambassador to Saudi Arabia, "we are essentially supporting a quasi-feudal devolution of authority to armed enclaves, which exist at the expense of central government authority."[319] Informal Sunni militia leaders received resources from the United States that otherwise would not have been available to them. Even as this forced an AQI retreat, it allowed these militias to survive and thrive as local patronage units in a way that otherwise would not have been possible.

While it would be easy to give al-Maliki the full responsibility for this situation because of his failure to integrate the SOI into the state, US government officials shared in the accountability. As analyst Toby Dodge described the program in 2007, "The U.S. military is now essentially circumventing the Iraqi government."[320] The United States extracted some concessions from the Iraqi government on SOI integration but also knowingly worked around the GOI, finessing the lack of state-to-state cooperation for the sake of expediency. Washington outsourced Iraqi state sovereignty in Sunni neighborhoods to the SOI without first garnering the GOI's real approval.

No one has suggested a better practical alternative at an operational level during a bloody civil war when US forces in Iraq found themselves enmeshed in an unexpected counterinsurgency war against AQI. Temporary cooperation with warlords may have been the only way to stop attacks against both the government and the civilian population. Given GOI sectarianism and the weaknesses of the Iraqi Army at that point, cooperation had to be initiated and sustained by a powerful outside military actor like the United States.

The underlying issue, then, is not the *operational* wisdom of the SOI program. Instead it is whether anyone could reasonably have expected this to lead to *strategic* reconciliation and long-term security for Iraq. The SOI policy may have been the "least bad choice" that was available, given the situation at hand in Iraq in 2006. From that perspective, the goal may have been simply to get out before the cost became too high, and leave a relatively low-functioning Iraqi state basically to its own devices. If this is correct, then US policy in Iraq followed a long-standing historical pattern of military interventions by liberal democracies, including many recent peace enforcement operations.[321]

Until the archives of the US-Iraq negotiation process (and the associated political negotiations within the Bush administration between 2007 and 2008) are opened at some future date, what we cannot know is whether Washington could have done anything to make the SOI integration process turn out differently. Could the United States have done more to mediate conflicts or provide reassurance between Sahwa and SOI leaders and the GOI? Did Washington miss opportunities to pressure or cajole the GOI into moving more quickly to integrate SOI members into Iraqi state security forces—for example, by linking issues across security and other negotiations? We know that US military commanders watched the arrest rates of SOI members very carefully, and quietly intervened in some egregious or politically sensitive cases to secure a release. But could the United States have negotiated a different status of forces agreement or Strategic Framework Agreement with the GOI in late 2008—for example, by keeping some near-term US military presence in mixed Sunni-Shia urban areas to provide more oversight of government actions?[322] These questions were mirrored in late 2011, when US negotiators under President Barack Obama failed to gain Iraqi agreement on the legal immunity provision that would have been necessary for a continuing US military presence in the country.

While history awaits the answers to these questions, a number of lessons can be drawn from this case for future conflicts. First, as in the case of Pakistan's FATA, the traditional authority of Iraqi tribal leaders was long ago distorted by empires and states into warlordism. Even though tribal identification still had real meaning and a significant part of the population turned to tribal elders to help solve problems, tribal norms had been easily subverted by outside offers of money and power. This should serve as a caution for anyone hoping to "work with the tribes" in the belief that they form a legitimate traditional authority structure in any state that has witnessed empire or dictatorship. Tribal "local power brokers" can be criminals, and lighting rods for political resentment and violence. Outside actors must recognize that when they work with such leaders they are engaged in the same kind of manipulation now, with the same potential for unintended blowback.

Next, warlords usually don't change their spots to become liberal democrats. One like Abu Abid may lead a heroic uprising and then turn around to brutalize his own population, and that shouldn't be surprising. Others may use political office to feed their force-based patronage networks, fighting over business contracts or election results. As long as warlords have outside support they will use it in their own interests, and if that support vanishes they will seek a replacement. They worked with

Saddam, with AQI, and with the United States and the coalition, and the ideology of the outsider didn't much matter. Perhaps the best outcome going forward would be the failure of these Sunni warlords to find an alternative external patron, leaving them with too few resources to carry on their previous pattern of behavior.

It is not clear that even a welcoming Iraqi government could have overcome this pattern by simply integrating private militias into state police forces. Real integration would require the old incentives for force-based patronage to disappear. In one sense, the al-Maliki government had the right idea when it thought about breaking up the militias and sending individuals to various locations around the country. To succeed, though, this would have required a country where Sunnis didn't have to fear retribution from their Shia militia enemies, and where government leaders were not beholden to radical and furious Shia constituents and supporters. If the GOI had used all the intelligence held by its various agencies and searched through the personnel files of SOI leaders, with some effort it probably could have found a way to win key Sunni network members over to its side, replacing external patronage with state patronage as Saddam had done before to ensure their continued loyalty. Al-Maliki lacked the political incentive to do so, though. In states where sectarian or ethnic hatred is entrenched, warlordism may be all that is achievable.

Most crucially, outside actors must not conflate short-term operational military success with long-term strategic success and reconciliation. Operational success was accomplished by US military forces who cajoled Sunnis to switch sides, or perhaps more accurately when the United States was used as a tool by Sunnis who wanted to switch sides anyway and drive AQI out. Strategic success could only be accomplished by Iraqis themselves, acting on behalf of their own interests and their own hopes and fears for the future, and not by outsiders.

Reconciliation will certainly take more than a generation, and may not be possible at all given Iraq's fractured, violent, and tragic recent history and its intrusive Iranian neighbor. The best that can be hoped for in the medium term is that both the Shia-led government and the Sunni militias recognize that it is not in their interests to attack or destabilize each other. As of 2011 that recognition seemed sadly lacking, as attacks against Shia sites and arrests of SOI leaders continued. An old Iraqi tribal proverb says: "He who takes vengeance after forty years may have acted too soon." The proverb might be updated for current times to say: "He who takes vengeance too soon may find himself threatened by warlords who seek external support."

Conclusion

Lessons and Hypotheses

This chapter draws together findings from the various cases, integrating the conclusions and policy lessons from previous chapters, to propose a number of generalizable hypotheses about warlordism and sovereignty in the modern world. I use the term "hypotheses" here because these case studies are a theory-generating exercise. They delve deeply into a few policy-relevant examples. A conclusive test of the arguments drawn from them would require applying the hypotheses to a much broader range of cases.

My goals are twofold: to lay the foundation for a framework that can guide future scholarship on warlords and states, and to provide a reference for policy makers who choose (or are forced) to work with warlords in practice in the future. The hypotheses fall into three basic categories: the origins of warlords, the stability of warlordism as an equilibrium point inside weak states, and the consequences (both useful and dangerous) of working with warlords in regions that are difficult to govern.

Origins

Hypothesis 1. Potential specialists in violence are always among us. Warlords emerge whenever state (or state-like) security institutions are too weak to effectively control territory.

Warlordism, as this book's opening epigraph from David Herrmann asserts, is the "default condition of humanity." Self-interested specialists in violence will always be present in any population, as the widespread nature of organized crime around the globe makes clear. Individuals

[187]

willing and able to use force and patronage will always be on the lookout for opportunities to employ their chosen talents against people who lack protection. When state (or state-like) security institutions atrophy or are corrupted on a particular piece of territory, someone is bound to seize that opportunity to try to become a warlord, especially if no alternative group with strong norms of governance steps forward to present a legitimate alternative to the state (one example of such alternative, norm-based governance is found in Somaliland, described in chapter 2).

It would be ideal if we could predict the exact conditions that spawn warlords. Political scientists prefer theories that explain variance across cases, so scholars would like to know what explains whether or not warlords will emerge in a given situation—for example, following regime collapse or civil war. The wide variety of career pathways followed by warlords suggests that this is impossible.

In the past, warlords were often preexisting "big men" or bosses who foisted themselves on intervening states, as individuals from the FATA did toward the British Empire. Yet often states themselves create the conditions for warlords to emerge along various routes. The Pakistani state did this first by constitutional primogeniture, but later by empowering Islamist radicals who had no official state role. The Georgian cases show that significant variation occurs even inside the same state and regime at the same point in history: one warlord, Aslan Abashidze, came to power by rising through the ranks of the Soviet Communist Party establishment, while the other, Emzar Kvitsiani, was a jailbird gang leader in Soviet times whose rise occurred by chance out of the geography of warfare. In Iraq too there was much variation, with some Sunni warlords arising from a tribal base manipulated by Saddam Hussein, and others emerging fully armed from his disintegrating security forces. The extreme case is when warlords are created practically from whole cloth by state leaders, as in the case of Chechnya's Ramzan Kadyrov under President Putin.

Warlords come to power along many different pathways. The key is that they are individual specialists in violence who seize opportunities when they find them. This means that policy makers should be on the lookout for warlordism any time a state collapses. Warlordism is especially likely when a collapsing state has practiced clientelism, lacks a strong tradition of institutions and governance, and has a fragmented society.

Hypothesis 2. Empires and states often subvert traditional tribal norms to create tribal warlordism for the sake of expediency.

The history of the FATA demonstrates that both the British Empire and the modern Pakistani state were able to subvert Pashtun tribal norms by offering patronage opportunities to those who threatened them. Rather than maintaining the traditional equality of all honorable Pashtun men, tribal leaders became hereditary "official" maliks. They relied on external payments and political agent–sanctioned khasadar militias, not the good opinion of all their tribesmen, for their power. They took "double benefits" by employing and benefiting their own family members with the humanitarian aid they accepted. Similarly the history of Iraq demonstrates that from the time of the Ottoman Empire onward, and again under the British, tribes and their leaders were manipulated by offers of money and power. Saddam Hussein created "fake sheiks" and "tribes made in Taiwan," trading favors for loyalty and allowing friendly tribal leaders to operate non-state militias useful for smuggling and other forms of criminality.

Tribal culture did not lose all meaning in either of these cases, despite the fact that tribal structures were long subverted by state patronage. Both in the FATA and in rural areas of Iraq, norms of kinship, of seeking the blessing and conflict resolution skills of tribal elders, and of avoiding tribal shame, remained quite strong. Clanship and kinship also play important roles in the other cases considered here: the closest advisors and highest-ranking assistants of the warlords in Georgia and Chechnya were clan or kin members, and in both Georgian locations the state-supporting challengers to each warlord came with kin in tow.

It would nonetheless be a mistake in any of these cases to assume that power balances among and within tribal, clan, or kin groups were socially agreed upon and based on long-standing traditional norms. Policy makers need to be clear-eyed and vigilant about the question of who benefits from their interactions with tribal leaders, especially in any country with a history of empire or other forms of nondemocratic rule. While it may make sense from a public relations standpoint—for example, for US military officers to talk about "the tribes" of Iraq as if they are a collective community—individual specialists in violence (and their immediate families) may benefit disproportionately from aid or alliance relationships in a way that is seen as unfair by other locals. The well-being of the rest of the tribe may or may not be the primary consideration of these individuals; the individuals who receive the aid have an incentive to deceive donors on this point. While supporting these individuals may help ensure immediate stability, it may also breed resentment, and resentment among those who are not favored may lead to long-term instability and violence. This may be something especially important for policy makers to consider in the aftermath of the 2011 Arab Spring, since tribalism continued to play an apparently important political role in Libya, for example.

Hypothesis 3. Warlords depend on external patronage; their power as individuals collapses when patronage is withdrawn.

The most important commonality across all of the cases presented here is that state leaders (either domestic or foreign) found it in their interests to work with, rather than against, individuals who were willing and able to use force to defend their personal control over a small piece of territory. In other words, whether or not warlordism endures fundamentally depends on the choices of states. Policy makers need to be aware that they are making that choice.

Creating and nurturing warlords may seem like the only option in difficult circumstances, but warlords only thrive when states (or other external actors like Al Qaeda) support them. They need external patronage to survive. Even warlords who sit on their own stores of natural wealth have to cross into or through state territory to conduct trade and participate in the economy. At a minimum they need safe passage—in other words, tolerance from state security institutions—in order to conduct their activities. In each of the cases considered here, one or another state or other external patron provided a lot more than just safe passage. Warlords in these narratives thrived by controlling the disbursal of state development assistance (in the FATA, Upper Kodori, and Chechnya), by receiving military aid from external patrons (in Ajara and in the case of the Sunni warlords of Iraq), and by diverting customs revenues or avoiding taxation (in every case included here).

When states withdraw their patronage, warlords flounder. The clearest examples of this are the cases from post-Soviet Georgia. The withdrawal of patronage by the Georgian state, when it was accompanied by well-informed outreach to members of the warlords' networks and rivals, left them with no alternative bases of local support. Abashidze lost his Russian supporters too, and Kvitsiani's family could only hope to return to Upper Kodori if Russian-supported Abkhazia made the choice to work with them. The Pakistani and Iraqi cases also buttress this hypothesis. Without the strong support of the Pakistani state, the tribal warlords of FATA could not maintain their social clout or in many cases their lives. Without the support of either the domestic Iraqi government or the US military, Sunni warlords fell to infighting and appeared once again to seek support from externally funded Islamist radicals.

In this sense, warlords are indeed paper tigers, as the NATO diplomat cited in chapter 1 claimed to be true in Afghanistan. Their own internal patronage networks cannot function without an external link, provided either domestically by their titular home state, or from across an international border. This reinforces the argument of chapter 2 concerning the fundamental difference between warlords during the feudal era in Europe and warlords in the post-1950 system of universal sovereignty. Warlords in the universal state system are not self-sufficient. A self-sufficient "local power broker" would have to rely on the support of his or her own citizenry. As Charles Tilly wrote, the need to collect taxes from one's own population to survive and thrive is what led to genuine state-building and governance in European history. Today's warlords are parasites who are protected by states and thrive on state weakness.

Hypothesis 4. The withdrawal of one patron leads warlords to search for a replacement.

The problem with the claim that warlords are paper tigers is that there are often so many potential external benefactors who can strengthen the warlords' teeth and claws. Warlords are dependent on external patronage, but external patronage opportunities are often abundant. The threat that warlords can turn to someone else for support often contributes to the decision by state leaders to play the benefactor role themselves, in the belief that they have no choice.

If the British Empire or the Pakistani state after independence had withdrawn their support, warlords in the FATA would have turned to Afghanistan (or the external armies that coveted Afghanistan) for support. The result may have been the expansion of the Afghan land mass and Pakistan's loss of FATA. Pakistan would have seen that as an unacceptable growth of the influence of a rival, since Islamabad has long interpreted events in Afghanistan in terms of Indian influence, and this might have led to major war. In Georgia, the threat of Russian hegemony sustained Tbilisi's support for Abashidze and Kvitsiani throughout the Shevardnadze era. It was only by cooperating with that external Russian state that Saakashvili got rid of Abashidze, and his failure to do so in the case of Kvitsiani may have helped provoke the 2008 war with Russia. In Iraq, Sunni warlords were originally supported by Saddam Hussein's state. They had hoped to gain support against the new state's Shia leaders from AQI; when this proved detrimental to their interests, they turned to the US-led military coalition as their external patron. When one patron failed, abused them, or deserted them, they sought another, and Sunni warlords were likely to seek a replacement for the US Sons of Iraq program as it wound down.

The only potential anomaly among the cases considered here is the absence of an immediate and obvious alternative patron—someone other than Putin and the Russian state—for Ramzan Kadyrov in Chechnya.

This makes it even more puzzling that Putin decided to elevate Ramzan to power, since there was no external pressure on Chechen territory that required it. The incentive structure here leads me to predict that Ramzan should use the opportunity of the leeway Russia gave him to search for alternative external patrons, as an insurance policy against Putin (or Putin's eventual decline in power). Russia's rivals, if they were paying attention, should have been courting him.

> Hypothesis 5. Information about local patronage networks (and how they may be diverted or supplanted) is the key weapon for states wishing to topple warlords.

In the only case in modern history where state leaders first supported warlords on their own territory and then successfully overthrew them and reestablished genuine sovereignty, Georgia, detailed local information about the political economy of warlord territory was vital for the success of the overthrow. Mikheil Saakashvili knew how Ajara worked because his university classmate and friend, Levan Varshalomidze, came out of Ajara's elite under Abashidze. Saakashvili's administration knew how Upper Kodori worked because of repeated negotiations conducted with local residents by Irakli Alasania when Kvitsiani was away in Tbilisi. The new Georgian state also had access to old KGB and Georgian intelligence service files that may have proved useful in dealing with these two men and their networks. These facts are not usually presented in the dominant narrative of Saakashvili's actions. Instead most analysts prior to this book have seen Saakashvili's ability to overthrow Abashidze and Kvitsiani as stemming from his popular support alone. But Saakashvili's successes were a two-stage process: first he had to oust the warlords, and then he had to win over the networks that had benefited from warlord patronage to the side of the state.

In contrast, in the FATA in Pakistan, state leaders lacked much access to the territory. They lacked legal access under the constitution, and physical access because they would be attacked if they entered without permission. Outside of reports by the political agents, who were probably themselves included in the official maliks' patronage networks, Pakistan's leaders had no detailed information about internal conditions in the FATA. State leaders did manage to create and empower a competing set of local power brokers in the FATA, the radical Islamists, but leaders' lack of good access to the region helped those new local power brokers escape state control, much like Frankenstein's monster.

In Chechnya, Kadyrov constantly pushed to have outside Russian security forces leave, and eventually they mostly did, giving him freedom of action without much oversight. The only place his plans seem to have gone awry was when an apparent assassination attempt against his rival Isa Yamadayev was thwarted in Moscow. Isa Yamadayev was apparently saved by the Russian police, but this happened outside of Chechen territory, and in the heart of Russia where state domestic intelligence sources would have the most information and control. While Putin's government would certainly have had old KGB and FSB records about Kadyrov and his allies and rivals, the Kadyrovs came to power out of an anarchic rebellion and episodic civil war that lasted for close to a decade. Unlike the situation in Georgia, where the reach of the state was temporarily broken by the anarchy of 1991–92 but was otherwise relatively stable over the course of the Shevardnadze era, Chechnya was a volatile tinderbox. The quality of Russian information about the situation in Chechnya would have been fragmentary, dependent on what was gathered by outside troops who lacked the trust of locals. As Kadyrov gained control over the security forces, and in the process his own clan rivals, independent Russian information must have shrunk considerably.

In Iraq it remains unclear how much information the Shia-dominated government leaders retained about Sunni warlords. The US military did not give the government of Iraq all the biometric data it had collected from SOI members, for fear that doing so would lead to retributive attacks against them. Rosters of SOI participants' names were turned over to the IFCNR, the state agency responsible for integrating them into the security forces, but the fingerprints and retinal scans that the United States collected were not shared with the government, at least outside of Al Anbar. Furthermore, the United States relied for its own vetting procedures on the word of tribal leaders about the *future* behavior of SOI recruits, not about their past behavior or misdeeds. This means that US records were never very thorough or complete. At the same time, though, Shia supporters of the Iraqi government dominated the new Interior Ministry from its inception in 2003. The old state police forces were never disbanded the way the military was after the fall of Saddam Hussein, and this makes it likely that some old police and domestic intelligence records from his totalitarian regime also survived intact. This may leave the future Iraqi state in a position closer to that of Saakashvili than that of the Pakistani state, in terms of the information available to it, should it decide to take further action to weed through former SOI members.

States with intrusive domestic intelligence services will find it easiest to control and overthrow warlords. Once warlords have successfully evaded the state's ability to monitor and collect information about them, they may have essentially made themselves necessary for the continuation of stability in their regions. Policy makers need to be aware that the more autonomy warlords are given, the harder it will be to get rid of them.

Hypothesis 6. Warlords have a particular incentive to gain legal control over security provision on their territory because this drastically limits the state's information about their activities.

In both the FATA and Chechnya, warlords gained a fair amount of legal control over security provision on their territories. In the FATA this was institutionalized in Pakistan's constitution: Pakistani security forces lacked the legal right to enter the FATA except in extraordinary circumstances. That meant that Pakistani intelligence about the FATA was limited and could be manipulated by the political agents and official maliks, or by the state-supported Islamist militants who supplanted them. In Chechnya this was institutionalized by a series of presidential decrees that gave the kadyrovtsy more and more control over the regional interior ministry forces, internal intelligence, and counterterrorism efforts, even though the province on paper remained subordinate to Russian law.

In Georgia the autonomy of warlord security forces was never fully institutionalized. Abashidze seized de facto control over the appointment of border guards, police, and other supposedly federal officials on Ajaran territory, but his right to do so was never made official. Saakashvili demonstrated this when he held military parades and exercises on the border of Ajara and sent his own federal interior ministry forces in to arrest the wayward railroad official. In Upper Kodori the Monadire militia of Kvitsiani was at times recognized as part of the defense or interior ministries, and its role was even codified in an international treaty with Russia. Yet legal control over security on the territory never quite escaped Tbilisi, even when the physical access of Georgian state officials was limited by threat. For example, state interior ministry employees always lived in Kodori.

In Iraq the effort by the United States to institutionalize the relationship between the government of Iraq and the Sons of Iraq units faced all kinds of legal roadblocks by the Iraqi state. The Sahwa movement in Al Anbar did effectively become a legal institution since local Sunni tribes were able to gain the right to control policing there. This was not surprising since the state never had any hope of directly controlling Al Anbar given the dominance of the Sunni population there and its long history of autonomy. Elsewhere in Iraq, while the al-Maliki government signed off on the agreement to integrate the SOI, it put up every possible resistance to actually implementing the agreement, using intelligence vetting, budgetary shortfalls, and unattractive job assignments to delay and limit the legally sanctioned rights of Sunni SOI units in the new state.

This hypothesis suggests that the government of Iraq may have in some sense acted wisely on behalf of its own interests by not allowing

Sunni SOI units to become the state police in their own areas of mixed Sunni-Shia communities. Once warlords obtain legal sanction for their security provision activities, it becomes almost impossible for the state to obtain good information about what goes on. The choice may nonetheless have worsened the overall security situation in the country, as Sunni SOI members felt abandoned, betrayed, and hostile as a result of the state's earlier promises. The only resolution to this dilemma would have required the state to protect Sunni individuals more reliably.

> Hypothesis 7. Populist leaders without strong opposition movements or democratic oversight will have the easiest time replacing warlordism with negotiated state rule.

Saakashvili's success is the only clear evidence for the hypothesis that leaders without opposition or democratic oversight will have the easiest time ousting warlords. Saakashvili could hand-select new leaders for warlord territories, change the constitution to neuter regional democratic opposition to his moves, threaten coercion through military force movements, and negotiate immunity deals that were credible because they were not transparent. He could thereby bolster his allies without much public discussion or dissent in Tbilisi. This hypothesis suggests that Russia would be another case where this could happen: Putin or someone like him could choose a replacement for Kadyrov and negotiate deals inside Chechnya without risking much political dissent in Moscow. It would take a highly risk-acceptant leader to do this, though, since consensus in Moscow would likely break down if the effort failed and Chechnya once again became anarchic.

While neither Pakistan nor Iraq are institutionalized democracies today, leaders in both countries have faced significant and debilitating opposition, especially on questions relating to security issues in the territories considered here. Pakistan's president cannot decree a solution to the status of the FATA, and Iraq's prime minister cannot decree a solution to the SOI issue in mixed Shia-Sunni areas. In both cases leaders face well-resourced and strongly divided national and provincial parliaments, as well as security forces whose ultimate control and loyalty is unclear. States that have a hard time acting quickly and consistently will find it difficult to control warlords on their territory.

> Hypothesis 8. Humanitarian aid given to warlord territories will be controlled by warlord patronage networks and will not build loyalty to the state. Providing incentives for labor migration to state-controlled territories may better showcase the advantages of sovereign control.

This hypothesis must remain tentative, since it arises out of the only case where there is clear evidence to back it, namely Pakistan's FATA. Humanitarian aid given to the official maliks was misused in the 1970s and directed toward their own individual profit. More recent evidence indicates that international aid to the FATA has also not always been used fairly to benefit the population as a whole. This does not mean that giving humanitarian aid to the FATA is a bad thing. It is better to feed, educate, and heal people as best as can be done, given the current power structure, than to leave everyone without assistance. It simply means that aid is not likely to be a mechanism for political change.

At the same time, the opportunity for illegal migration to Dubai and other Persian Gulf regions during the oil boom of the early 1970s was seized by ordinary residents of the FATA. They used the opportunity to bring relative wealth to their families, and to establish homes in the settled regions of the North-West Frontier Province and its capital of Peshawar. If a global recession and the war in Afghanistan had not interrupted that process, the society might have evolved in a very different direction. Economic opportunity, when it is dangled just outside warlord zones, can lead to evolutionary development within.

Georgia too offered a fair amount of opportunity for residents of Ajara and Upper Kodori to see the good things that happened on state-controlled territory. In Georgia's case, popular enthusiasm for Saakashvili served to showcase the advantages of sovereign control, especially as the support of the United States and other Western states led to construction projects and other opportunities for wealth-generation there. When Tbilisi tried to make "Upper Abkhazia" a showcase to attract Abkhazians back to Georgia, Russia interpreted it as a taunt, and this probably helped provoke Russian military action in 2008. But one could imagine a quieter version of encouraging Upper Kodori well-being that would have served the same purpose better.

In the Chechnya case, as in the FATA in the 1970s, a fair amount of the aid sent by the state for social development purposes seemed to find its way into private pockets, in this case those of Ramzan. Chechens did migrate for work to Moscow and other Russian cities in droves. But they were treated badly there, subjected to police harassment and ethnically motivated street violence and murder. Chechens were not shown much of the benefits of sovereign statehood in Russia.

In Iraq the Commander's Emergency Response Program was explicitly designed to provide patronage to "local power brokers." The aid was distributed as those individuals saw fit, for the purpose of building individual alliances. Now it remains to be seen how well Sunnis are integrated into state labor opportunities. In 2009 and 2010, many former

SOI members complained that they were offered only unattractive or unsafe jobs by the government of Iraq. The analysis presented here suggests that this was a terrible mistake on the part of the government. If that government had instead made work for Sunni SOI members attractive and profitable, and provided safeguards against sectarian reprisal to allow migration elsewhere in the country, it might have wooed the Sunni population away from the warlords who wished to control their neighborhoods.

THE UTILITY OF WARLORDS FOR SECURITY

Hypothesis 9. Warlords may become irreplaceable in minority population areas when ethnic or sectarian tension is high.

Saakashvili's job in Georgia was made much easier by the fact that residents of Ajara and Upper Kodori considered themselves as Georgian as anyone else. Georgia never fought a war against either Ajarans or the residents of Upper Kodori. Each region had unique cultural attributes, but the populations there did not fear ethnic retribution. It was therefore straightforward for Saakashvili to find locals who were willing to allow the state back in. Most likely that would have been true for Shevardnadze as well; he was needlessly intimidated by threats of "clan warfare" in the warlord regions.

Russian Chechens and Iraqi Sunnis were in a much different category. Not only were they minorities within their home countries, but they also fought brutal civil wars against the majority population, and inherited histories of major confrontations. In such cases submitting to warlords may be seen by the local population as a better choice than submitting to a hostile state bent on revenge and retribution. Building the kind of mutual trust that is necessary for genuine state sovereignty in such cases is difficult, and in both of these recent cases the choices made by state leaders instead exacerbated sectarianism and ethnic tension.

Pakistan is a middle case. Islamabad has not gone to war explicitly against "Pashtunistan" as an ethnic territory. But the Pashtuns, especially those living in the FATA, have always been considered outsiders by many in Pakistan. Despite their long integration into the economy and armed forces of Pakistan, FATA Pashtuns will likely still be held at arms' length by many other Pakistanis, and vice versa. Indeed the evidence indicates that this was one of the challenges Pakistani military forces faced in their 2009 incursion into the FATA to try to oust Islamist militants: even though they were fellow citizens of Pakistan, some FATA residents saw them as an external invasion force. Building trust with the Pashtuns will be difficult for Pakistani leaders, and this will complicate any future transition of the FATA into a "normal" state province.

This intervening variable of ethnic tension or sectarianism does not mean that warlord rule on particular territories is inevitable. It does not even mean that the local population would prefer warlordism to state penetration in the abstract. For example, many Pashtuns retained homes in both the FATA and the settled North-West Frontier Province, many Chechens worked in Moscow and other Russian cities, and many Sunnis cooperated with Shias in their daily lives and commerce in Iraq. It does mean, however, that once warlordism is established on a minority territory, state leaders who wish to restore sovereignty need to focus on reconciliation and inclusion of that minority population. Otherwise the choices that state leaders make can strengthen the appeal and perceived legitimacy of warlords as the providers of security and patronage.

Hypothesis 10. Middleman warlords can serve a positive role as transnational buffers, maintaining stability in contested border regions.

The positive role that warlords played as buffers was an unexpected finding from two of the cases considered here, Upper Kodori in Georgia and the FATA in Pakistan. In Upper Kodori, Kvitsiani's militia was effectively written into the Treaty of Moscow as the local security force that patrolled the mountain passes dividing Georgia proper from breakaway Abkhazia. His forces acted as a tripwire, providing information to the Georgian state about Russian overflights, bombing, and incursions, but also reassuring the Abkhaz side that a safety zone separated their territory from the Georgian military. Once Kvitsiani was ousted, the balance shifted, and in 2008 Russian forces rolled right over the weaker Georgian forces and took the territory.

For the FATA case there is less direct information about the role that the official maliks played in maintaining a border buffer. It is a good bet, however, that both Afghan state forces earlier in the century and Soviet forces from 1979 to 1989 would have thought twice about trying to navigate the treacherous mountain passes in the face of tribal hostility. The deal reached between Islamabad and the official maliks allowed Pakistan to concentrate its military forces elsewhere, on the conflict with India over Kashmir, rather than having to worry that its neighbor to the northwest would seize its territory. It was the breakdown of that deal and the empowerment of Islamist warlords that allowed Al Qaeda foreigners to enter and create a new security problem for Pakistan.

Both of these cases also suggest a potential downside to the otherwise positive border buffer role of warlordism: the stability that warlords provide allows state leaders to ignore ongoing border tensions by putting them on the backburner. In Georgia the border issue with Abkhazia never went away, and came back to bite Tbilisi with a vengeance during the 2008 war with Russia when Upper Kodori was lost. In Afghanistan neither Hamid Karzai nor the Taliban recognized the legitimacy of the Durand Line, so the issue of Pashtunistan remained on the table more than sixty years after the establishment of the state of Pakistan. Taking the border issue off the immediate agenda does not solve what is a real security problem. Instead it can help turn border disputes into long-term frozen conflicts.

Hypothesis 11. Warlords create resentment by impeding fair outcomes. Supporting them risks long-term destabilizing violence as a result.

Even though there are some potential security benefits to working with warlords when they are tripwires for border conflicts, and when no other alternative is believed to be cost-effective, it should be remembered that warlord patronage separates a chosen elite from everyone else. Beyond the negative humanitarian implications of supporting such social stratification, policy makers need to keep the long-term practical implications of this choice in mind. It is likely that radical Islamism in Pakistan's FATA was fostered in part by the double benefits that the state gave the official maliks, and their lack of concern about the criminal justice system for ordinary people. It is likely that terrorism and insurgency in the North Caucasus were fostered in part by the brutal methods of Ramzan Kadyrov, and a desire for revenge against him and his Russian patrons. It is likely that political violence in Iraq in 2010 and 2011 was at least partly sparked by internal battles and rivalry within and around the SOI and Sahwa movements, and by those who resented the relative local power or wealth of some SOI leaders.

None of these cases led to all-out civil war. But the degree of suffering and even death (including among state security forces and innocent bystanders) was significant. Warlords do not just use violence themselves; they can also provoke violent reactions from those they exclude. Policy makers who bargain with warlords cannot ignore this consequence of their choice.

OVERALL IMPLICATIONS

Which role warlords will play in either furthering or threatening stability and security depends on a variety of factors. Under particular conditions warlords, especially when they are already entrenched on a piece of territory, may very well serve important roles in maintaining the peace. Yet they are unlikely to become state builders, and their territories will remain underdeveloped, with economies skewed toward their own patronage networks. This will create resentment among those excluded, especially as global communication becomes ever easier and everyone can see how other people live. Warlord actions will also continue to undermine state strength, by bleeding bureaucratic resources and customs revenue away from state control, and by fostering criminality.

The convenience of warlordism can lead state failure to become an equilibrium point for state leaders—in other words, a static situation where no one who has any power has an incentive to replace warlordism with institution building. Cooperation with warlords should therefore be pursued only when it is understood that lasting state failure is the likely consequence, when warlords truly are the least bad alternative. The problem is that it is easy for state leaders to reach that conclusion without thinking creatively about alternative scenarios, especially when the long-term consequences seem so far off that they are easily left to a successor.

It is my hope that US and other policy makers do not continue unthinkingly to choose the "default option" of working with warlords when they face new crises around the world. In 2011 the most pressing new cases for this concern were states buffeted by the Arab Spring, especially Libya and Yemen, where no cohesive rebel governance alternative to the shattered old regimes appeared on the immediate horizon. Warlordism spawned by the drug trade also appeared to be threatening the peace in Mexico, and remained a concern in some areas of Brazil and Colombia. In each of these Latin American cases, instability followed a decision by state leaders to confront a situation that their predecessors had tolerated or supported; state action disrupted a balance between rival warlords. One could imagine similar major policy dilemmas with crucial international security implications if the North Korean or Iranian or Pakistani states were to collapse in the future and fragmented security forces began battling each other for control over nuclear material.

When approaching warlords, policy makers must keep in mind that short-term stability is not the same thing as long-term security, and that military operational success is not the same thing as strategic political success. Most important, warlords in the modern world are not future state-builders. Working with them means outsourcing state sovereignty, and once granted it is hard to reel back in. When supported by external patronage, warlordism instead takes on a life of its own.

Notes

1. WARLORDS: AN INTRODUCTION

1. Sally Neighbor, "Warlords' Unwelcome Return," *Australian*, February 27, 2010.

2. For trenchant criticism of this choice, see Laura Secor, "The Pragmatist," *Atlantic Monthly* 294, no. 1 (July/August 2004), 44; and Astri Suhrke, Kristian Berg Harpviken, and Arne Strand, *Conflictual Peacebuilding: Afghanistan Two Years after Bonn*, Report 2004: 4 (Oslo: International Peace Research Institute, 2004).

3. For a prominent argument that the US should cooperate with warlords, see Andrew J. Bacevich, "Afghanistan: What's Our Definition of Victory?," *Newsweek*, Dec. 8, 2008. For the argument that the warlords should have been and could have been sidelined, see Kathy Gannon, "Afghanistan Unbound," *Foreign Affairs* 83, no. 3 (May/June 2004): 35–46.

4. Keith Stanski, " 'So These Folks Are Aggressive': An Orientalist Reading of 'Afghan Warlords,' " *Security Dialogue* 40, no. 1 (2009): 73–94; and Stanski, "A Discursive Critique of the 'Warlord' Concept," paper prepared for delivery at the 50th Annual Convention of the International Studies Association, New York, February 2009. The classic claim that Western scholars who study the developing world are by definition creating an "Other" was made by Edward W. Said, *Orientalism* (New York: Random House, 1978).

5. Kimberly Marten, "Warlords," in *The Changing Character of War*, ed. Hew Strachan and Sibylle Scheipers (New York: Oxford University Press, 2011), 302–14. My definition has developed over time; for an earlier version, see Marten, "Warlordism in Comparative Perspective," *International Security* 31, no. 3 (Winter 2006/2007): 41–73.

6. Arthur Waldron, "The Warlord: Twentieth-Century Chinese Understandings of Violence, Militarism, and Imperialism," *American Historical Review* 96, no. 4 (Oct. 1991): 1073–1100.

7. Lucian W. Pye, *Warlord Politics: Conflict and Coalition in the Modernization of Republican China* (New York: Praeger, 1971).

8. Akbar S. Ahmed, *Social and Economic Change in the Tribal Areas, 1972–1976* (New York: Oxford University Press, 1977), 22.

9. Max Weber uses the term "warlord" to describe a typical charismatic relationship. Weber, *Economy and Society: An Outline of Interpretive Sociology, vol. 1*, ed. Guenther Roth and Claus Wittich (Berkeley: University of California Press, 1978), 241–45.

10. William Reno, *Warlord Politics and African States* (Boulder: Lynne Rienner, 1998).

11. Antonio Giustozzi, *The Debate on Warlordism: The Importance of Military Legitimacy*, Discussion Paper 13 (London: London School of Economics Crisis States Development Research Centre, 2005), 1–2.

12. Tom Coghlan, "Fearless Female Warlord Now Has UN in Her Sights," *Daily Telegraph*, February 18, 2006, http://www.telegraph.co.uk/; and Matt Dupee, "Taliban 'Shadow' Governor Slain; Female Warlord Surrenders," *Long War Journal*, July 11, 2008, http://www.longwarjournal.org/.

13. Diego Gambetta, *The Sicilian Mafia: The Business of Private Protection* (Cambridge: Harvard University Press, 1996).

14. Sudhir Venkatesh describes a social system in a set of housing projects on the south side of Chicago that replicates warlordism. Venkatesh, *Gang Leader for a Day: A Rogue Sociologist Takes to the Streets* (New York: Penguin, 2008).

15. Stephen D. Krasner divides the definition of sovereignty into four types, two of which are domestic sovereignty and international legal sovereignty. Krasner, *Sovereignty: Organized Hypocrisy* (Princeton: Princeton University Press, 1999). Some neoclassical realists recognize that domestic and international legal sovereignty do not always equate; see "Introduction," in *Neoclassical Realism, the State and Foreign Policy*, ed. Jeffrey W. Taliaferro, Steven E. Lobell, and Norrin M. Ripsman (New York: Cambridge University Press, 2009), 25.

16. Max Weber, "The Profession and Vocation of Politics," in *Weber: Political Writings*, ed. Peter Lassman and Ronald Speirs (New York: Cambridge University Press, 1994), 310–12. Also see "The Types of Legitimate Domination," chapter 3 in Weber, *Economy and Society: An Outline of Interpretive Sociology, vol. 1*, 212–301.

17. For seminal scholarly discussions of state weakness in Africa, see Robert H. Jackson and Carl G. Rosberg, "Why Africa's Weak States Persist: The Empirical and the Juridical in Statehood," *World Politics* 35, no. 1 (October 1982): 1–24; Crawford Young, "The African Colonial State and Its Political Legacy," in *The Precarious Balance: State and Society in Africa*, ed. Donald Rothchild and Naomi Chazan (Boulder: Westview, 1988), 25–66; Robert H. Jackson, *Quasi-states: Sovereignty, International Relations and the Third World* (New York: Cambridge University Press, 1993); and Jeffrey Herbst, *States and Power in Africa: Comparative Lessons in Authority and Control* (Princeton: Princeton University Press, 2000).

18. Allen Hicken, "Clientelism," *Annual Review of Political Science* 14 (2011), 302–3.

19. Harrison Wagner, *War and the State: The Theory of International Politics* (Ann Arbor: University of Michigan Press, 2007); Douglass C. North, John Joseph Wallis, and Barry R. Weingast, *Violence and Social Orders: A Conceptual Framework for Interpreting Recorded Human History* (New York: Cambridge University Press, 2009).

20. For example, the Republic of Bashkortostan in Russia. See Ildar Gabdrafikov and Henry E. Hale, "Bashkortostan's Democratic Moment? Patronal Presidentialism, Regional Regime Change, and Identity in Russia," in *Reconstruction and Interaction of Slavic Eurasia and Its Neighboring Worlds*, ed. Osamu Ieda and Uyama Tomoshiko (Sapporo, Japan: Hokkaido University Slavic Research Center, 2006), 75–102; and Ellen Barry, "Russia Strongman to Retire as Kremlin Replaces Regional Leaders," *New York Times*, July 14, 2010.

21. Gambetta, *Sicilian Mafia*, 2.

22. This is based on Weber's definition of charismatic authority. Weber, *Economy and Society, vol. 1*, 241–45.

23. This was part of Weber's definition of "charismatic" leadership. See S. N. Eisenstadt, *Max Weber: On Charisma and Institution Building* (Chicago: University of Chicago Press, 1968).

24. Stathis N. Kalyvas, in his otherwise careful study of new and old civil wars, conflates rebels who loot for a cause with warlords who loot for personal gain. See "'New' and 'Old' Civil Wars: A Valid Distinction?," *World Politics* 54, no. 1 (October 2001): 99–118, especially p. 105.

25. John MacKinlay, "Defining Warlords," in *Peacekeeping and Conflict Resolution*, ed. Tom Woodhouse and Oliver Ramsbotham (London: Frank Cass, 2000), 48–62; Gordon Peake, "From Warlords to Peacelords?," *Journal of International Affairs* 56, no. 2 (Spring 2003): 181–91; Sasha Lezhnev, *Crafting Peace: Strategies to Deal with Warlords in Collapsing States* (Lanham, MD: Lexington Books, 2005); and Giustozzi, "Debate on Warlordism." Mary Kaldor, *New and Old Wars: Organized Violence in a Global Era*, 2nd ed. (Stanford: Stanford University Press, 2007), does not use the term "warlord," but her definition of "new wars" argues that the non-state actors who fight them will be predatory in a way that differs from the insurgents of old.

26. Reno, *Warlord Politics and African States*; Reno, "Mafiya Troubles, Warlord Crises," in *Beyond State Crisis? Postcolonial Africa and Post-Soviet Eurasia in Comparative Perspective*, ed. Mark R. Beissinger and Crawford Young (Baltimore: Johns Hopkins University Press, 2002), 105–28.

27. James E. Sheridan, *China in Disintegration: The Republican Era in Chinese History, 1912–1949* (New York: Free Press, 1975).

28. Mancur Olson, "Dictatorship, Democracy, and Development," *American Political Science Review* 87, no. 3 (September 1993): 567–76.

29. Antonio Giustozzi, "War and Peace Economies of Afghanistan's Strongmen," *International Peacekeeping* 14, no. 1 (January 2007): 75–89, argues that what he calls "warlords" can evolve into what he calls "strongmen" over time, with the distinction being based on the degree of social legitimacy exercised. Also see Paul Jackson, "Warlords as Alternative Forms of Governance," *Small Wars and Insurgencies* 14, no. 2 (Summer 2003): 131–50; and Ken Menkhaus, "Local Security Systems in Somali East Africa," in *Fragile States and Insecure People? Violence, Security, and Statehood in the Twenty-First Century*, ed. Louise Andersen, Bjørn Møller, and Finn Stepputat (New York: Palgrave/Macmillan, 2007), 67–97.

30. "State failure" is a poorly defined concept across a large and disparate literature, but for my purposes here I will use it to mean the failure to establish domestic sovereignty. For a review of the concept of state failure, see Kimberly Marten, "Failing States and Conflict," in *The International Studies Encyclopedia, vol. 4*, ed. Robert A. Denemark (Hoboken, NJ: Wiley-Blackwell, 2010), 2012–22.

31. For examples of this argument, see Gambetta, *Sicilian Mafia*; Phil Williams, ed., *Russian Organized Crime: The New Threat?* (London: Frank Cass, 1997); and Vadim Volkov, *Violent Entrepreneurs: The Use of Force in the Making of Russian Capitalism* (Ithaca: Cornell University Press, 2002).

32. For a discussion of this phenomenon in Sicily, see Gambetta, *Sicilian Mafia*, 34–52. This phenomenon is apparent in Afghanistan as well; see Giustozzi, "War and Peace Economies of Afghanistan's Strongmen."

33. Dexter Filkins, "With U.S. Aid, Warlord Builds Afghan Empire," *New York Times*, June 6, 2010.

34. Dexter Filkins, "U.S. Said to Fund Afghan Warlords to Protect Convoys," *New York Times*, June 21, 2010.

35. Samuel P. Huntington, *Political Order in Changing Societies* (New Haven: Yale University Press, 1968), 18, citing Aristotle's *Politics*.

36. See Daniel H. Nexon, *The Struggle for Power in Early Modern Europe: Religious Conflict, Dynastic Empires and International Change* (Princeton: Princeton University Press, 2009), 43–48. Nexon notes that the patronage networks of early modern Europe were challenged and disrupted frequently, and that the stability they offered was therefore temporary at best.

37. Sheridan, *China in Disintegration*, 12–16.

38. Report of the Senate Armed Services Committee, *Inquiry into the Role and Oversight of Private Security Contractors in Afghanistan*, 111th Congress, 2nd Session, September 28, 2010, http://info.publicintelligence.net/SASC-PSC-Report.pdf.

39. This logic derives from Olson, "Dictatorship, Democracy, and Development." For an application of this argument to a different set of issues, see Kimberly Marten Zisk, *Weapons, Culture, and Self-Interest: Soviet Defense Managers in the New Russia* (New York: Columbia University Press, 1997). For a case-by-case application to various examples of warlordism, see Marten, "Warlordism in Comparative Perspective."

40. Robert Axelrod, *The Evolution of Cooperation* (New York: Basic Books, 1984).

41. Gambetta, *Sicilian Mafia*, 22–24.

42. Pye, *Warlord Politics*, 54; Sheridan, *China in Disintegration*, 78–79.

43. Huntington, *Political Order in Changing Societies*.

44. See Allen W. Johnson and Timothy Earle, *The Evolution of Human Societies: From Foraging Group to Agrarian State* (Stanford: Stanford University Press, 1987).

45. Hendrik Spruyt, *The Sovereign State and Its Competitors* (Princeton: Princeton University Press, 1994). Spruyt argues that long-distance traders of bulky, hard-to-protect goods were most likely to take political action against arbitrary feudal rule in the medieval era.

46. Peter D. Little, *Somalia: Economy without State* (Bloomington: Indiana University Press, 2003).

47. Douglass C. North and Robert Paul Thomas, *The Rise of the Western World: A New Economic History* (New York: Cambridge University Press, 1973).

48. Paul Collier, V. L. Elliott, Håvard Hegre, Anke Hoeffler, Marta Reynal-Querol, and Nicholas Sambanis, *Breaking the Conflict Trap* (Washington: World Bank, 2003).

49. Huntington, *Political Order in Changing Societies*, 21.

50. Reno, *Warlord Politics and African States*; Giustozzi, "War and Peace Economies of Afghanistan's Strongmen"; Charles King, "The Benefits of Ethnic War: Understanding Eurasia's Unrecognized States," *World Politics* 53, no. 4 (July 2001): 524–52; Peter Andreas, *Blue Helmets and Black Markets: The Business of Survival in the Siege of Sarajevo* (New York: Cornell University Press, 2008).

51. Krasner, *Sovereignty*.

52. David A. Lake, *Hierarchy in International Relations* (Ithaca: Cornell University Press, 2009).

53. Alexander Cooley and Hendrik Spruyt, *Contracting States: Sovereign Transfers in International Relations* (Princeton: Princeton University Press, 2009).

54. Joel S. Migdal, *State in Society: Studying How States and Societies Transform and Constitute One Another* (New York: Cambridge University Press, 2001); Catherine

Boone, "States and Ruling Classes in Postcolonial Africa: The Enduring Contradictions of Power," in *State Power and Social Forces: Domination and Transformation in the Third World*, ed. Joel S. Migdal, Atul Kohli, and Vivienne Shue (New York: Cambridge University Press, 1994), 108–40.

55. Krasner, *Sovereignty*, 7.

56. Joel S. Migdal, "The State in Society: An Approach to Struggles for Domination," in *State Power and Social Forces*, ed. Migdal, Kohli, and Shue, 13–14.

57. For the view that many African "tribal chiefs" were in fact themselves the product of colonialism, see Mahmood Mamdani, *Citizen and Subject: Contemporary Africa and the Legacy of Late Colonialism* (Princeton: Princeton University Press, 1986).

58. Karen Barkey, *Bandits and Bureaucrats: The Ottoman Route to State Centralization* (New York: Cornell University Press, 1994).

59. Karen Barkey, *Empire of Difference: The Ottomans in Comparative Perspective* (New York: Cambridge University Press, 2008).

60. Nexon, *Struggle for Power in Early Modern Europe*, mentions "violence-wielding patrons" and "warlords" on p. 41.

61. Examples include A. S. Kanya-Forstner, *Conquest of the Western Sudan: A Study in French Military Imperialism* (London: Cambridge University Press, 1969); Anthony Clayton, *The British Empire as a Superpower, 1919–39* (London: Macmillan, 1986); Brian McAllister Linn, *Guardians of Empire: The U.S. Army and the Pacific, 1902–1940* (Chapel Hill: University of North Carolina Press, 1997); Linn, "Cerberus' Dilemma: The U.S. Army and Internal Security in the Pacific, 1902–1940," in *Guardians of Empire: The Armed Forces of the Colonial Powers, c. 1700–1964*, ed. David Kilingray and David E. Omissi (New York: Manchester University Press, 1999), 114–36; Philip D. Curtin, *The World and The West: The European Challenge and the Overseas Response in the Age of Empire* (New York: Cambridge University Press, 2000); and Moshe Gershovich, *French Military Rule in Morocco: Colonialism and its Consequences* (London: Frank Cass, 2000).

62. For example "Taylorland" under warlord Charles Taylor occasionally included chunks of neighboring states, in addition to most of Liberia. Reno, *Warlord Politics*, 92.

63. Charles Tilly, "Reflections on the History of European State-Making," in *The Formation of National States in Western Europe*, ed. Charles Tilly (Princeton: Princeton University Press, 1975), 23–24.

64. James C. Scott, *The Art of Not Being Governed: An Anarchist History of Upland Southeast Asia* (New Haven: Yale University Press, 2009).

65. Thomas Hobbes, *Leviathan* (New York: Oxford University Press, 2008), 84. First published 1651.

66. Daniel Benjamin and Steven Simon, *The Age of Sacred Terror: Radical Islam's War against America* (New York: Random House, 2002).

67. Ken Menkhaus and Jacob N. Shapiro, "Non-State Actors and Failed States: Lessons from Al-Qa'ida's Experiences in the Horn of Africa," in *Ungoverned Spaces*, ed. Clunan and Trinkunas, 77–94.

68. I have attempted to follow the theory development and process-tracing path originally set by Alexander George. See Alexander L. George and Andrew Bennett, *Case Studies and Theory Development in the Social Sciences* (Cambridge: MIT Press, 2004).

69. Analysts often refer to Ramzan Kadyrov by his first name. I will follow that practice here to distinguish him from his father, Akhmad Kadyrov.

2. Warlords and Universal Sovereignty

1. Douglass C. North, *Institutions, Institutional Change, and Economic Performance* (New York: Cambridge University Press, 1990).

2. Guenther Roth, "Personal Rulership, Patrimonialism, and Empire-Building in the New States," *World Politics* 20, no. 2 (January 1968): 194–206; and Georgi M. Derluguian, *Bourdieu's Secret Admirer in the Caucasus: A World-System Biography* (Chicago: University of Chicago Press, 2005).

3. Harrison Wagner, *War and the State: The Theory of International Politics* (Ann Arbor: University of Michigan Press, 2007); Douglass C. North, John Joseph Wallis, and Barry R. Weingast, *Violence and Social Orders: A Conceptual Framework for Interpreting Recorded Human History* (New York: Cambridge University Press, 2009).

4. Michael Mousseau, "Market Prosperity, Democratic Consolidation, and Democratic Peace," *Journal of Conflict Resolution* 44, no. 4 (August 2000): 472–507; Mousseau, "Market Civilization and Its Clash with Terror," *International Security* 27, no. 3 (Winter 2002–2003): 5–29; and Mousseau, "The Social Market Roots of Democratic Peace," *International Security* 33, no. 4 (Spring 2009): 52–86.

5. North, Wallis, and Weingast, *Violence and Social Orders*.

6. Charles Tilly, "War Making and State Making as Organized Crime," in *Bringing the State Back In*, ed. Peter B. Evans, Dietrich Rueschemeyer and Theda Skocpol (New York: Cambridge University Press, 1985), 169–91.

7. Charles Tilly, "Reflections on the History of European State-Making," in *The Formation of National States in Western Europe*, ed. Charles Tilly (Princeton: Princeton University Press, 1975), 3–83.

8. Kimberly Marten, "Warlordism in Comparative Perspective," *International Security* 31, no. 3 (Winter 2006/2007): 41–73.

9. James C. Scott, *The Art of Not Being Governed: An Anarchist History of Upland Southeast Asia* (New Haven: Yale University Press, 2009).

10. Norbert Elias, *The Civilizing Process: Sociogenic and Psychogenetic Investigations*, rev. ed. (Malden, MA: Blackwell, 2000), 185–362.

11. Hendrik Spruyt, *The Sovereign State and Its Competitors* (Princeton: Princeton University Press, 1994).

12. Elias, *The Civilizing Process*, 236.

13. Saskia Sassen, *Territory, Authority, Rights: From Medieval to Global Assemblages*, updated ed. (New York: Princeton University Press, 2006).

14. Joseph R. Strayer, *On the Medieval Origins of the Modern State* (Princeton: Princeton University Press, 1970); and Gianfranco Poggi, *The Development of the Modern State: A Sociological Introduction* (Stanford: Stanford University Press, 1978), 19–21.

15. Jan Glete, *War and the State in Early Modern Europe: Spain, the Dutch Republic and Sweden as Fiscal-Military States, 1500–1660* (New York: Routledge, 2002).

16. James B. Collins, *The State in Early Modern France*, 2nd ed. (New York: Cambridge University Press, 2009), 10–20.

17. Elias, *The Civilizing Process*, 192, 205, 235.

18. Ibid., 263–64.

19. Spruyt, *Sovereign State and Its Competitors*, 77–79.

20. Robert Jackson, *Sovereignty* (Malden, MA: Polity, 2007), 49–50.

21. Sassen, *Territory, Authority, Rights*, 87.

22. Julia Adams, *The Familial State: Ruling Families and Merchant Capitalism in Early Modern Europe* (Ithaca: Cornell University Press, 2005), 14–15.

23. While Spruyt, *Sovereign State and Its Competitors*, and Adams, *Familial State*, both emphasize alliances made with merchants, Collins, *State in Early Modern France*, and Sassen, *Territory, Authority, Rights*, note that kings also incorporated the nobility into political alliances in France in particular.

24. Alan Harding, *Medieval Law and the Foundations of the State* (New York: Oxford University Press, 2002), 222; Adams, *Familial State*, 16.

25. Samuel E. Finer, "State- and Nation-Building in Europe: The Role of the Military," in *The Formation of National States in Western Europe*, ed. Charles Tilly (Princeton: Princeton University Press, 1975), 84–163. Also see Martin van Creveld, *The Rise and Decline of the State* (New York: Cambridge University Press, 1999), 59–125.

26. Sassen, *Territory, Authority, Rights*, while not using the term "warlord," describes this as being the historical process that occurred. This is consonant with Tilly's arguments about the co-development of war-fighting capabilities and capitalism; see Tilly, *Coercion, Capital, and European States, AD 990–1992* (Malden, MA: Blackwell, 1992).

27. Glete, *War and the State in Early Modern Europe*.

28. Jeffrey Herbst, "Responding to State Failure in Africa," *International Security* 21, no. 3 (Winter 1996/1997): 120–44, suggests that statehood may be an inappropriate institution for sub-Saharan Africa. No one, however, has proposed a workable alternative. An additional call for alternatives to statehood is made by *Ungoverned Spaces: Alternatives to State Authority in an Era of Softened Sovereignty*, ed. Anne L. Clunan and Harold A. Trinkunas (Stanford: Stanford University Press, 2010), but the volume does more to describe stateless territories than to advocate alternatives to statehood.

29. Scott, *Art of Not Being Governed*, 11.

30. Robert H. Jackson and Carl G. Rosberg, "Why Africa's Weak States Persist: The Empirical and the Juridical in Statehood," *World Politics* 35, no. 1 (October 1982): 1–24; Tanisha M. Fazal, *State Death: The Politics and Geography of Conquest, Occupation, and Annexation* (New York: Princeton University Press, 2007).

31. Parag Khanna, "Future Shock? Welcome to the Coming Middle Ages," *Financial Times*, December 28, 2010.

32. For historical examples, see Mary Backus Rankin's description of Republican-era Chinese warlords, in "State and Society in Early Republican Politics, 1912–18," *China Quarterly*, no. 150 (June 1997), 270; Antonio Giustozzi's description of post-2001 Afghanistan, in "War and Peace Economies of Afghanistan's Strongmen," *International Peacekeeping* 14, no. 1 (January 2007): 75–89; and, in regard to Emzar Kvitsiani of the Kodori Gorge in Abkhazia discussed later in this book, Mikheil Saakashvili, "Georgian President Promises to Crush Rebel Militia Leader," interview on Imedi TV (Tbilisi), July 24, 2006, as reported by the BBC News Worldwide Monitoring News Service.

33. For the argument that it might, see Sheri Berman, "From the Sun King to Karzai: Lessons for State Building in Afghanistan," *Foreign Affairs* 89, no. 2 (March/April 2010): 2–9.

34. Reno, *Warlord Politics and African States*, 79–111.

35. See Lloyd E. Eastman, "Nationalist China during the Nanking Decade, 1927–1937," in *The Nationalist Era in China, 1927–1949*, Eastman et al. (New York: Cambridge University Press, 1991), 8–11, and Ramon H. Myers, "The Chinese State During the Republican Era," in *The Modern Chinese State*, ed. David Shambaugh (New York: Cambridge University Press, 2000): 42–72.

36. For a literature review on the concepts of authority and governance, see Deborah D. Avant, Martha Finnemore, and Susan K. Sell, "Who Governs the Globe?" in *Who Governs the Globe?*, ed. Avant, Finnemore and Sell (New York: Cambridge, 2010), 1–31. Also see David A. Lake, "Rightful Rules: Authority, Order, and the Foundations of Global Governance," *International Studies Quarterly* 54 (September 2010): 587–613.

37. Vadim Volkov, *Violent Entrepreneurs: The Use of Force in the Making of Russian Capitalism* (Ithaca: Cornell University Press, 2002).

38. Dipali Mukhopadhyay, *Warlords as Bureaucrats: The Afghan Experience*, Carnegie Papers 101 (Washington: Carnegie Endowment for International Peace, August 2009).

39. Dipali Mukhopadhyay, "Disguised Warlordism and Combatanthood in Balkh: The Persistence of Informal Power in the Formal Afghan State," *Conflict, Security and Development* 9, no. 4 (December 2009): 535–64.

40. Carlotta Gall, "In Afghanistan's North, Ex-Warlord Offers Security," *New York Times*, May 17, 2010.

41. Institute for War and Peace Reporting, "Warlords Reemerging in North," December 17, 2009, "Crime Wave Alarms Balkh Residents," June 3, 2010, " 'Rogue Police' Reports in Afghan North," March 8, 2011, and "Afghan Police Criticized Over Mazar-e Sharif Violence," April 14, 2011, http://www.unhcr.org/refworld/.

42. Adam Pain, *Opium Poppy Strikes Back: The 2011 Return of Opium in Balkh and Badakhshan Provinces* (Kabul: Afghanistan Research and Evaluation Unit, July 2011).

43. Ken Menkhaus, "Governance without Government in Somalia: Spoilers, State Building, and the Politics of Coping," *International Security* 31, no. 3 (Winter 2006/2007), 91–93; Mark Bradbury, *Becoming Somaliland: Reconstructing a Failed State* (Bloomington: Indiana University Press, 2008), 94–95.

44. Edgar O'Ballance, *The Red Army of China* (New York: Praeger, 1962), 57–63; and Gregor Benton, *New Fourth Army: Communist Resistance along the Yangtze and the Huai, 1938–41* (Berkeley: University of California Press, 2000), 42–72.

45. Charles Tilly, "Reflections on the History of European State-Making," in *The Formation of National States in Western Europe*, ed. Charles Tilly (Princeton: Princeton University Press, 1975), 3–83.

46. The first prominent work that argued that quasi-states were protected by the international system from existential warfare was Robert H. Jackson and Carl G. Rosberg, "Why Africa's Weak States Persist: The Empirical and the Juridical in Statehood," *World Politics* 35, no. 1 (October 1982): 1–24. Also see Robert H. Jackson, *Quasi-states: Sovereignty, International Relations and the Third World* (New York: Cambridge University Press, 1990); and Jeffrey Herbst, *States and Power in Africa: Comparative Lessons in Authority and Control* (Princeton: Princeton University Press, 2000), especially pp. 114–15.

47. The concept of the rentier state was first proposed by Hossein Mahdavy, "Patterns and Problems of Economic Development in Rentier States: The Case of Iran," in *Studies in Economic History of the Middle East*, ed. M. A. Cook (London: Oxford

University Press, 1970), 428–67, and was developed by Terry Lynn Karl, *The Paradox of Plenty: Oil Booms and Petro-States* (Berkeley: University of California Press, 1997).

48. Tilly, "War Making and State Making as Organized Crime," 172.

49. The model is developed by Deborah Avant, *The Market for Force: The Consequences of Privatizing Security* (New York: Cambridge University Press, 2005).

50. Stathis N. Kalyvas, *The Logic of Violence in Civil War* (New York: Cambridge University Press, 2006), 173–209.

3. Ungoverned Warlords: Pakistan's FATA in the Twentieth Century

1. The NWFP was renamed Khyber Pakhtunkhwa in April 2010. Because this chapter focuses on historical events, the NWFP name will be retained throughout.

2. Remarks by Ahmed Rashid to the United States Institute of Peace Afghanistan Working Group, "Sanctuary? The Afghanistan-Pakistan Border and Insurgency in the 1980s, 90s and Today," Washington, DC, Dec. 7, 2007, audio recording available at http://www.usip.org/.

3. J. Michael McConnell, *Annual Threat Assessment of the Intelligence Community for the Senate Armed Services Committee*, SASC ATA 2008-IC Statement for the Record, February 27, 2008, http://www.dni.gov/testimonies/20080227_testimony.pdf.

4. Anwar Iqbal, "Bush Calls Fata Most Dangerous Region," *Dawn* (Pakistan), April 13, 2008; Iqbal, "New 9/11 to Come from Fata: U.S. General," *Dawn*, May 23, 2008; Petraeus's testimony is available for streaming at www.youtube.com, "Petraeus Says Greatest Threat to U.S. Comes from Pakistan," C-SPAN 3.

5. Max Weber, "The Profession and Vocation of Politics," in *Weber: Political Writings*, ed. Peter Lassman and Ronald Speirs (New York: Cambridge University Press, 1994), 313–14. Akbar S. Ahmed argued in 1980 that the Pashtun tribal code made Weber's "charismatic leadership" label inappropriate. See Ahmed, *Pukhtun Economy and Society: Traditional Structure and Economic Development in a Tribal Society* (Boston: Routledge & Keegan Paul, 1980), 96.

6. International Crisis Group, "Pakistan: Countering Militancy in FATA," Asia Report no. 178 (October 21, 2009), 4 http://www.crisisgroup.org.

7. Alexander L. George and Andrew Bennett, *Case Studies and Theory Development in the Social Sciences* (Cambridge: MIT Press, 2005), 86.

8. Allen Hicken, "Clientelism," *Annual Review of Political Science* 14 (2011), 299–300.

9. Samuel P. Huntington, *Political Order in Changing Societies* (New Haven: Yale University Press, 1968).

10. "Pashtun" and "Pukhtun" are equivalent words for the ethnic group in question, reflecting the southern and northern pronunciation respectively. I have chosen "Pashtun" because it is the more familiar term for today's US readership, given its frequent use in news articles on Afghanistan. British imperial authorities incorrectly used the offensive term "Pathan" to refer to this ethnic group.

11. Ahmed Rashid, *Taliban: Militant Islam, Oil and Fundamentalism in Central Asia* (New Haven: Yale, 2000), esp. pp. 84–94; Mariam Abou Zahab and Olivier Roy, *Islamist Networks: The Afghan-Pakistan Connection*, trans. John King (New York: Columbia University Press, 2004), 69–70; Zahid Hussain, *Frontline Pakistan: The Struggle with Militant Islam* (New York: Columbia University Press, 2007); Thomas H. Johnson

and M. Chris Mason, "Understanding the Taliban and Insurgency in Afghanistan," *Orbis* 52, no. 1 (Winter 2007): 71–89; Thomas H. Johnson and M. Chris Mason, "No Sign until the Burst of Fire: Understanding the Pakistan-Afghanistan Frontier," *International Security* 32, no. 4 (Spring 2008): 41–77; and Ty L. Groh, "A Fortress without Walls: Alternative Governance Structures on the Afghan-Pakistan Frontier," in *Ungoverned Spaces: Alternatives to State Authority in an Era of Softened Sovereignty*, ed. Anne L. Clunan and Harold A. Trinkunas (Stanford, CA: Stanford University Press, 2010), 95–112. Some anthropologists avoid using the word "tribe" because it can appear condescending, and because it was British imperial authorities who first used the term to classify the Pashtuns. No condescension is intended here. The term accurately captures the predominant segmentary agnatic kinship social structure of the Pashtuns, which long predated the British and continues to influence the politics and culture of the geographic area today. Pashtun elites accepted and made advantageous use of the British terminology from the colonial era onward, and hence it would be naïve to view the classification as a unilateral imperial imposition. See Sana Haroon, *Frontier of Faith: Islam in the Indo-Afghan Borderland* (New York: Columbia University Press, 2007), 25–30; and Paul Titus, "Honor the Baluch, Buy the Pushtun: Stereotypes, Social Organization and History in Western Pakistan," *Modern Asian Studies* 32, no. 3 (July 1998): 657–87.

12. The Haqqani family fits the definition of tribal warlords. See Joshua Partlow, "Haqqani Insurgent Group Proves Resilient Foe in Afghan War," *Washington Post*, May 31, 2011.

13. Salman Masood, "Pakistan Lifts Longtime Ban on Political Activities in Restive Tribal Areas," *New York Times*, Aug. 15, 2009.

14. International Crisis Group, "Pakistan: Countering Militancy," 5.

15. Akbar S. Ahmed, *Religion and Politics in Muslim Society: Order and Conflict in Pakistan* (New York: Cambridge University Press, 1983), 7–8; Stephen Alan Rittenberg, *Ethnicity, Nationalism, and the Pakhtuns: The Independence Movement in India's North-West Frontier Province* (Durham, NC: Carolina Academic Press, 1988); and Onam-ur-Rahim and Alain Viaro, *Swat: An Afghan Society in Pakistan* (Karachi: City Press, 2002).

16. Warren Swidler, "Economic Change in Baluchistan: Processes of Integration into the Larger Economy of Pakistan," in *Pakistan's Western Borderlands: The Transformation of a Political Order*, ed. Ainslie T. Embree (Durham, NC: Carolina Academic Press, 1977), 85–108; Noor al Haq, "Northwest Tribal Belt of Pakistan," in *Federally Administered Tribal Areas of Pakistan*, Islamabad Policy Research Institute Paper 10 (Islamabad: IPRI, 2005), 12.

17. Rittenberg, *Ethnicity, Nationalism, and the Pakhtuns*, 31–33.

18. Ibid., 43–46.

19. Onam-ur-Rahim and Viaro, *Swat*, 177.

20. Akbar S. Ahmed, *Social and Economic Change in the Tribal Areas, 1972–1976* (New York: Oxford University Press, 1977), 22; Onam-ur-Rahim and Viaro, *Swat*, 105–7.

21. Lal Baha, *N.W.F.P. Administration under British Rule, 1901–1919* (Islamabad: National Commission on Historical and Cultural Research, 1978), 143, 160.

22. For a discussion of institutional reforms in the PATA over time, see Joshua T. White, "The Shape of Frontier Rule: Governance and Transition, from the Raj to the Modern Pakistani Frontier," *Asian Security* 4, no. 3 (2008): 219–43.

23. Robert LaPorte Jr., "Urban Groups and the Zia Regime," *in Zia's Pakistan: Politics and Stability in a Frontline State*, ed. Craig Baxter (Boulder: Westview, 1985), 8.

24. Ahmed, *Pukhtun Economy and Society*, 119–41. Also see David M. Hart, *Guardians of the Khaibar Pass: The Social Organization and History of the Afridis of Pakistan* (Lahore: Vanguard, 1985), 15–16.

25. Hart, *Guardians of the Khaibar Pass*, 70–72.

26. Onam-ur-Rahim and Viaro, *Swat*, 102.

27. Ahmed, *Religion and Politics in Muslim Society*, 27.

28. Benedicte Grima, *Secrets from the Field: An Ethnographer's Notes from North Western Pakistan* (Bloomington, IN: Author House, 2004), 42–43.

29. Ahmed, *Pukhtun Economy and Society*, 5.

30. Onam-ur-Rahim and Viaro, *Swat*, 103.

31. Titus, "Honor the Baluch, Buy the Pushtun," 669.

32. Shahid Javed Burki, "What Migration to the Middle East May Mean for Pakistan," *Journal of South Asian and Middle Eastern Studies* 3, no. 3 (Spring 1980), 54; Jonathan S. Addleton, *Undermining the Centre: The Gulf Migration and Pakistan* (Karachi: Oxford University Press, 1992), 31–38.

33. C. G. P. Rakisits, "Centre-Province Relations in Pakistan under President Zia: The Government's and the Opposition's Approaches," *Pacific Affairs* 61, no. 1 (Spring 1988), 86; Titus, "Honor the Baluch, Buy the Pushtun," 674–77.

34. Baha, *N.W.F.P. Administration under British Rule*, 135–36; Ahmed, *Pukhtun Economy and Society*, 63.

35. Haroon, *Frontier of Faith*, 36–37, 67–68.

36. Ibid., 15–17.

37. D. Donald, "Notes on the Adam Khel Afridis (1901)," in *Colonial Reports on Pakistan's Frontier Tribal Areas*, ed. Robert Nichols (New York: Oxford, 2005), 66.

38. A beautiful display of this cultural tendency is found in the Enlightenment Gallery of the British Museum in London, where all sorts of items are labeled and categorized and placed into appropriate boxes and cases. See http://www.britishmuseum.org/explore/galleries/themes/room_1_enlightenment.aspx.

39. Baha, *N.W.F.P. Administration under British Rule*, 34; Haroon, *Frontier of Faith*, 27.

40. Ahmed, *Social and Economic Change in the Tribal Areas*, 47.

41. A detailed description of this history is provided by Baha, *N.W.F.P. Administration under British Rule*. What amounts to a restating of her research findings is provided by Noor al Haq, "Northwest Tribal Belt of Pakistan," in *Federally Administered Tribal Areas of Pakistan*, Islamabad Policy Research Institute Paper 10 (Islamabad: IPRI, 2005), 1–27.

42. Baha, *N.W.F.P. Administration under British Rule*, 100.

43. Ibid., 109, 127–31.

44. For examples of this, see ibid., 35–37.

45. Haroon, *Frontier of Faith*, 23.

46. Baha, *N.W.F.P. Administration under British Rule*, 38.

47. F. W. Johnston, "Notes on Wana (1903)," in *Colonial Reports on Pakistan's Frontier Tribal Areas*, ed. Robert Nichols (New York: Oxford, 2005), 47, 49.

48. Rittenberg, *Ethnicity, Nationalism, and the Pakhtuns*, 56–57.

49. This point is made well by Haroon, *Frontier of Faith*, 25–30.

50. Rashid Ahmad Khan, "Political Development in the FATA: A Critical Perspective," in *Tribal Areas of Pakistan: Challenges and Responses*, ed. Pervaiz Iqbal Cheema and Maqsudul Hasan Nuri (Islamabad: Islamabad Policy Research Institute, 2005), 27; C. Christine Fair and Peter Chalk, "Pakistan," in *Securing Tyrants or Fostering Reform? U.S. Internal Security Assistance to Repressive and Transitioning Regimes*, ed. Seth G. Jones, et al. (Santa Monica: RAND, 2006), 10–12; Naveed Ahmad Shinwari, *Understanding FATA: Attitudes towards Governance, Religion & Society in Pakistan's Federally Administered Tribal Areas* (Peshawar: Community Appraisal and Motivation Program, 2008), 3, http://www.understandingfata.org/.

51. Ahmed, *Pukhtun Economy and Society*, 146; Shinwari, *Understanding FATA*, 19.

52. Hart, *Guardians of the Khaibar Pass*, 141–43.

53. Maqsudul Hasan Nuri, "Federally Administered Tribal Areas (FATA): Pakistan's Post-9/11 Politico-Strategic Response," in *Federally Administered Tribal Areas of Pakistan*, IPRI, 59.

54. Shinwari, *Understanding FATA*, 17.

55. Khan, "Political Development in the FATA," 30; Imtiaz Gul, "FATA—A Futuristic View," in *Tribal Areas of Pakistan*, ed. Cheema and Nuri, 151.

56. Azmat Hayat Khan, "FATA," in *Tribal Areas of Pakistan*, ed. Cheema and Nuri, 96–97.

57. Mumtaz A. Bangash, "FATA: Towards a New Beginning," in *Tribal Areas of Pakistan*, ed. Cheema and Nuri, 63; Gul, "FATA—A Futuristic View," in ibid., 156.

58. Shinwari, *Understanding FATA*, 57.

59. Nuri, "Federally Administered Tribal Areas," 53.

60. Bangash, "FATA," 64; Ashfaq Yusufzai, "Pakistan: Sealing of Plaza Sparks Fight against Colonial Law," InterPressService (IPS) Newswire, April 10, 2008.

61. Fair and Chalk, "Pakistan," 156.

62. "Final Report: Gender Based Action Research Study 2003 on Initiating and Implementing Women and Children Development Program in FATA," prepared for the Khwendo Kor nongovernmental organization and submitted to the Canadian International Development Agency Pakistan Office, Islamabad, January 2006, 24–25.

63. Khan, "Political Development in the FATA," 41; Shinwari, *Understanding FATA*, 5.

64. Ahmed, *Pukhtun Economy and Society*, 143.

65. Ahmed, *Social and Economic Change in the Tribal Areas*, 49.

66. Shinwari, *Understanding FATA*, 73.

67. Ahmed, *Religion and Politics in Muslim Society*, 35.

68. Shinwari, *Understanding FATA*, 66.

69. International Crisis Group, "Pakistan: Countering Militancy," 15.

70. Ahmed, *Pukhtun Economy and Society*, 142–44.

71. Gul, "FATA—A Futuristic View," 153. Also see Shinwari, *Understanding FATA*, 1.

72. International Crisis Group, "Pakistan: Countering Militancy," 11.

73. Ahmed notes that road-building efforts were met with force in the 1930s, in *Pukhtun Economy and Society*, 339.

74. Selig S. Harrison, "Nightmare in Baluchistan," *Foreign Policy* 32 (Autumn 1978), 151–54.

75. Rashid Ahmed Khan, "FATA after Independence: 1947–2001," in Noor ul Haq, Rashid Ahmed Khan, and Maqsudul Hasan Nuri, *Federally Administered Tribal Areas of Pakistan*, Islamabad Policy Research Institute Paper 10 (March 2005): 35.

76. Khan, "Political Development in the FATA," 36.

77. Johnson and Mason, "No Sign until the Burst of Fire," 69.

78. Khan, "FATA after Independence," 39.

79. Khan, "Political Development in the FATA," 36.

80. Fazal-ur-rahim Marwat, "The Genesis of Change and Modernization in Federally Administered Tribal Areas (the FATA) of Pakistan," *Islamabad Policy Research Institute (IPRI) Journal* 7, no. 2 (Summer 2007), 75.

81. Ahmed, *Social and Economic Change in the Tribal Areas*, 9, 61.

82. Ibid., 3.

83. Ahmed, *Religion and Politics in Muslim Society*, 101; Charles H. Kennedy, "Rural Groups and the Stability of the Zia Regime," in *Zia's Pakistan*, ed. Baxter, 31.

84. Marwat, "The Genesis of Change and Modernization in the FATA," 75.

85. Ibid.

86. LaPorte, "Urban Groups and the Zia Regime," 15.

87. Khan, "Political Developments in the FATA," 37; Khan, "FATA after Independence," 39.

88. The author is grateful to C. Christine Fair for the suggestion that a comparison of these sources would be useful in answering this question.

89. Both the definitions of some terms and the polling methods used in the two census periods differed. In the 1972 version, the political agents provided population estimates and individuals were not polled; the 1981 version was the first time that individual households were queried. See *1981 Census Report of Federally Administered Tribal Areas (the FATA)* (Islamabad: Pakistan Population Census Organization Statistics Division, 1984), preface (no page number). In the 1972 report, "irrigated" areas were reported, in addition to "cultivated" areas; in the 1981 report there is no discussion of "irrigated" areas, so no comparison of agricultural development assistance effects is possible. Also, there were some changes in district designations between the two reports.

90. "FATA: Socio Economic Indicators," table, available at the FATA Secretariat website, http://fata.gov.pk/.

91. Ahmed, *Religion and Politics in Muslim Society*, 101. This statement is repeated almost word for word in Marwat, "The Genesis of Change and Modernization in the FATA," 75.

92. Haider Zaman, "Problems of Education, Health and Infrastructure in FATA," in *Tribal Areas of Pakistan*, ed. Cheema and Nuri, 73.

93. International Crisis Group, "Pakistan: Countering Militancy," 16.

94. Shinwari, *Understanding FATA*, 1.

95. Zaman, "Problems of Education, Health and Infrastructure in FATA," 86–87.

96. Khan, "FATA after Independence," 33–34.

97. Bangash, "FATA," 43–69; Mumtaz Alvi, "Fata Legislators May Demand Provincial Status," *The News* (Pakistan), April 4, 2008; Sohail Khan, "Abolition of 10 Clauses of FCR Suggested," *The News*, April 10, 2008; White, "The Shape of Frontier Rule."

98. Johnson and Mason, "Understanding the Taliban," 80; Johnson and Mason, "No Sign until the Burst of Fire," 41–77.

99. Ahmed, *Pukhtun Economy and Society*, 106–14.

100. Rittenberg, *Ethnicity, Nationalism, and the Pakhtuns*, 10.

101. For useful discussions of Sufism, see Karen Armstrong, *A History of God: The 4,000-Year Quest of Judaism, Christianity and Islam* (New York: Ballantine Books, 1993), 225–35; Rashid, *Taliban*, 84, who talks about its moderating influence in historical Afghanistan; Ahmed, *Journey into Islam: The Crisis of Globalization* (Washington, DC: Brookings, 2007), 33; and William C. Chittick, John O. Voll, and Kazuo Ohtsuka, "Sufism: Sufi Thought and Practice," in *The Oxford Encyclopedia of the Islamic World*, ed. John L. Esposito (New York: Oxford University Press, 2009).

102. Haroon, *Frontier of Faith*, 33–66.

103. Ibid. 37, 71, 77.

104. Rittenberg, *Ethnicity, Nationalism, and the Pakhtuns*, 36–37.

105. Haroon, *Frontier of Faith*, 60–67.

106. Barbara Daly Metcalf, *Islamic Revival in British India: Deoband, 1860–1900* (Princeton: Princeton University Press, 1982), 100–111.

107. Metcalf, *Islamic Revival*. The Deobandi movement was related to the broader Islamist renewal movement that percolated throughout the nearby Ottoman Empire, which sought a return to Koranic roots to bring justice to ordinary people suffering under outside oppression. See Noah Feldman, *The Fall and Rise of the Islamic State* (New York: Princeton University Press, 2008).

108. Metcalf, *Islamic Revival*, 136.

109. Haroon, *Frontier of Faith*, 39–48, 60–62, 66–67.

110. Jon W. Anderson, "Khan and Khel: Dialectics of Pakhtun Tribalism," in *The Conflict of Tribe and State in Iran and Afghanistan*, ed. Richard Tapper (New York: St. Martin's Press, 1983), 143–44.

111. Ahmed, *Pukhtun Economy and Society*, 167; Ahmed, *Religion and Politics in Muslim Society*, 26; Haroon, *Frontier of Faith*, 71.

112. Hart, *Guardians of the Khaibar Pass*, 89.

113. Haroon, *Frontier of Faith*, 67–68.

114. Ahmed, *Social and Economic Change in the Tribal Areas*, 50.

115. Addleton, *Undermining the Centre*, 45–47.

116. Zahid Hussain, *Frontline Pakistan: The Struggle with Militant Islam* (New York: Columbia University Press, 2007), 14–15.

117. Ahmed, *Religion and Politics in Muslim Society*, 49–87.

118. Hussain, *Frontline Pakistan*, 17–18; Fair and Chalk, *Fortifying Pakistan*, 24; Johnson and Mason, "No Sign until the Burst of Fire," 70.

119. Addleton, *Undermining the Centre*, 47.

120. Rodney W. Jones, "The Military and Security in Pakistan," in *Zia's Pakistan*, ed. Baxter, 78; Steve Coll, *Ghost Wars: The Secret History of the CIA, Afghanistan, and Bin Laden* (New York: Penguin, 2004), 61–62; Johnson and Mason, "No Sign until the Burst of Fire," 70.

121. Zahab and Roy, *Islamist Networks*, 22–27; Hussain, *Frontline Pakistan*, 77–78; Fair and Chalk, *Fortifying Pakistan*, 24.

122. Coll, *Ghost Wars*, 63–68, 89–106, 125–37, 149; Johnson and Mason, "No Sign until the Burst of Fire," 70–71.

123. Hussain, *Frontline Pakistan*, 80.

124. Marwat, "The Genesis of Change and Modernization in the FATA," 77.

125. Hussain, *Frontline Pakistan*, 85–86.

126. Shinwari, *Understanding FATA*, 41; Rashid, *Descent into Chaos*, 268.

127. Hussain, *Frontline Pakistan*, 78.

128. Khan, "Political Developments in the FATA," 39.

129. Marwat, "The Genesis of Change," 76.

130. Fair and Chalk, *Fortifying Pakistan*, 13; Hussain, *Frontline Pakistan*, 77–79; Ashley J. Tellis, "Pakistan—Conflicted Ally in the War on Terror," Carnegie Endowment for International Peace Policy Brief 56 (December 2007), 2.

131. Johnson and Mason, "Understanding the Taliban," 75.

132. Zahab and Roy, *Islamist Networks*, 13, 47.

133. Hussain, *Frontline Pakistan*, 78. Also see Rashid, *Taliban*, 89.

134. Marwat, "The Genesis of Change," 80–81.

135. Hussain, *Frontline Pakistan*, 78.

136. Daniel A. Kronenfeld, "Afghan Refugees in Pakistan," *Journal of Refugee Studies* 21, no. 1 (2008): 43–63.

137. Onam-ur-Rahim and Viaro, *Swat*, 7.

138. Grant M. Farr, "The Effect of the Afghan Refugees on Pakistan," in *Zia's Pakistan*, ed. Baxter, 95–96.

139. Farr, "The Effect of the Afghan Refugees," 98; Kronenfeld, "Afghan Refugees in Pakistan," 45.

140. Kronenfeld, "Afghan Refugees in Pakistan," 45–49, 54.

141. Farr, "Effect of the Afghan Refugees," 102, 103.

142. Kronenfeld, "Afghan Refugees in Pakistan," 52.

143. Rashid, *Taliban*, 86, 90, 184–93.

144. Asad Munir, "Waziristan Crisis," *The News*, May 27, 2006; International Crisis Group, "Pakistan: Countering Militancy," 10.

145. Nuri, "Federally Administered Tribal Areas," 50.

146. International Crisis Group, "Pakistan: Countering Militancy," 4.

147. Hussain, *Frontline Pakistan*, 77.

148. Gul, "FATA—A Futuristic View," 152; Haroon Rashid, "Vice-and-Virtue Battle in Khyber Valley," BBC News, Aug. 26, 2004, http://news.bbc.co.uk/; Ahmed Rashid, *Descent into Chaos: The United States and the Failure of Nation Building in Pakistan, Afghanistan and Central Asia* (New York: Viking, 2008), 249; Sami Yousafzai and Ron Moreau, "Where 'The Land Is on Fire,'" *Newsweek*, June 16, 2008.

149. Addleton, *Undermining the Centre*, 11–12. A large number of Pakistani laborers remained in the Persian Gulf in the first decade of the twenty-first century; see Syed Mohammed Ali, "Development: Protecting our Migrant Workforce," *Daily Times*, April 1, 2008. However, there is no hard data that is publicly available about their numbers or current economic impact, and certainly no study of how many are illegal migrants from the FATA.

150. Haris Gazdar, "A Review of Migration Issues in Pakistan," unpublished paper prepared for the Regional Conference on Migration, Development and Pro-Poor Policy Choices in Asia, June 2003, Dhaka, Bangladesh, 11, http://www.livelihoods.org/.

151. Shahid Javed Burki, "Pakistan's Sixth Plan: Helping the Country Climb out of Poverty," *Asian Survey* 24, no. 4 (April 1984), 417; Haris Gazdar, "A Review of Migration Issues in Pakistan," 10. The NWFP in particular had out-migration that appears to have been two to three times more a percentage of its population than the Pakistani average; see Addleton, *Undermining the Centre*, 89.

152. Addleton, *Undermining the Centre*, 52.

153. Marwat, "The Genesis of Change and Modernization in the FATA," 74.

154. Jonathan Addleton, "The Role of Migration in Development: Pakistan and the Gulf," *Fletcher Forum* 5, no. 2 (Summer 1981): 319–32; Rashid Amjad, "Impact of Workers' Remittances from the Middle East on Pakistan's Economy: Some Selected Issues," *Pakistan Development Review* 25, no. 4 (Winter 1986): 757–82; Shahnaz Kazi, "Domestic Impact of Remittances and Overseas Migration: Pakistan," Asian Regional Program on International Labor Migration Working Paper 7, RAS/85/009 (New Delhi: UN Development Program/International Labor Organization Asian Employment Program, 1988), 2.

155. Gazdar, "A Review of Migration Issues in Pakistan," 10.

156. Kennedy, "Rural Groups," 42.

157. Addleton, *Undermining the Centre*, 89–92.

158. Kazi, "Domestic Impact," 38–39; Onam-ur-Rahim and Viaro, *Swat*, 209.

159. Akbar S. Ahmed, "The Arab Connection: Emergent Models of Social Structure among Pakistani Tribesmen," *Asian Affairs* 12, no. 2 (June 1981), 168.

160. Burki, "What Migration to the Middle East May Mean," 49.

161. LaPorte, "Urban Groups and the Zia Regime," 18.

162. Addleton, *Undermining the Centre*, 138–50.

163. Kazi, "Domestic Impact," 10–11, 20–23; Addleton, *Undermining the Centre*, 195–99.

164. Addleton, *Undermining the Centre*, 171–72, 190.

165. Hart, *Guardians of the Khaibar Pass*, 91.

166. Gazdar, "A Review of Migration Issues in Pakistan," 6.

167. John Adams, "Pakistan's Economic Performance in the 1980s: Implications for Political Balance," in *Zia's Pakistan*, ed. Baxter, 59.

168. Addleton, *Undermining the Centre*, 195.

169. International Crisis Group, "Pakistan: Countering Militancy," 8.

170. Ahmed, "The Arab Connection," 168, 171.

171. Ahmed, *Religion and Politics in Muslim Society*, 100–101.

172. International Crisis Group, "Pakistan: Countering Militancy," 19–20.

173. Johnson and Mason, "No Sign until the Burst of Fire."

174. Ahmed, *Pukhtun Economy and Society*, 97–98.

175. Onam-ur-Rahim and Viaro, *Swat*, 165n20.

176. Hart, *Guardians of the Khaibar Pass*, 79.

177. Onam-ur-Rahim and Viaro, *Swat*, 123, 186.

178. Ahmed, *Pukhtun Economy and Society*, 122.

4. THE GEORGIAN EXPERIMENT WITH WARLORDS

1. For excellent descriptions of the nationalist militias, their origins, and their demise, see David Darchiashvili, "The Army-Building and Security Problems in Georgia," June 1997, http://www.nato.int/acad/fellow/95–97/darchais.pdf; Darchiashvili, "Georgian Defense Policy and Military Reform," in *Statehood and Security: Georgia after the Rose Revolution*, ed. Bruno Coppieters and Robert Legvold (Cambridge: MIT Press, 2005), 117–52; Darchiashvili, "Security Sector Reform in Georgia, 2004–2007," Caucasus Institute for Peace, Democracy and Development Paper, Tbilisi, 2008; and Christoph Zürcher, "Georgia's Time of Troubles, 1989–1993," in *Statehood and Security*, ed. Coppieters and Legvold, 83–116.

2. Kathleen Collins, "The Logic of Clan Politics: Evidence from the Central Asian Trajectories," *World Politics* 56, no. 2 (January 2004): 224–61.

3. Elizabeth Fuller, "Georgia," in *Nations in Transit 2009* (Budapest: Freedom House, 2009), 211–28.

4. Stephen D. Krasner, *Sovereignty: Organized Hypocrisy* (Princeton: Princeton University Press, 1999).

5. Georgi M. Derluguian, "The Tale of Two Resorts: Abkhazia and Ajaria Before and Since the Soviet Collapse," in *The Myth of 'Ethic Conflict': Politics, Economics, and 'Cultural' Violence*, ed. Beverly Crawford and Ronnie D. Lipshutz (Oakland, CA: University of California International and Area Studies Digital Collection, 1998), 263, 276–77.

6. Mathijs Pelkmans, *Defending the Border: Identity, Religion, and Modernity in the Republic of Georgia* (Ithaca: Cornell University Press, 2006), 96–97, 101, 105, 107, 113.

7. International Crisis Group, "Saakashvili's Ajara Success: Repeatable Elsewhere in Georgia?," ICG Europe Briefing, Tbilisi/Brussels, August 18, 2004, 2, http://www.crisisgroup.org/.

8. This theme came up repeatedly in my interviews in Batumi and with Ajarans living in Tbilisi, September and October 2009.

9. Georgi M. Derluguian, *Bourdieu's Secret Admirer in the Caucasus: A World-System Biography* (Chicago: University of Chicago Press, 2005), 230.

10. Monica Duffy Toft, *The Geography of Ethnic Violence: Identity, Interests, and the Indivisibility of Territory* (Princeton: Princeton University Press, 2003),108–9.

11. Toft, *The Geography of Ethnic Violence*, 111; Derluguian, *Bourdieu's Secret Admirer*, 231; Julie A. George, "Minority Political Inclusion in Mikheil Saakashvili's Georgia," *Europe-Asia Studies* 60, no. 7 (September 2008), 1157.

12. International Crisis Group, "Saakashvili's Ajara Success," 2–3.

13. Elizabeth Fuller, "Aslan Abashidze: Georgia's Next Leader?" *RFE/RL Research Report* 2, no. 44 (November 5, 1993): 23–26, http://www.rferl.org/.

14. Derluguian, "The Tale of Two Resorts," 280; Pelkmans, *Defending the Border*, 110–12.

15. Fuller, "Aslan Abashidze."

16. Author's interviews with Giorgi Targamadze (now chairman of the Christian Democratic Movement of Georgia and a member of the Georgian parliament, and formerly an anchor for TV-Ajara and a leader of Abashidze's Revival Party), Tbilisi, September 22, 2009; and with Giorgi Masalkini (now associate professor of philosophy at Batumi State University, member of the Republican Party, and twice formerly a member of the Ajaran Supreme Soviet), Batumi, September 30, 2009.

17. Toft, *Geography of Ethnic Violence*, 111.

18. Derluguian, *Bourdieu's Secret Admirer*, 231.

19. Toft, *Geography of Ethnic Violence*, 111–12; Pelkmans, *Defending the Border*, 111.

20. Jonathan Wheatley, *Georgia from National Awakening to Rose Revolution: Delayed Transition in the Former Soviet Union* (Burlington, VT: Ashgate, 2005), 58–59.

21. David Hearst, "Babu, God, Grandad, Potentate, Leader, President . . . and Chef," *Guardian* (UK), March 13, 2004.

22. Author's interview with Masalkini; author's interview with Davit Berdzhenishvili (a leader of the Republican Party from Ajara), Tbilisi, September 28, 2009.

23. Wheatley, *Georgia from National Awakening to Rose Revolution*, 59.

24. International Crisis Group, "Saakashvili's Ajara Success," 3n16.

25. Nick Paton Walsh, "After the Revolution," *Guardian*, May 13, 2004.

26. George, "Minority Political Inclusion," p. 1157.

27. Fuller, "Aslan Abashidze," 24.

28. Reportedly no one died in these attacks. Author's interviews with Masalkini and Berdzhenishvili.

29. Fuller, "Aslan Abashidze," 25.

30. Derluguian, *Bourdieu's Secret Admirer in the Caucasus*, 232.

31. Author's interview with Mamuka Kakaladze and Zaza Davitadze (leaders of the Ajaran branch of the Movement for a Just Georgia), Batumi, September 30, 2009.

32. Thornike Gordadze, "Georgian-Russian Relations in the 1990s," in *The Guns of August 2008: Russia's War in Georgia*, ed. Svante E. Cornell and S. Frederick Starr (Armonk, NY: M. E. Sharpe, 2009), 35.

33. Fuller, "Aslan Abashidze."

34. "Russia Turns up the Heat on Georgia," *Asia Times Online*, October 29, 1999, http://www.atimes.com/c-asia/AJ30Ago1.html.

35. Darchiashvili, "Georgian Defense Policy and Military Reform," 132–33; Jaba Devdariani and Wojciech Bartuzi, "Ajaria Showdown Raises Prospect of Renewed Civil Strife in Georgia," *Eurasia Insight*, March 15, 2004; Ian Traynor, "Buoyant Georgian President Charms Putin into U-Turn," *Guardian* (UK), March 22, 2004.

36. "Saakashvili Sets Ultimatum to Abashidze, Threatens to Isolate Adjara," *Civil Georgia*, March 15, 2004, http://www.civil.ge/.

37. Author's interview with Archil Gegeshidze (a high-ranking foreign affairs and security advisor during the Shevardnadze era, and now a senior fellow at the Georgian Foundation for Strategic and International Studies), Tbilisi, September 22, 2009; author's interview with Zurab Kachkachishvili (a long-standing Georgian Foreign Ministry official and spokesperson and now Georgia's first ambassador to India), Tbilisi, September 23, 2009.

38. International Crisis Group, "Saakashvili's Ajara Success," 3.

39. Lincoln A. Mitchell, *Uncertain Democracy: U.S. Foreign Policy and Georgia's Rose Revolution* (Philadelphia: University of Pennsylvania Press, 2009), 55.

40. Ibid., 43–46.

41. Ghia Nodia, "Georgia: Dimensions of Insecurity," in *Statehood and Security*, ed. Coppieters and Legvold, 55.

42. International Crisis Group, "Saakashvili's Ajara Success," 5.

43. Maya Beridze, "Regional Party Plays Wild Card Role in Parliamentary Campaign," *Eurasia Insight*, October 29, 2003.

44. Mitchell, *Uncertain Democracy*, 59.

45. Mitchell, *Uncertain Democracy*.

46. Jean-Christophe Peuch, "Georgia: New Controversy over Vote Counting Heightens Tensions," Radio Free Europe/Radio Liberty, November 7, 2003.

47. "Georgia: Thousands Rally in Tbilisi in Support of President," Radio Free Europe/Radio Liberty, November 18, 2003; Zurab Karumidze's interview with David Zurabishvili, in *Enough! The Rose Revolution in the Republic of Georgia, 2003*, ed. Zurab Karumidze and James V. Wertsch (Hauppauge, NY: Nova Science Publishers, 2005), 63–64.

48. This was a real potential flashpoint for violence, especially since the protesters were carrying clubs. Zurab Karumidze's interview with Richard Miles, former US ambassador to Georgia, in *Enough!*, ed. Karumidze and Wertsch, 6.

49. Giorgi Kandelaki, *Georgia's Rose Revolution: A Participant's Perspective*, Special Report 167 (Washington: United States Institute of Peace, 2006).

50. Author's telephone interview with Mark Mullen (former head of the National Democratic Institute in Georgia and an eyewitness to the Rose Revolution in Tbilisi), August 19, 2009; author's interview with Levan Ramishvili (chairman of the pro-Saakashvili Liberty Institute and an organizer of the Rose Revolution), Tbilisi, September 27, 2009.

51. "Georgia Protests Detention of Defense Ministry Officials in Adjaria," *Newsline* (Radio Free Europe/Radio Liberty), September 29, 1999.

52. Nick Paton Walsh, "After the Revolution," *Guardian* (UK), May 13, 2004.

53. Pelkmans, *Defending the Border*, 179–80.

54. International Crisis Group, "Saakashvili's Ajara Success," 4.

55. "Adjar Leader Sets Conditions for Participation in Georgian Parliament," *Newsline* (Radio Free Europe/Radio Liberty), January 25, 1999; "Shevardnadze against Free Trade Zone," *Civil Georgia*, March 11, 2003; author's interview with Vladimer Papava (the former minister of the economy who was sent by Shevardnadze to negotiate with Abashidze about the free economic zone in 1999), Tbilisi, September 24, 2009.

56. Author's interview with Vano Nakaidze (formerly head of the Georgian State Oil Company and then deputy minister of economic development), Tbilisi, September 28, 2009.

57. International Crisis Group, "Saakashvili's Ajara Success," 4.

58. Giorgi Sepashvili, "Greenoak Buys Georgian Shipping Co. for $107 mln," *Civil Georgia*, December 20, 2004.

59. Author's interview with Nakaidze.

60. Martin Kettle, "Hillary's Brothers Warned Off Georgia," *Guardian* (UK), September 18, 1999.

61. "Adzhar Leader Incriminated in Georgian Merchant Fleet Scandal," *Newsline* (Radio Free Europe/Radio Liberty), August 4, 1999; Liz Fuller, "Is Tbilisi Seeking a Pretext to Neutralize Abashidze?" *Caucasus Report* (Radio Free Europe/Radio Liberty) 2, no. 31 (August 6, 1999).

62. International Crisis Group, "Saakashvili's Ajara Success," 3; Pelkmans, *Defending the Border*, 204. The relevant clan names were Abashidze, Gogitidze, Bakuridze, and Bladadze, according to Wheatley, *Georgia from National Awakening to Rose Revolution*, 115.

63. Derluguian, *Bourdieu's Secret Admirer*, 232.

64. Lincoln Mitchell, unpublished trip report, November 2003.

65. Archil Gegeshidze, "Georgia's Regional Vulnerabilities and the Ajaria Crisis," *Insight Turkey*, April 2004; author's interviews with Gegeshidze and Kachkachishvili.

66. "Ajaran Leader Calls Batumi University an Opposition Breeding Ground," BGI News Agency (Tbilisi), August 14, 1996, as reported by the BBC Summary of World Broadcasts, August 17, 1996.

67. International Crisis Group, "Saakashvili's Ajara Success," 3, 4–5.

68. Tsotne Bakuria, "Shadowy Nuclear Trail," *Washington Times*, March 29, 2006.

69. Author's e-mail interview, May 2009.

70. For a hint of this, see David Hearst, "Babu, God, Grandad, Potentate, Leader, President."

71. Mitchell, unpublished trip report.

72. Liz Fuller, "Aslan and Avtandil," *Caucasus Report* 5, no. 30 (September 13, 2002).

73. Nato Oniani interview with Eduard Shevardnadze, Georgian Radio (Tbilisi), February 20, 1995, as reported by the BBC Summary of World Broadcasts (hereafter BBC), February 22, 1995.

74. "Nuttily Naughty," *Economist*, October 28, 2000, http://www.economist.com.

75. Pelkmans, *Defending the Border*, 195–213; Mitchell, unpublished trip report; author's interview with Gigi Tsereteli (deputy chairman of parliament), Tbilisi, September 21, 2009. Some of the new facilities *were* used by those who could pay, like a beautiful state-of-the-art tennis club.

76. "Nuttily Naughty."

77. Pelkmans, *Defending the Border*, 68–69, 180–93.

78. Catherine Boone, "States and Ruling Classes in Postcolonial Africa: The Enduring Contradictions of Power," in *State Power and Social Forces: Domination and Transformation in the Third World*, ed. Joel S. Migdal, Atul Kohli, and Vivienne Shue (New York: Cambridge University Press, 1994), 108–40.

79. Mitchell, *Uncertain Democracy*, 85.

80. "Abashidze Cuts Ties with Tbilisi," *Civil Georgia*, November 24, 2003.

81. Daan van der Schriek, "Ajaria Issue Creates Conundrum for Georgia's New Leaders," *Eurasia Insight*, December 4, 2003.

82. Jaba Devdariani, "Abashidze Faces Pressure to Adjust to Georgia's New Political Reality," *Eurasia Insight*, January 13, 2004; Wojciech Bartuzi, "In Troublesome Georgian Province, Fears Grow Amidst Deep Discord," *Eurasia Insight*, January 20, 2004.

83. Nick Paton Walsh, "Georgia Pins Hopes on Poll," *Guardian* (UK), January 3, 2004; Walsh, "Separatists Give Georgian Leader First Headache," *Guardian*, January 9, 2004.

84. Author's e-mail interview with a knowledgeable US diplomat who wishes to remain off the record, May 2009.

85. "U.S. Ambassador Visits Batumi," *Civil Georgia*, December 23, 2003.

86. International Crisis Group, "Saakashvili's Ajara Success," 6.

87. Bartuzi, "In Troublesome Georgian Province, Fears Grow"; Jean-Christophe Peuch, "Georgia: Groups Working Toward Regime Change in Restive Georgia," Radio Free Europe/Radio Liberty, January 22, 2004.

88. "Saakashvili Attended Military Parade in Adjara," *Civil Georgia*, January 25, 2004.

89. "Tbilisi Concerned over Tensions in Adjara," *Civil Georgia*, January 28, 2004.

90. "Protestors Rally against Probe of Omega Group," *Civil Georgia*, February 19, 2004.

91. Jaba Devdariani, "Government Using Carrots and Sticks in Georgia's Anti-Corruption Drive," *Eurasianet Business and Economics*, March 17, 2004.

92. International Crisis Group, "Saakashvili's Ajara Success," 6.

93. "More Violence Reported in Adjara," *Civil Georgia*, February 23, 2004.

94. Maya Beridze, "Political Tension Rises between Georgian Government and Recalcitrant Region of Ajaria," *Eurasia Insight*, March 2, 2004.

95. "Tbilisi, Batumi Up Ante in War of Words," *Civil Georgia*, March 9, 2004.

96. "Tensions Increase, as Saakashvili Barred from Entering Adjara," *Civil Georgia*, March 14, 2004.

97. "Saakashvili Gives Ultimatum to Renegade Leader," Radio Free Europe/Radio Liberty, March 14, 2004, Nick Paton Walsh, "Georgia Edges Close to Civil War," *Guardian* (UK), March 15, 2004; Giorgi Sepashvili and Tea Gularidze, "Fear Prevails in Batumi," *Civil Georgia*, March 15, 2004; "Adjara under Partial Blockade," *Civil Georgia*, March 15, 2004; "Banks Banned to Operate in Adjara," *Civil Georgia*, March 16, 2004.

98. "Batumi Naval Blockade Enforced," *Civil Georgia*, March 16, 2004.

99. Traynor, "Buoyant Georgian President Charms Putin into U-Turn."

100. Daan van der Schriek, "As Ajarian Leader Backpedals, Saakashvili Threatens to Revive Economic Blockade," *Eurasia Insight*, March 22, 2004.

101. "Batumi-Based Military Unit Mutinies," *Civil Georgia*, April 20, 2004.

102. "More Officers Refuse to Obey Renegade Commander," *Civil Georgia*, April 21, 2004.

103. "MPs Urge Government to Disarm Militia in Adjara," *Civil Georgia*, April 24, 2004.

104. "46 Soldiers of Abashidze's Elite Troops Flee Adjara," *Civil Georgia*, April 27, 2004.

105. Nick Paton Walsh, "Georgia on the Brink of Civil War," *Guardian* (UK), April 26, 2004.

106. "Coast Guard Holds Exercises," *Civil Georgia*, April 28, 2004.

107. "Interior Minister Threatens with 'Police Operation' in Adjara," *Civil Georgia*, April 28, 2004.

108. Giorgi Sepashvili, "Sensing Abashidze Weakness, Tbilisi Treads a Tough Line," *Civil Georgia*, April 29, 2004.

109. While this had great symbolic importance, the Choloki River is actually a shallow and narrow stream.

110. "Adjara Blows up Key Bridges, Cuts Road Links," *Civil Georgia*, May 2, 2004.

111. Tom Parfitt, "Georgia's Rebels Ready for War," *Guardian* (UK), May 4, 2004.

112. Nick Paton Walsh, "Adzharia Militia Beat up Students," *Guardian* (UK), May 5, 2004.

113. Nick Paton Walsh, "Adzharian Leader Flees Georgia, Says President," *Guardian* (UK), May 6, 2004.

114. "Batumi Oil Terminal Mined," *Civil Georgia*, May 5, 2004; "Tbilisi Dispatched Mine Clearers to Adjara," *Civil Georgia*, May 5, 2004.

115. Sergei Blagov, "Amid Celebration in Batumi, Georgian Authorities Move to Reassert Authority in Ajaria," *Eurasia Insight*, May 6, 2004.

116. Daan van der Schriek, "Georgia Moves Swiftly to Erase Abashidze Legacy in Ajaria," *Eurasia Insight*, May 11, 2004. Dumbadze was later reportedly exchanged to Russia for a group of Georgian troops taken prisoner during the August 2008 war, and lived in Moscow afterward.

117. Author's interview with Tsereteli.

118. Author's interviews with Levan Ramishvili (chairman of the Liberty Institute and a leader of the Rose Revolution), Tbilisi, September 27, 2009; with Masalkini; and with Kakaladze and Davitadze.

119. Eter Turadze, "Ajaria: Concern over Missing Funds," Institute for War and Peace Reporting, Caucasus Reporting Service no. 263, November 25, 2004, http://www.iwpr.net/.

120. Imedi TV (Tbilisi), May 10, 2004, as reported by the BBC.

121. International Crisis Group, "Saakashvili's Ajara Success," 11; George, "Minority Political Inclusion," 1160–61.

122. Author's interview with Levan Varshalomidze (governor of Ajara), Batumi, September 30, 2009.

123. "Adjara's Local Parliament Convened," *Civil Georgia*, December 2, 2008.

124. "Saakashvili Meets Clinton," *Civil Georgia*, September 22, 2009; "Batumi-Based TV in Tax Dispute with State," *Civil Georgia*, October 15, 2009, and "Ombudsman Meets Finance Minister over Batumi-Based TV's Tax Dispute," *Civil Georgia*, October 30, 2009.

125. Law on Government, Government of the Autonomous Republic of Adjara, http://www.adjara.gov.ge/eng/.

126. Imedi TV (Tbilisi), March 17, 2005, as reported by the BBC. This was confirmed by author's interview with Levan Varshalomidze.

127. His name is Eldar Varshalomidze. "Batumi-Based TV in Tax Dispute with State."

128. Giorgi Sepashvili, "Adjara Leadership Accused of Media Censorship, 'Clan-Based' Governance," *Civil Georgia,* March 3, 2005.

129. Imedi TV (Tbilisi), October 19, 2004, as reported by the BBC.

130. Maka Malakmadze, "Father and Son Arrested for Following the Order of the President," Human Rights Centre (Tbilisi), April 28, 2009, as reported by Human-rights.ge: Web Portal on Human Rights in Georgia, http://www.humanrights.ge.

131. "How Varshalomidzes [*sic*] Got Hold of a Three Story House," Human Rights Centre (Tbilisi), June 27, 2009, as reported by Humanrights.ge: Web Portal on Human Rights in Georgia, http://www.humanrights.ge.

132. Rustavi-2 TV (Tbilisi), August 15, 2006, as reported by the BBC.

133. *Mid-Term (2006–2010) Programme for Social and Economic Development of Gulrip-shi District Kodori Gorge of the Autonomous Republic of Abkhazia,* Autonomous Republic of Abkhazia [in Exile] Ministry of Economy, Tbilisi, 2006, Annex 10.

134. Imedi TV (Tbilisi), October 19, 2004, as reported by the BBC.

135. "Finance Minister in Georgia's Ajaria Resigns," Kavkasia-Press News Agency (Tbilisi), April 29, 2005, as reported by the BBC.

136. Kimberly Marten, "Russian Efforts to Control Kazakhstan's Oil: The Kumkol Case," *Post-Soviet Affairs* 23, no. 1 (January-March 2007): 18–37.

137. Author's interview with Levan Varshalomidze.

138. Sebastian J, "Batumi Aquarium/Henning Larsen Architects," *Arch Daily,* August 12, 2010, http://www.archdaily.com/73022/batumi-aquarium-henning-larsen-architects.

139. Author's interview with Levan Varshalomidze.

140. Author's interview with Berdzhenishvili.

141. "Is Adjar Leader in Danger of Being Killed?" *Newsline* (Radio Free Europe/Radio Liberty), April 8, 1999.

142. Liz Fuller, "Georgian President Summons His Envoy for Abkhazia," and "Who Details His Mediation Success," *Newsline* (Radio Free Europe/Radio Liberty), October 1, 2002; "Georgia Set to Reject Adjar Leader's Abkhaz Peace Proposal," *Caucasus Report* 5, no. 34 (October 11, 2002).

143. "Georgia: New Pro-Russian Party Vows to Crush Opposition," Rustavi-2 TV (Tbilisi), December 17, 2002, as reported by the BBC.

144. "Ajaran Leader Returns from Mediation Mission in Moscow—Georgian Report," Prime-News Agency (Tbilisi), November 14, 2002, as reported by the BBC.

145. "Lebed in Adjaria," *Newsline* (Radio Free Europe/Radio Liberty), July 19, 1999.

146. "Moscow Mayor and Georgian Regional Head Set Cooperation Areas," Russian Economic News, November 6, 2001, Lexis/Nexis Academic Universe online database.

147. "Russian TV Exposes Moscow Mayor's Property Interests in Ajaria," Ren TV (Moscow), March 18, 2004, as reported by the BBC.

148. Simon Ostrovsky, "Adzharia's Fortunes Lure New Masters," *Moscow Times,* March 31, 2004.

149. "Ajarian Leader Visiting Moscow, Russia," RIA Economic News, February, 2003, Lexis/Nexis Academic Universe news database.

150. Wojciech Bartuzi, "Ajaria Showdown Raises Prospect of Renewed Civil Strife in Georgia," *Eurasia Insight*, March 15, 2005.

151. Jaba Devdariani, "Developing Abashidze, Georgia's President Raises Stakes," *Eurasia Insight*, November 14, 2003.

152. "Burjanadze, Abashidze Discussed Disputed Visa Regime," *Civil Georgia*, December 11, 2003.

153. "Moscow Backs Abashidze, Slams 'Extremist' Forces in Adjara," *Civil Georgia*, January 21, 2004.

154. "Moscow Accuses Tbilisi of Trying to Oust Adjarian Leader," *Civil Georgia*, March 12, 2004.

155. Liz Fuller, "Prompting Warning from Russia," *Newsline* (Radio Free Europe/Radio Liberty), February 26, 2004. A knowledgeable US diplomat who wishes to remain off the record does not "recall any credible evidence that the Russians had militarily reinforced the Batumi Base"; author's e-mail interview, May 2009.

156. "Saakashvili Gives Ultimatum to Renegade Leader."

157. "Saakashvili: Russian Visit Great Success," *Civil Georgia*, February 12, 2004.

158. Traynor, "Buoyant Georgian President Charms Putin into U-Turn;" author's e-mail interview with a knowledgeable US diplomat, May 2009.

159. "Adjara Suffers Blockade," *Civil Georgia*, March 16, 2004.

160. Simon Ostrovsky, "Adzharian Leader Revels in Defiance," *Moscow Times*, March 22, 2004.

161. Walsh, "Adzharian Leader Flees Georgia."

162. Zurab Karumidze, interview with Eduard Shevardnadze, in *Enough!*, ed. Karumidze and Wertsch, 31.

163. Nick Paton Walsh, "After the Revolution," *Guardian* (UK), May 13, 2004.

164. Ostrovsky, "Adzharia's Fortunes Lure New Masters."

165. Irakly Areshidze, "Did Russia and Georgia Make a Deal over Ajaria?" *Eurasia Insight*, May 19, 2004.

166. Sergei Blagov, "Amid Celebration in Batumi, Georgian Authorities Move to Reassert Authority in Ajaria," *Eurasia Insight*, May 6, 2004.

167. "Georgia Suspends Ban on Russia's WTO Accession," *Civil Georgia*, February 24, 2004.

168. "Russia's Big Business Comes to Georgia," *Civil Georgia*, May 28, 2004.

169. "Bendukidze's Gone!" *The Messenger* (Tbilisi English-language newspaper), February 12, 2009, http://www.messenger.com.ge/.

170. Sergei Blagov, "To Secure Future, Georgia Banks on Russian Business," EurasiaNet.org, June 3, 2004, http://www.eurasianet.org/.

171. Elizabeth Owen, "Georgia: Pankisi's Chechens Worry about Implications of Tbilisi-Moscow Rapprochement," *Eurasia Insight*, May 18, 2004; Areshidze, "Did Russia and Georgia Make a Deal?"

172. Andrei Illarionov, "The Russian Leadership's Preparation for War, 1999–2008," in *Guns of August 2008*, ed. Cornell and Starr, 55.

173. Nikolai Sokov notes how vulnerable the Russian bases on Georgian territory were. See Sokov, "The Withdrawal of Russian Military Bases from Georgia: Not Solving Anything," *PONARS Policy Memo* 363, June 2005, http://csis.org/files/media/csis/pubs/pm_0363.pdf.

174. Kodori is its Georgian name; Kodor is its Abkhazian name. Kodori is the standard international usage, and will be used here.

175. Elizabeth Owen, "Georgia: Abkhazia Reasserts Control over Upper Kodori Gorge," *Eurasia Insight*, October 16, 2008.

176. *Mid-Term (2006–2010) Programme for Social and Economic Development of Gulripshi District Kodori Gorge of the Autonomous Republic of Abkhazia*, 6.

177. Charles King, *The Ghost of Freedom: A History of the Caucasus* (New York: Oxford University Press, 2008).

178. Derluguian, "Tale of Two Resorts," 266–67; King, *Ghost of Freedom*, 215.

179. Derluguian, "Tale of Two Resorts," 268.

180. Louise Shelley, "Georgian Organized Crime," in *Organized Crime and Corruption in Georgia*, ed. Louise Shelley, Erik R. Scott and Anthony Latta (New York: Routledge, 2007), 51–52.

181. Jaba Devdariani, "Barbs over Kidnapping Reach Dangerous Pitch in Georgia," *Eurasia Insight*, June 23, 2003.

182. Author's interviews with Gia Tarkhan-Mouravi (an academic physicist and geographer, and also a native of the mountains, who was involved with the 1993 refugee rescue operations), Tbilisi, September 23, 2009; Irakli Alasania (former head of the Government of Abkhazia in Exile, a lead negotiator with Abkhaz and Kodori authorities early in the Saakashvili regime, former Georgian ambassador to the United Nations, and now an opposition political leader), Tbilisi, September 24, 2009; and Davit Darchiashvili (currently an MP with Saakashvili's governing party, and an academic expert on Georgian security issues and the rise of militias in the early 1990s), Tbilisi, September 25, 2009.

183. Nodia, "Georgia: Dimensions of Insecurity," 52.

184. The Gali region was a partial exception. See Tom Trier, Hedbig Lohm and David Szakony, *Under Siege: Inter-Ethnic Relations in Abkhazia* (New York: Columbia University Press, 2011), 45–54.

185. Devdariani, "Barbs over Kidnapping Reach Dangerous Pitch."

186. "Georgia Denies Attacks on Russian Peacekeepers," *Civil Georgia*, April 7, 2002.

187. "Guerrilla Group Surrenders Arms," *Civil Georgia*, February 11, 2004.

188. "Nadareishvili, Kvitsiani Trade Accusations on Kodori UN Kidnapping," *Civil Georgia*, June 19, 2003.

189. Author's interview with Tarkhan-Mouravi, and her not-for-attribution interview with a knowledgeable native of Upper Kodori who lives in Tbilisi, September 2009.

190. Author's not-for-attribution interview with a knowledgeable native of Upper Kodori who lives in Tbilisi.

191. Georgian President Mikheil Saakashvili made this accusation in a much later television interview; "Georgian President Promises to Crush Rebel Militia Leader," Imedi TV (Tbilisi), July 24, 2006, as reported by the BBC News Worldwide Monitoring News Service. These accusations were confirmed in the author's interview with

Paata Zakareishvili (a Georgian government representative responsible for negotiating refugee and return-of-remains issues following the Abkhaz war in 1993, and now a human rights NGO leader), Tbilisi, September 23, 2009.

192. Author's interviews with Tarkhan-Mouravi and with Temuri Yakobashvili (minister for state reintegration), Tbilisi, September 29, 2009.

193. Author's interview with Zakareishvili.

194. Author's interviews with Tarkhan-Mouravi, Zakareishvili, and Darchiashvili; and interview with Shota Utiashvili (head of the Interior Ministry's information and analytical department), September 25, 2009.

195. Text of Agreement on a Cease-fire and Disengagement of Forces, published in *Svobodnaya Gruziya* (Tbilisi, in Russian), May 17, 1994, as reported by the BBC, May 31, 1994.

196. "Georgian Rebel Leader Profiled," Rustavi-2 TV, July 23, 2006, as reported by the BBC.

197. Georgi Putkaradze, "Fugitive Georgian Official's Emergence in Abkhazia Linked to Provocation," *Rezonansi* (Tbilisi newspaper), June 24, 2008, as reported by the BBC.

198. Author's interviews with Gegeshidze, Utiashvili, and Alasania, as well as a not-for-attribution interview with a very knowledgeable official.

199. Saakashvili made this accusation without putting a dollar figure on it ("Georgian President Announces Transfer of Abkhaz Government-in-Exile") and this was confirmed by the author's interview with Alasania and her not-for-attribution interview with a very knowledgeable official. Utiashvili supplied the dollar figure in his interview with the author.

200. "Sabotage on Russia-Georgia Power Line Said to Have Been Planned in Tbilisi," Prime-News Agency (Tbilisi), February 1, 2003, as reported by the BBC.

201. Author's interview with Utiashvili.

202. "Georgian President Appoints Representative in Kodori Gorge," Prime-News Agency (Tbilisi), August 8, 2000, as reported by the BBC.

203. "Kodori Holds the Key to Abkhazia," *Civil Georgia*, October 24, 2001.

204. Darchiashvili, "Georgian Defense Policy and Military Reform," 148.

205. Devdariani, "Barbs over Kidnapping Reach Dangerous Pitch."

206. "Georgian Minister Dismisses Russian Explanation for Abkhazia Troop Deployment," Prime-News Agency (Tbilisi), April 16, 2002, as reported by the BBC.

207. Shelley, "Georgian Organized Crime," 55.

208. "Russian Peacekeepers Resume Patrolling of Georgia's Kodori Gorge," Interfax News Agency (Moscow), April 26, 2005, as reported by the BBC. While Georgia denied the accusations about the 2001 Chechen activities in Kodori at the time, a Japanese journalist later confirmed them with a photo record. "Japanese Journalist Tells a Story of Pankisi Hideout," *Civil Georgia*, March 6, 2003.

209. "Georgian President's Envoy Discusses Details of Russian-Abkhaz Border Incident," Rustavi-2 TV (Tbilisi), July 31, 2002; and "Abkhaz Separatist Troops Leave Georgian-Controlled Area," Kavkasia-Press News Agency (Tbilisi), August 26, 2002, both as reported by the BBC.

210. "Locals Ensuring Security of Kodori Gorge, Georgian President's Envoy Says," Prime-News Agency (Tbilisi), April 24, 2003, as reported by the BBC.

211. Saakashvili made this accusation; "Georgian President Announces Transfer of Abkhaz Government-in-Exile to Kodori," Imedi TV (Tbilisi), July 27, 2006, as reported by the BBC. It was confirmed by the author's interviews with Zakareishvili, Utiashvili, and Alasania.

212. Devdariani, "Barbs over Kidnapping Reach Dangerous Pitch."

213. Dexter Filkins, "Kidnappers in Separatist Georgian Region Free 4 U.N. Workers," *New York Times*, June 12, 2003.

214. Devdariani, "Barbs over Kidnapping Reach Dangerous Pitch."

215. "'Crime Bosses' Helped Free Abducted UN Observers—Georgian MP," Prime-News Agency (Tbilisi), June 15, 2003, as reported by the BBC. Oniani was arrested in Moscow in 2009 after his crime ring in Spain was broken up by local police in 2006.

216. Krasner, *Sovereignty.*

217. Author's e-mail interview, May 2009.

218. Author's not-for-attribution interview with a knowledgeable native of Upper Kodori who lives in Tbilisi.

219. "Authorities Dismiss Rumours about Sacking of Georgian Governor of Abkhaz Gorge," Rustavi-2 TV (Tbilisi), March 8, 2004, as reported by the BBC.

220. "Georgia to Restore Local Military Unit in Kodori Gorge after Russian Overflights," Rustavi-2 TV (Tbilisi), September 14, 2004, as reported by the BBC.

221. Author's interview with Alasania.

222. "Presidential Representative Position in Kodori Gorge Abolished," *Civil Georgia*, December 4, 2004.

223. "Georgian-Backed Abkhaz Government to Rule Kodori Gorge," Kavkasia-Press News Agency (Tbilisi), December 4, 2004, as reported by the BBC.

224. "Power Line Damaged in Kodori," Civil Georgia news service, January 18, 2005, and "'Saboteurs' Damage Power Line," *Civil Georgia*, February 7, 2005.

225. "Georgian Defence Chief Wants to Rid Army of Local Paramilitary Units," Imedi TV (Tbilisi), April 26, 2005, as reported by the BBC.

226. "Paper: Okruashvili, Alasania at Odds over Military Unit in Kodori," *Civil Georgia*, July 5, 2005.

227. "Georgia: Tbilisi-Backed Abkhaz Authorities Appoint Envoy in Kodori Gorge," Mze TV (Tbilisi), May 23, 2005, as reported by the BBC.

228. Author's interview with Zakareishvili.

229. "Georgian Official Stresses Importance of Direct Contacts with Abkhaz," Imedi TV (Tbilisi), July 12, 2005, as reported by the BBC.

230. "Okruashvili Speaks of 'Intrigues' against Him," *Civil Georgia*, July 11, 2005.

231. "Alasania's UN Appointment Triggers Controversy," *Civil Georgia*, June 13, 2006.

232. Marina Vashakmadze, "Transcript of RFE/RL Interview with Georgia's Irakli Alasania," Radio Free Europe/Radio Liberty, January 5, 2009.

233. "Sabotage Blamed for Power Line Damage," *Civil Georgia*, March 27, 2006.

234. "Energy Minister Comments on Damage to Power Line," and "Saakashvili Speaks about Prison Riot, Hails Police," both *Civil Georgia*, March 27, 2006.

235. "Former Militia Head Says Authorities Plan Assault on Georgian-Controlled Gorge," Kavkas-Press (Tbilisi), July 22, 2006, as reported by the BBC.

236. "Rebel Former Official Rules out Compromise with Georgian Government," Imedi TV (Tbilisi), July 23, 2006, as reported by the BBC.

237. "Rebel Militia Leader Claims US Pressure on Georgia over Abkhazia Gorge," Rustavi-2 TV (Tbilisi), July 23, 2006, as reported by the BBC.

238. "Georgian Speaker Says Rebel Militia Leader Has Little Popular Support," Rustavi-2 TV (Tbilisi), July 23, 2006, as reported by the BBC.

239. "Georgian President Promises to Crush Rebel Militia Leader."

240. "Russia Warns Georgia against Use of Force in Rebel Gorge," Interfax-AVN (Moscow), July 25, 2006, as reported by the BBC.

241. C. J. Chivers, "Georgia Sends Troops to Subdue Rebel Militia," *New York Times*, July 26, 2006.

242. "Russia Warns Georgia against Use of Force"; Chivers, "Georgia Sends Troops."

243. "Georgian Minister Accuses Russia of 'Close Contacts with Kodori Rebels," Rustavi-2 TV (Tbilisi), July 31, 2006, as reported by the BBC.

244. "Rebel Warlord's Sister in Custody," *Civil Georgia*, July 31, 2006.

245. "Reports: Group of Rebels Escape into Abkhaz-Controlled Territory," *Civil Georgia*, August 5, 2006.

246. Author's interview with Utiashvili, and a not-for-attribution interview with a knowledgeable Georgian official.

247. "Georgian President Announces Transfer of Abkhaz Government-in-Exile to Kodori," Imedi TV (Tbilisi), July 27, 2006, as reported by the BBC.

248. Author's interview with Utiashvili.

249. Author's not-for-attribution interview with a knowledgeable Georgian official.

250. Author's interview with Utiashvili.

251. Because what follows is speculative, I have chosen to leave these comments off the record.

252. Author's not-for-attribution interview with a knowledgeable Georgian official.

253. "UN, Russian Observers Begin Patrolling Disputed Georgian Gorge," RIA Novosti (Moscow), October 12, 2006, as reported by the BBC.

254. "Abkhaz Official Says UN Inspection Found 550 Georgian Police in Kodori," Interfax (Moscow), October 13, 2006, as reported by the BBC.

255. "Russian Peacekeepers Say Georgia Carrying out Illegal Engineering Work in Kodori," ITAR-TASS (Moscow), December 14, 2006, as reported by the BBC.

256. "'Abkhazia against Georgia' Proposal to Open UN Post in Upper Kodori Gorge," Apsnypress (Sukhumi), July 18, 2007, as reported by the BBC.

257. "Wanted Warlord Threatens Partisan Warfare in Kodori," *Civil Georgia*, September 11, 2006; "Paper Reports Clash in Kodori," *Civil Georgia*, September 20, 2006; and "Wanted Warlord Claims Responsibility for Kodori Shelling," *Civil Georgia*, November 2, 2006.

258. "Rebel Militia Leader Calls on Georgia to Withdraw Forces from Kodori Gorge," Interfax, November 1, 2006, as reported by the BBC.

259. "Senior Georgian MP Says Kodori Rebel Leader Is Russia's Stooge," Kavkas-Press (Tbilisi), November 8, 2006, as reported by the BBC.

260. "Nine Parties to Contest Georgian Local Self-Government Elections," Channel 1 TV (Tbilisi), August 31, 2006, as reported by the BBC.

261. *Mid-Term (2006–2010) Programme for Social and Economic Development of Gulripshi District Kodori Gorge of the Autonomous Republic of Abkhazia*, Autonomous Republic of Abkhazia [in Exile] Ministry of Economy, Tbilisi, 2006.

262. Michael Schwirtz, "A Battle for Hearts and Minds Sets off a Building Boom," *New York Times*, October 9, 2006.

263. Table 2a, "Statement of Government Operations," FY 2006 Expenses on Social Benefits, 597 million GEL; available as a downloadable Excel document under "Annual Data" at the Ministry of Finance website, http://www.mof.ge/en/3992. Throughout 2006, the GEL exchange rate was between 1.7 and 1.8 for 1 US dollar.

264. David R. Sands, "U.S. Stands by Decision on Kodori Gorge," *Washington Times*, October 19, 2006.

265. "Georgian Military Expert Says Kodori Raid 'Major Lesson,' Airspace Unprotected," Rezonansi (Tbilisi newspaper), March 15, 2007, as reported by the BBC.

266. Giorgi Putkaradze, "Fugitive Georgian Official's Emergence in Abkhazia Linked to Provocation," Rezonansi (Tbilisi newspaper), June 24, 2008, as reported by the BBC.

267. "Georgian Interior Minister on Clash in Abkhazia's Kodori Gorge," Rusatvi-2 TV (Tbilisi), September 20, 2007; "Georgia Says It Killed Four in Kodori Clash, Suspects Russia," Rustavi-2 TV July 9, 2008; both as reported by the BBC.

268. "Georgian Reports Say Russian Paratroopers Deployed near Kodori Gorge," Kavkas-Press (Tbilisi), May 11, 2008, as reported by the BBC; "Gather Round the Gorge: Georgia and Russia," *Economist*, May 17, 2008, http://www.economist.com.

269. Elza Tsiklauri, interview with Mamuka Areshidze, "There is Danger that Two Fronts Will Be Opened for Georgia," Rezonansi (Tbilisi newspaper), July 11, 2008, as reported by the BBC.

270. Giorgi Putkaradze, "Kvitsiani in Sukhumi?" Rezonansi (Tbilisi newspaper), June 24, 2008, as reported by the BBC.

271. Nino Kekelia, "Georgian Units in Kodori May Be Replaced by an International Police Force," Rezonansi (Tbilisi newspaper), July 22, 2008, as reported by the BBC.

272. International Crisis Group, "Russia vs. Georgia: The Fallout," Europe Report 195, Tbilisi/Brussels, August 22, 2008, 3.

273. Michael Schwirtz, "Abkhazia Wrests Gorge from Preoccupied Georgia," *New York Times*, August 18, 2008.

274. Author's not-for-attribution interview with a very knowledgeable official.

275. Irma Choladze and Natia Kuprashvili, "Kodori Gorge Refugees in Limbo," Institute for War and Peace Reporting, Caucasus Reporting Service no. 477, January 22, 2009, http://www.iwpr.net/.

276. Summary of Abkhaz press compiled by BBC Monitoring, November 3, 2008.

277. Author's interview with Utiashvili.

278. Trier, Lohm and Szakonyi, *Under Siege*, 47–49, 50.

279. "Sokhumi Sets up Abkhaz Administration in Kodori," *Civil Georgia*, September 3, 2008; "Separatists Appoint Wanted Criminal as Governor of Occupied Region," Rustavi-2 television, September 3, 2008, http://www.rustavi2.com/.

280. "Georgian TV Reports Abkhaz Separatist Official's Murder," Rustavi-2 TV, Tbilisi, February 13, 2009, as reported by the BBC.

281. Owen, "Georgia: Abkhazia Reasserts Control."

282. Author's interview with Utiashvili.

283. Kenneth A. Schultz and Barry R. Weingast, "Limited Governments, Powerful States," in *Strategic Politicians, Institutions, and Foreign Policy*, ed. Randolph M. Siverson (Ann Arbor: University of Michigan Press, 1998), 15–49.

284. Matthew Devlin, "Seizing the Reform Moment: Rebuilding Georgia's Police, 2004–2006," Innovations for Successful Societies Policy Note, Princeton University (2010), 7–9, http://www.princeton.edu/successfulsocieties.

5. Chechnya: The Sovereignty of Ramzan Kadyrov

1. Renat Abdullin, interview with Ramzan Kadyrov, "Ramzan Kadyrov: Umarov Is Wounded but Not Dead," *Izvestia* newspaper website, July 8, 2009, as reported by the BBC Worldwide Monitoring service (hereafter, the BBC); "Street in Chechnya's Capital Named after Putin," Ekho Moskvy radio (Moscow), October 5, 2008, as reported by the BBC.

2. "Chechnya's Kadyrov Given Title 'Head of Republic,' Not President," RIA Novosti press service in English, September 2, 2010.

3. "Chechen Leader Denies Reported Plans to Unite Chechnya, Ingushetia," Interfax news agency (Moscow), June 24, 2009; and Vladimir Mukhin, "Without Precise Targeting, War on Terror in North Caucasus Is Impossible," *Nezavisimaya Gazeta*, June 25, 2009; both as reported by the BBC.

4. Michael Schwirtz, "Russian Anger Grows over Chechnya Subsidies," *New York Times*, October 8, 2011.

5. Emil Souleimanov, interviewed by Jesse Tatum, "The Current Trend of the Kremlin Is to Rather Formally Distance Itself from the North Caucasus," *Caucasian Review of International Affairs* 4, no. 1 (Winter 2010): 87–90.

6. Joel S. Migdal, "The State in Society: An Approach to Struggles for Domination," in *State Power and Social Forces: Domination and Transformation in the Third World*, ed. Joel S. Migdal, Atul Kohli, and Vivienne Shue (New York: Cambridge University Press, 1994), 7–34; Catherine Boone, *Political Topographies of the African State: Territorial Authority and Institutional Choice* (New York: Cambridge University Press, 2003); Sheri Berman, "From the Sun King to Karzai: Lessons for State Building in Afghanistan," *Foreign Affairs* 89, no. 2 (March/April 2010): 2–9.

7. Ildar Gabdrafikov and Henry E. Hale, "Bashkortostan's Democratic Moment? Patronal Presidentialism, Regional Regime Change, and Identity in Russia," in Osamu Ieda and Uyama Tomoshiko, eds., *Reconstruction and Interaction of Slavic Eurasia and Its Neighboring Worlds* (Sapporo, Japan: Hokkaido University Slavic Research Center, 2006), 75–102; Ellen Barry, "Russia Strongman to Retire as Kremlin Replaces Regional Leaders," *New York Times*, July 14, 2010.

8. For in-depth descriptions of the motives and course of the first Chechen war, see Anatol Lieven, *Chechnya: Tombstone of Russian Power* (New Haven: Yale University Press, 1998), and Carlotta Gall and Thomas de Waal, *Chechnya: Calamity in the Caucasus* (New York: New York University Press, 1998). For comparisons of the political motives behind the two wars, see Matthew Evangelista, *The Chechen Wars: Will Russia Go the Way of the Soviet Union?* (Washington: Brookings Institution Press, 2002), and Mikhail A. Alexseev, "Back to Hell: Civilian-Military 'Audience Costs' and

Russia's Wars in Chechnia," in *Military and Society in Post-Soviet Russia*, ed. Stephen L. Webber and Jennifer G. Mathers (Manchester: Manchester University Press, 2006), 97–113.

9. The best description and analysis of this process is found in James Hughes, *Chechnya: From Nationalism to Jihad* (Philadelphia: University of Pennsylvania Press, 2007).

10. For prominent Western analyses of this conspiracy theorizing, see Andrew Jack, *Inside Putin's Russia: Can There Be Reform without Democracy?* (New York: Oxford University Press, 2004), and Peter Baker and Susan Glasser, *Kremlin Rising: Vladimir Putin's Russia and the End of Revolution* (New York: Scribner, 2005), 55.

11. Mikhail Trepashkin, interview by Dmitrii Volchek for the US government–supported Radio Liberty (Radio Svoboda) news program "Itogi Nedeli," January 12, 2007, www.svobodanews.ru/articleprintview/424178.html.

12. Anna Politkovskaya, *A Small Corner of Hell: Dispatches from Chechnya* (Chicago: University of Chicago Press, 2003); Hughes, *Chechnya*, 119–20. For an in-depth analysis of the range of tactics used by Russian forces, see Mark Kramer, "The Perils of Counterinsurgency: Russia's War in Chechnya," *International Security* 29, no. 3 (Winter 2004/2005): 5–63.

13. Hughes, *Chechnya*, 121.

14. Aleksei Malashenko, *Ramzan Kadyrov: Rossiiskii Politik Kavkazskoi Natsional'nosti* [Ramzan Kadyrov: A Russian Politician with a Caucasian Face] (Moscow: Moscow Carnegie Center, 2009), 23.

15. Politkovskaya, *Small Corner of Hell*, 140; Georgi M. Derluguian, *Bourdieu's Secret Admirer in the Caucasus: A World-System Biography* (Chicago: University of Chicago Press, 2005), 255.

16. Liz Fuller, "Putin Names Interim Chechen Leader," Radio Free Europe/Radio Liberty (RFE/RL) *Caucasus Report* 3, no. 24 (June 16, 2000), http://www.rferl.org/.

17. Press accounts do not reveal when Akhmad Kadyrov went to Mecca. For a report of the first Russian visit, see "Mufti Babahan Commenting on Pilgrimage to Mecca," TASS, August 9, 1988.

18. Politkovskaya, *Small Corner of Hell*, 140.

19. Simon Saradzhyan, "Pro-Moscow Chechens Oppose Kadyrov," *Moscow Times*, June 20, 2000; Evangelista, *The Chechen Wars*, 85.

20. Dmitri V. Trenin and Aleksei V. Malashenko with Anatol Lieven, *Russia's Restless Frontier: The Chechnya Factor in Post-Soviet Russia* (Washington: Carnegie Endowment for International Peace, 2004), 34, 37; Derluguian, *Bourdieu's Secret Admirer in the Caucasus*, 255.

21. Trenin and Malashenko with Lieven, *Russia's Restless Frontier*, 32, 36.

22. Anna Badkhen, "Chechen Religious Leader Shot Dead," *Moscow Times*, June 17, 2000.

23. Yevgenii Krutikov, "Mufti in Exile," *Izvestiya*, October 9, 1999, as reported by the Russian Press Digest news service.

24. Trenin and Malashenko with Lieven, *Russia's Restless Frontier*, 37.

25. Emma Gilligan, *Terror in Chechnya: Russia and the Tragedy of Civilians in War* (Princeton: Princeton University Press, 2010), 65, 84.

26. Jack, *Inside Putin's Russia*, 123.

27. "Kadyrov Fends off Babich," *North Caucasus Analysis* (Jamestown Foundation) 4, no. 2 (January 31, 2003), http://www.jamestown.org/December.

28. Jack, *Inside Putin's Russia*, 122–23; Baker and Glasser, *Kremlin Rising*, 300–301.

29. Jack, *Inside Putin's Russia*, 123.

30. Darrell Slider, "Politics in the Regions," in *Development in Russian Politics 6*, ed. Stephen White, Zvi Gitelman and Richard Sakwa (New York: Palgrave Macmillan, 2005), 176.

31. "Kadyrov Takes over Special-Police Unit," *North Caucasus Analysis* (Jamestown Foundation) 4, no. 19 (May 29, 2003); http://www.jamestown.org/.

32. Hughes, *Chechnya*, xiii.

33. Daniel H. Nexon, *The Struggle for Power in Early Modern Europe: Religious Conflict, Dynastic Empires and International Change* (Princeton: Princeton University Press, 2009), 116.

34. Gilligan, *Terror in Chechnya*, 83–85.

35. Jack, *Inside Putin's Russia*, 125. Kramer, "The Perils of Counterinsurgency," 46, in contrast, argues that the success of the assassination reflects only the carelessness of Akhmad's security forces.

36. Vlad Trifonov, "The Bomb Blast Effect," *Kommersant* (Moscow), May 16, 2004, http://www.kommersant.com/.

37. "Sentence Executed: A Political Assassination," *Kommersant*, May 14, 2004.

38. Malashenko, *Ramzan Kadyrov*, 19.

39. Gordon M. Hahn, *Russia's Islamic Threat* (New Haven: Yale University Press, 2007), 34.

40. "Profile: Alu Alkhanov," BBC News, October 5, 2004, http://news.bbc.co.uk/.

41. "Beskadyrovshchina," Lenta.ru news service, May 2, 2006, http://lenta.ru/.

42. Aleksei Nikolskii and Yelena Rudneva, "Abramov Stepped Aside for Kadyrov," *Vedemosti* (Moscow), March 1, 2006, as reported by the RusData Dialine press digest (hereafter RusData).

43. Andrei Riskin, "A Son Should Go into Politics, Too," *Nezavisimaya Gazeta*, December 9, 2005, as reported by RusData.

44. Nikolskii and Rudneva, "Abramov Stepped Aside."

45. Ivan Sukhov, "Legislative Base Is Being Prepared in Chechnya for a Pre-Term Resignation of Alu Alkhanov," *Vremya Novostei*, May 12, 2006, as reported by Rus-Data.

46. "Kadyrov raspustil 'kadyrovstsev' [Kadyrov Set Free the kadyrovtsy]," Lenta.ru news service, April 29, 2006; Vladimir Mukhin and Andrei Riskin, "Ramzan Kadyrov Lost His Guards," *Nezavisimaya Gazeta*, May 3, 2006, as reported by RusData.

47. Aleksandr Zheglov and Sergei Mashkin, "Deadly Enemy," *Kommersant*, November 20, 2006, as reported by RusData.

48. Aleksandr Sidyachko, "Cousin for a Premier," *Gazeta* (Moscow), March 9, 2007, as reported by RusData.

49. Jason Lyall, "Are Coethnics More Effective Counterinsurgents? Evidence from the Second Chechen War," *American Political Science Review* 104, no. 1 (February 2010): 1–20.

50. Gilligan, *Terror in Chechnya*, 84–85.

51. Kira Latukhina and Anastasia Kornya, "Successful Amnesty Will Increase Kadyrov's Chances," *Vedomosti*, August 21, 2006, as reported by RusData.

52. C. J. Chivers, "To Smother Rebels, Arson Campaign in Chechnya," *New York Times*, September 29, 2008.

53. According to the Russian human rights organization Memorial, these statements were made at a meeting with parents that was broadcast on the Vajnakh Chechen television channel, April 7, 2010; http://www.memo.ru/eng/news/2010/07/08/080710.htm (page discontinued).

54. "Chechen Terror Family Chief Splits from Sons, Backs Kremlin," *Australian*, October 19, 2009.

55. Roland Dannreuther and Luke March, "Chechnya: Has Moscow Won?" *Survival* 50, no. 4 (August./September 2008): 97–112.

56. C. J. Chivers, "Slain Exile Detailed Cruelty of the Ruler of Chechnya," *New York Times*, February 1, 2009.

57. C. J. Chivers, "Top Chechen Gave Order for Abduction, Austria Says," *New York Times*, April 28, 2010.

58. Gilligan, *Terror in Chechnya*, 87.

59. Ivan Sukhov, "The Old Guard," *Vremya Novostei* (Moscow), July 29, 2009, as reported by the BBC.

60. Ivan Sukhov, "New Chechen Regime," *Vremya Novostei* (Moscow), May 8, 2009, and Aleksandr Gamov, "Ramzan Kadyrov: We Have Cornered the Rebels and We Will Put an End to Them Soon," *Komsomol'skaya Pravda*, September 16, 2009, both as reported by the BBC.

61. Gilligan, *Terror in Chechnya*, 85.

62. See "In the Court of the Chechen King," *People and Power*, Al Jazeera English television, October 21, 2009, http://www.youtube.com/ and "Ramzan Patriotic Club Part 2," *Highlights of the Week with Chrystal Callahan*, November 16, 2009, http://www.youtube.com/.

63. Fuller, "Putin Names Interim Chechen Leader."

64. Hughes, *Chechnya*, 118–19.

65. "Russian Politicians Survive Gun Attack in Chechnya," Interfax news agency (Moscow) in English, August 15, 2003, as reported by the BBC.

66. Ekho Moskvy Radio, May 31, 2004, as reported by the BBC.

67. Simon Saradzhyan, "Pro-Moscow Chechens Oppose Kadyrov," *Moscow Times*, June 20, 2000.

68. Mark Franchetti, "I'm Next on Chechnya's Death List," *Times* (London), May 10, 2009.

69. Yulia Maksimova, Eduard Yermolov, and Viktor Paukov, "Vostok Feels Kadyrov's Wrath," *Vremya Novostei*, April 16, 2008, as reported by RusData.

70. Ksenia Solyanskaya, "Kadyrov Gets Rid of Important Opponent," *Gazeta.ru*, May 14, 2008, as reported by RusData.

71. Musa Muradov, "Chechnya's Special Forces Suffer Layoffs," *Kommersant*, June 25, 2008, as reported by RusData.

72. Sergei Mashkin, "Chechen Hero of Russia Declared a Murderer," *Kommersant*, August 7, 2008, as reported by RusData.

73. Michael Schwirtz, "Former Rebel in Chechnya Is Killed in Moscow," *New York Times*, September 25, 2008.

74. "Chechen President's Deadly Foe Killed in Moscow," *Gazeta.ru*, September 26, 2008, as reported by RusData.

75. "Russia: A Chechen Assassination," STRATFOR, September 25, 2008.

76. Franchetti, "I'm Next on Chechnya's Death List."

77. Ellen Barry and Michael Schwirtz, "Killings of Chechen Leader's Foes May Test Kremlin's Will or Power to Restrain Him," *New York Times*, April 7, 2009.

78. Barry and Schwirtz, "Killings of Chechen Leader's Foes."

79. Ellen Barry, "Russia: Chechen Leader Taps Successor," *New York Times*, September 25, 2009.

80. Mark Franchetti, "Chechnya's President 'Ordered Me to Kill Rival,'" *Times* (London), May 2, 2010.

81. William Finnegan, "Letter from Mexico: Silver or Lead," *New Yorker*, May 31, 2010, 39, claims that local officials are given a choice: "Take a bribe or a bullet."

82. Amie Ferris-Rotman, "Chechen Leader, Rival Make Surprise Peace Deal," Reuters, August 24, 2010; "Kadyrov Expresses Condolences to Family of Late Commander Sulim Yamadayev," RIA Novosti press service, August 25, 2010.

83. Ivan Sukhov, "New Chechen Regime," *Vremya Novostei* (Moscow), May 8, 2009, as reported by the BBC.

84. In 2006 "in the North Caucasus" was dropped from the title. Ivan Sukhov, "New Chechen Regime," *Vremya Novostei* (Moscow), May 8, 2009, as reported by the BBC.

85. Trenin and Malashenko with Lieven, *Russia's Restless Frontier*, 40.

86. Kramer, "Perils of Counterinsurgency," 13–15.

87. Andrei Soldatov, "Kontrol' nad Chechnei peredan, no ne FSB" [Control over Chechnya has been transferred, but not to the FSB], *Ezhednevnyi Zhurnal* (Moscow), October 12, 2009, http://www.ej.ru/.

88. Sukhov, "New Chechen Regime."

89. Soldatov, "Kontrol' nad Chechnei peredan."

90. Decree no. 116, "O merakh po protivodesitviyu terrorizmu [On Measures for Countering Terrorism], February 15, 2006, with amendments from August 2, 2006, available at *Prezident. Ukazy* on the East View database. The clearest discussion of these orders and of changes in the command arrangements made over time is found in "Bor'ba s terrorizmom/Chechnya" [Struggle with terrorism/Chechnya], on the Agentura.ru website, http://studies.agentura.ru/tr/russia/sk/chechnya/.

91. This was outlined in point 6v of Decree no. 116 of 2006.

92. Andrei Soldatov, "The FSB's Provincial Empire: Reform of State Security Directorates in Russian Regions Urged," *Yezhednevnyi Zhurnal*, December 20, 2009, http://www.agentura.ru/english/dosie/fsb/regions.

93. Musa Muradov, "Vladimir Putin Leaves Chechnya to Ramzan Kadyrov," *Kommersant*, August 10, 2006, as reported by RusData.

94. Aleksandr Artemyev, Ilya Azar, and Roman Badanin, "An End to the War," *Gazeta.ru*, April 16, 2009, as reported by the BBC; Michael Schwirtz, "Russia Announces End of Operation in Chechnya," *New York Times*, April 17, 2009.

95. Schwirtz, "Russia Announces End of Operation in Chechnya."

96. Artemyev, Azar, and Badanin, "An End to the War."

97. Abdullin, interview with Ramzan Kadyrov.

98. Vladimir Georgievich Mukhin, "Tainaya chechenskaya voina" [Secret Chechen War]," *Nezavisimaya Gazeta* (Moscow), October 13, 2009.

99. Artemyev, Azar, and Badanin, "An End to the War."

100. Soldatov, "Kontrol' nad Chechnei peredan."

101. "Russia: Control of Chechnya's Operational Staff Handed over to FSB," ITAR-TASS News Agency (Moscow), October 7, 2009, as reported by the BBC.

102. "Bor'ba s terrorizmom/Chechnya" [Struggle with terrorism/Chechnya], on the Agentura.ru website, http://studies.agentura.ru/tr/russia/sk/chechnya/.

103. Abdullin, interview with Kadyrov.

104. Interfax news agency (Moscow), November 11, 2009, and December 14, 2009, as reported by the BBC.

105. Tatyana Stanovaya, "The 'Pension' Reform of the MVD," Politkom.ru website, February 24, 2010, as reported by the BBC on March 1, 2010.

106. Stanovaya, "Pension Reform."

107. "Kadyrov Seeks to Expel Illegal Migrants and Russian Police," Radio Free Europe/Radio Liberty, March 14, 2010.

108. Ekho Moskvy (Moscow) radio station, November 14, 2009, as reported by the BBC.

109. Liz Fuller, "Moscow, Chechnya See Next Stage of War against Terrorism Differently," Radio Free Europe/Radio Liberty, April 20, 2010.

110. See the reports on the Chechen Wahhabist rebel website, "Scandal: Kaydrov Publicly Criticized Medvedev for the North Caucasian District," January 22, 2010, and "Kremlin's Governor-General in the Caucasus Publicly Reprimanded Kadyrov," March 6, 2010, http://www.kavkazcenter.com/. Also see Natal'ia Gorodetskaia, "Aleksandr Khloponin Khochet Ob'edinit' Severnyi' Kavkaz i Sdelat' ego Chast'iu Rossii [Aleksandr Khloponin Wants to Unify the North Caucasus and Make his Own Part of Russia], *Kommersant Daily* 37, March 4, 2010.

111. Aleksandr Ryklin, "Brother Yamadayev's Shadow," *Yezhednevnyi Zhurnal*, May 15, 2009, as reported by the BBC.

112. Abdullin, interview with Ramzan Kadyrov.

113. Artemyev, Azar, and Badanin, "An End to the War."

114. "International Certificate Goes to Grozny Airport," *Chechnya Today*, November 13, 2009, http://chechnyatoday.com/; Andrei Kovalevskii and Igor Bakharev, "Foreign Planes Will Be Landing at Grozny," *Gazeta.ru*, November 6, 2009, as reported by the BBC.

115. "Historic Flight Leaves Chechnya," BBC News, November 16, 2009.

116. Grozny airport director Sultan Gambulatov, in "Chrystal Callahan—Grozny International Airport," April 5, 2010, a film clip apparently produced for Grozny Television; www.youtube.com/.

117. Soldatov, "Kontrol' nad Chechnei peredan."

118. Gambulatov, in "Chrystal Callahan: Grozny International Airport."

119. Mark Feygin, "Far from Moscow: Little Algeria," *Yezhednevnyi Zhurnal,* August 24, 2009, as reported by the BBC.

120. Kovalevskii and Bakharev, "Foreign Planes Will be Landing at Grozny."

121. Trenin and Malashenko with Lieven, *Russia's Restless Frontier,* 11.

122. Personal communication with the author, June 2010.

123. "Chrystal Callahan—Grozny International Airport."

124. Abdullin, interview with Ramzan Kadyrov.

125. A. A. Nesterenko, responses to media questions concerning the opening of the Chechen Republic's representative offices in a number of European countries, Russian Ministry of Foreign Affairs website, September 11, 2009, as reported by the BBC.

126. Ibragim Kerimov, interview with Ramzan Kadyrov, "Chechnya without Threats," *Rossiisskaya Gazeta,* February 12, 2010, as reported by the BBC on February 17, 2010.

127. Anna Arutunyan, "Return of the Prodigal Oligarchs," *Moscow News,* March 1, 2010.

128. "Telman Ismailov Considers Investing in Chechen Projects," *St. Petersburg Times,* February 19. 2010.

129. Gorodetskaia, "Aleksandr Khloponin Khochet Ob'edinit' Severnyi' Kavkaz."

130. Liz Fuller, "Chechnya Remains Bound to Moscow by Economic Weakness," Radio Free Europe/Radio Liberty, April 22, 2009.

131. Trenin and Malashenko with Lieven, *Russia's Restless Frontier,* 37–38.

132. "Chechen Premier Blames Moscow for Failed Chechen Recovery," *Kommersant,* October 1, 2005, as reported by the BBC.

133. Sergei Ryabukhin, report of the audit of the Chechen budget for January–June 2007, in Chetnaya Palata Rossiiskoi Federatsii [Audit Chamber of the Russian Federation], *Arkhiv Byulleteniia Chetnoi Palati,* no. 5, 2008, http://www.ach.gov.ru/.

134. Gordon M. Hahn, "The *Jihadi* Insurgency and the Russian Counterinsurgency in the North Caucasus," *Post-Soviet Affairs* 24, no. 1 (2008), 10.

135. "Russia to Set up Federal Body to Oversee Rebuilding of Georgia's Rebel Region," Interfax news agency (Moscow), December 25, 2008, as reported by the BBC.

136. Fuller, "Is Chechen Leader Losing Moscow's Trust?" For details of Mikhail Savchin's appointment to this post, see Dzhambulat Are, "Commissioner for Kadyrov's Rights," *Prague Watchdog,* December 1, 2008, http://www.watchdog.cz/.

137. Jane Armstrong, "Fealty to the Kremlin Suits War-Weary Chechens," *Globe and Mail* (Toronto), February 22, 2008.

138. Gregory Feifer, "The Price of Progress—Life in Kadyrov's Grozny Permeated by Fear," Radio Free Europe/Radio Liberty, August 11, 2009; and Anna Badkhen, "From Chechnya, a Cautionary Tale," *Boston Globe,* March 11, 2010.

139. Ilya Varlamov, "In Pictures: A Rare Glimpse of Grozny," BBC News, http://www.bbc.co.uk/news/world-europe-11455058.

140. Sophia Kishkovsky, "Tolstoy Recalled Fondly in Chechen Museum," *New York Times*, January 2, 2010.

141. Armstrong, "Fealty to the Kremlin."

142. Ruslan Kutayev, interviewed by Ivan Sukhov, "Russia's Behavior towards the Peoples of the Caucasus Is Dishonest," *Vremya Novostei*, April 15, 2008, as reported by the BBC.

143. Jonathan Littell, "Corruption in Chechnya," interview by *Prague Watchdog*, May 18, 2009, http://www.watchdog.cz/.

144. Kutayev interviewed by Sukhov, "Russia's Behavior."

145. Gamov, "Ramzan Kadyrov."

146. Littell, "Corruption in Chechnya."

147. Mark Dunn and Adrian Dunn, "Bloody Hands on Cup Money: Push to Withhold Dictator's $420,000," *Herald Sun* (Australia), November 20, 2009.

148. Maryam Arbiyeva, "Ramzan Kadyrov Inaugurated as Chechnya's New President," *Gazeta* 62, no. 1 (April 6, 2007), as reported by RusData.

149. Abdullin, interview with Ramzan Kadyrov.

150. Elise Giuliano, *Constructing Grievance: Ethnic Nationalism in Russia's Republics* (Ithaca: Cornell University Press, 2011).

151. Lieven, *Chechnya*; Gall and de Waal, *Chechnya*; Evangelista, *The Chechen Wars*; and Hughes, *Chechnya*.

152. Malashenko, *Ramzan Kadyrov*, 16.

153. Alexey Malashenko, "The Two Faces of Chechnya," *Carnegie Moscow Center Briefing* 9, no. 3 (July 2007), 3.

154. This possibility was hinted at by Lilia Shevtsova, *Russia: Lost in Transition* (Washington: Carnegie Endowment for International Peace, 2007), 281, and is sometimes heard as a rumor circulating among Kadyrov's detractors.

155. Vicken Cheterian, *War and Peace in the Caucasus: Ethnic Conflict and the New Geopolitics* (New York: Columbia University Press, 2008), 228.

156. Hughes, *Chechnya*, 24, 65; Gall and de Waal, *Chechnya*, 108.

157. "Gantemirov Gets Out of Prison Early," *Moscow Times*, September 11, 1999.

158. Hughes, *Chechnya*, 63.

159. Thomas de Waal, "What Follows Victory?" *Moscow Times*, December 11, 1999; Yevgenia Albats, "Power Play: Thugs Occupy Power Vacuum in Chechnya," *Moscow Times*, January 27, 2000.

160. Trenin and Malashenko with Lieven, *Russia's Restless Frontier*, 37.

161. Hughes, *Chechnya*, 124.

162. Simon Saradzhyan, "Chechen Leaders Unite at Kazantsev's Demand," *Moscow Times*, July 22, 2000.

163. "Gantamirov Named Chechnya's Press and Information Minister," *Jamestown Foundation Monitor* 8, no. 31 (February 13, 2002).

164. Gilligan, *Terror in Chechnya*, 84.

165. "Kadyrov versus Gantamirov: Trouble Brewing," *North Caucasus Analysis* (Jamestown Foundation) 6, no. 22 (June 7, 2005).

166. Jan H. Kalicki, "Oil on the Silk Road," *World Today* 56, no. 8/9 (August/September 2000), 27–28.

167. Abdullin, interview with Kadyrov.

168. "Russia: Oil," U.S. Energy Information Administration Country Analysis Briefs, May 2008, http://www.eia.doe.gov/emeu/cabs/Russia/Oil.html.

169. Derluguian, *Bourdieu's Secret Admirer in the Caucasus*, 256.

170. Dar'ia Pyl'nova and Dmitrii Shkrylev, "Voina za Chechenskuiu Neft'" [The War over Chechen Oil], *Novaia Gazeta* 9 (January 30, 2009), East View database.

171. Roman Kupchinsky, "Stolen Oil and Purchased Guns," Radio Free Europe/Radio Liberty, October 25, 2005.

172. Politkovskaya, *A Small Corner of Hell*, 166–73.

173. Ibid., 140; Gregory Feifer, "The Price of Progress: Life in Kadyrov's Grozny Permeated by Fear," Radio Free Europe/Radio Liberty, August 11, 2009.

174. Pyl'nova and Shkrylev, "Voina za Chechenskuiu Neft'."

175. Abdullin, interview with Ramzan Kadyrov.

176. Pyl'nova and Shkrylev, "Voina za Chechenskuiu Neft'."

177. Pyl'nova and Shkrylev, "Voina za Chechenskuiu Neft'."

178. Kutayev, interviewed by Sukhov, "Russia's Behavior"; "Rosneft to Build Oil Refinery in Chechnya," *Daily Telegraph*, February 23, 2010.

179. Kerimov, interview with Kadyrov, "Chechnya without Threats."

180. Quoted by Barry and Schwirtz, "Killings of Chechen Leader's Foes."

181. Lyall, "Are Coethnics More Effective Counterinsurgents?," 9.

182. This data has been compiled by the Human Rights and Security Initiative of the Center for Strategic and International Studies, "Violence in the North Caucasus," Washington, DC, August 2009, http://csis.org/files/publication/ViolenceNorth CaucasusAugust2009.pdf, and Gordon M. Hahn, "The Caucasus Emirate's Summer 2009 Suicide Bombing Campaign," *Islam, Islamism, and Politics in Eurasia Report* (Monterey Institute of International Studies) 1, no. 3 (November 27, 2009).

183. Paul Goble, "Chechnya Is More Violent Than Reported," *Moscow Times*, October 28, 2010.

184. Valery Dzutsev, "Kadyrov's Forces Accused of Aiding the Insurgency and Obstructing Federal Forces," *Eurasia Daily Monitor* (Jamestown Foundation) 7, no. 138 (July 19, 2010).

185. Gordon M. Hahn, "Comparing the Level of Caucasus Emirate Terrorist Activity in 2008 and 2009," *Islam, Islamism and Politics in Eurasia Report* (Monterey Institute of International Studies) 8 (February 5, 2010).

186. "Chechnya without CTO: 292 Casualties in 320 Days," *Caucasian Knot*, March 2, 2010, http://www.eng.kavkaz-uzel.ru/.

187. David Nowak, "Chechen Rebels Claim Russian Train Bombing," *Washington Post*, December 2, 2009.

188. Ivan Sukhov, "This War Will Never Be Over," *Vremya Novostei* (Moscow), June 24, 2009, as reported by the BBC; Dmitry Trenin as quoted by Catherine Belton, "Chechen

Leader's Strong-Arm Tactics Sow Chaos in Caucasus," *Financial Times*, July 18–19, 2009.

189. Sergei Markedonov, "Ramzan the Tamer," *Gazeta.ru*, July 1, 2009, as reported by the BBC.

190. Sergei Markedonov, quoted by Paul Goble, "Chechnya Far from Peaceful and Far Less under Russian Control in Year Since Moscow Ended 'Counter-Terrorist Operation' There," *Window on Eurasia*, http://windowoneurasia.blogspot.com, April 15, 2010.

191. Philip P. Pan, "Medvedev Decries Chechen Killings," *Washington Post*, August 15, 2009.

192. "Russia in the Lead in 2009 by Number of Claims Submitted to ECtHR," *Caucasian Knot*, January 29, 2010, http://www.eng.kavkaz-uzel.ru/.

193. "Special Unit Set up to Probe Chechen Disappearances," ITAR-TASS News Agency, March 2, 2010, as reported by the BBC.

194. Liz Fuller, "Is Ramzan Kadyrov's Star on the Wane?" *Caucasus Report*, Radio Free Europe/Radio Liberty, February 1, 2010.

195. Dmitrii Yefimovich Furman, "Feudal Borders of Power Hierarchy," *Nezavisimaya Gazeta*, September 9, 2009, as reported by the BBC.

196. Ellen Barry, "Echoes of a Grim Past: Chechnya and Its Neighbors Suffer a Relapse," *New York Times*, August 30, 2009.

197. Emil Souleimanov and Ondrej Ditrych, "The Internationalization of the Russia-Chechen Conflict: Myths and Reality," *Europe-Asia Studies* 60, no. 7 (September 2008): 1199–1222, esp. 1217–20.

198. Hahn, "The *Jihadi* Insurgency," 27.

199. Liz Fuller, "Is Chechen Leader Losing Moscow's Trust?" Radio Free Europe/Radio Liberty, April 7, 2009.

200. "In the Court of the Chechen King."

201. Hughes, *Chechnya*.

202. Littell, "Corruption in Chechnya."

203. Ivan Semashko, "Kadyrov Thinks Chechen Women Should Observe Traditional Dress Code," *Noviye Izvestiia*, no. 167 (September 14, 2007), as reported by RusData; "Chechen President Restricts Vodka Sales," *Moscow Times*, February 19, 2009.

204. Amie Ferris-Rotman, "Analysis: Sharia Law Threatens Moscow Control in Muslim Chechnya," Reuters, August 26, 2010.

205. Aleksey Makarkin, "The Islamization of a 'Problematical' Subject," Politkom.ru website, September 16, 2009, as reported by the BBC on September 23, 2009.

206. "In the Court of the Chechen King."

207. "Chechen President Comes to Saudi Arabia for Religious Pilgrimage," RIA Novosti press service, July 11, 2010.

208. "Paintball Attacks on Women Prompt Outrage," Reuters, June 18, 2010.

209. Elena Milashina, "Den' Chechenskoi Zhenshchiny [Chechen Women's Day]," *Novaya Gazeta* 105, September 22, 2010, http://www.novayagazeta.ru/data/2010/105/08.html.

210. Malashenko, "The Two Faces of Chechnya."

211. Ibid.; Dmitry Butrin, Musa Muradov and Alvina Kharchenko, "Ramzan Kadyrov Chooses Freedom," *Kommersant* (Moscow) no. 166 (September 8, 2006), as reported by RusData.

212. Anders Åslund, "The End of the Putin Model," *Washington Post*, February 26, 2010.

213. Claire Egg, "Tide of Protest Engulfs More Russian Cities," Radio Free Europe/Radio Liberty, March 10, 2010.

214. RIA Novosti (in Russian), published in *Rossiisskaya Gazeta* (Moscow), February 12, 2010, http://www.rg.ru/.

215. "Russian 2010 Budget Balanced if Oil at $95 per Barrel—Kudrin (Part 2)," Interfax news agency (Moscow), May 15, 2010.

216. Paul Goble has monitored the current Russian discussion of this issue in his *Windows on Eurasia* blog, for example on March 23, 2009, and May 24, 2010; http://windowoneurasia.blogspot.com.

217. "Russian Envoy to North Caucasus Calls for More Effective Use of Budget Funds," RIA Novosti (in Russian) and ITAR-TASS (in English) news agencies, February 24, 2010, as reported by the BBC.

218. "Ramzan Kadyrov Inaugurated as Head of Chechnya for Second Term," ITAR-TASS News Agency, April 5, 2011.

219. Hahn, "The *Jihadi* Insurgency," 35.

220. Lyall's painstaking research of each reported "sweep" campaign in Chechnya between 2000 and 2005 suggests that the tactics used by Russian and Chechen units were similar, and that if anything the Russian units were more indiscriminate in their use of violence. Lyall, "Are Coethnics More Effective Counterinsurgents?"

221. Robert A. Pape, Lindsey O'Rourke, and Jenna McDermit, "What Makes Chechen Women So Dangerous?" *New York Times*, March 31, 2010.

222. American Committee for Peace in the Caucasus, "The Yevkurov Experiment," November 18, 2009, http://www.peaceinthecaucasus.org/sites/default/files/pdf/Yevkurov_Assessment.pdf.

6. It Takes Three: Washington, Baghdad, and the Sons of Iraq

1. I will refer to the groups in question simply as "Sunni," in line with common practice in the United States. The Kurds of Iraq are also mostly Sunni, but are not Arab.

2. Timothy Williams and Duraid Adnan, "Sunnis in Iraq Allied with U.S. Quitting to Rejoin Rebels," *New York Times*, October 17, 2010.

3. Ned Parker, "Al Qaeda in Iraq Rises Again," *Los Angeles Times*, September 13, 2010; and Timothy Williams, "Insurgent Group in Iraq, Declared Tamed, Roars," *New York Times*, September 27, 2010.

4. "Iraqi Civilian Casualties Estimated at Wartime Low," *New York Times*, December 30, 2010.

5. International Crisis Group, *Loose Ends: Iraq's Security Forces between U.S. Drawdown and Withdrawal*, Middle East Report 99, October 26, 2010, 6, http://www.crisisgroup.org/.

6. Najim Abed Al-Jabour and Sterling Jensen, "The Iraqi and AQI Roles in the Sunni Awakening," *Prism* (journal of the National Defense University Center of Complex Operations) 2, no. 1 (December 2010): 3–18.

7. Marc Lynch, "Explaining the Awakening: Engagement, Publicity, and the Transformation of Iraqi Sunni Political Attitudes," *Security Studies* 20, no. 1 (Spring 2011): 1–37.

8. International Crisis Group, *Loose Ends,* 33n190.

9. Jim Michaels, *A Chance in Hell: The Men Who Triumphed over Iraq's Deadliest City and Turned the Tide of War* (New York: St. Martin's Press, 2010), pp. 143, 174.

10. Lynch, "Explaining the Awakening."

11. Farook Ahmed, "Sons of Iraq and Awakening Forces," *Institute for the Study of War Backgrounder* 23, February 21, 2008, http://www.understandingwar.org/. For striking visual evidence of each of these patterns, see the charts included in US Department of Defense, "Measuring Stability and Security in Iraq," Report to Congress in accordance with the Department of Defense Appropriations Act 2008 (Section 9010, Public Law 109–289), March 7, 2008, 18–22, http://www.defense.gov/pubs/.

12. Multi-National Forces Iraq, slides accompanying prepared testimony of David H. Petraeus before the US Congress on the situation in Iraq, September 10–11, 2007, esp. slide 8, http://www.defense.gov/pubs/.

13. Stephen Biddle, "Stabilizing Iraq from the Bottom Up," prepared remarks, testimony before the US Senate Committee on Foreign Relations, 110th Congress, April 2, 2008, 7; Biddle, "Patient Stabilized?" *National Interest,* March/April 2008, 22.

14. For the argument that sectarian tensions in Iraq qualified as a civil war, see James D. Fearon, "Iraq: Democracy or Civil War?" testimony before the US House of Representatives Subcommittee on National Security, Emerging Threats, and International Relations, September 15, 2006, http://cisac.stanford.edu/publications/iraq_democracy_or_civil_war; and Fearon, "Iraq's Civil War," *Foreign Affairs* 86, no. 2 (March/April 2007): 2–15.

15. Julian E. Barnes and Adam Entous, "U.S., NATO Look to Use Local Police in Afghanistan," *Wall Street Journal,* September 16, 2010.

16. Carlotta Gall, "NATO Seeks Afghan Police in South," *New York Times,* November 13, 2010; Jon Lee Anderson, "Letter from Khost: Force and Futility," *New Yorker* 87, no. 13 (May 16, 2011).

17. Andrew Rathmell, Olga Oliker, Terrence K. Kelly, David Brannan, and Keith Crane, *Developing Iraq's Security Sector: The Coalition Provisional Authority's Experience* (Santa Monica: RAND, 2005), 65–71, and David C. Gompert, Terrence K. Kelly, and Jessica Watkins, *Security in Iraq: A Framework for Analyzing Emerging Threats as U.S. Forces Leave* (Santa Monica: RAND, 2010).

18. Biddle, "Stabilizing Iraq from the Bottom Up."

19. Author's interview with Stephen Biddle, Washington, DC, May 25, 2010. Also see Thomas E. Ricks, *The Gamble: General David Petraeus and the American Military Adventure in Iraq, 2006–2008* (New York: Penguin, 2009), 208.

20. Michaels, *Chance in Hell,* 135.

21. James Warden, "Transitions Aren't Easy for Sons of Iraq," *Stars and Stripes,* Mideast ed., September 24, 2008.

22. See "Al-Anbar Progress?," *People and Power,* Al Jazeera English television, September 9, 2007, http://www.youtube.com/.

23. Keiko Sakai, "Tribalization as a Tool of State Control in Iraq: Observations on the Army, the Cabinets, and the National Assembly," in *Tribes and Power: Nationalism and Ethnicity in the Middle East*, ed. Faleh Abdul-Jabar and Hosham Dawod (London: Saqi, 2003), 139–40.

24. Kevin M. Woods et al., *Iraqi Perspectives Report: Saddam's Senior Leadership on Operation Iraq Freedom from the Official U.S. Joint Forces Command Report* (Annapolis: US Naval Institute Press, 2006).

25. Ibid., 3–4.

26. Nora Boustany, "Anti-Regime Riots, 30 Deaths Reported in Iraqi Province," *Washington Post*, June 2, 1995. Also see Austin Long, "The Anbar Awakening," *Survival* 50, no. 2 (April/May 2008), 76.

27. Woods et al., *Iraqi Perspectives Report*.

28. Woods et al., *Iraqi Perspectives Report*, 53–54, 149.

29. Dexter Filkins, "Complexity of Iraq Insurgency Helps it to Survive," *New York Times*, December 2, 2005.

30. Ahmed S. Hashim, *Insurgency and Counterinsurgency in Iraq* (Ithaca: Cornell University Press, 2006), esp. pp. 184 and 201.

31. Nora Bensahel et al., *After Saddam: Prewar Planning and the Occupation of Iraq* (Santa Monica: RAND, 2008), 140–41; James Dobbins, "Occupying Iraq: A Short History of the CPA," *Survival* 51, no. 3 (June/July 2009), 141.

32. For an example of this claim, see Nir Rosen, *The Triumph of the Martyrs: A Reporter's Journey into Occupied Iraq* (Washington, DC: Potomac Books, 2008), 138.

33. Dobbins, "Occupying Iraq," 157.

34. Lin Todd et al., *Iraq Tribal Study—Al Anbar Governorate: The Albu Fahd Tribe, the Albu Mahal Tribe and the Albu Issa Tribe*, completed under contract with the US Department of Defense, June 18, 2006, p. ES-12 (Executive Summary, p. 12), http://www.comw.org/warreport/fulltext/0709todd.pdf.

35. Bensahel et al., *After Saddam*, 141.

36. Special Inspector General, Iraq Reconstruction, *Hard Lessons: The Iraq Reconstruction Experience*, ed. Stuart W. Bowen Jr. (Washington, DC: US Government Printing Office, 2009), 250.

37. David Cloud and Greg Jaffe, *The Fourth Star: Four Generals and the Epic Struggle for the Future of the United States Army* (New York: Random House Crown Publishers, 2009), 238–39.

38. Kimberly Kagan, *The Surge: A Military History* (New York: Encounter Books, 2009), 6.

39. Special Inspector General, *Hard Lessons*, 252.

40. International Crisis Group, *Loose Ends*, 6–8 and 14–17.

41. Cloud and Jaffe, *Fourth Star*, 239.

42. "Battle for Baghdad's Belt," *Jane's Terrorism and Security Monitor*, March 6, 2009.

43. Kenneth Katzman, "Al Qaeda in Iraq: Assessment and Outside Links," Congressional Research Service Report for Congress, RL32217, Washington, DC, August 15, 2008, 9–10, 10–11, available http://www.dtic.mil/.

44. An unsigned letter claiming that attacks against the Shia were engineered to provoke a spiral of violence was found by US troops in February. US officials

reported that the letter was written by AQI leader Abu Musab al-Zarqawi and addressed to senior Al Qaeda leaders abroad. One prominent analyst argues that it was probably not Zarqawi who wrote it, but instead Iraqi Sunni insurgents who wished to gain more Al Qaeda support for their activities. See Evgenii Novikov, "Baathist Origins of the Zarqawi Letter," *Terrorism Monitor* (Jamestown Foundation) 2, no. 6 (March 24, 2004), http://www.jamestown.org/.

45. For descriptions of the Saddam era, see Woods, et al., *Iraqi Perspectives Report*, 4, 55.

46. Sabah al-Sattam Effan Fahran al-Shurji al-Aziz, in *Al-Anbar Awakening, Vol. II: Iraqi Perspectives*, ed. Gary W. Montgomery and Timothy S. McWilliams (Quantico, VA: US Marines Corps University, 2009), 144.

47. Katzman, "Al Qaeda in Iraq," 9–10.

48. Brian Fishman, ed., *Bombers, Bank Accounts, and Bleedout: Al-Qa'ida's Road In and Out of Iraq* (West Point: Combating Terrorism Center, 2008), 12, http://www.ctc.usma.edu/harmony/pdf/Sinjar_2_July_23.pdf.

49. Rosen, *Triumph of the Martyrs*, 41–43.

50. Ibid., 59, 66.

51. Mahan Abedin, "Iraq's Divided Insurgents," *Mideast Monitor* 1, no. 1 (February 2006), http://www.mideastmonitor.org/.

52. Lydia Khalil, "Leader of 1920 Revolution Brigades Killed by Al-Qaeda," *Terrorism Focus* (Jamestown Foundation) 4, no. 9 (April 10, 2007).

53. Nir Rosen, "Iraq's Jordanian Jihadis," *New York Times*, February 19, 2006.

54. Katzman, "Al Qaeda in Iraq," 12.

55. Fishman, ed., *Bombers, Bank Accounts, and Bleedout*, 12.

56. Lynch, "Explaining the Awakening," 9–10.

57. Katzman, "Al Qaeda in Iraq," 13.

58. Col. David Sutherland, interviewed by Kimberly Kagan, Institute for the Study of War, October 25, 2007; http://www.understandingwar.org/.

59. Jacob Shapiro, "Bureaucratic Terrorists: Al-Qa'ida in Iraq's Management and Finances," in *Bombers, Bank Accounts, and Bleedout*, ed. Fishman, 74.

60. Katzman, "Al Qaeda in Iraq," 16.

61. Author's telephone interview with Omar al-Shahery, former deputy director general of defense intelligence in the Iraqi Ministry of Defense, May 18, 2010.

62. Williams, "Insurgent Group in Iraq."

63. Michaels, *Chance in Hell*, 196–98.

64. Shapiro, "Bureaucratic Terrorists," 66–80.

65. I am grateful to Austin Long for this point.

66. This was reported on combat journalist Michael Yon's blog, "Drilling for Justice," *Michael Yon Online Magazine*, June 24, 2007, http://www.michaelyon-online.com/drilling-for-justice.htm, and repeated independently in author's telephone interview with Omar al-Shahery, June 30, 2010.

67. David J. Kilcullen, "Anatomy of a Tribal Revolt," *Small Wars Journal Blog*, August 29, 2007, http://www.smallwarsjournal.com/; Kilcullen, "Field Notes on Iraq's Tribal Revolt against al-Qa'ida," *CTC Sentinel* (Combating Terrorism Center at West Point)

1, no. 11 (October 2008): 1–5; "Iraq's 'Al Qaeda Widows' Seek Help, Rehabilitation," *Radio Free Europe/Radio Liberty Iraq Report*, October 1, 2010, http://www.rferl.org/.

68. Michael R. Gordon, "G.I.'s Forge Sunni Tie in Bid to Squeeze Militants," *New York Times, July 6, 2007.*

69. Alissa J. Rubin and Stephen Farrell, citing Lt. Col. Michael Getchell, "Awakening Councils by Region," *New York Times*, December 22, 2007; Nir Rosen, "The Myth of the Surge," *Rolling Stone*, March 6, 2008, quoting an unnamed US Army officer talking about Abu Salih in the Baghdad neighborhood of Dora.

70. Author's telephone interview with Omar al-Shahery, May 18, 2010.

71. Author's telephone interview with Col. John W. Charlton, May 12, 2010.

72. Biddle, "Stabilizing Iraq from the Bottom Up," 10; Biddle, "Patient Stabilized?," 23; author's interview with Lt. Col. (Ret.) John Nagl, Washington, DC, August 30, 2010.

73. Author's interview with Charlton.

74. Michael Gisick, "CLC Recruiting Drive Targets Detainees," *Stars and Stripes*, Mideast ed., February 3, 2008.

75. Rosen, *Triumph of the Martyrs*, 181–83.

76. Phil Williams, *Criminals, Militias, and Insurgents: Organized Crime In Iraq* (Carlisle, PA: US Army War College Strategic Studies Institute, 2009), 226, http://www.strategicstudiesinstitute.army.mil/.

77. Williams, *Criminals, Militias, and Insurgents*, 49.

78. Alissa J. Rubin, "Guns Go Silent after 24-Hour Face-Off in Baghdad," *New York Times*, March 29, 2009.

79. Lt. Col. David Buckingham, quoted by Geoff Ziezulewicz, "U.S. Troops, Iraqi Army Work to Secure Baghdad District after Militia Leader's Arrest," *Stars and Stripes*, Mideast ed., April 5, 2009.

80. Ghaith Abdul-Ahad, "Meet Abu Abed: The US's New Ally against al-Qaida," *Guardian* (UK), November 10, 2007.

81. Bill Ardolino, "In Pictures: Patrolling the Shorja Market with the Sons of Iraq," *Long War Journal*, May 12, 2008, http://www.longwarjournal.org/.

82. For a bald statement of the idea that patronage is a key component of authority in Arab tribal culture, see Carl Salzman, *Culture and Conflict in the Middle East* (Amherst, NY: Humanity Books, 2008). This was a frequent theme raised in the author's own interviews with Americans who had worked with the SOI.

83. Hosham Dawod, "The 'State-ization' of the Tribe and the Tribalization of the State: The Case of Iraq," in *Tribes and Power*, ed. Abdul-Jabar and Dawod, 113.

84. Kilcullen, "Anatomy of a Tribal Revolt."

85. Ricks, *The Gamble*, 195–96.

86. Rory Stewart, *The Prince of the Marshes, and Other Occupational Hazards of a Year in Iraq* (New York: Harcourt, 2006), 47–52.

87. Center for Army Lessons Learned, *Operation Iraqi Freedom Initial Impressions Report*, no. 04–13, May 2004, 39, http://www.globalsecurity.org/.

88. Michaels, *Chance in Hell*, 1.

89. Todd et al., *Iraq Tribal Study.*

90. Toby Dodge, *Inventing Iraq: The Failure of Nation Building and a History Denied* (New York: Columbia University Press, 2003), 75.

91. Austin Long, "War Comes to Al Anbar: Political Conflict in an Iraqi Province," paper prepared for delivery at the International Studies Association Annual Convention, New York, February 2009.

92. Faleh A. Jabar, "Sheikhs and Ideologues: Deconstruction and Reconstruction of Tribes under Patrimonial Totalitarianism in Iraq, 1968–1998," in *Tribes and Power*, ed. Abdul-Jabar and Dawod, 75.

93. Todd et al., *Iraq Tribal Study*, 3-17 (chap. 3, p. 17).

94. Jabar, "Sheikhs and Ideologues," 76.

95. Dodge, *Inventing Iraq*, 111.

96. Sakai, "Tribalization as a Tool of State Control in Iraq"; author's telephone interview with Omar al-Shahery, May 18, 2010.

97. Amatzia Baram, "Neo-Tribalism in Iraq: Saddam Hussein's Tribal Policies 1991–96," *International Journal of Middle East Studies* 29 (1997), 3–4.

98. Jabar, "Sheikhs and Ideologues," 80.

99. Dawod, "The 'State-ization' of the Tribe," 120–21.

100. Jabar, "Sheikhs and Ideologues," 82; Baram, "Neo-Tribalism in Iraq," 2.

101. Baram, "Neo-Tribalism in Iraq," 5–8, 19.

102. Todd et al., *Iraq Tribal Study*, 3-38 (chap. 3, p. 38); Baram, "Neo-Tribalism in Iraq," 20.

103. Jabar, "Sheikhs and Ideologues," 74.

104. Todd et al., *Iraq Tribal Study*, 5-53–54 (chap. 5, pp. 53–54); author's telephone interview with Omar al-Shahery, May 18, 2010.

105. Todd et al., *Iraq Tribal Study*, 5-50 (chap. 5, p. 50); 5-51 (chap. 5, p. 51); author's telephone interview with Omar al-Shahery, May 18, 2010.

106. Todd et al., *Iraq Tribal Study*, 4-4 (chap. 4, p. 4).

107. Ibid., 5-47 (chap. 5, p. 47).

108. Baram, "Neo-Tribalism in Iraq," 12, 13.

109. Williams, *Criminals, Militias, and Insurgents*, 25–26.

110. Jabar, "Sheikhs and Ideologues," 77–78.

111. Todd et al, *Iraq Tribal Study*, ES-5 (Executive Summary, p. 5), 3-37 (chap. 3, p. 37), 2-2 (chap. 2, p. 2).

112. Ibid., 2-36–40 (chap. 2, pp. 36–40).

113. Michaels, *Chance in Hell*, p. 155.

114. Austin Long, "Why Anbar Voted for Allawi," *Middle East Channel* (*Foreign Policy* blog), April 5, 2010, http://mideast.foreignpolicy.com/.

115. Author's telephone interview with Lt. Gen. John R. Allen, June 18, 2010.

116. Michaels, *Chance in Hell*, especially comments made by Petraeus, 92–93.

117. Author's telephone interview with Omar al-Shahery, May 18, 2010.

118. George Tenet with Bill Harlow, *At the Center of the Storm: My Years at the CIA* (New York: Harper Collins, 2007), 418–19, 440–41; author's telephone interview with

Omar al-Shahery, May 18, 2010. Al-Shahery helped arrange one major meeting in 2004 that had no lasting impact.

119. Author's telephone interview with Omar al-Shahery, June 30, 2010.

120. Lynch, "Explaining the Awakening," 28–29.

121. Kilcullen, "Anatomy of a Tribal Revolt"; Kilcullen, "Field Notes."

122. Wissam Abd al-Ibrahim al-Hardan al-Aethawi (former first deputy of the Sahwa movement), in *Al-Anbar Awakening, Vol. II: Iraqi Perspectives*, 56; Michaels, *Chance in Hell*; author's telephone interview with Omar al-Shahery, May 18, 2010.

123. Biddle, "Stabilizing Iraq from the Bottom Up," 6–7.

124. Rosen, "Myth of the Surge."

125. "An Interview with Raymond T. Odierno," *Prism* 1, no. 2 (March 2010), 147.

126. Author's interview with Charlton.

127. John A. McCary, "The Anbar Awakening: An Alliance of Incentives," *Washington Quarterly* 32, no. 1 (January 2009), 44; Kagan, *The Surge*; Michaels, *Chance in Hell*.

128. Al-Jabouri and Jensen, "Iraqi and AQI Roles in the Sunni Awakening."

129. Michael R. Gordon, "101st Airborne Scores Success in Northern Iraq," *New York Times*, September 4, 2003; Mark Martins, "No Small Change of Soldiering: The Commander's Emergency Response Program (CERP) in Iraq and Afghanistan," *Army Lawyer*, February 2004 (DA PAM 27-50-369), 8–9; Linda Robinson, *Tell Me How This Ends: General David Petraeus and the Search for a Way out of Iraq* (New York: Public Affairs, 2008), 68–72; Carter Malkasian, "Counterinsurgency in Iraq: May 2003–January 2007," in *Counterinsurgency in Modern Warfare*, ed. Daniel Marston and Carter Malkasian (New York: Osprey Publishing, 2008), 243.

130. Thomas E. Ricks, "The Lessons of Counterinsurgency," *Washington Post*, February 16, 2006; George Packer, "Letter from Iraq: The Lesson of Tal Afar," *New Yorker* 82, no. 8 (April 10, 2006), 49–65; Malkasian, "Counterinsurgency in Iraq," 251–52; Bing West, *The Strongest Tribe: War, Politics, and the Endgame in Iraq* (New York: Random House, 2008), 84–88.

131. Carter Malkasian, "Signaling Resolve, Democratization, and the First Battle of Fallujah," *Journal of Strategic Studies* 29, no. 3 (June 2006): 423–52; Malkasian, "Did the Coalition Need More Forces in Iraq?," *Joint Forces Quarterly* 46, no. 3 (2007), 121–23; Malkasian, "Counterinsurgency in Iraq," 247–48; and West, *Strongest Tribe*, 50–53, 88–93, 286. For a scathing view of the Fallujah Brigade episode in particular, see Rosen, *Triumph of the Martyrs*, 139–40, 150–59. For confirmation of CIA involvement, see Stephen Manning, "CIA Chief: Military Strikes offer Lessons," *USA Today*, September 17, 2008; I am grateful to Austin Long for this citation.

132. Jeanne F. Hull, *Iraq: Strategic Reconciliation, Targeting, and Key Leader Engagement* (Carlisle, PA: US Army War College Strategic Studies Institute, 2009), 2, http://www.strategicstudiesinstitute.army.mil/.

133. Author's telephone interview with Keith Mines (US State Department governance coordinator in Al Anbar Province from August 2003 to February 2004), April 19, 2010.

134. Hull, *Iraq*, 2.

135. Elaine M. Grossman, "New Bush Strategy in Iraq Will Aim to Shield Public from Insurgents," *Inside the Pentagon*, November 3, 2005. For a critique of the PRTs in

practice, see Blake Stone, "Blind Ambition: Lessons Learned and Not Learned in an Embedded PRT," *Prism* 1, no. 4 (September 2010): 147–58.

136. For examples of what this meant on the ground, see Packer, "Letter from Iraq," 50, and Michaels, *Chance in Hell*, 3.

137. Biddle, "Stabilizing Iraq from the Bottom Up," 3.

138. For examples, see Nir Rosen, "An Ugly Peace: What Changed Iraq," *Boston Review* 34, no. 6 (November/December 2009): 17–21.

139. Drew Brown, "Commanders Warn Groups of Infiltration," *Stars and Stripes*, European ed., February 6, 2008.

140. Raymond Odierno, interviewed by David Feith, "How the Surge Was Won," *Wall Street Journal*, September 18–19, 2010; Michaels, *Chance in Hell*.

141. Lynch, "Explaining the Awakening," 7–8.

142. Author's interview with Allen.

143. Author's telephone interview with Col. Richard D. Welch, former chief of the Reconciliation and Engagement Program with the US Division Center in Baghdad, June 24, 2010.

144. Author's interview with Allen; West, *Strongest Tribe*, 293–94.

145. Greg Jaffe, "Tribal Connections," *Wall Street Journal*, August 8, 2007.

146. Michael Gisick, "U.S. Tries to Bridge Gap between Iraqi Rivals," *Stars and Stripes*, Mideast ed., February 19, 2008.

147. Author's interview with Allen.

148. "U.S. Strategy in Iraq," James Fallows's hosting of *The Charlie Rose Show* on PBS television, March 31, 2006, http://video.google.com/, including comments by Fallows, Lt. Col. (ret.) Lewis Sorley, and Nagl; Ricks, *The Gamble*, 12–30.

149. West, *Strongest Tribe*, 173–74.

150. Packer, "Letter from Iraq," 53–54.

151. One of Petraeus's first speeches to commanders focused on reconciliation. See Cloud and Jaffe, *Fourth Star*, 257.

152. Hull, *Iraq*.

153. Author's interview with Welch.

154. Hull, *Iraq*, 2–4, 13.

155. Odierno's role is emphasized by Kagan, *The Surge*, esp. p. 197.

156. Kagan, *The Surge*, 32, 37–38.

157. Author's interview with Charlton.

158. The new manual was developed by a group of officers and civilian consultants led by Conrad Crane and Nagl under the direction of both Petraeus and Mattis. *Counterinsurgency Field Manual*, US Army Field Manual 3-24 (chap. 3, p. 24) and Marine Corps Warfighting Publication 3-33.5 (chap. 3, p. 33.5) (Chicago: University of Chicago Press, 2007). There are only two lines mentioning outreach to insurgents, on 5-12 (chap. 5, p. 12) and 5-30 (chap. 5, p. 30; Table 5-8); neither uses the word "reconciliation."

159. Author's interview with Nagl.

160. "Rumsfeld's Memo of Options for the Iraq War," *New York Times*, December 3, 2006. The Pentagon confirmed the authenticity of the memo.

161. Author's interview with Nagl.

162. Kimberly Kagan, "The Anbar Awakening: Displacing al Qaeda from Its Stronghold in Western Iraq," Institute for the Study of War, Iraq Report 3, April 5, 2007, 4, http://www.understandingwar.org/report/anbar-awakening.

163. Rosen, "Iraq's Jordanian Jihadis"; Rosen, *Triumph of the Martyrs*.

164. Long, "Anbar Awakening"; McCary, "Anbar Awakening."

165. Long, "Anbar Awakening," 7–8; McCary, "Anbar Awakening," 47.

166. In-depth examples include Long, "Anbar Awakening"; McCary, "Anbar Awakening"; Ricks, *The Gamble*, 62–72; and Michaels, *A Chance in Hell*.

167. McCary, "Anbar Awakening," 47.

168. Author's interview with Allen. Also see Alissa J. Rubin, "Sunni Sheik Who Backed U.S. in Iraq Is Killed," *New York Times*, September 14, 2007.

169. Author's interview with Allen.

170. Long, "War Comes to Al Anbar," 11.

171. Rosen, *Triumph of the Martyrs*.

172. Malkasian, "Signaling Resolve."

173. Author's telephone interview with Omar al-Shahery, June 30, 2010.

174. The timeline is chronicled by Todd et al., *Iraq Tribal Study*, 4-32 to 4-35 (chap. 4, pp. 32–35); Long, "Anbar Awakening," 78–79; and West, *Strongest Tribe*, 101–2.

175. Todd et al., *Iraq Tribal Study*, 4-32 (chap. 4, p. 32).

176. Long, "Anbar Awakening," 78.

177. Michaels, *Chance in Hell*, 124–32.

178. Long, "Anbar Awakening," 78.

179. West, *Strongest Tribe*, 101–2.

180. West, *Strongest Tribe*, 102.

181. This paragraph relies on Michaels, *Chance in Hell*, 98–100.

182. Ibid., 101–2.

183. Ibid., 93–94, 103.

184. Ibid., 136–38.

185. West, *Strongest Tribe*, 213–40; quotation is from p. 214.

186. Kagan, "The Anbar Awakening," 5; Michaels, *Chance in Hell*, 22–23.

187. Ahmad Bezia Fteikhan al-Rishawi (paramount sheik of the Albu Risha tribe), in *Al-Anbar Awakening, Vol. II: Iraqi Perspectives*, 46

188. Author's interview with Charlton.

189. Ibid.

190. The information contained in the next two paragraphs all comes from Michaels, *Chance in Hell*, but is not presented chronologically in the book.

191. Michaels, *Chance in Hell*, 105.

192. Jaffe, "Tribal Connections."

193. Wissma Abd al-Ibrahim al-Hardan al-Aethawi, former first deputy of the Sahwa, *Al-Anbar Awakening, Vol. II: Iraqi Perspectives*, 57.

194. Michaels, *Chance in Hell*, 149, 150–52.

195. Ahmed, "Sons of Iraq and Awakening Forces," 8.

196. "Anbar Province Opens First Iraqi Police Academy," *Stars and Stripes*, Mideast ed., June 7, 2007.

197. Monte Morin, "You Will Not Have One Roadside Bomb," *Stars and Stripes*, Mideast ed., March 3, 2007.

198. The story in the rest of this paragraph comes from Jaffe, "Tribal Connections."

199. West, *Strongest Tribe*, 259.

200. Author's interview with Allen.

201. Thamer Ibrahim Tahir al-Assafi (Ramadi city council member and member of the Council of Muslim Scholars) in Al Anbar, in *Al-Anbar Awakening, Vol. II, Iraqi Perspectives*, 35.

202. Majed Abd al-Raaza Ali al-Sulayman, in *Al-Anbar Awakening, Vol. II: Iraqi Perspectives*, 132–33.

203. Rubin, "Sunni Sheik Who Backed U.S."

204. Ricks, *The Gamble*, 221.

205. Sudarsan Raghavan, "Maliki, Petraeus Visit Insurgent Hotbed in Iraq," *Washington Post*, March 14, 2007.

206. Michaels, *Chance in Hell*, 225, 229.

207. Rubin, "Sunni Sheik Who Backed U.S."

208. Ali Hatim Abd al-Razzaq Ali al-Sulayman al-Assafi, in *Al-Anbar Awakening, Vol. II: Iraqi Perspectives*, 211–12.

209. Sudarsan Raghavan, "Rise of Awakening Groups Sets off a Struggle for Power among Sunnis," *Washington Post*, July 4, 2008.

210. Liz Sly, "Iraq's Sunni Awakening Movement Takes First Place in Anbar Province Elections," *Chicago Tribune*, March 8, 2009.

211. Sam Dagher, "Old Problems Persist Despite New Leadership in Iraq's Anbar Province," *New York Times*, September 13, 2009.

212. The phrase was used by Allen, author's interview.

213. William S. McCallister, "Sons of Iraq: A Study in Irregular Warfare," *Small Wars Journal*, September 8, 2008, http://smallwarsjournal.com/.

214. McCallister, "Sons of Iraq."

215. "Baghdad's Morgues Working Overtime," Associated Press, November 12, 2006. This was highlighted by Nagl in author's interview.

216. Kagan, *The Surge*, 30.

217. For a useful interactive map of sectarian neighborhoods in Baghdad, see BBC News, "Baghdad: Mapping the Violence," http://news.bbc.co.uk/2/shared/spl/hi/in_depth/baghdad_navigator.

218. Kagan, *The Surge*, 37–38.

219. Author's not-for-named-attribution interview with an American responsible for working with the government of Iraq on SOI integration issues, July 13, 2010.

220. Robinson, *Tell Me How This Ends*, 219; author's telephone interview with Omar al-Shahery, June 30, 2010.

221. This included Sheik Sattar and Sehik Heiss of Ramadi. See Rubin, "Sunni Sheik Who Backed U.S.," and Jaffe, "Tribal Connections."

222. Author's interview with Welch.

223. Richard A. Oppel Jr. et al., "Iraq Takes Aim at Leaders of U.S.-Tied Sunni Groups," *New York Times*, August 22, 2008.

224. Zeke Minaya, "Pragmatism Paves Way for Progress," *Stars and Stripes*, Mideast ed., September 3, 2007.

225. West, *Strongest Tribe*, 297; Robinson, *Tell Me How This Ends*, 231.

226. Robinson, *Tell Me How This Ends*, 231–32; Kagan, *The Surge*, 49.

227. Robinson, *Tell Me How This Ends*, 234–37.

228. Author's interview with Welch.

229. Robinson, *Tell Me How This Ends*, 241–51.

230. Author's interview with Welch.

231. One example is Mashhadani. Geoff Ziezulewicz, "Empowered by the U.S., Imprisoned by Iraqis," *Stars and Stripes*, Mideast ed., September 24, 2009.

232. Andrew W. Koloski and John S. Kolasheski, "Thickening the Lines: Sons of Iraq, a Combat Multiplier," *Military Review,* January/February 2009, 45–46, 48.

233. Bill Ardolino, "In Pictures: Patrolling the Shorja Market with the Sons of Iraq," *Long War Journal*, May 12, 2008, http://www.longwarjournal.org/.

234. John Vandiver, "One is Sunni and One Shiite," *Stars and Stripes*, Mideast ed., May 9, 2008.

235. The information in this paragraph comes from Ned Parker, "The Rise and Fall of a Sons of Iraq Warrior," *Los Angeles Times*, June 29, 2008.

236. International Crisis Group, *Loose Ends*, 26.

237. Quoted in Ned Parker, "Iraq Seeks Breakup of Sunni Fighters," *Los Angeles Times*, August 23, 2008.

238. Sutherland, interviewed by Kagan.

239. Author's interview with Col. David Sutherland, New York City, August 5, 2010.

240. Sutherland, interviewed by Kagan.

241. Garrett Therolf, "Colonel Reaches out to Iraqi Sheiks," *Los Angeles Times*, July 10, 2007.

242. Kimberly Kagan, "The Battle for Diyala," Institute for the Study of War, Iraq Report, February 11, 2007–April 25, 2007, 4; http://www.understandingwar.org/report/battle-diyala.

243. Solomon Moore, "Security Collapses in Diyala Province," *Los Angeles Times*, January 7, 2007.

244. Sutherland, interviewed by Kagan.

245. Richard A. Oppel Jr., "Sectarian Rifts Foretell Pitfalls of Iraqi Troops' Taking Control," *New York Times*, November 21, 2006.

246. Kagan, "Battle for Diyala," 4; "Greywolf: Making a Difference," briefing slides prepared for Sutherland (no date given), 7, Institute for the Study of War, http://www.understandingwar.org/files/SutherlandBriefingSlides.pdf.

247. Sutherland, interviewed by Kagan; author's interview with Sutherland.

248. "Greywolf: Making a Difference," 17.

249. Alexandra Zavis, "Offensive in Baqubah," *Los Angeles Times*, June 24, 2007.

250. Author's interview with Sutherland.

251. Sutherland, interview by Kagan; Therolf, "Colonel Reaches out to Iraqi Sheiks"; author's interview with Sutherland.

252. Therolf, "Colonel Reaches out to Iraqi Sheiks."

253. Sam Dagher, "Risky US Alliances in Iraq," *Christian Science Monitor*, July 17, 2007.

254. Sutherland, interviewed by Kagan. Also see "Greywolf: Making a Difference," 4.

255. Therolf, "Colonel Reaches out to Iraqi Sheiks."

256. Solomon Moore, "A Promising Province in Iraq Is Now a Tinderbox," *Los Angeles Times*, January 3, 2007.

257. Dagher, "Risky US Alliances in Iraq."

258. Kagan, "Battle for Diyala," 8.

259. Michael R. Gordon, "G.I.'s Forge Sunni Tie in Bid to Squeeze Militants," *New York Times*, July 6, 2007.

260. Kagan, "Battle for Diyala," 9.

261. Author's interview with Sutherland.

262. "Greywolf: Making a Difference," 11.

263. Alexandra Zavis, "Ira's Civilian Guards Eye Each Other," *Los Angeles Times*, February 22, 2008.

264. Sutherland, interviewed by Kagan; Gordon, "G.I.'s Forge Sunni Tie."

265. Michael R. Gordon, "Iraq Hampering U.S. Bid to Widen Sunni Police Role," *New York Times*, October 28, 2007.

266. Oppel et al., "Iraq Takes Aim at Leaders of U.S.-Tied Sunni Groups"; Saif Rasheed and Tina Susman, "Iraq, U.S.-Funded Militias at Loggerheads," *Los Angeles Times*, September 12, 2008; "The Maliki Government Confronts Diyala," *Institute for the Study of War Backgrounder*, no. 34 (September 23, 2008).

267. Ned Parker, "Baqubah Still a Minefield of Iraqi Sectarian Tensions," *Los Angeles Times*, December 7, 2008.

268. Kagan interview of Sutherland; Joel Wing, "The Islamic Party's Victory in Diyala," *Musings on Iraq*, February 9, 2009, http://musingsoniraq.blogspot.com/.

269. Michal Harari, "Uncertain Future for the Sons of Iraq," *Institute for the Study of War Backgrounder*, August 3, 2010, 1.

270. Author's interview with Welch.

271. Author's not-for-named-attribution interview, July 13, 2010.

272. Quoted in Hoda Jasim and Rahma al Salem, "The Awakening Council: Iraq's Anti-al-Qaeda Sunni Militias," *Asharq Alawsat* (London), December 29, 2007.

273. Michael R. Gordon, "Iraq Hampering U.S. Bid to Widen Sunni Police Role," *New York Times*, October 28, 2007.

274. Author's interview with Charlton.

275. Catherine Dale, *Operation Iraqi Freedom: Strategies, Approaches, Results, and Issues for Congress*, Report 7–5700, Congressional Research Service, April 2, 2009, 120, http://www.fas.org/sgp/crs/natsec/RL34387.pdf.

276. Author's interview with Charlton.

277. Wissam, in *Al-Anbar Awakening, Vol. II: Iraqi Perspectives*, 59.

278. Author's interview with Allen.

279. For an example, see the Ministry of Reintegration representative interviewed, "Al-Anbar Progress."

280. Author's not-for-named-attribution interview, July 13, 2010.

281. Sadiq al-Rikabi, quoted by the International Crisis Group, *Loose Ends*, 26.

282. Dale, *Operation Iraqi Freedom*, 121.

283. Michael Gisick, "Money Man Keeps Citizens' Groups Going," *Stars and Stripes*, Mideast ed., March 10, 2008.

284. Leo Shane III, "Sons of Iraq Evolving into New Roles," *Stars and Stripes*, Mideast ed., August 30, 2008.

285. Harari, "Uncertain Future for the Sons of Iraq," 2. There is variation in the published data on integration levels, but data published by the Institute for the Study of War is usually considered reliable by US military officers.

286. International Crisis Group, *Loose Ends*, 26.

287. "Diala Police Begins [*sic*] Integration of 18,000 Sahwa Fighters," Aswat Al-Iraq newswire in English, March 23, 2010.

288. Author's interview with Welch.

289. Dale, *Operation Iraqi Freedom*, 120. Also see Charles Levinson, "Woman Controls Iraq's Security Forces," *USA Today*, February 5, 2008.

290. Cloud and Jaffe, *Fourth Star*, 230.

291. Quoted in Levinson, "Woman Controls Iraq's Security Forces."

292. Levinson, "Woman Controls Iraq's Security Forces."

293. Author's not-for-named attribution interview, July 13, 2010.

294. Harari, "Uncertain Future for the Sons of Iraq," 2.

295. Dale, *Operation Iraqi Freedom*, 121.

296. James Warden, "Some Sons Get Head Start on New Jobs," *Stars and Stripes*, Mideast ed., November 4, 2008.

297. Farook Ahmed, "Sons of Iraq and Awakening Forces," *Institute for the Study of War Backgrounder* 23, February 21, 2008, 12.

298. Author's not-for-named-attribution interview, July 13, 2010. For a description of the variety of Iraqi state intelligence agencies, see International Crisis Group, *Loose Ends*, 8–12.

299. Author's interview with Welch.

300. Kim Gamel, "Iraqi Budget Woes Force Security Hiring Freeze," Associated Press, March 20, 2009.

301. International Crisis Group, *Loose Ends*, 26.

302. Shane, "Sons of Iraq Evolving into New Roles."

303. John Nagl, Colin Kahl, and Shawn Brimley, "How to Exit Iraq," *New York Times*, September 5, 2008.

304. Heath Druzin, "Sons of Iraq Still Waiting on Promises," *Stars and Stripes*, Mideast ed., May 9, 2009.

305. International Crisis Group, *Loose Ends*, 26.

306. Author's interview with Welch.

307. Williams and Adnan, "Sunnis in Iraq."

308. Ahmed, "Sons of Iraq and Awakening Forces," 12.

309. An unnamed US military intelligence staff officer, quoted in Michael Gisick, "Sons of Iraq Face Weakened Power," *Stars and Stripes*, Mideast ed., January 3, 2010. Also see Harari, "Uncertain Future for the Sons of Iraq," 2.

310. Williams and Adnan, "Sunnis in Iraq."

311. Author's interview with Welch.

312. Steven Lee Myers, "Gunmen Rob Baghdad Jewelry Stores in Sight of Checkpoints," *New York Times*, May 26, 2010; Timothy Williams and Durad Adnan, "Robbery Rampage Kills 4 Jewelry Stop Owners in Iraq," *New York Times*, June 27, 2010.

313. This could happen, for example, if the groups were infiltrated by the so-called Men of the Army of Al Naqshbandia Order. That organization, led by high-ranking officers of the Saddam Hussein era, continued to fight US troops in northern Iraq long after relative calm had appeared elsewhere. See Tim Arango, "G.I.s Find Bullets Still Flying at Outpost in Iraq," *New York Times*, May 15, 2010. It also appeared that AQI was attempting a comeback; Ned Parker, "Al Qaeda in Iraq Rises from the Ashes," *Los Angeles Times*, September 13, 2010.

314. Nir Rosen, "If America Left Iraq," *Atlantic Monthly*, December 2005, 42–46.

315. Author's not-for-named-attribution interview, July 13, 2010.

316. Biddle, "Stabilizing Iraq from the Bottom Up"; Biddle, "Patient Stabilized?"; Gompert, Kelly, and Watkins, *Security in Iraq*, 33.

317. Jim Michaels, "Iraq to Spend $13B on U.S. Arms, Equipment," *USA Today*, September 1, 2010. Nagl highlighted this point in the author's interview with him.

318. International Crisis Group, *Loose Ends*, 6.

319. Quoted by Rosen, "The Myth of the Surge."

320. Quoted by Roula Khalaf, "Anbar Is Made Safer but Critics Query the Cost," *Financial Times*, September 8–9, 2007.

321. Kimberly Marten, *Enforcing the Peace: Learning from the Imperial Past* (New York: Columbia University Press, 2004).

322. The texts of the agreements signed on November 17, 2008, are available online: "Strategic Framework Agreement for a Relationship of Friendship and Cooperation between the United States of America and the Republic of Iraq," GlobalSecurity.org, http://www.globalsecurity.org/military/library/policy/national/iraq-strategic-framework-agreement.htm, and "Agreement Between the United States of America and the Republic of Iraq On the Withdrawal of United States Forces from Iraq and the Organization of Their Activities during Their Temporary Presence in Iraq," GlobalSecurity.org, http://www.globalsecurity.org/military/library/policy/dod/iraq-sofa.htm.

Index

Note: Page numbers in *italics* indicate illustrations; those with a *t* indicate tables.

Abadi, Haidar, 175
Abashidze, Aslan, 64, 68–86, 99–101,
    188–91, 194; as Abkhazian envoy, 83;
    clan of, 75–77; exile of, 80, 84–86; and
    Gamsakhurdia, 70; and Kvitsiani, 89;
    militia of, 71–72, 79–80; overthrow of,
    79–82, 103, 192; Revival Party of,
    73–74, 76, 77, 79, 83; rise of, 69–73;
    and Rose Revolution, 74, 77, 80, 84;
    Russian support of, 72–73, 83–86,
    103; and Saakashvili, 74, 77–80,
    82–83, 99–101; and Shevardnadze,
    72–77, 99
Abashidze, Giorgi, 76, 85
Abashidze, Mehmet, 70
Abkhazia, 64, 83, 87, 198; economic devel-
    opment of, 96–98, 100; government in
    exile of, 92, 93; map of, *66*; tourism in,
    88; Upper, 94–99, 196. *See also* Upper
    Kodori
Abramov, Sergei, 110, 122, 129
"Abu Abid" (Saif Sa'ad Ahmed al-
    Ubaydi), 152, 173, 174, 185
Abu Fahd tribe, 164, 166
Abu Ghraib, 172, 173
Abu Mahal tribe, 165–66
Abu Nasir tribe, 154
Abu Nimr tribe, 165
Abu Risha, Sattar, 167–70
Adulami, Khalid, 178
Afghanistan, 9–10, 18–19, 24–25, 101, 196;
    Local Police Initiative in, 143; map of,
    32; NATO mission in, 1–3, 27; and
    "Pashtunistan," 46; refugees from, 55;

Soviet invasion of, 1, 34, 51, 53–54, 61;
    Taliban of, 10, 31, 34–36, 39, 56, 61,
    199. *See also* FATA
Africa, sub-Saharan, 4, 5, 26, 28–29, 140,
    207n28
Afridi tribe, 41, 59
Ahmad, Sheik, 170
Ahmed, Akbar S., 3, 39, 47, 51, 52, 62
Ajara (Georgia), 68–86, 99, 190; Abashidze
    in, 68–86; economic development in,
    81–84; history of, 68–69; map of, *66*;
    nationalism in, 197; Russian bases in,
    72–73, 84; territorial control in, *68*,
    70–72, 75, 194. *See also* Batumi
Akhmad. *See* Kadyrov, Akhmad-Hadji
Alasania, Irakli, 92–93, 190, 225n182
Alford, Dale, 166
Alkhanov, Alu, 110, 111, 116
Alkhanov, Ruslan, 110, 114
Allen, John R., 160, 169
Al Qaeda, 190; and bin Laden, 148; in
    FATA, 31, 37, 54, 61, 198; in Iraq, 18,
    139–52, 157–79, 183–86, 191; in Soma-
    lia, 15
Ameriyah Knights, 173, 176
Anbar People's Committee, 166–68
Anderson, Jon, 51
Andreas, Peter, 12
Arab Spring (2011), 183, 189, 200
Argvliani, Bacho, 94, 98, 99
Armenia, *66*, 75, 84
Association of Muslim Scholars (AMS),
    148–49
Atta Mohammad Noor, 27